LEARNING AND STUDY STRATEGIES

Issues in Assessment,
Instruction, and
Evaluation

EDUCATIONAL PSYCHOLOGY

Allen J. Edwards, Series Editor

Department of Psychology
Southwest Missouri State University
Springfield, Missouri

A complete list of titles in this series is available from the publisher on request.

LEARNING AND STUDY STRATEGIES

Issues in Assessment, Instruction, and Evaluation

Edited by

Claire E. Weinstein

Department of Educational Psychology
College of Education
University of Texas
Austin, Texas

Ernest T. Goetz

Department of Educational Psychology
College of Education
Texas A&M University
College Station, Texas

Patricia A. Alexander

Department of Educational Curriculum and Instruction
College of Education
Texas A&M University
College Station, Texas

Academic Press
San Diego New York Boston
London Sydney Tokyo Toronto

Academic Press, Inc.
A Division of Harcourt Brace & Company
525 B Street, Suite 1900, San Diego, California 92101-4495

United Kingdom Edition published by
ACADEMIC PRESS INC. (LONDON) LTD.
24-28 Oval Road, London NW1 7DX

Library of Congress Cataloging-in-Publication Data

Learning and study strategies: issues in assessment, instruction, and
  evaluation / edited by Claire E. Weinstein, Ernest T. Goetz,
  Patricia A. Alexander.
    p.   cm.
  Includes index.
  ISBN 0-12-742460-1   (alk. paper)
    1. Learning—Congresses.   2. Study, Method of—Congresses.
3. Cognitive styles—Congresses.   4. Individualized instruction-
-Congresses.   I. Weinstein, Claire E.   II. Goetz, Ernest T.
III. Alexander, Patricia A.
LB1060.L4235   1988   87-24219
370.15—dc19   CIP

PRINTED IN THE UNITED STATES OF AMERICA
   96 97 BB 9 8 7 6 5 4

To those who have taught us a zest for living
and a zest for learning—our parents and our mentors

Mama and Papa Weinstein
Burton and Meredith Goetz
Memaw and Honey Mullins
Richard C. Anderson
Ruth Garner
Arthur W. Melton
Wilbert J. McKeachie
Frank W. Wicker
Merlin C. Wittrock

CONTENTS

PART III. APPROACHES TO INSTRUCTION IN LEARNING AND STUDY STRATEGIES

PART IV. EVALUATION OF RESEARCH AND PRACTICE IN LEARNING AND STUDY STRATEGIES

CONTRIBUTORS

PATRICIA A. ALEXANDER   Department of Educational Curriculum and Instruction, Texas A&M University, College Station, Texas 77843

ANNA UHL CHAMOT   InterAmerica Research Associates, Rosslyn, Virginia 22209

DONALD F. DANSEREAU   Department of Psychology, Texas Christian University, Fort Worth, Texas 76129

RUTH GARNER   Department of Curriculum and Instruction, University of Maryland, College Park, Maryland 20742

ERNEST T. GOETZ   Department of Educational Psychology, Texas A&M University, College Station, Texas 77843

VICTORIA CHOU HARE   University of Illinois at Chicago, College of Education, Chicago, Illinois 60680

BEAU FLY JONES   North Central Regional Educational Laboratory, Winnetka, Illinois 60093

RICHARD E. MAYER   Department of Psychology, University of California, Santa Barbara, Santa Barbara, California 93106

BARBARA L. McCOMBS   Denver Research Institute, University of Denver, Denver, Colorado 80208

W. J. McKEACHIE   Department of Psychology, University of Michigan, Ann Arbor, Michigan 48109

CURTIS MILES   Piedmont Technical College, Greenwood, South Carolina 29648

J. MICHAEL O'MALLEY   InterAmerica Research Associates, Rosslyn, Virginia 22209

DAVID R. PALMER   Department of Educational Psychology, University of Texas, Austin, Texas 78712

DOUGLAS J. PALMER   Department of Educational Psychology, Texas A&M University, College Station, Texas 77843

SCOTT G. PARIS   Department of Psychology, University of Michigan, Ann Arbor, Michigan 48109

RALPH E. REYNOLDS   Department of Educational Studies, University of Utah, Salt Lake City, Utah 84112

ERNST Z. ROTHKOPF   Research Department, Bell Laboratories, Murray Hill, New Jersey 07974

ROCCO P. RUSSO   InterAmerica Research Associates, Rosslyn, Virginia 22209

DIANE LEMONNIER SCHALLERT   Department of Eduational Psychology, University of Texas, Austin, Texas 78712

RONALD R. SCHMECK   Department of Psychology, Southern Illinois University, Carbondale, Illinois 62901

LARRY L. SHIREY   Department of Educational Psychology, Stanford University, Stanford, California 94305

GLORIA STEWNER-MANZANARES   InterAmerica Research Associates, Rosslyn, Virginia 22209

CLAIRE E. WEINSTEIN   Department of Educational Psychology, University of Texas, Austin, Texas 78712

VICTOR L. WILLSON   Department of Educational Psychology, Texas A&M University, College Station, Texas 77843

JOHN E. WILSON   Greenville Independent School District, Greenville, Texas 75401

PETER WINOGRAD   Department of Curriculum and Instruction, University of Kentucky, Lexington, Kentucky 40506

M. C. WITTROCK   Department of Education, University of California, Los Angeles, California 90024

STEPHEN A. ZIMMERMANN   Department of Educational Psychology, University of Texas, Austin, Texas 78712

PREFACE

Research into the cognitive strategies required for effective knowledge acquisition, storage, and use has exploded during the past few years. Work on study strategies, once an isolated and largely atheoretical area of prescriptive manuals and race-horse training studies, has suddenly blossomed into an interdisciplinary topic of considerable theoretical and practical concern. Drawing upon advances in fields such as cognitive, developmental, educational, and social psychology, current research on learning and study strategies reflects concerns about cognitive, metacognitive, and affective aspects of the learner and the instructional task and interactions between learners and tasks.

Learning and Study Strategies reflects the theoretical diversity and interdisciplinary nature of current research on the cognitive strategies of autonomous learning. Topics such as metacognition, attribution theory, self-efficacy, direct instruction, attention, and problem solving are discussed by leading researchers of learning and study strategies. Further, the contributors to this volume acknowledge and address the concerns of educators at the primary, secondary, and postsecondary school levels. This blend of theory and practice is an important feature of this volume.

Learning and Study Strategies is organized around three critical issues: assessment of an individual's strategic behaviors, delivery of strategy instruction, and evaluation of strategy instruction and research. The discussion begins with two stage-setting chapters. McKeachie examines the need for strategy training in terms of current conditions in our schools and colleges. Mayer examines the conceptual bases of learning strategies, drawing particularly on cognitive psychology.

In the section on assessment, Weinstein, Zimmermann, and Palmer review assessment instruments and describe the development and evaluation of the Learning and Study Strategies Inventory (LASSI). Palmer and Goetz argue that in order to understand studiers' selection and use of strategies we must examine their beliefs about self and strategies. Garner cautions about the use of self-reports of strategy selection and implementation. Reynolds and Shirey report studies that circumvent Garner's concerns by the use of on-line measures to examine the role of attention in studying.

The section on instruction represents a variety of approaches. Dansereau outlines his research on cooperative learning, in which the students teach each other (and themselves). Winograd and Hare review work on direct instruction of strategies, in which the teacher delivers explicit information about strategy use to the students. McCombs calls for strategy instruction that combines cognitive, metacognitive, and affective components. Schmeck discusses the consideration of individuals' strategies in the context of his model of learning styles in order to reconcile strategy instruction with individuals' differing styles and personalities. Schallert, Alexander, and Goetz examine implicit strategy instruction provided by instructors and texts in college courses. O'Malley, Russo, Chamot, and Stewner-Manzanares examine the role of strategies in the learning of English as a second language. Jones describes efforts to develop curriculum for the Chicago Public Schools that translates advances in "laboratory" research into gains in the classroom.

Evaluation of strategy instruction and research is considered from methodological, theoretical, and applied perspectives. Willson critically examines experimental designs and statistical techniques employed in the area and suggests alternative procedures that address some of the problems and gaps. Rothkopf ponders what effective strategies are "really like" and what is required to get students to use them. Wittrock views the work on learning and study strategies as reflective of current theoretical views in cognitive psychology, notably his generative process model. Paris considers the theoretical models and metaphors that have guided strategy research and the ways in which they have constrained this research. The chapters by Wilson and Miles express the need to provide information and instructional techniques for learning and study strategies to the educational practitioners in primary, secondary, and postsecondary schools. Wilson and Miles also discuss the pitfalls that threaten such translation and implementation.

The intended audience for this volume is primarily educators and researchers in higher education. More specifically, this book should be of interest to individuals whose areas of interest include comprehension, instruction, learning, and memory. Instructors of study skills and developmental reading courses should also profit from reading this volume, as should teacher trainers and public school resource personnel.

The chapters included in this volume were originally presented at a conference funded by the Basic Research Program of the Army Research Institute, jointly sponsored by the University of Texas and Texas A&M University, and held at the Texas A&M University campus during October 1984.

The editors and authors would like to express their deep appreciation to the members of these institutions who worked so hard to help make the conference and the book a success and, we hope, an important contribution to the field. In particular, we would like to thank Robert Sasmor and Judith Orasanu from the Army Research Institute, Mollie Banks and Michael Thomas from the University of Texas, and Michael Ash and William Peters from Texas A&M University.

I

INTRODUCTION: TWO PERSPECTIVES ON LEARNING AND STUDY STRATEGIES

THE NEED FOR
STUDY STRATEGY TRAINING

W. J. McKeachie

Why do students need training in study strategies? Clearly, there are individual differences in the way students study, and Weinstein (Ch. 3, this volume) and others (Weinstein & Mayer, 1986) have demonstrated that these differences in study strategies are related to differences in achievement. "A" students study in ways different from those of "C" and "D" students.

It is all too easy to assume, however, because "A" students differ from less able students in study strategies, that their success is due to these strategies. It is conceivable that the causal relationships here are reversed. It may well be that "A" students use different strategies because they already have a good grasp of the material, and are able to use more sophisticated strategies than those of students who lack sufficient background and ability. Perhaps students learn by trial and error to use those strategies that fit their own level of ability, background, and sophistication.

The relationship is one in which effective study strategies usually result in greater learning. This is demonstrated by a number of studies in which students were taught to use more effective study strategies with a resultant improvement in achievement (Kulik et al., 1983). Such training has been going on for many years. Wellesley College had a course in 1894, and courses in reading and study skills proliferated in the 1930s. If work on study strategies has been going on for 90 years why should we have a conference on study strategies at just this point in history?

The answer, I believe, lies in theoretical developments perhaps even more than in the area of practice. Through the 90 years of history of teaching study skills, general rules of study skills have evolved. As the Kulik et al. (1983) study demonstrated, these recipes, or rules, have brought about success often enough to have become a fairly well established part of the college and university scene. What is different today is that we have a better theoretical understanding of the reasons these study strategies work. Cognitive psychology has developed a set of laboratory research studies and theoretical concepts that are much closer to the natural learning settings in which study strategies have been applied. I have given talks about applying principles of

3

LEARNING AND STUDY STRATEGIES: ISSUES IN
ASSESSMENT, INSTRUCTION, AND EVALUATION

learning to college teaching for many years. In fact, I well remember an occasion when I was speaking to presidents of colleges and universities in New England. When I finished, Victor Butterfield, President of Wesleyan University, immediately popped up and said, "Bill, if these principles are so good, why aren't psychologists better teachers?"

I countered with the observation that not all chemists were good cooks. The problem was not only a gap between theory and practice but also some serious limitations to the theory. As I noted some years later in my paper, "The Decline and Fall of the Laws of Learning" (McKeachie, 1974), the principles of reinforcement, contiguity, and exercise were good first steps in identifying variables affecting learning, but they were useful only within certain limiting bounds. Derived from animal laboratories in which possible "confounding" variables were controlled, the principles were not universally applicable in real-life educational settings, where the interactions with the confounding variables made a substantial difference.

Within the past two decades, experimental, developmental, and instructional psychologists have increasingly turned from animal to human subjects; from studies of classical and operant conditioning to studies of meaningful verbal learning; from highly artificial laboratory settings to natural learning settings; or to laboratory settings that are more closely related to learning in the real world. A substantial body of research and theory has emerged under the general rubric, *cognitive psychology*. As a result, we can now apply the conceptual frameworks used in cognitive psychology to an understanding of the bases for the effectiveness of traditional study strategies training.

Moreover, the area of training students in cognitive skills is relevant to one of the hot theoretical and research issues of the day. A generation ago most psychologists believed that intelligence was relatively fixed, largely determined by heredity, and well measured by intelligence tests. In the ensuing years, each of these beliefs has been called into question. Whereas each belief probably has a kernel of truth, the debate has largely moved from attacks upon these beliefs to questions about the best ways of describing individual differences in learning and problem-solving abilities, and about the degree to which general abilities or skills can be trained. It is clear that much high-level intellectual functioning depends upon high levels of prior knowledge and experience in a paricular domain. While most of us believe that cognitive abilities can be generalized beyond a special field of knowledge, it is still not very clear to what extent learning and problem-solving abilities can be generalized, and what kind of training produces generalization. Thus, both theoreticians and practitioners have a real stake in work in the area of this conference.

By holding a conference at this time, we can reasonably hope to establish the conditions under which study strategies training can be effective, identify the variables that influence the effectiveness of particular strategies, and assess the kinds of changes in cognitive processing that result from students' applications of study habits. Thus, there are good reasons to have a special interest in study strategy training at this time, not only for cognitive psychologists but also for counselors concerned with helping students to improve their performance.

The conceptual, theoretical, and research interests in cognitive strategies are not the only reason that study strategy training is now in the limelight. The last one and a half decades have been marked by increasing public concern about the improvement of education, and particularly the education of those who, for one reason or another, enter the higher levels of education with abilities and strategies that handicap them in achieving success. In many such cases, one of the problems is that neither home backgrounds nor schools have helped young adults become aware of alternative ways of approaching learning situations, and of options other than increasing or decreasing one's effort as one approaches different learning situations. Education is frequently directed in ways that provide students with opportunities to carry out elaboration, self-monitoring or other strategies, but seldom is any explicit attention given to helping students become aware that they have a choice in types of learning strategies that may be employed. In general, educational activities are teacher-directed and students learn to conform to the teacher's directions without any conscious thought about why the teacher directs them to carry out certain activities.

Moreover, teachers themselves do not think teaching involves the development of more effective repertoires of learning strategies. Students are directed to carry out certain learning activities, but grades and other feedback to the students are primarily directed to the correctness of the outcome, rather than to the strategy used to achieve the result. Students seldom get directed training and practice in developing study strategies. Rather, they stumble upon effective strategies only when, by chance, they vary their approach and find that one method works better than others.

Current motivation theory also enters the picture. Because students' own theories of intelligence and learning often involve the notion that failure to learn is the result of low innate ability, they attribute their failures to stable, unchangeable factors which they can do nothing about. Their motivation to learn is low because they feel it is useless to try. Changing attributions and self-concepts to include the idea that needed skills can be developed may have a significant effect upon motivation.

A more pragmatic reason for the current interest in teaching more effective learning strategies is demographic. College and university administrators all across the country know about the leveling off of the 18- to 22-year-old population and the expected decrease in this age group during the next few years. If colleges and universities are to survive, most need to be more effective in recruiting and retaining students. Whereas many colleges and universities perceived their function in earlier years as screening out those students who lacked the ability to compete successfully for good grades, they are now sending out recruiters to bring in the very type of applicants they turned away in previous decades. Thus, there is now administrative support for teaching more effective learning strategies to students who might previously have been rejected.

Two other topical issues lend support to the learning strategies movement. Despite President Reagan's laissez-faire attitude toward disadvantaged groups, schools and colleges have generally retained a commitment toward increased educational opportunities for minorities. Almost all institutions, however, have found that many minority group members are not well prepared for university work. At my own university, which has one of the highest percentages of blacks in the Big Ten (but still lower than our goal), our attrition rate for black students is substantially higher than that for nonminority students, despite efforts to provide academic and emotional support. Among the strong supporters of my "Learning to Learn" course are the administrators responsible for minorities. But minority students are not the only ones who need more effective learning strategies. Even at the time of Binet, teachers and school officials were concerned about children who were not able to keep up with the other pupils in normal classroom studies. Today, the movement to improve education for "slow learners" has burgeoned—sometimes by simply taking them out of regular classrooms to ease the task of teachers—but usually with an effort to improve their learning. Programs for the "slow learners," or "learning disabled," include members of minority groups, but the majority are white and come from all reaches of society. Research has already shown that these children can be trained in more effective study strategies. The challenge for research is to understand the problems of transfer and effective use of study strategies beyond the training situation.

The second topical issue providing support for training is the current concern about university sports. Star athletes, possessing less adequate academic abilities than those characteristic of other students, are often admitted to selective universities. Once on campus, they are expected to devote 30 or 40 hours a week to conditioning and practice, leaving limited time for study. During their sport's season of competition, they are forced to miss many classes because of games played away from the school. Thus, achieving academic success is made almost impossible. To keep athletes academically eligible, athletic departments route them into "easy A" courses, postpone required general education courses, and sometimes resort to dishonesty. Because of widely publicized scandals, some university administrators have taken a more active interest in the degree of exploitation of college athletes and have exerted pressures to increase the possibility that athletes can obtain a decent education. This, too, has been a factor supportive of the "learning strategies" movement.

My personal interest in teaching study strategies has been influenced by my own research. For more than 30 years I have been concerned about students whose performance is impaired by excessive anxiety, particularly anxiety about achievement tests. Our research has revealed some techniques to help these students perform better on tests. Other researchers have also developed methods of reducing anxiety, but even when such students have learned to relax and control their feelings of anxiety, their performance has not improved. Our more recent research indicates that such students perform poorly on tests not simply because they are anxious but because they are poorly prepared. Highly anxious students study, but they study ineffectively, memorizing details and reading and rereading. Do anxious students not know about more effective methods? Do they lack sufficient confidence in their skill to try them? Are they so anxious that they have become rigid rather than flexible in their choice of learning strategies? It may be that there are different types of anxious students, some included in each of these categories. In any case, I see study strategy training as an important vehicle for gaining further understanding of test-anxious students, and helping them.

What can we hope to accomplish in this conference? I anticipate that I myself will learn a good deal. Two of the things I would like to learn are the nature of training required for skill development and the effective use of learning strategies. Recently, Claire Weinstein and I wrote concluding chapters for the book by Holley and Dansereau (1984) on spatial learning strategies. The information presented in that book clearly demonstrates that spatial strategies can be an important aid in learning, and that in order for spatial strategies to be more effective than nonspatial strategies, students need a lot of practice in automatizing the particular spatial strategy they are learning, the amount of time necessary for this being approximately 12 to 24 hours.

Those of us who now teach learning strategies have a pretty good catalogue of strategies that can be effective. We do not, however, have a clear picture of the amount of training needed to develop sufficient skills in each strategy in order for it to be more effective than the alternatives used by students previously.

Moreover, we have a strong tendency to bring with us, from the earlier days of study skill training, the presumption that what we are teaching are "skills," with the connotation that these skills are superior to the presumably "skill-less" condition of the learner who has not yet been trained in study skills. I like the term "strategy" because it indicates that what we are teaching are alternative modes of learning, which can be chosen when appropriate for the task. The term "strategy" implies that we need to learn more about the conditions under which a particular strategy should be chosen. For example, what strategies are best to use when one is dealing with difficult or unfamiliar material, compared to easy, familiar material? What strategies are most effective for different kinds of students? To what degree is the student's prior knowledge, verbal ability, mathematical ability, motivation, or other individual characteristics variables important in determining what strategy is most likely to be effective? How do we teach students to diagnose both themselves and the situation in order to make effective choices?

These sorts of questions lead into another area of research that seems to me particularly important. It is the area currently best represented by Barbara McCombs's (1984) work on motivational strategies, and by the work in Europe and in the United States on the influence of anxiety upon cognitive processes. There is much evidence from research on anxiety that individuals are less inclined to take risks and vary behavior when they are highly anxious. To what degree does learning strategy training need to take anxiety into account? Are there cases where the important first task is to deal directly with techniques for coping with anxiety, rather than to develop skills that may give the individual a greater sense of self-efficacy and lower anxiety? How does a student's sense of self-efficacy affect his or her learning of study strategies, and how does increasing competence in study strategies affect a student's sense of self-efficacy?

A closely related area concerns approaches directed toward attributions for failure and success. Some teaching in learning strategies courses is designed to direct students away from attributing their failures to fixed, stable causes, such as low ability; and rather toward attributing success and failure to the use, or lack of use, of effective, learnable learning strategies. To what degree do we need to couple skill training with direct attention to attributions of learners?

I have asked a lot of questions, but I am convinced that they are highly interrelated. We cannot simply teach the knowledge of learning strategies; we must also provide the practice necessary to expand the strategies into well-developed skills; and in turn, we must attend to the motivational variables that will determine whether or not these strategies are chosen wisely and used effectively.

I am sure that we will not answer all of these questions in this conference. I am confident, however, that the papers that follow will make thoughtful contributions to study strategy training, and that our interactions will result in increased sophistication in this area.

REFERENCES

Holley, C. D., & Dansereau, D. F. (1984). *Spatial learning strategies: Techniques, applications, and related issues.* Orlando, FL: Academic Press.

Kulik, C. L., Kulik, J., & Schwalb, B. J. (1983). College programs for high-risk and disadvantaged students: A meta-analysis of findings. *Review of Educational Research, 53,* 397–414.

McCombs, B. L. (1984). Processes and skills underlying continuing intrinsic motivation to learn: Toward a definition of motivational skills training interventions. *Educational Psychologist, 19,* 199–218.

McKeachie, W. J. (1974). The decline and fall of the laws of learning. *Educational Researchers, 3,* 7–11.

Weinstein, C. E., & Mayer, R. E. (1986). The teaching of learning strategies. In M. Wittrock (Ed.), *Handbook of research on teaching* (pp. 315–327). New York: Macmillan.

LEARNING STRATEGIES: AN OVERVIEW

Richard E. Mayer*

The list of educational goals for schools is a long one. Included are the transmission of knowledge, the nurture of social and personal development, the enhancement of motor and artistic skills, and the improvement of the student's intellect. It is this latter goal—improving the student's mind—that is perhaps the most illusive, and that is the focus of this volume.

There is a disappointing history of educational programs aimed at teaching students how to learn (Mayer, 1987a). From the Latin School Movement of the 1600s (Rippa, 1980) to the massive Head Start Program of the 1960s (Caruso et al., 1982), there has been little or no evidence of success. The current revival of interest in studying learning strategies is based on a long-standing premise that our schools should help students learn to successfully control their cognitive processes, including learning to learn, to remember, and to think. Unlike the older programs, such as Latin Schools or Head Start, however, current programs on learning strategies can be based on our growing understanding of how people learn. Thus, in order to successfully pursue the goal of teaching students how to learn, it is useful to understand the learning process, i.e., what goes on in the learner's head during learning.

Learning strategies can be defined as behaviors of a learner that are intended to influence how the learner processes information. Examples include underlining of key ideas in a passage, outlining of the ideas in a lecture, or trying to put some newly learned information into one's own words.

The purpose of this paper is to provide a conceptual overview of learning strategies, with special focus on cognitive issues. First, the paper presents three basic models of learning, and then the paper focuses on four components in the models—instruction, learning processes, learning outcomes, and performance. Second, the paper briefly describes how learning strategy

*This paper was written while the author was on sabbatical leave at the Center for the Study of Reading, University of Illinois. The author's address is: Richard E. Mayer, Department of Psychology, University of California, Santa Barbara, CA 93106.

LEARNING AND STUDY STRATEGIES: ISSUES IN ASSESSMENT, INSTRUCTION, AND EVALUATION

training can affect the process and outcome of learning, with special emphasis on an examplary research study. The paper concludes with a discussion of
future research needs. For more detailed literature reviews, see Cook and
Mayer (1983) and Weinstein and Mayer (1986).

I. THREE VIEWS OF LEARNING

Because learning strategies are intended to influence the process of learning, any useful theory of learning strategies must be based on an underlying
theory of human learning. In this section, we briefly investigate three major
types of theories of learning—quantitative, qualitative, and behaviorist.

A. HOW MUCH IS LEARNED?

Figure 1 shows a simplified version of a quantitative theory of learning.
This model consists of four main elements: instruction, learning process,
learning outcome, and performance. Instruction is presented to the learner.
The learner processes the incoming information. Some of the information is
encoded in memory. This information can be used to answer questions or
solve problems. If the learner processes the information more successfully,
then more will be learned (or it will be learned more strongly); if the learner
processes the information less successfully, then less will be learned. Thus,
learning strategy training would be aimed at influencing how successfully
the learner processes the instructional material; the effects of this processing
would be quantitative, that is, would influence "how much" is learned.

B. WHAT IS LEARNED?

Figure 2 shows a simplified version of a qualitative theory of learning. As
with the previous theory, this theory consists of four elements: instruction,
learning process, learning outcome, and performance. If the learner pro-

Instruction		Learning process		Learning outcome		Performance
good	→	heavy processing	→	many nodes	→	good retention and transfer
poor	→	light processing	→	few nodes	→	poor retention and transfer

FIG. 1. A quantitative approach to learning.

Instruction		Learning process		Learning outcome		Performance
instruction for attention	→	pay attention overall	→	many nodes	→	good retention
instruction for guiding attention	→	pay selective attention	→	many nodes of selected type	→	good retention of selected type
instruction for organizational rehearsal	→	organize	→	internal connections	→	good inference question answering & poor retention of original order
instruction for generative encoding	→	elaborate	→	external connections	→	good transfer & poor verbatim retention

FIG. 2.   A qualitative approach to learning.

cesses the information in one way, this will result in one kind of learning outcome; if the learner processes the information in another way, this will result in a different kind of outcome. For example, a verbatim reciting of each word in a lesson might lead to better performance on a test of verbatim recognition, while active paraphrasing might lead to better performance on a test requiring inferences from the lesson (Mayer & Cook, 1980). Thus, learning strategy training would be aimed at influencing the selection of a type of processing that is appropriate for the learner's anticipated goals. The effects of this processing would be qualitative, that is, would influence "what kind" of learning outcome is acquired.

C.   How Much Behavior Is Acquired?

To this list of models we could add a behaviorist model in which the two cognitive elements—learning process and learning outcomes—are ignored. According to this model, the performance on a post-test depends solely on the amount of instruction that is presented. None of the contributors to this volume supports this view of the learner as an empty bucket into which knowledge may be poured.

These three models of learning represent three fundamentally different views of learning strategies. The first model suggests a place for learning strategies in improving the overall amount of learning. Learning strategies programs based on this model of learning are aimed at increasing "how much" is learned. The second model suggests that students must learn how to select a learning strategy that is appropriate for a given goal. Learning strategies programs based on this model of learning are aimed at influencing "what kind" of learning takes place. Finally, the "bucket" model rejects the usefulness of learning strategies, since what goes on in the learner's head during the act of instruction is not important. A major research issue implied by these distinctions is the determination of the most useful model for describing the effects of learning strategies.

II.   FOUR COMPONENTS IN LEARNING

This section of the chapter investigates how learning strategies may be related to four components of learning: instruction, learning processes, learning outcomes, and performance.

A.   INSTRUCTION

The first component is instruction. Instruction refers to any sequence of events that is intended to help a person learn something. Weinstein and Mayer (1986) have distinguished between teaching of learning strategies for basic kinds of tasks and for complex kinds of tasks. Basic learning refers to learning of isolated facts, such as "2 + 2 = 4" or "the capital of California is Sacramento." Complex learning refers to the learning of integrated bodies of knowledge, such as a lesson on the nitrogen cycle or on how radar works. A previous review (Weinstein & Mayer, 1986) has suggested that learning strategies appropriate for one type of learning situation may not be appropriate for another.

B.   LEARNING PROCESSES

Let us continue by examining a simple information-processing model of the learner, as shown in Fig. 3. As you can see, this model consists of three memory stores represented by boxes (sensory memory (SM), short-term memory (STM), and long-term memory (LTM)) as well as four control processes represented by arrows (attention, rehearsal, encoding, and retrieval). Although this model is open to criticism (Klatzky, 1983), let us explore it as a potentially useful framework for our current purposes.

1.   Attention

Information from the outside world, such as from instructional materials or a teacher's lecture, enters the system through sensory memory. For example, if the learner is reading a textbook, then the printed words are

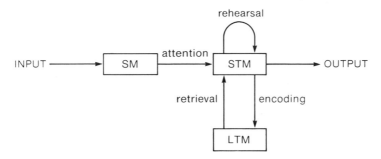

FIG. 3.   An information processing system.

represented in a visual sensory memory. Since information in this store fades rapidly, the learner must pay attention. By attending to a particular piece of information in SM, the learner is able to transfer that information to short-term memory. According to the quantitative model, learning strategies aimed at the process of attention can influence how much attention is paid, and thus, how much information reaches STM. For example, a motivated reader may pay attention to more information than an unmotivated reader. According to the qualitative model, learning strategies aimed at the process of attention can influence selective attention, and thus which kind of information reaches STM. For example, a learner who is reading a textbook could focus mainly on topic sentences, or on definitions of key terms.

2.   Rehearsal

Once information has reached STM, a learner may actively think about the material. Since information in STM fades, it is necessary to actively rehearse the material. According to the quantitative model, learning strategies aimed at the process of rehearsal can influence how much rehearsal takes place, and thus, how long information can be held in STM. Therefore, more rehearsal leads to more information being available for storage in STM. According to the qualitative model, learning strategies aimed at the process of rehearsal can influence the type of rehearsal that takes place, and thus, the type of information held in STM. For example, a learner could rehearse by trying to find causal links connecting the ideas presented in textbook material, or by trying to memorize a verbatim definition.

3.   Encoding

The next step is to transfer the information from STM into LTM, i.e., the process of encoding. Information held in LTM is permanent, but may be difficult to retrieve due to interference. According to the quantitative model, learning strategies aimed at the process of encoding can influence how fast information is encoded and how much is encoded. According to the qualitative model, learning strategies can also influence the quality of the encoding process, that is, the degree to which the new information is integrated with existing knowledge. For example, in learning a mathematical equation, the information can be encoded as presented or can be integrated with existing knowledge about the variables in the equation.

4. Retrieval

Finally, retrieval refers to transferring knowledge from LTM to STM. According to the quantitative model, retrieval of prior knowledge during learning could affect the overall amount learned, but would not affect how the information is stored in LTM. According to the qualitative model, the outcome of learning depends on both what is presented and the existing knowledge with which it is assimilated. Therefore, the type of existing knowledge that is retrieved and used in an assimilative context during learning would influence what is learned. For example, in learning a new programming language, a learner could retrieve prior knowledge about how a calculator works.

C. LEARNING OUTCOMES

The foregoing section hypothesizes that differences in the learner's cognitive processing during learning can affect what is learned. For example, the quantitative model suggests that the amount of attention paid, the amount of rehearsal, and the strength of encoding each can affect how much is learned. In contrast, the qualitative model suggests that attentional processes can affect the selection of information, rehearsal processes can affect the internal connections that are built within this new information, and encoding processes can affect the integration of new information with existing knowledge. These differences in learning outcomes are discussed in this section. In particular, three aspects of the learning outcome will be examined: the number of nodes, internal connections, and external connections.

1. Number of Nodes

A straightforward way of describing what is learned is to list the information that has been acquired. If each unit of knowledge is considered to be a node, then learning outcomes can be described in terms of the number of nodes. For example, many analyses of learning from prose view each node as an idea unit (e.g., see Britton & Black, 1985), that is, a simple event, action, or state. According to the quantitative model, learning strategies can influence the number of nodes that are acquired. According to the qualitative model, learning strategies can influence not only the overall number of nodes but also which nodes are acquired.

2. Internal Connections

In addition to describing how many nodes are acquired, we can describe the internal structure or relations among the nodes. For example, in learning about the nitrogen cycle, a learner may build internal connections indicating the causal relations among steps in the cycle (see Mayer et al., 1984). The quantitative model does not deal with internal connections, since it focuses only on how many nodes are acquired. In contrast, the qualitative model suggests that differences in the kind of rehearsal can lead to differences in the internal connections that a learner builds.

3. External Connections

Finally, learning outcomes can differ with respect to how well the new information is related to existing knowledge. For example, in learning about the nitrogen cycle, a learner may build external connections indicating an analogy between nature and a man-made factory (see Mayer et al., 1984). Again, the quantitative model does not deal with external connections, because it focuses only on how many nodes are acquired. The qualitative model, however, suggests that differences in the kind of encoding process can lead to differences in the external connections that a learner builds.

In summary, the quantitative model focuses on how many nodes are acquired, whereas the qualitative model focuses on which nodes are acquired, how they are related to one another, and how they are related to existing knowledge.

D. PERFORMANCE

Learning processes and learning outcomes are cognitive events that can be only indirectly studied. Differences in learning outcomes that result from differences in the learning process, however, should be related to observable differences in learners' post-test performance. In this section, we explore two types of performance measures: quantitative and qualitative.

1. Quantitative Measures

A straightforward way to evaluate the outcome of learning is to give the learner a test of how much is learned. Examples include a recall test (with overall amount recalled as the main measure), a recognition test (with overall amount correct as the main measure), and a question answering test (with overall amount correct as the main measure). These tests are quantitative because they are aimed at providing an overall measure of how much is learned. This type of dependent measure is most appropriate for the quantitative model of learning.

2.   Qualitative Measures

In contrast, the qualitative model of learning predicts that differences in processing will lead to differences in the quality of learning outcomes. To measure differences in selective attention, recall or recognition tests can be scored by category, with special focus on which types of information are learned. To measure differences in internal connections, recall or recognition tests can be scored for degree of verbatim retention and degree of inference. For example, students who have built useful internal connections may be expected to produce more inferences but to be less able to retain the information in verbatim form. Finally, to measure differences in external connections, transfer tests, including both near and far transfer items, can be given. For example, students who have built useful external connections might be expected to excel on far transfer, but not on problems identical to those given during instruction (see Mayer, 1984, 1987b).

III.   CAN STUDENTS LEARN TO MANIPULATE THEIR COGNITIVE PROCESSES?

The central question in the learning strategy literature is whether or not students can learn how to control their own cognitive processes during learning. In this section, we explore examples of potentially learnable techniques for selecting information (i.e., controlling attention), building internal connections (i.e., controlling rehearsal and encoding), and building external connections (i.e., controlling retrieval, rehearsal, and encoding).

A.   TECHNIQUES FOR SELECTING INFORMATION

Some learning strategies may be aimed mainly at helping the learner to focus attention on certain kinds of information. For example, activities such as student underlining of prose material (e.g., see Rickards & August, 1975) may serve to focus the student's attention. Techniques aimed mainly at focusing attention should have their strongest effects on dependent measures of retention of the target information. In recent reviews (Mayer, 1984, 1987b), I noted that techniques for selecting information may also serve to limit attention and reduce the amount of connection building. Thus, I recommended that selection strategies should be taught when the goal of learning is to retain specific target information; and that training of these strategies would be particularly useful when learners are not experienced in determining which information is important.

B. TECHNIQUES FOR BUILDING INTERNAL CONNECTIONS

Some learning strategies are aimed mainly at building internal connections among elements in the presented material, that is, building a logical structure or outline of the material to be learned. Under some circumstances, training in how to write an outline of a lecture or lesson can encourage a learner to connect and organize the ideas in a text (e.g., see Dansereau et al., 1979). Techniques that mainly affect the building of internal connections should affect retention (i.e., main ideas in the outline should be retained better) and should affect students' ability to make inferences. In recent reviews (Mayer, 1984, 1987b), I noted that organizational strategies tend to be most effective when the reader is unfamiliar with the material to be learned.

C. TECHNIQUES FOR BUILDING EXTERNAL CONNECTIONS

Finally, some learning strategies may be aimed mainly at building connections between the new information and existing knowledge. For example, Resnick and Ford (1981) describe this process as *mapping* between information to be learned and a familiar model or analogy. Training learners how to elaborate on presented material is one example of an integration strategy (e.g., see Wittrock, 1974). Techniques aimed mainly at enhancing integration of old and new knowledge may not enhance verbatim retention, since the verbatim material is modified to fit in with existing knowledge. These techniques, however, should have a positive effect on measures of transfer, such as creative problem solving. When the goal of learning is to be able to apply what is learned to new situations, then integration strategies may be useful. I have previously pointed out, however, that not all elaboration or analogy activities are equally effective (Mayer, 1979).

In summary, different learning strategies may have different goals ranging from selection of target of information to building internal connections to building external connections.

IV. AN EXAMPLE

As an example, let us consider a recent study (Cook, 1982) aimed at teaching students how to select relevant information and build internal connections. The subjects were junior college students enrolled in a science course, with the material being unfamiliar for most of the students.

Cook noted that expository prose found in science textbooks is often presented within text structures, such as the following:

1. Generalization: a main idea is presented along with other sentences that support, clarify, or extend that idea.
2. Enumeration: a list of facts is presented.
3. Sequence: a description of a series of events or steps in a process is presented.
4. Classification: a procedure for separating items into categories is given.
5. Compare/contrast: the similarities or differences between two or more things are discussed.

In order to empirically test the reliability of these five types of expository prose structures, Cook instructed some college students in the recognition of each structure, while other students received no training. On a test, all subjects were asked to sort 20 science passages into five groups based on the structure of the material (rather than content). The trained group correctly sorted 79% of the passages compared to 61% for the control group. These results support the idea that students can be taught to recognize prose structures.

The next step in Cook's research was to develop a 10-hour strategy-training program to help junior college students recognize and outline prose structures found in their own science textbooks. Students received extensive practice in outlining each type of structure, with feedback given after each attempt. A control group received no training, but took the same science course.

In order to assess the effectiveness of her strategy training, Cook gave all students a pretest and a post-test. In both tests, students read passages (different from those given during training) and then tried to recall the information (recall test), and solve problems based on the information in the passage (problem solving test). On the recall test, the trained subjects showed a pretest-to-post-test gain of 11% on recall of important information, and a loss of 4% on recall of unimportant information; in contrast, the control group showed a pretest-to-post-test gain of 0% in important information and a gain of 3% on recall of unimportant information. Apparently, the training was successful in helping students focus on important information. On the problem-solving test, the trained group showed a pretest-to-post-test gain of

24% compared to a 3% loss for the control group. The training was also apparently successful in helping students build connections needed for making inferences.

V. RESEARCH ISSUES

As stated in the Introduction, learning strategies are behaviors that are intended to manipulate a person's cognitive processes during learning. Cook's (1982) study is an example of a successful strategy-training program in which there is evidence of students learning to select relevant information and build connections. The study, however, also points to many of the unresolved issues and problems in the learning strategies field.

First, we need better techniques for describing and evaluating learning strategies, including techniques for describing the cognitive processes and outcomes of learning. In the Cook study, for example, it is not clear whether the training affected the building of internal connections (which was the intended purpose) or the building of external connections. Similarly, we need dependent measures that are sensitive to changes in learners' processes and outcomes. Looking only at overall percent correct or percent retention does not achieve this goal.

Second, we need a research base concerning the question of whether it is better to provide training in general learning strategies, independent of subject matter domains, or to provide training in specific strategies, within the context of subject matter domains. This issue has also been hotly debated within the problem-solving training literature (e.g., see Tuma & Reif, 1980). In the Cook study, the latter approach was used with some success; however, this result does not demonstrate that general strategy training is ineffective.

VI. GENERAL CONCLUSION

The study of learning strategies, as described in this volume, involves an attempt to understand how to help learners improve their ability to learn, to remember, and to think. In a previous volume, Lochhead and Clement (1979) pointed out that there is a long and somewhat disappointing history concerning teaching of these skills. What is new with the current interest in learning strategies is that it can be based on an emerging cognitive theory of human learning and memory. This chapter has provided an overview of how cognitive theory can enhance the study of learning strategies, and how the study of learning strategies can help refine cognitive theory. The chapters that follow in this volume provide many promising examples of this reciprocal process.

REFERENCES

Britton, B. K., & Black, J. B. (1985). *Understanding expository prose*. Hillsdale, NJ: Erlbaum.
Caruso, D. R., Taylor, J. J., & Detterman, D. K. (1982). Intelligence research and intelligent policy. In D. K. Detterman, & R. J. Sternberg (Eds.). *How and how much can intelligence be increased?* (pp. 45–65). Norwood NJ: Ablex.
Cook, L. K. (1982). The effects of text structure on the comprehension of scientific prose, unpublished doctoral dissertation, University of California, Santa Barbara.
Cook, L. K., & Mayer, R. E. (1983). Reading strategy training for meaningful learning from prose. In M. Pressley, & J. Levin (Eds.). *Cognitive strategy research: Educational applications* (pp. 87–131). New York: Springer-Verlag.
Dansereau, D. F., Collins, K. W., McDonald, B. A., Holley, C. D., Garland, J., Diekoff, G. M., & Evans, S. H. (1979). Evaluation of a learning strategy system. In H. F. O'Neill, & C. D. Spielberger (Eds.). *Cognitive and affective learning strategies*. New York: Academic Press.
Klatzky, R. (1983). *Human memory*. New York: Freeman.
Lochhead, J., & Clement, J. (1979). *Cognitive process instruction*. Philadelphia: Franklin Institute Press.
Mayer, R. E. (1979). Can advance organizers influence meaningful learning? *Review of Educational Research, 49*, 371–383.
Mayer, R. E. (1984). Aids to text comprehension. *Educational Psychologist, 19*, 30–42.
Mayer, R. E. (1987a). The elusive search for teachable aspects of problem solving. In J. A. Glover, & R. R. Ronning (Eds.). *Historical foundations of educational psychology* (pp. 327–347). New York: Plenum Press.
Mayer, R. E. (1987b). Instructional variables that influence cognitive processes during reading. In B. K. Britton, & S. M. Glynn (Eds.), *Executive control processes in reading* (pp. 201–216). Hillsdale, NJ: Erlbaum.
Mayer, R. E., & Cook, L. K. (1980). Effects of shadowing on prose comprehension and problem solving. *Memory & Cognition, 8*, 101–109.
Mayer, R. E., Dyck, J., & Cook, L. K. (1984). Techniques that help readers build mental models from science text. *Journal of Educational Psychology, 76*, 1089–1105.
Resnick, L., & Ford, W. (1981). *The psychology of mathematics for instruction*. Hillsdale, NJ: Erlbaum.
Rickards, J. P., & August, G. J. (1975). Generative underlining strategies in prose recall. *Journal of Educational Psychology, 67*, 860–865.
Rippa, S. A. (1980). *Education in a free society*. New York: Longman.
Tuma, D. T., & Reif, F. (1980). *Problem solving and education*. Hillsdale, NJ: Erlbaum.
Weinstein, C. E., & Mayer, R. E. (1986). The teaching of learning strategies. In M. C. Wittrock (ed.), *Handbook of research on teaching* (3rd ed. pp. 315–327). New York: Macmillan.
Wittrock, M. C. (1974). Learning as a generative process. *Educational Psychologist, 11*, 87–94.

II

ISSUES IN THE ASSESSMENT OF LEARNING AND STUDY STRATEGIES

ASSESSING LEARNING STRATEGIES: THE DESIGN AND DEVELOPMENT OF THE LASSI

Claire E. Weinstein, Stephen A. Zimmermann, and David R. Palmer

In response to the increasing numbers of academically underprepared students entering American colleges and universities, many institutions have created programs to remedy student deficiencies (Noel & Levitz, 1982). Traditionally, most of the programs established to remedy academic deficiencies have focused on basic skills in mathematics, reading, communication, and study habits and attitudes. There is another set of competencies necessary for effective learning, however, that includes the strategies and skills students need to manage and monitor their own learning in a variety of contexts.

Current research has demonstrated that one way to influence the manner in which students process new information and acquire new skills is to instruct them in the use of learning strategies (Dansereau, 1985; also Ch. 7, this volume; Dansereau et al., 1979; Jones, Ch. 13, this volume; Jones et al., 1984; Mayer, Ch. 2, this volume; McCombs, 1981; also Ch. 9, this volume; McKeachie, Ch. 1, this volume; Weinstein, 1978; Weinstein & Mayer, 1985; Weinstein & Underwood, 1984; Wittrock, 1978, 1985; also Ch. 16, this volume). A number of issues arise, however, in adapting the findings from these research studies for use in improving an individual's ability to benefit from instruction. One major issue in this area relates to assessment. The successful implementation and evaluation of a learning strategies training program requires a reliable and valid means for measuring students' deficits and progress. An accurate diagnosis of students' entry-level learning strategies deficits can be used to create individualized prescriptions for training, and subsequent assessments can be used to evaluate the effectiveness of that training.

The purpose of this paper is to identify some of the current issues in learning strategies assessment and to present a description of the design and development of a specific instrument created to address some problems encountered in diagnosing student deficits. In the following section, several

LEARNING AND STUDY STRATEGIES: ISSUES IN
ASSESSMENT, INSTRUCTION, AND EVALUATION

research and practical issues relating to self-report inventories that assess learning strategies use will be briefly examined. The validity of this type of instrument in an applied setting (such as a study improvement course) will also be discussed. Next, the initial design and development of the Learning and Study Strategies Inventory (LASSI) will be presented. (For a more detailed discussion, see Weinstein et al., 1983.) Data on the reliability, validity, and norms for this instrument will also be provided.

I.   ISSUES IN THE ASSESSMENT OF LEARNING STRATEGIES

Currently, the majority of instruments available for assessing learning strategies focus on the individual's study practices. These instruments are generally used in high school or post-secondary educational or training settings for a number of purposes, including:

1. Prediction of academic performance;
2. Counseling students concerning their study practices;
3. Screening or criterion measures for study skills courses.

Several study skills instruments are available commercially. A review of these instruments (Schulte & Weinstein, 1981) reveals that most of them cover traditional areas of study skills, such as note taking, time management, work habits, and student attitudes toward school and study. Generally, these instruments use a self-report format and sample a broad range of topics within the area of study skills. For those instruments that provide such data, reliability is generally found to be in the acceptable (Anastasi, 1976) range of .80 and above. Subscales, however, partially due to their shorter length, are often found to have somewhat lower reliability (.46 to .93).

Most of these inventories have used what Svensson (1977) terms a "correlational" approach. That is, they seek to find behaviors or activities that are correlated with successful studying, but may not be the direct cause of successful learning. Such a correlational approach is reflected by the manner in which study skills inventories are typically constructed and validated. For example, Carter (1958) constructed his California Study Methods Survey by weighting items on the basis of how well they distinguished between students with high and low grade point averages who had similar IQ and achievement test scores. A similar procedure was used in selecting items for the Survey of Study Habits and Attitudes (Brown & Holtzman, 1967), the Effective Study Test (Brown, 1964), and the College Adjustment and Study Skills Inventory (Christensen, 1968).

Whereas all of these inventories predict grade-point average from a low to moderate degree (.19 to .60), they do not yield information about how the student learns, but rather the conditions under which he or she does it best. Svensson (1977) distinguished this correlational approach from a functional approach which seeks to find qualitative differences in students' study habits that may affect learning outcomes. For instance, Svensson found that students learned reading passages by either attending to specific details of the text or by searching for overall meaning. He found that a student's strategy for reading influenced both the amount and type of information recalled from the text.

After an extensive review of both commercially available and experimental instruments conducted as part of our work on the Cognitive Learning Strategies Project, the following conclusions were reached:

1. Across study skills inventories, there seems to be no consistent definition of study skills. The term includes a broad range of topics, and inventories vary in their coverage of these topics. In addition, the specific topics covered by a particular inventory often are not specified.
2. Although several inventories have subscales that measure specific topics within study skills (e.g., note taking, scheduling), the reliability of the subscales is often so low that the subscales cannot be used separately.
3. Most of the recommended or "good" study practices in study skills inventories have not been empirically validated. Therefore, a high score on a study skills inventory does not necessarily mean that a student's study practices are effective.
4. No measure has been validated for use as a diagnostic tool. The majority of validity studies have demonstrated the usefulness of a given instrument as a predictor of academic achievement.
5. Most of the instruments can be easily faked. That is, students who want to give the impression that they use effective learning strategies can respond to the instrument in ways that do not provide accurate information about their actual strategy use.
6. Although recent research has suggested that there are two components to effective study—consistent and regular study, and an "active" learning style—most items in published inventories deal primarily with the first component.

Given these problems, a major goal of our current work on the Cognitive Learning Strategies Project has been to develop an instrument to help educators and trainers diagnose strengths and weaknesses in students' learning and study strategies in order to provide individualized remedial training. To accomplish this goal, an instrument is needed that:

1. Assesses a broad range of topics within the area of learning strategies in a reliable and valid manner;

2. Assesses covert and overt behaviors that are related to learning and that can be altered through training;
3. Reflects the current state of the art in learning strategy research and cognitive psychology;
4. Is validated for use as a diagnostic instrument.

For the past 5 years we have been developing an instrument to try to meet as many of these criteria as possible. We call this measure the Learning and Study Strategies Inventory (LASSI).

II.   LASSI—EARLY DEVELOPMENTAL STAGES

An analysis of the instruments reviewed by Schulte and Weinstein (1981) revealed that the topics encompassed by the terms "study skills" and "learning strategies" vary considerably from inventory to inventory. Because there was no consensus concerning definitional components of various study strategies or skills, the initial phases of this research involved attempting to create a categorization scheme. One of the early steps in this process was to survey the topics included in published study skills books, manuals, and programs.

A.   SURVEY OF PUBLISHED STUDY SKILLS MATERIALS

Forty-seven study skills books, manuals, and program guides were collected. A list of component topics was compiled from the tables of contents and subject headings used in those materials. A modified Delphi technique (Udinsky et al., 1981) was used to reach a consensus among four judges participating in this phase of the work. This method required the judges to examine the materials, create their own set of potential categories, and then review the other judges' results to determine if they wanted to change any of their own responses. This method was repeated three times until a consensus was reached among three doctoral students and a professor who served as judges. Table 1 lists the 19 general categories that resulted from the final revision of the categorical scheme.

B.   DEVELOPMENT OF AN ITEM POOL

The first step in the creation of an item pool was to collect items from the published, unpublished, and experimental instruments gathered by Schulte and Weinstein (1981). Individual items from these existing inventories were typed on index cards for sorting and categorization purposes. Additional

TABLE 1 Categorical Scheme for Data from a
Survey of Published Study Skills Materials

Classroom behavior
Concentration
Frustration and anxiety
Instructor/student interaction
Learning strategies and techniques
Library skills
Motivation
Note taking, summaries, outlines, and book marking
Perceived deficits/Desire to take course
Problem-solving
Reading comprehension
Reading speed
Scheduling and organization
School attitudes and attributions
Study environment
Tests and examinations
Vocabulary
Work habits
Writing skills

sources for potential items included other research and development experts in this area and items from the State-Trait Anxiety Inventory (Spielberger et al., 1970) and the Test Attitude Inventory (Spielberger et al., 1978). Items not appropriate for an instrument using a self-report format were eliminated from the pool. A total of 645 items remained.

The 645 potential items were sorted by the judges into the categories identified in the previous section. During this process two major problems became apparent: first, many items were exact or close duplicates of other items; second, a number of items fit into more than one category (e.g., scheduling time as a test-taking strategy). The first problem was resolved by eliminating duplicate items. The second problem was left to be addressed after the initial pilot tests, when the category scheme could be revised based on the descriptive and correlational data collected. In addition, items that did not directly deal with study practices (e.g., items about personality characteristics) and items whose content concerned an aspect of study or previous behavior and experience that could not be altered and, therefore, could not be a target for remediation (e.g., "My parents read to me as a child.") were eliminated. Items that were confusing, compound items (those containing more than one question or statement in the same item), and poorly worded items were rewritten by specialists in tests and measurement. This selection process reduced the pool of potential items to 291. These 291 items were then converted to a forced-choice mode using a true–

false format, with approximately half the items worded positively and approximately half worded negatively. (This decision was later changed, and a Likert-type scale was used after the initial pilot testing.)

III. PRELIMINARY PILOT TEST

A preliminary pilot test was conducted to evaluate administration procedures and to begin collecting psychometric data about the items. Following the conversion of all items to a true–false format, they were randomly divided into three sets of 97 items each and typed as three separate instruments (due to a concern about time) for pilot testing. Pilot subjects were requested to complete one of these three instruments, to respond to the Marlowe–Crowne Social Desirability Scale (Crowne & Marlowe, 1964), and to complete a postexperimental questionnaire. The Marlowe–Crowne Social Desirability Scale was included to provide data about the relationship between responses to individual items and the degree to which subjects displayed a social desirability response set. This type of response set is a major problem for self-report instruments in the area of learning strategies. It was decided that one way to reduce this problem was to eliminate potential LASSI items that had significant correlations (positive or negative) with the measure of social desirability. The postexperimental questionnaire was included to gather data from the participants concerning perceived weaknesses, problem questions, and suggested modifications. Correlations with other available data, such as Scholastic Aptitude Test (SAT) scores or high school rank, were not used as selection criteria since very few relationships were significant or meaningful. It was decided that cumulative grade point average (GPA) would be the most recent measure and, therefore, most likely to be reflective of current study practices.

In addition to eliminating items from the potential pool, a number of items were also added to the pool. The sources for these new items included: a survey of current research literature in cognitive psychology, responses from students on the postexperimental questionnaire, suggestions from practitioners, and students' responses to an open-ended questionnaire (the Learning Activities Questionnaire: Weinstein et al., 1980).

A. REFORMATTING THE LASSI

The data were analyzed to yield several different measures:

1. The percentage of participants responding true or false to each item in each set;

2. Correlation coefficients for the relation between scores for each item and cumulative GPA, SAT Verbal Scores, SAT Math Scores, and high school rank [there were too few American College Test Assessment Program (ACT) scores reported to use this data];
3. Correlation coefficients for the relation between each Marlowe–Crowne Social Desirability Scale.

In addition, participants' responses to the postexperimental questionnaire were also tabulated and summarized. The most consistent finding was that students were uncomfortable with a true–false format.

After consulting with two psychometricians, a decision was made to reformat the scale. A 5-point Likert-type format was used for this and all subsequent versions of the LASSI. In some cases, this change necessitated rewording items. These changes were made, and the new item pool was then reviewed by two content matter experts and two psychometricians. On the basis of their comments, as well as a second review of the items by the project team, further revisions were made.

The new set of potential LASSI items was then independently recategorized by three judges. The judges then met to resolve their differences and to create a revised set of categories to reduce the overlap created in the original set. Table 2 lists the 14 general categories that resulted from this revision of the categorial scheme. This revised form of the LASSI contained at least seven items for each general category. The total number of items for this version was 149.

TABLE 2   Categorical Scheme for Revised
LASSI Items after Preliminary Pilot Test

Anxiety
Attitude
Comprehension monitoring
Concentration
Information processing
Motivation
Note taking/outlining
Reading
Scheduling
Selecting main ideas
Self-management
Study environment
Test strategies
Work habits

IV.   REVISION OF THE LASSI ITEM POOL

On the basis of the data obtained during the preliminary pilot test of the LASSI, criteria were established for eliminating items from the potential item pool, and several new items were added. (Responses to each of these new items also correlated with scores on the Marlowe–Crowne Social Desirability Scale as part of another study.)

A.   ITEM SELECTION CRITERIA

Items were eliminated if they met any of the following criteria:

1. The item's correlation with the Marlowe–Crowne Social Desirability Scale was above .50.
2. The item's correlation with cumulative GPA was not significant at the .10 probability level.
3. The content of the item dealt with an area that was more conveniently measured in a reliable and valid manner by an objective or performance assessment. (Based on this criteria a small number of items dealing with vocabulary and library skills were eliminated.)

A second pilot test instrument was created by rewording some randomly selected items to create an approximately equal distribution of positively and negatively worded statements, and then randomly ordering the items (with the constraint that two similar items from the same category did not appear consecutively).

V.   SECOND PILOT TEST

Given the large number of revisions after the preliminary pilot test, a second pilot test was conducted to evaluate the administration procedures and to examine the properties of the items on the revised instrument. The descriptive data collected and the student comments made during the feedback portion of the administration sessions were used to establish criteria for selecting items for the field test version of the LASSI.

A.   ITEM SELECTION CRITERIA

Items were eliminated if they met any of the following three criteria:

1. If two items from the same category had highly similar wording and highly similar response patterns, one of the items was eliminated.

2. The item dealt with a very specialized skill, such as creating a bibliography for a term paper.
3. Responses to the item were limited to one or two contiguous points on the scale.

This process resulted in the elimination of 19 items. It should also be noted that at that time the name of the instrument was changed from the Learning and Study "Skills" Inventory to the Learning and Study "Strategies" Inventory. It was believed that this term was both more inclusive and more reflective of the strategic nature of many of the items.

B. PRELIMINARY TEST–RETEST RELIABILITY

As a first step in examining the psychometric properties of the LASSI, a study was undertaken to establish the test–retest reliability of the instrument. Ninety-six students drawn from several sections of an introductory educational psychology course at the University of Texas at Austin participated. Participants met in groups of 7 to 25 for two 1-hour sessions, separated by a 3- to 4-week interval. The participants were given 45 minutes in which to complete the instrument. Six students were unable to complete both sessions, and their data were eliminated from the analysis. A test–retest correlation of .88 for the total instrument was computed.

VI. CONSTRUCTION OF THE LASSI SCALES

Using the data from several field tests, the number of items was reduced from 130 to 90, and 10 scales measuring different clusters of learning strat-

TABLE 3   Coefficient Alpha and Number of Items for Each of the LASSI Scales

Scale	No. of items	Alpha
Anxiety	10	.82
Attitude	4	.60
Concentration	8	.82
Information processing	17	.88
Motivation	14	.87
Scheduling	5	.69
Selecting main ideas	4	.61
Self-testing	5	.64
Study aids	8	.69
Test strategies	13	.83

egies and study attitudes were developed. (See the Appendix for a sample of the items from the final 90-item version of the LASSI.) The first step in the development of these scales was accomplished by a team of experts who grouped the items according to a particular theme or factor. This process was repeated several times. Refinements were made in the groupings using the coefficient alphas (an upper-limit estimate of the test–retest reliability). Items were added or deleted to obtain a maximum coefficient alpha for each scale. The data were from the Fall 1982 incoming freshman class at a small private college in the eastern United States. A total of 850 students participated, with complete data available for 783 students. The coefficient alpha and the number of items for each scale are presented in Table 3. (A brief description of each of the scales can be found in the Appendix.)

VII.   TEST–RETEST RELIABILITY

In the study previously described, estimates of the reliability with the 130-item LASSI were obtained. Since no new items were added to obtain the 90-item LASSI, this data bank was reanalyzed for the final version of the LASSI. The participants were allowed 45 minutes to complete the instrument. The correlations and number of participants with complete data available are given in Table 4 for each scale.

VIII.   VALIDITY AND NORMS

The validity of the LASSI has been examined using several different approaches. First, the scale scores have been compared, where possible, to

TABLE 4   Test–Retest Data for the Final Version of the LASSI

Scale	r	n
Anxiety	.81	95
Attitude	.64	96
Concentration	.80	95
Information processing	.79	95
Motivation	.79	95
Scheduling	.77	96
Selecting main ideas	.64	95
Self-testing	.66	96
Study aids	.70	96
Test strategies	.79	95

other tests or subscales measuring similar factors. For example, scores on the Information Processing Scale of the LASSI have been correlated with scores on the Elaborative Processing Scale of Schmeck's Inventory of Learning Processes (1977) (r = .60). Second, several of the scales have been validated against performance measures. For example, scores on the Selecting Main Ideas scale have been compared to students' scores on selecting main ideas from texts and other readings (r = .40 and above). Finally, the LASSI has been subjected to what might be called "user validity." Professors, counselors, advisors, and developmental educators at more than ten different colleges and universities have used the LASSI on a trial basis. The results have been very good; potential users report few, if any, administration problems and a high degree of usefulness in their setting. These results have encouraged us to proceed with the development of norms and reporting formats.

As part of our own work on the Cognitive Learning Strategies Project we have also examined the usefulness of the LASSI for an undergraduate course in learning-to-learn. This course is designed to help academically underprepared and educationally disadvantaged students who either are experiencing, or are predicted to experience academic problems while attending the University of Texas. This 3-credit, elective course is offered as part of the regular program in the Department of Educational Psychology. Because the class is taught in a group consisting of approximately 30 students in each section, a major problem has been to create or find methods that can be used to diagnose particular student problems and direct remediation and enrichment activities.

Over the course of four academic semesters, the LASSI was used as part of a battery of measures administered to all students entering the learning skills course. [Other measures included the Survey of Study Habits and Attitudes (Brown & Holtzman, 1967), the Trait Anxiety Inventory portion of the State-Trait Anxiety Inventory (Spielberger et al., 1970), the Test Attitude Inventory (Spielberger et al., 1978), and the Nelson-Denny Reading Test, either form C or D (Brown et al., 1973)]. The data obtained from these administrations of the LASSI were used in two major ways. First, the data provided guidelines for individual prescriptions (many of the assignments in this class are individualized to help target the material to students' own needs). Use of the profiles from the LASSI, and the comparison of individual student profiles to the norms helped to identify those areas in which a student may be particularly weak. This information was used to help select the individual topics to be emphasized for that individual.

The second major use was to help guide the curriculum development efforts for the course. In the analysis of group data collected over the four semesters, several patterns emerged. For example, an overwhelming number of students who took this course were extremely deficient in information-processing strategies. This led to an increased emphasis on the use of cognitive strategies for knowledge acquisition, which in turn, led to higher achievement scores.

We are currently examining these and additional data to study the patterns that seem to emerge from our population. We will be using these data to continue to improve the course and to investigate alternative groupings of students for course labs or sections.

IX. CONCLUDING COMMENT

The development of any learning strategies instrument is an ongoing process. The research and development activities described in this chapter are continuing under the sponsorship of the United States Army Research Institute for the Behavioral and Social Sciences. Current work is focusing on:

1. Additional studies of scale validities,
2. The development of new items for those scales that presently have fewer than ten items (e.g., study aids),
3. The development of reporting formats and forms,
4. The development of student profiles.

Given the increasing needs of many of our students, it is urgent that this type of work continue. As researchers continue to identify and understand the psychological dimensions of academic competencies and their assessment, they must also be prepared to translate these findings into forms that will further the goals of our society while furthering the goals of science. Helping people to become independent learners who assume responsibility for their own learning and know how to direct and manage their study activities, in school or on-the-job, must be a democracy's major educational priority in a rapidly changing world.

X. APPENDIX: BRIEF DESCRIPTIONS OF LASSI SCALES AND SAMPLE ITEMS

Anxiety
Often worries about school; may worry so much that it is hard to concentrate; easily discouraged about grades; tense about school and studying for tests; nervous even when well prepared.
    Sample items:

1. Worrying about doing poorly interferes with my concentration on tests.

2. When I begin an examination, feel pretty confident that I will do well.
3. Even when I'm well prepared for a test, I feel very anxious.

Attitude
Attitude about and interest in college.
   Sample items:

1. Success in school is very important to me.
2. I feel confused and undecided as to what my educational goals should be.
3. In my opinion, what is taught in my courses is not worth learning.

Concentration
Ability to concentrate, pay close attention, listen carefully and think about what is being said; not easily distracted.
   Sample items:

1. I often find that I have been reading, but don't know what it was about.
2. I concentrate fully when studying.
3. I find that during lectures I think of other things and don't really listen to what is being said.

Information processing
Uses imaginal and verbal elaboration; thinks about how new information fits with what is already known; interrelates new information; creates comparisons; thinks about the meaning of what is read and heard; translates information into one's own words; uses logic.
   Sample items:

1. I try to find relationships between what I am learning and what I already know.
2. When I study, I try to somehow organize the material in my mind.
3. When having difficulty recalling something, I make an effort to recall something else that might be related to it.

Motivation
Willingness to work hard; level of motivation for college; has a considerable degree of incentive; diligent; stays "on top of" work; self disciplined.
   Sample items:

1. I read the textbooks assigned for my classes.
2. I hurry my assignments, trying to get them out of the way rather than doing a good job.
3. I seem to be able to find all kinds of excuses for not studying.

Scheduling
Uses time well, is well organized, systematic in planning the use of time; productive in using time to the best advantage.

Sample items:

1. I only study when there is the pressure of a test.
2. I make good use of daytime study hours between classes.
3. At the beginning of a study period I organize my work so that I will use the time most effectively.

Selecting the main idea

Seems to be able to pick out key ideas and critical points in information read or heard; focuses on important points in what has been read.

Sample items:

1. My underlining is helpful when I review text material.
2. I have difficulty identifying the important points in my reading.
3. Often when studying, I seem to get lost in details and "can't see the forest for the trees."

Self-testing

Reviews information learned; reviews regularly; prepares for classes and learning.

Sample items:

1. I stop periodically while reading and mentally go over or review what was said.
2. I go over homework assignments when reviewing class materials.
3. I seldom review except just before tests.

Study aids

Makes use of a broad approach to learning, makes good use of aids to help learning; supplements learning with helpful techniques; makes good use of key words, practice exercises, sample problems, examples, headings, diagrams, etc., to help learning.

Sample items:

1. I do not work through practice exercises and sample problems.
2. When they are available, I attend group review sessions.
3. I make simple charts, diagrams, or tables to summarize material in my courses.

Test strategies

Approach toward taking tests and exams; generally prepares appropriately; reviews right materials; ties materials together well; flexible when necessary.

Sample items:

1. I think through the meaning of test questions before I begin to answer them.

2. I have difficulty adapting my studying to different types of courses.
3. When I take a test, I realize I have studied the wrong material.

ACKNOWLEDGMENTS

The research reported in this chapter was supported in part by Contracts No. MDA903-79-C-0391 and MDA903-82-C-0122 with the Army Research Institute for the Behavioral and Social Sciences. Views and conclusions contained in this chapter are those of the authors and should not be interpreted as necessarily representing the official policies, either expressed or implied, of the Army Research Institute, or of the United States government.

REFERENCES

Anastasi, A. (1976). *Psychological testing*. New York: Macmillan.

Brown, W. F. (1964). *Effective Study Test*. San Marcos, TX: Effective Study Materials.

Brown, W. F., & Holtzman, W. H. (1967). *Survey of Study Habits and Attitudes manual*. New York: The Psychological Corporation.

Brown, J. I., Nelson, M. J., & Denny, E. C. (1973). *Nelson–Denny Reading Test*. Boston: Houghton Mifflin.

Carter, H. D. (1958). *California Study Methods Survey*. Monterey, CA: California Test Bureau.

Christensen, F. A. (1968). *College Adjustment and Study Skills Inventory*. Berea, OH: Personal Growth Press.

Crowne, D. P., & Marlowe, D. (1964). *The approval motive*. New York: Wiley.

Dansereau, D. F. (1985). Learning strategy research. In J. Segal, S. Chipman, & R. Glaser (Eds.). *Relating instruction to basic research*. Hillsdale, NJ: Erlbaum.

Dansereau, D. F., Collins, K. W., McDonald, B. A., Holley, C. D., Garland, J., Diekhoff, G., & Evans, S. H. (1979). Development and evaluation of a learning strategy training program. *Journal of Educational Psychology, 71*, 64–73.

Jones, B. F., Amiran, M. R., & Katims, M. (1984). Embedding structural information and strategy instructions in reading and writing instructional texts: Two models of development. In J. Segal, S. Chipman, & R. Glaser (Eds.), *Relating instruction to basic research*. Hillsdale, NJ: Erlbaum.

McCombs, B. L. (1981). Transitioning learning strategies research into practice: Focus on the student in technical training, paper presented at the annual meeting of the American Educational Research Association, Los Angeles.

Noel, L., & Levitz, R. (Eds.). (1982). *How to succeed with academically underprepared students*. Iowa City: American College Testing Service National Center for Advancing Educational Practice.

Schmeck, R. R., Ribich, F., & Ramanaiah, N. (1977). Development of a self-report inventory for assessing individual differences in learning processes. *Applied Psychological Measurement, 1*, 413–431.

Schulte, A. C., & Weinstein, C. E. (1981). Inventories to assess learning strategies. In C. E. Weinstein (Chair), Learning strategies research: Paradigms and problems, symposium presented at the annual meeting of the American Educational Research Association, Los Angeles.

Spielberger, C. D., Gonzalez, H. P., Taylor, C. J., Algaze, & Anton, W. D. (1978). Examination stress and test anxiety. In C. D. Spielberger, & I. G. Sarason (Eds.), *Anxiety and stress* (Vol. 5). New York: Hemisphere/Wiley.

Spielberger, C. D., Gorsuch, R. L., & Luschene, R. E. (1970). *Manual for the State-Trait Anxiety Inventory.* Palo Alto, CA: Consulting Psychologists Press.

Svensson, L. (1977). On qualitative differences in learning: III—Study skill and learning. *British Journal of Educational Psychology, 47,* 233–243.

Udinsky, B. F., Osterlind, S. J., & Lynch, S. W. (1981). *Evaluation Resource Handbook: Gathering, analyzing, reporting data.* San Diego: EdITS.

Weinstein, C. E. (1978). Elaboration skills as a learning strategy. In H. F. O'Neil, Jr. (Ed.), *Learning strategies.* New York: Academic Press.

Weinstein, C. E., & Mayer, R. E. (1985). The teaching of learning strategies. In M. C. Wittrock (Ed.), *Handbook of research on teaching* (3rd ed.). New York: Macmillan.

Weinstein, C. E., Schulte, A. C., & Cascallar, E. C. (1983). The Learning and Studies Strategies Inventory (LASSI): Initial design and development, Technical Report, U.S. Army Research Institute for the Social and Behavioral Sciences, Alexandria, VA.

Weinstein, C. E., & Underwood, V. L. (1984). Learning strategies: The *how* of learning. In J. Segal, S. Chipman, & R. Glaser (Eds.), *Relating instruction to basic research.* Hillsdale, NJ: Erlbaum.

Weinstein, C. E., Wicker, F. W., Cubberly, W. E., Roney, L. K., & Underwood, V. L. (1980). Design and development of the Learning Activities Questionnaire, Technical Report No. 459, U.S. Army Research Institute for the Behavioral and Social Sciences, Alexandria, VA.

Wittrock, M. C. (1978). The cognitive movement in instruction. *Educational Psychologist, 13,* 15–29.

Wittrock, M. C. (1985). Student thought processes. In M. C. Wittrock (Ed.), *Handbook of research on teaching* (3rd ed.). New York: Macmillan.

SELECTION AND USE OF STUDY STRATEGIES: THE ROLE OF THE STUDIER'S BELIEFS ABOUT SELF AND STRATEGIES

Douglas J. Palmer and Ernest T. Goetz

Although definitions of cognitive strategies differ (see Paris, Ch. 17, this volume; Rothkopf, Ch. 15, this volume), the view that strategies are learner-initiated actions is a consistent, central feature (Underwood, 1978). The fact that learners' initiative or choice plays a crucial role in strategy definitions suggests a heavy emphasis on motivation in the study of strategy use. To date, however, little direct attention has been given to this area. The purpose of this paper is to consider the relationship between a selected set of motivational variables and strategy use. To accomplish this task, we will examine recent frameworks that consider the impact of learner variables on cognitive functioning, and propose a model of strategy use. Development of this model is based on recent work in attribution theory and self-efficacy theory, and on characteristics of learners who use or fail to use strategies. Individual sections of this paper will review these topics and describe their relationships to the model. Following this discussion, an investigation based on the proposed model will be briefly described. Finally, theoretical and training implications of this model will be discussed.

The failure of individuals to use strategies may not be merely the result of a lack of training. It has been repeatedly demonstrated that many pupils with significant learning problems who have participated in strategy training programs do not maintain or generalize their use (see Brown et al., 1983). Students' failure to use effective strategies in which they have received training may be due to the interplay of a variety of factors. There is recent evidence that learners' perceptions concerning strategy attributes may influence their decisions concerning strategy use (Pressley et al., 1982). For example, if a student believes that a strategy requires a great deal of effort, he or she may fail to use it. In addition, student perceptions of their own achievement attributes (cf. Weiner, 1976, 1979) may affect strategy use. The student who perceives himself or herself as incompetent may be disinclined

LEARNING AND STUDY STRATEGIES: ISSUES IN
ASSESSMENT, INSTRUCTION, AND EVALUATION

to attempt the use of any strategy. Further, the match between students' perceptions of their own personal attributes and of strategy attributes may subsequently influence learners' decision to use a strategy. For example, if a student perceives that a certain strategy requires a great deal of content-related knowledge and he or she sees that he or she doesn't have that knowledge, he or she may be less likely to employ this strategy when difficulties are encountered. Finally, perceived efficacy of learning strategies for obtaining a learning outcome may also affect the decision for strategy use (Kennedy & Miller, 1976). This paper will discuss each of these proposed determinants of strategy use.

To introduce the variables that will be discussed in this paper, consider the studying behavior of an individual student. This student, who has done well in her courses, is currently reading a literature assignment. At the end of the second page of her assignment, she realizes that she does not understand the author's message or intent. She sees herself as a competent, hard-working student, but she has a problem understanding this difficult passage. On the basis of past experience with difficult texts, she has learned that if at first you do not understand, selectively reread and take notes. She realizes that these strategies may take a little extra time, but she sees herself as a good student who tries hard and is willing to spend that extra time. Besides, she knows that this strategy works most of the time when she has problems understanding what she has read.

In contrast, consider a student who has had a history of academic difficulty. She sees herself as a poor student with limited competence and little interest in academic performance. When presented with a text that she has difficulty understanding, she does not try to use any strategies. She believes that you need to be a smart, industrious student to effectively learn and use study strategies, and since her self-concept does not include those attributes, she views strategies as not beneficial for her. In addition, she does not think those "learning tricks" really work anyway. She is convinced that the only students who use strategies are those so smart that they do not really need them.

To provide a context for our review and our model of strategy use, we want to conclude this prologue with a statement of assumptions that have guided our thinking. First, strategy use requires intentional, active, effortful investment on the part of the learner. Second, we are primarily concerned with individuals who fail to use a strategy even though they know its use could facilitate their performance. Third, we are focusing on strategy use for attainment of instructor-assigned educational outcomes (i.e., "cool/academic" cognition) that may differ from the more personal, learner-initiated activities of everyday problem solving. Fourth, we are addressing a rather narrow band of motivational concerns, rational cognitive-oriented variables.

This decision reflects our view that these learner cognitions are the primary motivational variables for subsequent learning activities (for a discussion of a broader range of motivational factors, including affect, see McCombs, Ch. 9, this volume).

I. CONCEPTUAL FRAMEWORKS

As the cognitive view has re-emerged and replaced behaviorism as the dominant approach within psychology, there has been an increasing role for the learner in accounts of learning and memory. For example, Jenkins's (1979) tetrahedral model has the learner as one of its four components, along with instruction, material, and criterial task (see also Brown et al., 1983). Jenkins's model provides a framework for the investigation of how characteristics of the learner interact with other aspects of the learning situation to determine learning outcomes.

Similarly, Flavell and Wellman (1977) proposed that individuals' performance may be influenced by their own perceived characteristics, task characteristics, strategy use, and the interactions among the three components. They suggested that the information remembered depends on who stores it (Person × Task), what strategy is best suited to him or her (Person × Strategy), and the task he or she must perform (Person × Strategy × Task).

Motivational variables were excluded from the set of person variables represented in these frameworks and the research that they inspired. Recently, however, there have been attempts to incorporate motivational variables into conceptual frameworks for learning and memory.

Humphreys and Revelle (1984) propose a model in which students' personality factors (i.e., impulsivity, achievement motivation, and anxiety) influence their motivation (e.g., arousal, on-task effort). In turn, these motivational variables affect students' performance on memory tasks by affecting the availability and allocation of learners' cognitive resources during learning. For example, if a task has multiple components, learners may reallocate resources from one aspect of the task to another (cf. Reynolds & Shirey, Ch. 6, this volume), perhaps sacrificing accuracy to increase response speed. Further, a learner may not allocate resources if the perceived benefits of improved performance are not judged as adequate, while increases in motivation may make cognitive resources more available.

Borkowski et al. (1987) have implicated the interaction between motivational and metamemory beliefs in explaining why some children, regardless of intellectual functioning, use strategies on transfer tasks and others do not. Reflecting the conceptualization of metamemory presented by Pressley et al. (1982), Borkowski et al. state that metamemory consists of the following interactive components: specific strategy knowledge, relational strategy knowledge, general strategy knowledge, and metamemory acquisition procedures. Specific knowledge for each strategy includes: (1) appropriate goals and objectives; (2) appropriate tasks; (3) the range of applicability; (4) expected performance gains; (5) effort required; and (6) enjoyment value. Borkowski and his colleagues assume that competent learners possess an ample repertoire of strategies and adequate specific knowledge of each. The available store of strategies and specific strategy knowledge enables the efficient selection and use of strategies that characterize the competent learner. Relational strategy knowledge, the second component of the model, refers to learners' understanding of the comparative merits of specific strategies to perform specific tasks. General strategy knowledge, the motivational component of the model, concerns learners' understanding that effort is required to use strategies and that an effortful strategy orientation will result in successful task performance. Borkowski et al. suggest that general strategy knowledge is affected by individuals' attributions for their performance on previous similar tasks. Metamemory acquisition procedures, the final metamemory component, concern learners' independent, spontaneous decisions of when and how to use a strategy.

A.   STRATEGY USE MODEL

Within the context of these recent attempts to include motivational variables in models of cognitive functioning, we propose a model of strategy use. As shown in Fig. 1, despite the restrictions imposed by the assumptions stated above, there are a number of components in this model. The critical elements are students' perceptions of task attributes, strategy attributes, and their own attributes as learners.

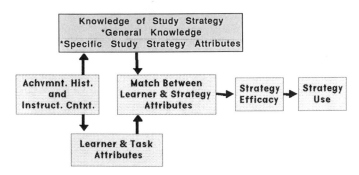

FIG. 1.   A model of study strategy use.

When confronted with academic tasks in instructional settings, students bring with them varying amounts of background knowledge and different histories of cognitive functioning and academic outcomes. These instructional and student characteristics, in turn, influence students' perceptions of themselves, the instructional task, and the cognitive strategies with which they are familiar and which they may employ. Weiner and his colleagues (see Weiner, 1972, 1974, 1979 for reviews) suggest that students' perceptions of achievement events include judgments concerning their own ability and effort, and task difficulty. In addition, we are proposing that learners view strategies as differing regarding the tasks to which they are appropriate and the level of learners' effort, intelligence, and prior knowledge required for effective use. In our model, the match between students' perceptions of learner attributes and strategy attributes affects their judgment of the personal effectiveness of the strategy, and ultimately, their decision to use it. We have defined match as the case where the perceived level of a learner's attribute meets or exceeds the perceived level required by the strategy. For example, if you view yourself to be not very smart, but believe that you do not need to be very smart in order to use a strategy, there is a match between strategy and learner attributes.

It is the nature of the strategy attributes and the concept of match between perceived strategy and learner attributes that set this model apart from the frameworks discussed above. While incorporating many components of the present model, Pressley et al. (1982) and Borkowski et al. (1987) ignore students' perceptions of their own cognitive ability and the ability required to effectively use strategies.

The concept of the match between learner and strategy attributes is similar to the distinction recently presented by Covington (1983) in a discussion of the role of attributions in metacognition and strategic behavior:

> Our understanding of such strategic self-management will be aided by an important distinction not sufficiently appreciated and frequently confused in the attribution literature. It involves the difference between attributions as *levels* and as *sources*. Attributional levels refers to the amount or degree of resources available to an individual for problem solving, such as the extent of one's ability or time available to study. In contrast, sources refers to the requirements for success at a given task. For example, assuming that outstanding ability is a key causal ingredient in success at solving a particular problem, does the person possess sufficient capacity to match the demands? (p. 155)

Development of this model was guided by theoretical and empirical work in attribution and self-efficacy theory and a consideration of the characteristics that differentiate individuals who use or fail to use appropriate strategies.

II. ATTRIBUTION THEORY

Kelley (1967) defined attribution as the process by which individuals interpret the causes of events in their environment. A basic assumption of attribution theorists is that people are motivated to understand the causes of events in their environments. Heider (1958), one of the pioneers of attribution theory, states that:

> Man is usually not content to register the observables that surround him; he needs to refer them as far as possible to the invariances of his environment. . . . The underlying causes of events, especially the motives of other persons, are the invariances of the environment that are relevant to him; they give meaning to what he experiences and it is these meanings that are recorded in his life space and are precipitated as the reality of the environment to which he then reacts. (p. 81)

Heider argued that subjective experiences are not only a legitimate object of study, but are essential for understanding how individuals see their world. As with other cognitive approaches to the study of human behavior, an underlying premise of attribution theory is that thought influences action. Therefore, an account of an individual's cognitive representation of the causes of an event may help explain what the individual does in that situation and in similar situations. Weiner (1972, 1974) contends that individuals' attributions for their performance influence their expectancy for future performance, persistence, affective reactions, and task choice.

A. ATTRIBUTIONS FOR COGNITIVE OUTCOMES: ANTECEDENTS AND CATEGORIES

Weiner and his colleagues have extensively examined individuals' attributions for achievement events (Weiner, 1972; 1974; 1976). Attributional researchers have reported that individuals systematically use a variety of information in forming attributions related to their performance (Frieze, 1976; Frieze & Weiner, 1971). The major antecedent cues for attributions include performance outcome, history of performance, and performance of others (Frieze, 1976). That is, your explanation for your performance on a test is influenced by how well you did on that test, how well you have done on other tests in the past, and how well others did in comparison to you.

Reviewing attributional studies that have used free-response procedures, Weiner (1979) reported that ability, effort, and task difficulty have been consistently identified as perceived causes of success and failure on academic tasks. Using an adaptation of Elig and Frieze's (1975) coding scheme, Weiner (1979) proposed that attributions for success and failure may be classified within a three-dimensional taxonomy of internality (internal or external), stability (fixed or variable), and controllability (controllable or uncontrollable). In this system, ability is classified as internal, fixed, and un-controllable. Effort is internal, variable, and controllable, and task difficulty is external, fixed, and uncontrollable.

Recently, Willson and Palmer (1983) examined whether or not the categorization of attribution statements by naive psychologists matches that of the attribution theorists. Undergraduate students provided causal statements immediately following feedback on their own actual test performance, and these statements were subsequently categorized by different students. Latent partition analysis was applied to the students' categorization to identify attributional clusters, and the clusters were then submitted to factor analysis. Willson and Palmer reported that students developed latent attributional clusters similar to these noted by Weiner (1974) (i.e., ability, effort, task characteristics, and chance). In contrast to Weiner's (1979) three-dimensional taxonomy, however, the factor analysis revealed that students' clusters were differentiated solely on the basis of success and failure.

B. ATTRIBUTION CONSEQUENCES: EXPECTANCY AND PERSISTENCE

McMahan (1973) and Weiner et al. (1976) noted a relationship between stable attributions and individuals' expectancy for future performance. That is, among individuals who attribute an outcome to stable causes, those who succeed tend to expect continued success, while those who fail expect continued failure. Attributions can be more important than the outcomes themselves in determining expectancies. Palmer and Willson (1982) found that objective performance measures and students' subjective success ratings predicted almost zero variance of students' expectancy for future performance. When attributions were included as predictors in the regressions, however, 26% of the variance in the students' expectancy was accounted for, with ability and task difficulty making the largest contributions. Thus, the studier who attributes failure on a test to lack of ability is unlikely to expect better results in the future.

Attributions have also been shown to affect persistence, including resistance to extinction (Rest, 1976; Weiner et al., 1972). Weiner (1979) argued that resistance to extinction is a function of causal attributions during the nonreinforcement phase. The attribution of nonreinforcement to unstable factors such as bad luck and not trying will increase resistance to extinction, while attributions such as lack of ability and task difficulty tend to decrease resistance to extinction (Rest, 1976). Thus, when faced with repeated failure, the studier's perceived causes of performance will influence how long the studier will continue to strive. Related to persistence, development of learned helplessness has been linked to attributional constructs (Abramson et al., 1978; Miller & Norman, 1979).

Maier and Seligman (1976) argued that exposure to uncontrollable aversive events produces motivational, emotional, and cognitive deficits in animals and humans. In humans, noncontingent failure on problem-solving tasks increases time to solution, trials to criterion, and number of errors, and produces feelings of anxiety and depression (Benson & Kennelly, 1976; Hiroto & Seligman, 1975; Klein et al., 1976; Miller & Seligman, 1975).

Maier and Seligman (1976) and Seligman (1975) proposed that learned helplessness is caused by individuals' expectancy of independence between their responses and outcome. Abramson et al. (1978) and Miller and Norman (1979) have elaborated the learned helplessness model. Drawing on attributional research, they have focused on individuals' causal attributions for aversive events as the crucial element in accounting for learned helplessness. Exposure to noncontingent aversive stimuli affects attributions of children (Dweck & Reppucci, 1973) and adults (Teasdale, 1978).

Ames and Lau (1982) investigated the relationship between college students' attributions for performance on the first exam in an introductory psychology course and their willingness to seek help for the next exam in that course by attending optional review sessions. Poor performance was associated with a greater likelihood of attendance. Although the effect of attributions failed significance overall, among poor performers, those who made help-relevant attributions were more likely to attend than those who made help-irrelevant attributions.

C.   ATTRIBUTION CONSEQUENCES: AFFECTIVE REACTIONS

When conditions prompt the learner to attribute failure to lack of ability (Tennen & Eller, 1977), or other internal, stable uncontrollable causes, the learner is likely to respond with apathy, resignation, helplessness, and depression (Weiner et al., 1978). The demeanor and behavior of many unsuccessful students might be described as academic learned helplessness. Weiner (1979) suggests there are three major sources of affect in an achievement situation: (1) general emotions tied directly to performance (i.e., good feelings as a result of success, bad feelings as a result of failure); (2) specific emotions associated with specific performance attributions (e.g., gratitude if success is due to others); and (3) self-esteem affective reactions (e.g., pride, shame, and competence) that are linked to the internal attributional dimension. Attributions also have been associated with students' anxiety concerning their performance. Arkin and Maruyama (1979) reported that for students who view themselves as successful, stable attributions (e.g., ability, test characteristics) were negatively correlated with anxiety. Among unsuccessful students, the more external their attributions, the more anxious they felt. That is, unsuccessful students became more anxious when they believed that their failure was due to factors outside of their control. Such anxiety can interfere with academic effectiveness. Sarason and Stoops (1978) found that students with high test anxiety were more self-centered and self-critical and produced more worry responses that interfered with information processing and attention to task-relevant cues than individuals with low test anxiety.

D.   ATTRIBUTION CONSEQUENCES: TASK CHOICE

Students' choices of tasks are also mediated by the students' perceived attributes. The learner's perceived level of competence influences task selection in a complex manner. Nicholls (1984) argues that both perceived level and conceptualization of competence influence an individual's achievement behavior. Nicholls identified two views of ability: simple mastery of tasks, or involving comparison with a normative reference group (cf. criterion-referenced and norm-referenced testing). Regardless of level of perceived ability, when students seek to demonstrate mastery they prefer tasks close to their own perceived level of competence, where one's highest level of competence might be demonstrated through maximum effort. When students seek comparison with a normative group, individuals with high perceived ability prefer tasks that are of normatively moderate or greater difficulty. On the other hand, students with low perceived ability avoid tasks of moderate difficulty due to high expectation for failure. Choice of either very easy or very difficult tasks enables them to avoid demonstrating low competence.

E.   ATTRIBUTIONS AND STUDY STRATEGY USE

In sum, individuals' attributions influence achievement-related variables including learners' expectations for future performance, task persistence, affective reactions, and task choice. We argue that these variables affect students' decisions about when and how to use strategies. Studiers who have low expectations for future performance, who are anxious and self-critical about their performance, who do not initiate studying efforts or fail to persist in these efforts, and who attempt tasks in which study strategies have limited chance of success are less likely to use effective strategies.

III.   SELF-EFFICACY THEORY

Conceptually and empirically linked to attribution research is the recent work by Bandura and his colleagues on self-efficacy (Bandura, 1978, 1982; Schunk, 1983). Bandura's primary assumption is that expectations of personal efficacy mediate peoples' actions. An efficacy expectation is the belief that one can successfully execute behaviors that produce desired outcomes. Bandura contends that these efficacy expectations influence: (1) individuals' choice of activities, causing them to avoid activities they believe exceed their capabilities, and undertake those they think they can perform; (2) how much effort people will expend; and (3) how long they will persist in the face of obstacles and aversive experiences. Bandura (1978) notes that efficacy expectations are affected by a variety of information including performance accomplishments, modeling, and verbal persuasion. Attributional content embedded within these sources of information may be an important antecedent for efficacy expectations (Schunk, 1983). Bandura argues that psychological interventions that influence subjects' self-efficacy expectations will affect subjects' behavior (Bandura, 1978, 1982). In fact, Bandura et al. (1975) reported that subjects tended to generalize their enhanced self-efficacy to other settings in which performance was negatively affected by their preoccupation with personal inadequacies. While there is only preliminary evidence relating strategy use and self-efficacy (e.g., Borkowski et al., 1987; McCombs, Ch. 9, this volume), we believe there are a number of implications of this area for study strategy training and research.

SELF-EFFICACY AND STRATEGY USE

Bandura and his colleagues have found that when presented with a difficult task, people who doubt their capability tend to give up. In contrast, those with a high sense of self-efficacy exert greater effort to meet the challenge (Bandura & Schunk, 1981; Schunk, 1981). These observations parallel descriptions of strategic and nonstrategic learners (Ryan, 1981; Borkowski et al., 1987). Bandura and Schunk (1981) found that self-efficacy and cognitive performance are enhanced when learners adopted attainable subgoals that lead to major goals rather than focusing directly on the more distant major goals.

Bandura (1978) notes that there may be times when efficacy expectations do not match performance. For example, if students underestimate the task demands, they may have high efficacy expectations but perform poorly on the task. This situation parallels a condition in which learners with limited metacognitive awareness (e.g., young children or learning-disabled pupils) fail to understand the nature of the task demands and overestimate their performance (Schneider, 1985; Wong, 1985). This metacognitive deficit has been identified as a major reason for the lack of strategy use within these populations. From the self-efficacy perspective, pupils may not use strategies because they think the task is easy and does not require special efforts.

The subsequent failure experiences may, in turn, lower their perception of personal efficacy.

Within the proposed model of strategy use, self-efficacy expectations involve the interaction or match between parallel self- and strategy-referent attributes. Students will have greater confidence in their capability to use a strategy if they perceive that they have the level of ability and effort required for effective use of the strategy, and that the strategy is appropriate for tasks like the one they are required to perform. Indirect empirical support for this contention may be found in a study by Fyans and Maehr (1979). They found that students who attribute their own success on achievement tasks to ability, effort, or luck will prefer tasks that they perceive as primarily determined by the same attribute. We are suggesting that the match of learner and strategy attributes conceptually forms the basis of individuals' decisions concerning whether or not they can use a strategy.

IV. LEARNER VARIABLES AND STRATEGY USE

Because of the nature of the disciplines, investigators in developmental psychology and special education focus upon learner characteristics, and the use of cognitive strategies has received a great deal of attention in these literatures during the last 15 years (e.g., Brown et al., 1983; Wong, 1985). In contrast, the relationship between learner characteristics and strategy use among adults has received only scattered and sporadic attention. There are, however, some recent investigations relating individual difference variables and adult learners' knowledge of, beliefs about, and use of strategies.

A. YOUNG AND LESS PROFICIENT LEARNERS

From their extensive review of research on memory in children, Brown et al. (1983) report that younger and less proficient pupils are less strategic in their learning efforts. They generally know fewer strategies and have little awareness of when and how to use the strategies they do know. These individuals also tend to evidence less awareness of their own capabilities and the nature of the tasks they are to perform (cf. Schneider, 1985; Wong, 1985). These deficits, however, have not been linked to maturational factors or a capacity deficit (Dempster, 1981). Rather, the nature of the youngsters' knowledge base may result in their relatively poor memory and limited strategy use (Chi, 1978). In areas where they are novices, youngsters have fewer available knowledge structures (i.e., schemata, chunks), with less information within each structure, and less integration (i.e., interconnections or links) across structures (Chi, 1976). Thus, they have less available knowledge to call upon, and that knowledge they do possess is less organized and less accessible.

Less proficient learners, such as pupils identified as learning-disabled or mildly retarded, have been described as "inactive learners," indicating the passive and disorganized nature of their approach to learning tasks (Torgesen, 1982). While limitations in their knowledge base may be a crucial determining factor, their strategy deficits also may reflect motivational factors. Results from a large-scale observational study of learning-disabled (LD) pupils indicated that the only common characteristic was their poor task orientation, including poor attention, concentration, effort, and persistence (McKinney et al., 1982). Weisz (1979) found that mentally retarded youngsters exhibited less persistence and response initiation. These behaviors reflect, in part, learned helplessness (e.g., Seligman, 1975). By definition, LD and mildly retarded pupils have a history of failure that may be an analog of the learned helplessness paradigm. LD pupils report attributions and display behavior patterns that are similar to those observed in learned helplessness studies (Pearl et al., 1980; Palmer et al., 1982). Licht (1983) contends that as a result of their history of failure, LD pupils may question their competence and the effect of effortful strategic attempts to learn.

B. ADULT LEARNERS

Despite the limited number of investigations that have examined individual difference variables and strategy use in adult learners, a variety of themes emerge. Specifically, adults' background knowledge, reading ability, metacognitive knowledge, and affect are associated with their use of strategies.

Students with more schooling report use of more and more varied strategies. In a study comparing graduate students, community college students, and army personnel with and without high school diplomas, graduate students displayed the greatest number and variety of strategies (Weinstein et al., 1980). Whereas each group reported high use of rote memorization, generative or elaborative strategies (i.e., imagery, elaboration, grouping) were most often reported by graduate students. Individuals with greater expertise in a specific domain also employ strategies that differ from those of individuals with less expertise. For example, novice physics problem solvers tend to rigidly employ a strategy that places heavy constraints on solution attempts, whereas experts exhibit greater flexibility and fewer strategic constraints (see Sweller et al. 1983 for a review).

Adults who are good readers report a greater number and variety of strategies (e.g., Hare, 1981; Smith, 1967). Good readers are also more likely to adapt their strategies to fit the purpose of a particular reading situation than are poor readers (Smith, 1967; Worden & Nakamura, 1982). This effective use of strategies appears to be related to their awareness of text structure and the reading process (Gambrell & Heathington, 1981; Goetz et al., 1983; Hiebert et al., 1983). Fischer and Mandl (1984) interviewed college students classified as good, average, or poor readers about their metacognitive awareness and study strategies during text processing. They found that good readers displayed a greater awareness of the nature of the task and their specific comprehension problems, and were more flexible in adapting their reading to deal with these problems. On the other hand, they found that poor readers reacted affectively to comprehension problems. When confronted with comprehension problems, poor readers were likely to view them as confirmation of failure expectations, rather than as cues to appropriate strategic activity; "Their poor performance can be described as a disposition to give up." (Fischer & Mandl, 1984, p. 241).

The potentially deleterious effects of learner affect were recently demonstrated by Ellis et al. (1984). For one group of subjects, depressed mood was experimentally induced prior to studying a list of sentences. Depressed mood reduced the effectiveness of elaborative encoding and cognitive effort. They concluded that a depressed mood can redirect learners' allocation of attention and reduce the amount of task-relevant processing during study.

To summarize, there appears to be an overlap in the results of strategy investigations with adult learners and young and atypical learners. Strategy use in each of these populations is affected by knowledge structure, strategy knowledge, and motivational factors. Academically capable learners appear to have more knowledge regarding, and make more use of, learning and study strategies than do their less able peers. The effective readers and studiers are more flexible and adaptive in their use of strategies and more aware of the variables that influence the appropriateness of specific strategies. Less able learners may be less likely to monitor and regulate the comprehension process, and more prone to emotional responses that interfere with learning. When faced with comprehension difficulties, less proficient learners may be more inclined to react affectively than effectively.

V. AN EMPIRICAL LOOK AT THE MODEL

Earlier, we introduced a model that illustrated how individuals' decisions to use a strategy are mediated by their perceptions of strategy, task, and personal attributes (see Fig. 1). As reflected in the literatures previously reviewed, various studies have looked at the relationships between one or a few of the variables in the model and strategy use. To provide a more comprehensive look at the model, we designed a study that examined the effect of the variables previously discussed within the temporal order proposed by our model of strategy use (Palmer & Goetz, 1983).

Subjects in this study were college students who had been counseled into a study skills course by academic advisors on the basis of high school transcripts, Scholastic Aptitude Test (SAT) scores, or other predictors that indicated the students would be academically "at risk." None of the subjects had participated in any study-strategy training activities prior to this investigation.

Subjects were randomly assigned a 100-word passage in one of four content areas at either the college or advanced level in a completely crossed, 4 × 2 design. The subjects were asked to "read and study the passage carefully, as we will be asking you some questions about it." Subjects answered four short-answer questions immediately after reading without referring back to the text. After answering the questions, subjects were shown model answers and asked to rate on a 12-point scale their perceived success or failure in the task. In light of their performance on the short-answer questions, subjects were asked to rate the following attributes: effort, intelligence, industriousness, prior knowledge, and task difficulty on 4-point Likert-type scales. For example, subjects were asked, "How much effort did you use when reading the text?"

Subsequently, subjects were asked a series of questions related to study strategies. The list of strategies queried was based on the work of Anderson (1980) and Weinstein (1978). Strategies were organized on a list under the headings of prereading, during reading, and post-reading activities. The students were asked to report which strategies they used when reading the text and how frequently they use these strategies when they read texts like the one they just read. Reported strategy use was high, with students reporting an average of 8.36 strategies each (cf. Weinstein et al., 1980).

Finally, subjects were asked to rate each of the 24 strategies on a variety of attributes. Specifically, they were asked how much intelligence, effort, industriousness, prior instruction in the strategy, and knowledge of text content would be required to effectively use each of the strategies. Students were also asked to rate how much they knew about using the strategies effectively, the level(s) of difficulty of text for which each would be appropriate, and how beneficial the use of each would be for understanding texts such as the one they had just read.

Answers to the essay questions were assigned scores of zero, one, or two, by two independent raters. The relationship of text content area, text level, and strategy use to performance on the short-answer essay questions was examined by means of a series of regression analyses conducted in a stagewise fashion. In the first stage, the text variables accounted for 25.0% of the variance in test performance. In the second stage, three of the strategies accounted for an additional 7% of the variance on test performance. The strategies were skimming the passage and anticipating the test (both pre-reading), and selective rereading.

MODELS OF STRATEGY USE

Separate analyses were conducted on each of the three strategies that were related to performance on the test. The effect of each of the hypothesized determinants of strategy use from the model illustrated in Fig. 1 was examined in a series of regression analyses performed in a stage-wise fashion. At each stage of the analysis except the first (an evaluation of text topic and level effects employing a General Linear Model approach), stepwise regression was used to evaluate all of the factors entered in that stage. These models accounted for 18.2, 21.0, and 9.2% of the variance in the use of skimming, anticipating the test, and selective rereading, respectively.

The final full models differed for each of the strategies studied. For skimming, general knowledge of the strategy, learners' perceptions of their industriousness, match between learner and strategy effort, match between learner and strategy industry, and strategy efficacy predicted strategy use. Anticipating the test was predicted by knowledge of the strategy, learner effort, perceived level of student industriousness required to effectively use the strategy, and strategy efficacy. For selective rereading, strategy knowledge was the sole predictor.

This study provides empirical support for the role of each component of the model in determining strategy use. The fact that the final model differed for each of the strategies investigated suggests that there may be no single model for how studiers come to select and employ strategies in instructional context. It should also be noted that the relatively homogeneous subject population (i.e., "at risk" college students) and the multitude of strategies and attributes queried (at the possible expense of subjects' willingness or ability to provide accurate information) may have resulted in an underestimate of the importance of model components.

VI.   IMPLICATIONS

With the study of cognition and emotion being reemphasized in psychology, there has been increased acknowledgment of and interest in the role of the human in human behavior. Developmental and cognitive psychologists have stressed the role of the person's knowledge of specific tasks, and his or her own cognitive processes and characteristics. Personality and developmental psychologists have been concerned with the role of motivational and emotional factors as determinants of a person's affective reactions, expectations, achievement-related behaviors, and cognitive outcomes. Various investigators concerned with atypical populations have also considered cognitive and affective constructs. With this accumulating body of research, it is becoming evident that there is a dynamic interplay between personality and cognition (see also Schmeck, Ch. 10, this volume). Furthermore, personality may be best viewed as an interaction of constitutional factors and prior learning that results in individual differences in cognitions about oneself and one's environment. In turn, these cognitions influence and are influenced by the environment (Endler & Magnusson, 1976; Mischel, 1973). It is a person's cognitions that play a central role in his/her model of strategy use.

Examining the theoretical and research literatures discussed above, we were struck by the many areas of potential convergence, and by how few of these have been noted or pursued. For the most part, researchers in each of the areas neither cite the work nor share the concerns of those in other areas. This fact is not surprising given the volume of literature that is being generated in each of the areas. To attempt to move between areas of research and domains of literature is indeed daunting. We believe that both affective and cognitive components influence students' performance on academic tasks. To understand the role of the studier in study behavior, we must consider how self-referent thought, knowledge of the task and topic, and strategic knowledge and beliefs combine and interact. Whereas recent efforts have been made to bring together cognitive and affective constructs, the approach we are advocating, as exemplified by our model, is both broader and narrower than current syntheses. It is broader in attempting to consider the many traditionally separated concerns discussed above. It is narrower in terms of couching the descriptions of self-referent thought and strategic knowledge in the context of specific attributes for a specific task and strategy. The potential benefits of such an approach are tempered by concern about the complexity of the description of strategy influences that may emerge. Further research is needed before the potential costs and benefits of this approach can be accurately assessed.

From the framework we have described, strategy training programs should consider, in part, learners' self-referent and strategy referent thought. Kurtz and Borkowski (1984) suggest that learners who perceive that their efforts will lead to success are more likely to use trained strategies in a transfer situation. Recent training efforts have included development of a separate attribution training component within a strategy training package (McCombs, Ch. 9, this volume) and effort attribution retraining activities that are integrated into strategy training procedures (Short & Ryan, 1984). Following from the model proposed in this paper, we suggest that training should attend to students' perceptions of their effort and ability attributes and their perceptions of parallel strategy attributes. Following instruction on the specific procedures required to perform the strategic behaviors, an assessment of the match between learners' perceived self- and strategy attributes may be conducted. This assessment activity would allow for a more individualized training program to produce a match between the learner and strategy attributes. For example, if a student perceives that he or she is sufficiently industrious to use the strategy but is not smart enough to effectively perform the strategic behavior, required training efforts should attend to modifying his or her perceptions of competence. These training activities may involve self-instructional training procedures (see Meichenbaum & Asarnow, 1979) that emphasize the linkage between competence and the learner's developing strategic behavior.

REFERENCES

Abramson, L., Seligman, M., & Teasdale, J. (1978). Learned helplessness in humans: Critique and reformulation. *Journal of Abnormal Psychology, 87,* 49–74.

Ames, R., & Lau, S. (1982). An attributional analysis of student help-seeking in academic settings. *Journal of Educational Psychology, 74,* 414–423.

Anderson, T. H. (1980). Study strategies and adjunct aids. In R. J. Spiro, B. C. Bruce, & W. F. Brewer (Eds.), *Theoretical issues in reading comprehension* (pp. 483–502). Hillsdale, NJ: Erlbaum.

Arkin, R. M., & Maruyama, G. M. (1979). Attribution, affect, and college exam performance. *Journal of Educational Psychology, 71,* 85–93.

Bandura, A. (1978). The self system in reciprocal determinism. *American Psychologist, 33,* 344–358.

Bandura, A. (1982). Self-efficacy mechanism in human agency. *American Psychologist, 37,* 122–147.

Bandura, A., Jeffery, R. W., & Gajdos, E. (1975). Generalizing change through participant modeling with self-directed mastery. *Behavior Research and Therapy, 13,* 141–152.

Bandura, A., & Schunk, D. H. (1981). Cultivating competence, self-efficacy, and intrinsic interest through proximal self-motivation. *Journal of Personality and Social Psychology, 41,* 586–598.

Benson, J. S., & Kennelly, K. J. (1976). Learned helplessness: The result of uncontrollable reinforcements or uncontrollable aversive stimuli? *Journal of Personality and Social Psychology, 34,* 138–145.

Borkowski, J. G., Johnston, M. B., & Reid, M. K. (1987). Metacognition, motivation, and the transfer of control processes. In S. J. Ceci (Ed.), *Handbook of cognitive, social, and neuropsychological aspects of learning disabilities.* Hillsdale, NJ: Erlbaum.

Brown, A. L., Bransford, J. D., Ferrara. R. A., & Campione, J. C. (1983). *Learning, remembering, and understanding.* In J. Flavell, & E. Mankman (Eds.), *Carmichael's manual of child psychology* (Vol. 1). New York: Wiley.

Chi, M. T. H. (1976). Short-term memory limitations in children: Capacity or processing deficits? *Memory and Cognition, 4,* 559–572.

Chi, M. T. H. (1978). Knowledge structures and memory development. In R. S. Siegler (Ed.), *Children's thinking: What develops?* (pp. 73–96). Hillsdale, NJ: Erlbaum.

Covington, M. V. (1983). Motivated cognitions. In S. G. Paris, G. M. Olson, & H. W. Stevenson (Eds.), *Learning and motivation in the classroom* (pp. 139–164). Hillsdale, NJ: Erlbaum.

Dempster, F. N. (1981). Memory span: Sources of individual and developmental differences. *Psychological Bulletin, 89,* 63–100.

Dweck, C. S., & Reppucci, N. D. (1973). Learned helplessness and reinforcement responsibility in children. *Journal of Personality and Social Psychology, 25,* 109–116.

Elig, T., & Frieze, I. (1975). A multi-dimensional scheme for coding and interpreting perceived causality for success and failure events: The CSPC. *JSAS Catalog of Selected Documents in Psychology, 5,* 313 (Manuscript #1069).

Ellis, H. C., Thomas, R. L., & Rodriguez, I. A. (1984). Emotional mood states and memory: Elaborative encoding, semantic processing, and cognitive effort. *Journal of Experimental Psychology: Learning, Memory, and Cognition, 10,* 470–482.

Endler, N., & Magnusson, D. (1976). Toward an interactional psychology of personality. *Psychological Bulletin, 83,* 956–974.

Fischer, P. M., & Mandl, H. (1984). Learner, text variables, and the control of text comprehension and recall. In H. Mandl, N. L. Stein, & T. Trabasso (Eds.), *Learning and comprehension of text* (pp. 213–254). Hillsdale, NJ: Erlbaum.

Flavell, J. H., & Wellman, H. M. (1977). Metamemory. In R. V. Kail, Jr., & J. W. Hagen (Eds.), *Perspectives on the development of memory and cognition* (pp. 3–33). Hillsdale, NJ: Erlbaum.

Frieze, I. H. (1976). Causal attributions and information seeking to explain success and failure. *Journal of Research in Personality, 10,* 293–305.

Frieze, I. H., & Weiner, B. (1971). Cue utilization and attributional judgments for success and failure. *Journal of Personality, 39,* 591–605.

Fyans, L. J., & Maehr, M. L. (1979). Attributional style, task selection, and achievement. *Journal of Educational Psychology, 71,* 499–507.

Gambrell, L. B., & Heathington, B. S. (1981). Adult disabled readers' metacognitive awareness about leading tasks and strategies. *Journal of Reading Behavior, 13,* 215–222.

Goetz, E. T., Palmer, D. J., & Haensly, P. A. (1983). Metacognitive awareness of text variables in good and poor readers. In J. A. Niles, & L. A. Harris (Eds.), *Searches for meaning in reading/language . processing. and instruction (Thirty-second Yearbook of the National Reading Conference)* (pp. 129–134). Rochester, NY: National Reading Conference.

Hare, V. C. (1981). Readers' problem identification and problem-solving strategies for high-and-low-knowledge comprehenders. *Journal of Reading Behavior, 13,* 359–365.

Heider, F. (1958). *The psychology of interpersonal relations.* New York: Wiley.

Hiebert, E. H., Englert, C. S., & Brennan, S. (1983). Awareness of text structure in recognition and production of expository discourse. *Journal of Reading Behavior, 15,* 63–79.

Hiroto, D. S., & Seligman, M. E. P. (1975). Generality of learned helplessness in man. *Journal of Personality and Social Psychology, 31,* 311–327.

Humphreys, M. S., & Revelle, W. (1984). Personality, motivation, and performance: A theory of the relationship between individual differences and information processing. *Psychological Review, 91,* 153–184.

Jenkins, J. J. (1979). Four points to remember: A tetrahedral model and memory experiments. In L. S. Cermak, & F. I. M. Craik (Eds.), *Levels of processing in human memory* (pp. 429–446). Hillsdale, NJ: Erlbaum.

Kelley, H. H. (1967). Attribution theory in social psychology. In D. Levine (Ed.), *Nebraska*

Symposium on motivation (Vol. 15, pp. 192–238). Lincoln, NE: University of Nebraska Press.

Kennedy, B. A., & Miller, D. J. (1976). Persistent use of verbal rehearsal as a function of information about its value. *Child Development, 47,* 566–569.

Klein, D. C., Fencil-Morse, E., & Seligman, M. E. P. (1976). Learned helplessness, depression, and the attribution of failure. *Journal of Personality and Social Psychology, 33,* 508–516.

Kurtz, B. E., & Borkowski, J. G. (1984). Children's metacognition: Exploring relations among knowledge, process, and motivational variables. *Journal of Experimental Child Psychology, 37,* 335–354.

Licht, B. G. (1983). Cognitive-motivational factors that contribute to the achievement of learning-disabled children. *Journal of Learning Disabilities, 16,* 483–490.

Maier, S. F., & Seligman, M. E. P. (1976). Learned helplessness: Theory and evidence. *Journal of Experimental Psychology: General, 105,* 3–46.

McKinney, J. D., McClure, S., & Feagans, L. (1982). Classroom behavior of learning disabled children. *Learning Disability Quarterly, 5,* 45–52.

McMahan, I. D. (1973). Relationships between causal attributions and expectancy of success. *Journal of Personality and Social Psychology, 28,* 108–114.

Meichenbaum, D., & Asarnow, J. (1979). Cognitive-behavioral modification and metacognitive development: Implications for the classroom. In P. C. Kendall, & S. D. Hollon (Eds.), *Cognitive behavioral interventions: Theory, research, and procedures* (pp. 11–35). New York: Academic Press.

Miller, I., & Norman, W. (1979). Learned helplessness in humans: A review and attribution-theory model. *Psychological Bulletin, 86,* 93–118.

Miller, W. R., & Seligman, M. E. P. (1975). Depression and learned helplessness in man. *Journal of Abnormal Psychology, 84,* 228–238.

Mischel, W. (1973). Toward a cognitive social learning reconceptualization of personality. *Psychological Review, 80,* 252–283.

Nicholls, J. G. (1984). Achievement motivation: Conceptions of ability, subjective experience, task choice, and performance. *Psychological Review, 91,* 328–346.

Palmer, D. J., Drummond, F., Tollison, P., & Zinkgraff, S. (1982). An attributional investigation of performance outcomes for learning-disabled and normal-achieving pupils. *The Journal of Special Education, 16,* 207–219.

Palmer, D., & Goetz, E. (1983). Students' perceptions of study strategy attributes as a mediator of strategy use, paper presented at the meeting of the American Educational Research Association, Montreal, Canada.

Palmer, D. J., & Willson, V. (1982). Prediction of attributional consequences in an actual achievement setting. *Contemporary Educational Psychology, 7,* 334–345.

Pearl, R., Bryan, T., & Donahue, M. (1980). Learning disabled children's attributions for success and failure. *Learning Disability Quarterly, 3,* 3–9.

Pressley, M., Borkowski, J. G., & O'Sullivan, J. T. (1982). Memory strategies are made of this, paper presented at the convention of the American Psychological Association.

Rest, S. (1976). Schedules of reinforcement: An attributional analysis. In J. H. Harvey, W. J. Ickes, & R. F. Kidd (Eds.), *New directions in attribution research* (Vol. 1, pp. 97–120). Hillsdale, NJ: Erlbaum.

Ryan, E. B. (1981). Identifying and remediating failures in reading comprehension: Toward an instructional approach for poor comprehenders. In G. E. MacKinnon, & T. G. Waller (Eds.), *Reading research: Advances in theory and practice* (Vol. 3, 223–261). New York: Academic Press.

Sarason, I. G., & Stoops, R. (1978). Test anxiety and the passage of time. *Journal of Consulting and Clinical Psychology, 46*, 102–109.

Schneider, W. (1985). Developmental trends in the metamemory-memory behavior relationship: An integrative review. In D. Forrest-Pressley, G. E. MacKinnon, & T. G. Waller (Eds.), *Metacognition, cognition, and human performance.* New York: Academic Press.

Schunk, D. H. (1981). Modeling and attributional effects on children's achievement: A self-efficacy analysis. *Journal of Educational Psychology. 73*, 93–105.

Schunk, D. H. (1983). Ability versus effort attributional feedback: Differential effects on self-efficacy and achievement. *Journal of Educational Psychology, 75*, 848–856.

Seligman, M. E. P. (1975). *Helplessness: On depression, development, and death.* San Francisco: Freeman.

Short, E. J., & Ryan, E. B. (1984). Metacognitive differences between skilled and less skilled readers: Remediating deficits through story grammar and attribution training. *Journal of Educational Psychology, 76*, 225–235.

Smith, H. K. (1967). The response of good and poor readers when asked to read for different purposes. *Reading Research Quarterly, 3*, 53–83.

Sweller, J., Mawer, R. F., & Ward, M. R. (1983). Development of expertise in mathematical problem solving. *Journal of Experimental Psychology: General, 112*, 639–661.

Teasdale, J. (1978). Effects of real and recalled success on learned helplessness and depression. *Journal of Abnormal Psychology, 87*, 155–164.

Tennen, H., & Eller, S. J. (1977). Attributional components of learned helplessness and facilitation. *Journal of Personality and Social Psychology, 35*, 265–271.

Torgesen, J. K. (1982). The learning disabled child as an inactive learner: Educational implications. *Topics in Learning & Learning Disabilities, 2*, 45–52.

Underwood, G. (1978). Concepts in information processing. In G. Underwood (Ed.) *Strategies of information processing,* pp. 1–22. New York: Academic Press.

Weiner, B. (1972). *Theories of motivation: From mechanism to cognition.* Chicago: Rand McNally.

Weiner, B. (1974). *Achievement motivation and attribution theory.* Morristown, NJ: General Learning Press.

Weiner, B. (1976). Attribution theory, achievement motivation, and the educational process. *Review of Educational Research, 42*, 201–215.

Weiner, B. (1979). A theory of motivation for some classroom experiences. *Journal of Educational Psychology, 71*, 3–25.

Weiner, B., Frieze, I., Kukla, A., Reed, L., Rest, S., & Rosenbaum, R. M. (1972). Perceiving the causes of success and failure. In E. E. Jones, D. E. Kanouse, H. H. Kelley, R. E. Nisbett, S. Valins, & B. Weiner (Eds.), *Attribution: Perceiving the causes of behavior* (pp. 95–120). Morristown, NJ: General Learning Press.

Weiner, B., Nirenburg, R., & Goldstein, M. (1976). Social learning (locus of control) versus attributional (causal stability) interpretations of expectancy of success. *Journal of Personality and Social Psychology, 44*, 52–68.

Weiner, B., Russell, D., & Lerman, D. (1978). Affective consequences of causal ascriptions. In J. H. Harvey, W. J. Ickes, & R. F. Kidd (Eds.), *New directions in attribution research* (Vol. 2, pp. 59–90). Hillsdale, NJ: Erlbaum.

Weinstein, C. E. (1978). Elaboration skills as a learning strategy. In H. F. O'Neil, Jr. (Ed.), *Learning strategies* (pp. 31–56). New York: Academic Press.

Weinstein, C. E., Wicker, F. W., Cubberly, W. E., Ramey, L. K., & Underwood, V. L. (1980). Design and development of the Learning Activities Questionnaire, Report No. 459, U.S. Army Research Institute for the Behavioral and Social Sciences, Alexandria, VA.

Weisz, J. (1979). Perceived control and learned helplessness among mentally retarded and nonretarded children: A developmental analysis. *Developmental Psychology, 15*, 311–319.

Willson, V. L., & Palmer, D. J. (1983). Latent partition analysis of attributions for actual achievement. *American Educational Research Journal, 20*, 581–589.

Wong, B. Y. L. (1985). Metacognition and learning disabilities. In D. Forrest-Pressley, G. E. MacKinnon, & T. G. Waller (Eds.), *Metacognition, cognition, and human performance.* New York: Academic Press.

Worden, P. E., & Nakamura, G. V. (1982). Story comprehension and recall in learning-disabled versus normal college students. *Journal of Educational Psychology, 74*, 633–641.

VERBAL-REPORT DATA ON COGNITIVE AND METACOGNITIVE STRATEGIES

Ruth Garner

Learners use a range of cognitive strategies to complete a variety of academic tasks. Flavell (1981) points out that metacognitive experiences often precede or follow strategy use. An example of the former is a reader's noting she cannot recall information already read, and then engaging in selective text reinspection to answer a text explicit question. An example of the latter is a learner's writing a succinct summary of a text and discovering he has not really differentiated important information from irrelevant detail. Flavell (1979) describes metacognitively sophisticated learners who carry out cognitive activities both to assess the progress of task completion and to complete the task. These learners are invoking both "metacognitive strategies" (designed to monitor cognitive progress) and "cognitive strategies" (designed to make cognitive progress). These learners have become "amateur psychologists" (Miller, 1983, p. 272).

It has once again become an important research activity for psychologists and educators to document cognitive and metacognitive strategies used by learners. After some years of "rejection of unobservables" (Floden, 1981, p. 78), information-processing psychology has made the structure and process of the human mind its subject of research activity. As Floden describes the current state of affairs, there is a "relegitimizing of talk about what goes on in students' heads" (1981, p. 105). Some strategic activities and outcomes are readily observable; other covert strategies are not. Some strategies have reliable behavioral indicants; others do not. Both readily observed and not so readily observed strategies are currently considered worthy objects of scientific investigation. Verbal-report data are particularly useful in that they give researchers a glimpse at covert strategic activity that is not accessible except as described by strategy users.

The purposes of this chapter are: (1) to define cognitive and metacognitive strategies, (2) to describe verbal-report research methods currently being used to externalize strategic activity, (3) to enumerate criticisms of current methods, and (4) to suggest alternative research methods for documenting strategic repertoires. Reading strategies will be particularly emphasized.

LEARNING AND STUDY STRATEGIES: ISSUES IN
ASSESSMENT, INSTRUCTION, AND EVALUATION

I. STRATEGIES: WHAT ARE THEY?

As Kail and Bisanz (1982) point out, a strategy is a sequence of activities rather than a single event. This means, among other things, that learners need to acquire both the component processes and a routine for organizing the processes. This fact alone helps explain the frequency of nonstrategic responses and the complexity of training strategic activities that both maintain and transfer. A recent finding from our research program is that many proficient and less proficient readers have acquired some, but not all, of the components of the text-lookback strategy, a cognitive strategy used at the question answering stage to remedy memory gaps for information in text (see Garner et al., 1984). Had we operationalized the strategy as a unitary activity, we would have a picture of users and nonusers, but we would have missed valuable information about extent of use and of further needs for instruction. This is but one of many strategies that have important component pieces that are acquired, refined, and integrated into strategic wholes.

An important feature of any strategy is that it is largely under the control of the learner. That is to say, though certain subroutines may be learned to a point of automaticity, strategies are generally deliberate, planned, consciously engaged-in activities. In this context, Paris et al. (1983) call them "skills under consideration" (p. 295). This means both that strategies require attentional resources that are not limitless, and that strategies can be examined, reported, and modified. Paris et al. remind us that in order for an activity to be considered strategic, it must be selected by a learner from alternative activities, and it must be intended to attain a goal, to complete a task. Strategic activities, they tell us, are neither accidental nor merely obedient.

Another significant aspect of any metacognitive or cognitive strategy is the need for flexible use. This means that knowing when to use a strategy is as important as knowing how to use it. Examples of failures in flexible use of strategies are plentiful: reinspecting text for questions cueing use of reader knowledge base; allocating extensive studying time to easy and difficult tasks alike; looking for signals of importance in text (e.g., headings, topic sentences, redundancy) as a prelude to summary writing, and having no strategic option to be used with poorly crafted texts that fail to provide obvious relevance cues; or formulating self-questions for text in instances where surveying questions provided by the author would do as well for both fostering and monitoring of comprehension.

A strong relation between metacognitive experiences and adept strategy use is suggested by Forrest-Pressley and Gillies (1983), who argue that metacognitive activity directs the flexible use of various strategies. That is, metacognitively sophisticated learners know whether or not the criterion task to be completed warrants the costly expenditure of time and effort involved in strategic processing. This decision about selective use of time and effort obviously has a motivational component (see Hale, 1983). As Paris and Lindauer (1982) remind us, learners often recognize the need to apply strategic remedies for task completion, but choose not to do so.

II. VERBAL-REPORT METHODS

In order to examine strategies employed by novices and experts, we need to devise means to externalize them in the instances where they are not readily observable. Two prominent methods currently used to externalize cognitive and metacognitive strategies are interviews and "think-aloud" procedures. Both can be classified as "verbal-report methods" in that learners tell receptive listeners (typically researchers) what they have on occasion thought and done, what they might think and do in a hypothetical situation, or what they are thinking and doing while completing a task at hand. Interviews produce retrospective verbalizations, for they elicit reports of cognitive and metacognitive activity already completed. Think-aloud procedures produce concurrent verbalizations about an activity that is temporarily interrupted for provision of the verbal report.

A. INTERVIEW TECHNIQUES

An early example of an interview technique is the Myers and Paris (1978) study of metacognitive knowledge about reading. For the study, a standard set of questions (e.g., "What makes someone a really good reader?," "Do you ever have to go back to the beginning of a paragraph or story to figure out what a sentence means? Why?") about knowledge of interacting person, task, and strategy variables was presented to second- and sixth-grade students. Clear differences in knowledge related to age and experience emerged. The younger children demonstrated far less awareness than the older children of the existence of various reading strategies and less sensitivity about when and how to use strategies.

Two other studies are similar in design and have yielded similar results. Forrest and Waller (1980) presented children at three reading proficiency levels in grades 3 and 6 with a standard set of questions. Again, demonstrated knowledge of strategies increased with grade (and with reading ability). It is important to note that younger/poorer readers sometimes reported the value of strategies, but only with repeated probing from the interviewer. Garner and Kraus (1981–1982) presented seventh-grade students at two reading proficiency levels with standardized questions. Good comprehenders provided more meaning-emphasis responses than poor comprehenders, and suggested certain strategies such as rereading of text with far greater frequency.

All three of these interview studies have produced consistent results of differences in strategic knowledge along the dimensions of age or reading proficiency; older, better readers have more knowledge of cognitive and metacognitive strategies than younger, less able readers. We cannot say, however, on the basis of these interview studies, that this superior knowledge is accompanied by superior use of a range of strategies.

B. THINK-ALOUD PROCEDURES

Think-aloud procedures are related to interviews, in that learners report on thoughts and actions, but they do so while engaged in cognitive processing. These verbal reports are elicited with instructions and probes that vary in generality (e.g., "Tell me what you are thinking and doing while you read this article," "Tell me if you use any strategies while reading," "Tell me if you have occasion to use strategy X while you read this article."). The sustained verbalizations are typically recorded on audiotape for analysis, and are often augmented by nonverbal behavior records. A large quantity of data is usually produced.

Olshavsky (1976–1977) was one of the first investigators to use a think-aloud procedure to study reading strategies. In her study, reader interest, reader proficiency, and writing style of text were factors of interest. Subjects, 10th-grade students, were required to think aloud (talk about the story content and about thoughts and actions) after each independent clause in the text. Verbal reports were audiotaped. Olshavsky argued that interference with the reading process was minimized in the study by inclusion of a practice session and by ensuring that the investigator said nothing during reading/verbalizing. No statistically significant differences were found for levels of interest, proficiency, or text type, but the method employed generated much interest in the research community.

Using Olshavsky's system of inserting red dots at stop-points, Garner and Alexander (1982) investigated college students' reporting of a strategy of attempting to discern during reading the questions to be answered after reading. They asked the undergraduates to read an eight-page expository text, stopping every other page at a red dot to report on reading and question-preparation activities. Half of the college students verbalized a question-formulation strategy. Scores on a question-answering task for these students were significantly superior to scores of students who failed to verbalize the strategy while reading.

Alvermann (1984) also applied the Olshavsky system to research on strategy use. Second-grade children read basal reader stories with think-aloud breaks at red dots placed after each sentence. Relative frequency of various strategies reported for each story grammar category remained fairly constant.

Hayes and Flower (1980) have used think-aloud procedures extensively to uncover the psychological processes used to complete composing tasks. They have inferred the existence of three major processes (planning, translating, and reviewing) that seldom occur in successive stages, but typically appear in some form in the verbal reports of competent writers. Protocols (transcripts of taped verbal reports) have often amounted to 20 pages for an hour's writing (Flower & Hayes, 1981). Many protocol segments are quite "meta" in flavor (e.g., "I'll just make a list of topics now," "Oh no. We need more organizing," "Better go back and read it over.").

Think-aloud procedures used to track reading or writing activities in the form of "running commentaries" (Baker & Brown, 1984, p. 24) require interpretive decisions. As Kail and Bisanz (1982) point out, data must be transcribed and categorized. Decisions about relevant and irrelevant information in protocols must be made. Reliability assessment for categorization of verbal data is an important step. Categorization usually serves as a prelude to quantitative analysis of the number of different strategies reported by members of groups of interest, such as young children/older children, and poor readers/proficient readers (Meichenbaum et al., 1979).

III. CRITICISMS OF VERBAL REPORTS AS DATA

Both interviews and think-aloud procedures have encountered criticism on a number of fronts. Some criticisms are aimed at both interview and think-aloud methods; others are targeted at only one of these methods for eliciting strategic information. General criticisms will be presented first.

Perhaps the most basic concern is the accessibility of cognitive and metacognitive processes for introspective analysis. As Nisbett and Wilson (1977) put it, one can "doubt people's ability to observe directly the workings of their own minds" (p. 232). We all have had the experience of generating relatively vague, inarticulate descriptions of processing, when called upon to produce them unexpectedly. As Ericsson and Simon (1980) argue in their paper on verbal-report data, recurrent processes that have become automated are particularly problematic in this regard. A number of subroutines of cognitive and metacognitive strategies "suffer" this fate, and as they become routinized, also become less reportable. The result is incomplete data, and (potentially) inappropriate inferences about strategic processing. Meichenbaum (1980) cautions us, in this regard, to always treat protocols as incomplete records of thinking, and to avoid the error of equating language with thought.

Verbal facility is a second major concern. When verbal-report data are collected from individuals with limited language skills, such as young children (Cavanaugh & Perlmutter, 1982) or some low-income learners (Feagans & Farran, 1981), verbalizing difficulties can mask strategic strengths. Considerable individual differences in tendency to verbalize also exist (see Miyake & Norman, 1979). Because verbal skills are not adequately developed in some learner groups, some nonverbal assessment of cognitive and metacognitive strategic knowledge may be in order. Yussen and Bird (1979), for instance, have presented pictorial, rather than verbal, stimuli to children.

Related to young children's nonproficiency in verbalizing is their inexperience in responding to highly general questions or probes (Yussen et al., 1982). They tend not to be "formal-definers," and are likely to respond to questions about cognition with information about just-experienced events. When asked such a general question as "What is reading?," they may refer to a very specific classroom practice or may just report that they "do not know." Yussen and his colleagues suggest that children are uncertain, in such an instance, about what aspect of reading they are expected to discuss. These young children may need to be given specific vignettes of strategic activities (perhaps presented with props) to which they can react with some referential certainty.

A third criticism aimed at these methods is that not only do learners sometimes know more than they can tell (an example is young children, as discussed above), but that learners on occasion tell more than they can know (Nisbett & Wilson, 1977). That is, learners report using cognitive and metacognitive strategies they do not demonstrate using (Cavanaugh & Borkowski, 1980; Garner & Reis, 1981; Waters, 1982). They "mimic" teacher instructional language (Forrest & Waller, 1980), often providing systematically erroneous reports of undemonstrated cognitive and metacognitive activity. They report what they perceive they ought to know or do, what they think ideal readers know and do, not what they in fact know or do. Ready repetition of seldom applied phonics rules is a good example of this phenomenon (Ryan, 1981). As Ericsson and Simon (1980) point out, in cases such as these, verbal reports may bear very little relation to actual processes.

Related to this concern is a fourth problem: the cueing offered by instructions and probes. Information about the social desirability of particular strategies can be conveyed by inadequately bland statements (Simon, 1979). An investigator can ask about use of a specific strategy, encouraging learners to respond affirmatively. The researcher, in other words, can provide a broad hint of the most desirable response. Again, the resulting verbal reports from subjects may bear only minimal relation to their actual strategic processing.

A fifth, and final, general concern about verbal-report data is that very few researchers examine the stability of responses over time (Cavanaugh & Perlmutter, 1982). This means that potentially unstable patterns of reporting are not discovered as such, and far-reaching interpretations of strategic activity may be too hastily drawn.

In sum, as Brown (1980) suggests, "eyewitness testimony is fallible, no less for the objects and events of the internal world than for the external" (p. 15). In certain situations for certain learners, reports of strategic processing are likely to be highly fallible. Avoiding those situations is a critical task facing researchers exploring problems in the area of cognitive and metacognitive strategies.

Two additional criticisms pertain only to interviews. One is that a large processing-reporting distance (i.e., a long time lapse between thinking/ doing and providing the verbal report of what was thought and done) allows memory failure to intrude as an explanation for skimpy reporting (White, 1980). As White suggests, much more may have been consciously processed than is present in the verbal-report record.

Garner (1982) designed an experiment involving use of summarizing strategies and reporting of strategic activity either immediately following task completion or 2 days later. Clear processing-report interval effects were found for college students. Though students did not differ in demonstrated summarization proficiency, same-day report subjects reported significantly more cognitive events than delayed report subjects. These results support the wisdom of White's (1980) admonition to minimize delay in eliciting reports. Such action would in turn minimize demands on learners' long-term memory store, demands almost certain to ensure incomplete reports or reports "hampered by extensive interference" (Ericsson & Simon, 1980, p. 226) from recent, untargeted cognitive events.

The second criticism made specifically of interview methods is that they often elicit responses to hypothetical situations that are difficult for young children to interpret. That is to say, no strategic activity is engaged, but reporting on potential activity is elicited. As Ericsson and Simon (1980) argue, probing for hypothetical states cannot tap learners' memories for their cognitive and metacognitive processes, for the information was never in memory.

A serious criticism has been lodged specifically against think-aloud procedures as well. Various critics have argued that the very disruption of the cognitive or metacognitive process to generate the verbal report alters the process in potentially nontrivial ways. To minimize disruption, infrequent interruptions and unobtrusive introspection methods are usually advocated (see Kellogg, 1982). Critics maintain that the process can still be broken down "into unrepresentative meaningless fragments" (Fischer & Mandl, 1982, p. 344) by the interruptions. This is a distinct possibility for research studies that include breaks after every clause of a short story (e.g., Olshav-sky, 1976–1977). Certainly, an agile reader might want to finish the story, to eliminate the interfering. Surely "thinking often *runs away* from speaking" (Ballstaedt & Mandl, 1984, p. 340).

A possible outcome is depressed verbalizing and, therefore, incomplete reporting of cognitive and metacognitive activity. As Cavanaugh and Perl-mutter (1982) suggest, the verbal reports in these cases can be both quan-titatively and qualitatively poor reflections of processing. Or, as Ericsson and Simon (1980) argue, "When subjects give indications that they are working under a heavy cognitive load, they tend to stop verbalizing or they provide less complete verbalizations." (pp. 242–243).

Some conditions for eliciting verbal reports of cognitive and metacognitive strategies are superior to others; the former produce more valid data for eventual interpretation. A number of guidelines for supportive reflective-access conditions have been suggested by Ericsson and Simon (1980) and others:

1. Tap information available in short-term or activated memory; responses will be more accurate and will not drastically diminish processing capaci-ty. In this regard, reduce strategy use–strategy report intervals, and ask learners to report on specific events, not on hypothetical situations. Avoid automated processes; by definition, conscious attention is not nec-essary for their activation.
2. Ask learners what they do and think, not why. The amount of inference required is thus constrained.
3. Recognize that some verbal reports may be incomplete, but may still contain useful information. Prompt full reporting in a noncueing fashion, and with minimal process disruption.
4. Consider methods that reduce verbalization demands, particularly in gathering information from young children.
5. Assess reliability of responses.
6. Use multimethod assessment. By using a set of different methods that do not share the same sources of error, researchers eventually collect con-vergent data on actual strategies used by learners. Observable nonverbal behaviors (e.g., eye movements) are an excellent companion database (see Flavell et al., 1981), particularly for work with young children. Com-bining verbal-report data on process with product data (e.g., underlined protocols, written summaries of text) is another useful approach (Alex-ander et al., 1984; Phifer & Glover, 1982).

The sixth guideline perhaps demands the most emphasis. As Kail and Bisanz (1982) put it, "no single approach is sufficient for unambiguous and compre-hensive identification of a person's cognitive strategies" (p. 252).

IV. OTHER METHODS FOR ASSESSING STRATEGIES

A number of creative methods have been used recently to explore strategic operations, either as alternatives to more traditional interview and think-aloud procedures or as means of generating corroborative data for the outcomes of the traditional verbal-report methods. Three specific methods will be presented in this paper: (1) "stimulated recall," using videotapes of learning situations; (2) peer tutoring to externalize strategic repertoires; and (3) optimal–nonoptimal production activities.

Peterson et al. (1982) modified earlier stimulated-recall techniques to study students' cognitive processes during a teaching-learning segment. They asked students in grades 5 and 6 to participate in two 1-hour sessions on probability concepts. Student behavior during the lessons was coded by three observers for a series of 20-second intervals; all lessons were videotaped as well. Following each lesson, students were interviewed individually using the stimulated-recall procedure. Interviews were audiotaped.

Students were asked questions about what they were doing or thinking at five different times during the lesson after they had viewed the five appropriate portions of the videotape of the lesson. Interviewers were given specified prompts. Trained coders coded interview protocols for later analysis. The stimulated-recall technique was employed to uncover covert cognitive processes not observable by either on-site coders or videotape viewers.

Student interview responses were coded into five major categories: (1) attending; (2) understanding; (3) reasons for not understanding; (4) cognitive strategies; and (5) teaching processes. A number of findings emerged. First, observed off-task behavior was unrelated to students' reports of attending or to scores on an achievement test in mathematics. (It should be pointed out that nearly all students were attending to the lesson nearly all of the time, and a ceiling effect on the attending variable diminished the likelihood of high, positive correlations of attending with other study variables.) Second, students who reported comprehending all of the material tended to perform well both on assigned seatwork and on the achievement test. (This is a good comprehension monitoring display.) Third, and very important from a metacognitive perspective, students who did not provide detailed explanations of comprehension problems tended to do poorly on seatwork and on the achievement test. Fourth, a broad range of general and specific strategies (e.g., reworking a problem, reading/rereading directions, asking for help) was reported. A strategy labeled "trying to understand the teacher or problem" that involved general problem-solving steps applied to the particular task and materials was significantly positively related to both seatwork and achievement test performance.

Peterson and her colleagues (1982) point out that the stimulated-recall method avoids some of the problems associated with traditional interview techniques. Most important in this regard, the viewing of the videotaped record of the lesson in this study was a "nondirective retrieval cue that served to enhance the veridicality of the reports" (p. 546). Though verbal facility remained a potential confounding factor, memory failure, hypothetical questions, and overcueing were arguably diminished in impact.

A different method used recently by Garner et al. (1983) to examine strategic repertoires of experts and novices is peer tutoring. This research group asked sixth-grade students at two reading proficiency levels to tutor same-sex, same-race fourth-grade students. No strategic activities were taught to the older students. Rather, existing cognitive and metacognitive strategies related to reinspection of text to answer questions were made overt as tutors were asked to show tutees how to read an expository text segment and answer a set of reader-based and text-based questions following the text.

An observer, "blind" to the reading proficiency level of tutors, audiotaped all sessions and coded both directing and reinforcing (of text reinspection) behaviors of the older students on a low-inference scoring grid. The observer sat some distance from the pair of children, and announced at the start of the sessions that she was unable to help with task completion.

Audiotapes were transcribed, and verbal and nonverbal behaviors noted by observers and tape listeners were tallied. Significant differences between proficiency groups on all reinspection strategic behaviors of interest were found. Proficient tutors encouraged their tutees to look back to the text for unrecalled information in instances cued by text-based questions, and to particular segments of text where the information appeared.

Garner et al. (1983) point out that findings of a positive relation between use of a text-reinspection strategy and global reading level from an earlier study (see Garner & Reis, 1981) were supported with an entirely different method. They advocate use of the tutoring paradigm to explore additional cognitive and metacognitive strategies, arguing that though verbal facility once again is implicated in task performance, teaching tutees about what tutors neither know nor do [i.e., the Nisbett & Wilson (1977) concern] is highly unlikely. Furthermore, assessment of knowledge and strategic action over time and across settings (with a variety of tutees) is possible. Finally, the situation is not hypothetical, and the strategic operations are not disrupted, either by a potentially cueing adult or by the need for a child to produce fragmented reports of processing.

A third method used recently is optimal–nonoptimal production. Garner (1985) adapted a method suggested by Bracewell (1983) to trace the reason for text summarization deficiencies among older students. Specifically, she wanted to know if learners are not aware of what makes a short summary acceptable or if learners cannot produce short summaries, despite being aware of factors that differentiate acceptable and unacceptable products.

The Bracewell (1983) method involves setting the task for learners to produce optimal and nonoptimal outcomes for a given activity (in our study, summarizing a written descriptive passage). Bracewell suggests, and we agree, that a learner with adequate awareness of demands for the outcome (a short summary) should create two products that differ in measurable ways. A learner with sufficient production ability should create an optimal product that can be rated as acceptable on a set of predetermined measures. Deficiencies in awareness and production are not mutually exclusive.

Students in 9th and 11th grades and undergraduate reading methods classes were asked to write "good" and "bad" summaries for a seven paragraph passage on the topic of misconceptions about objects in motion. Number of ideas judged as important present in the summary, number of words used, and integration level of important ideas were the dependent measures. For each measure, awareness and production scores were generated.

There was strong evidence that most high school and college learners are aware that important ideas from a passage should be included in a short summary; across age groups, 73% of the students differentiated optimal and nonoptimal summaries by including more important ideas in the optimal product. Learner ability to produce the key pieces of information from the passage in an optimal summary varied dramatically by age; 15% of 9th-grade students, 50% of 11th-grade students, and 93% of the college students included more than half of the ideas judged as important in their summaries. These distinctions in awareness and production were examined for the other dependent measures as well, in the interest of eventually prescribing very specific instructional remedies.

It is argued (see Garner, 1985) that the method worked well in generating data on awareness and production deficiencies. It is suggested that comparing awareness information yielded by this method with information gleaned in an interview or think-aloud setting might yield interesting information about strategic strengths and needs and about systematic underreporting or overreporting in traditional verbal-report methods.

In closing the discussion of these alternative methods for assessing strategies, it should be mentioned that the verbal component (either uttering a description of what was thought and done, providing oral explanation to a tutee, or writing a product that displays particular features) is not removed from the methods. Individuals with limited language facility are perhaps as handicapped in displaying cognitive and metacognitive strengths with these methods as they are with traditional interview and think-aloud methods. Some concerns do diminish, however: "telling more than they know," cueing from investigators, lack of reliability assessment, processing-reporting gap, hypothetical settings, and disruptions of process.

It is important in concluding a discussion of verbal-report data on cognitive and metacognitive strategies to make a strong statement in favor of collection of data from many sources. If we want to know, for instance, if learners at a particular age and proficiency level know that a short summary of a passage includes all of the important ideas from the passage, we can be far more certain of our conclusions if we: (1) ask them in an interview situation what one does when one writes a short summary; (2) require them to think aloud while preparing a short summary (or soon after while viewing a videotape of their summarizing); (3) ask them to teach younger students how to write short summaries; and (4) require them to write both good and bad summaries, to be assessed for the presence of important ideas. We can be more certain of our conclusions because the different sets of data are not vulnerable to the same sources of invalidity. In this manner, then, the important goal of identification of learners' strategic repertoires is achieved with less ambiguity than if any single method were applied.

REFERENCES

Alexander, P. A., Hare, V. C., & Garner, R. (1984). The effects of time, access, and question type on response accuracy and frequency of lookbacks in older, proficient readers. *Journal of Reading Behavior, 16,* 119–130.

Alvermann, D. E. (1984). Second graders' strategic preferences while reading basal stories. *Journal of Educational Research, 77,* 184–189.

Baker, L., & Brown, A. L. (1984). Cognitive monitoring in reading. In J. Flood (Ed.), *Understanding reading comprehension: Cognition, language, and the structure of prose* (pp. 21–44). Newark, DE: International Reading Association.

Ballstaedt, S., & Mandl, H. (1984). Elaborations: Assessment and analysis. In H. Mandl, N. L. Stein, & T. Trabasso (Eds.), *Learning and comprehension of text* (pp. 331–353). Hillsdale, NJ: Erlbaum.

Bracewell, R. J. (1983). Investigating the control of writing skills. In P. Mosenthal, L. Tamor, & S. A. Walmsley (Eds.), *Research on writing* (pp. 177–203). New York: Longman.

Brown, A. L. (1980). Metacognition, executive control, self-regulation and other even more mysterious mechanisms, unpublished manuscript.

Cavanaugh, J. C., & Borkowski, J. G. (1980). Searching for metamemory–memory connections: A developmental study. *Developmental Psychology, 16,* 441–453.

Cavanaugh, J. C., & Perlmutter, M. (1982). Metamemory: A critical examination. *Child Development, 53,* 11–28.

Ericsson, K. A., & Simon, H. A. (1980). Verbal reports as data. *Psychological Review, 87,* 215–251.

Feagans, L., & Farran, D. C. (1981). How demonstrated comprehension can get muddled in production. *Developmental Psychology, 17,* 718–727.

Fischer, P. M., & Mandl, H. (1982). Metacognitive regulation of text processing: Aspects and problems concerning the relation between self-statements and actual performance. In A.

Flammer, & W. Kintsch (Eds.), *Discourse processing* (pp. 339–351). Amsterdam: North-Holland.

Flavell, J. H. (1979). Metacognition and cognitive monitoring. *American Psychologist, 34,* 906–911.

Flavell, J. H. (1981). Cognitive monitoring. In W. P. Dickson (Ed.), *Children's oral communication skills* (pp. 35–60). New York: Academic Press.

Flavell, J. H., Speer, J. R., Green, F. L., & August, D. L. (1981). The development of comprehension monitoring and knowledge about communication. *Monographs of the Society for Research in Child Development, 46,* (5, Serial No. 192).

Floden, R. E. (1981). The logic of information-processing psychology in education. In D. C. Berliner (Ed.), *Review of Research in Education* (Vol. 9, pp. 75–109). Washington, DC: American Educational Research Association.

Flower, L., & Hayes, J. R. (1981). A cognitive process theory of writing. *College Composition and Communication, 32,* 365–387.

Forrest, D. L., & Waller, T. G. (1980). What do children know about their reading and study skills, paper presented at the annual meeting of the American Educational Research Association, Boston.

Forrest-Pressley, D. L., & Gillies, L. A. (1983). Children's flexible use of strategies during reading. In M. Pressley, & J. R. Levin (Eds.), *Cognitive strategy research: Educational applications* (pp. 133–156). New York: Springer-Verlag.

Garner, R. (1982). Verbal-report data on reading strategies. *Journal of Reading Behavior, 14,* 159–167.

Garner, R. (1985). Text summarization deficiencies among older students: Awareness or production ability? *American Educational Research Journal, 22,* 549–560.

Garner, R., & Alexander, P. (1982). Strategic processing of text: An investigation of the effects on adults' question-answering performance. *Journal of Educational Research, 75,* 144–148.

Garner. R., & Kraus, C. (1981–1982). Good and poor comprehender differences in knowing and regulating reading behaviors. *Educational Research Quarterly, 6,* 5–12.

Garner, R., Macready, G. B., & Wagoner, S. (1984). Readers' acquisition of the components of the text-lookback strategy. *Journal of Educational Psychology, 76,* 300–309.

Garner, R., & Reis, R. (1981). Monitoring and resolving comprehension obstacles: An investigation of spontaneous text lookbacks among upper-grade good and poor comprehenders. *Reading Research Quarterly, 16,* 569–582.

Garner, R., Wagoner, S., & Smith, T. (1983). Externalizing question-answering strategies of good and poor comprehenders. *Reading Research Quarterly, 18,* 439–447.

Hale, G. A. (1983). Students' predictions of prose forgetting and the effects of study strategies. *Journal of Educational Psychology, 75,* 708–715.

Hayes, J. R., & Flower, L. S. (1980). Identifying the organization of writing process. In L. W. Gregg, & E. R. Steinberg (Eds.), *Cognitive processes in writing* (pp. 3–30). Hillsdale, NJ: Erlbaum.

Kail, R. V., Jr., & Bisanz, J. (1982). Cognitive strategies. In C. R. Puff (Ed.), *Handbook of research methods in human memory and cognition* (pp. 229–255). New York: Academic Press.

Kellogg, R. T. (1982). When can we introspect accurately about mental processes? *Memory and Cognition, 10,* 141–144.

Meichenbaum, D. (1980). A cognitive-behavioral perspective on intelligence. *Intelligence, 4,* 271–283.

Meichenbaum, D., Burland, S.. Gruson, L., & Cameron, R. (1979). Metacognitive assessment, paper presented at the Conference on the Growth of Insight, Madison, WI.

Miller, P. H. (1983). *Theories of developmental psychology.* San Francisco: Freeman.

Miyake, N., & Norman, D. A. (1979). To ask a question, one must know enough to know what is not known. *Journal of Verbal Learning and Verbal Behavior, 18,* 357–364.

Myers, M., & Paris, S. G. (1978). Children's metacognitive knowledge about reading. *Journal of Educational Psychology, 70,* 680–690.

Nisbett, R. E., & Wilson, T. D. (1977). Telling more than we can know: Verbal reports on mental processes. *Psychological Review, 84,* 231–259.

Olshavsky, J. E. (1976–1977). Reading as problem solving: An investigation of strategies. *Reading Research Quarterly, 12,* 654–674.

Paris, S. G., & Lindauer, B. K. (1982). The development of cognitive skills during childhood. In B. W. Wolman (Ed.), *Handbook of developmental psychology* (pp. 333–349). Englewood Cliffs, NJ: Prentice-Hall.

Paris, S. G., Lipson, M. Y., & Wixson, K. K. (1983). Becoming a strategic reader. *Contemporary Educational Psychology, 8,* 293–316.

Peterson, P. L., Swing, S. R., Braverman, M. T., & Buss, R. (1982). Students' aptitudes and their reports of cognitive processes during direct instruction. *Journal of Educational Psychology, 74,* 535–547.

Phifer, S. J., & Glover, J. A. (1982). Don't take students' word for what they do while reading. *Bulletin of the Psychonomic Society, 19,* 194–196.

Ryan, E. B. (1981). Identifying and remediating failures in reading comprehension: Toward an instructional approach for poor comprehenders. In G. E. Mackinnon, & T. G. Waller (Eds.), *Reading research: Advances in theory and practice* (Vol. 3, pp. 223–261). New York: Academic Press.

Simon, H. A. (1979). Information processing models of cognition. *Annual Review of Psychology, 30,* 363–396.

Waters, H. S. (1982). Memory development in adolescence: Relationships between metamemory, strategy use, and performance. *Journal of Experimental Child Psychology, 33,* 183–195.

White, P. (1980). Limitations on verbal reports of internal events: A refutation of Nisbett and Wilson and of Bem. *Psychological Review, 87,* 105–112.

Yussen, S. R., & Bird, J. E. (1979). The development of metacognitive awareness in memory, communication, and attention. *Journal of Experimental Child Psychology, 28,* 300–313.

Yussen, S. R., Mathews, S. R., & Hiebert, E. (1982). Metacognitive aspects of reading. In W. Otto, & S. White (Eds.), *Reading expository material* (pp. 189–218). New York: Academic Press.

THE ROLE OF ATTENTION IN STUDYING AND LEARNING

Ralph E. Reynolds and Larry L. Shirey

I. INTRODUCTION

Parents, teachers, administrators, and politicians are growing increasingly concerned with the lack of good study and reading skills of teenagers (Hunter & Harmon, 1979). Two sources provide evidence to warrant this concern. Both *A Nation at Risk* (National Commission on Excellence in Education, 1982) and *On Further Examination: Report of the Advisory Panel on Scholastic Aptitude Test Score Decline* (1977) have documented a decline in literacy achievement at the secondary school level. At the same time, it is not known which study strategies are most effective. Though researchers have been investigating study skills for over 75 years, the research has been inconsistent and inconclusive (Anderson & Armbruster, 1984). Consequently, many students leave high school with few or no reading or study skills, and many universities offer extensive remedial programs in study skills for incoming students. It appears that traditional approaches to investigating study skills have not been totally successful.

A reason for this lack of success may be that study skills researchers have concentrated on the form of studying (i.e., assigning a strategy and looking at learning outcomes from a group that used the strategy and from a group that did not), instead of on the substance of studying. The underlying processes students go through while studying have not been thoroughly investigated. The view taken in this chapter is that these underlying processes are as important as traditional study skills themselves, if not more so. Techniques such as note taking, underlining, summarizing, outlining, and graphically relating concepts are attempts to integrate and understand information that apply only after processes such as identifying important information, attention allocation, and comprehension monitoring have been engaged. Our approach will be to look at attention allocation and text element importance and attempt to ascertain the nature of their individual and interactive effects on what students learn and retain from the process of studying.

Specifically, the purposes of this chapter are to propose a model of the

LEARNING AND STUDY STRATEGIES: ISSUES IN
ASSESSMENT, INSTRUCTION, AND EVALUATION

studying process, to offer empirical and conceptual support for this model, and to discuss the theoretical implications of the model.

II. WHAT IS EFFECTIVE STUDYING?

Studying and learning from written discourse have been investigated extensively over the past 75 years. Much of the early work focused on the use of questions as study aids (Distad, 1926; Germane, 1920). Later studies looked at the utility of note taking (Howe & Singer, 1975; Mathews, 1938), underlining (Arnold, 1942; Kulhavy et al., 1975), outlining (Barton, 1930; Willmore, 1966), and summarization (Germane, 1921; Stordahl & Christensen, 1956; see Anderson & Armbruster, 1984, for a review). In general, the results have been mixed. For each strategy described, approximately half the studies find that the strategy in question has a positive effect on learning and the other half suggest no positive effect.

There are several possible reasons for these contradictory findings. First, the methodology used in the studies was not uniformly good. Several studies (e.g., Arnold, 1942; Poppleton & Austwick, 1964) found no advantage in note taking over read-only controls; however, their procedures did not look at quality of notes taken or the processes involved in deciding which material was appropriate to note. Without this sort of information, the exact nature of the variables involved cannot be specified, making generalizable conclusions from these studies difficult. Are the negative results due to the lack of usefulness of note taking, are they simply indicative of lack of student note-taking skill, or do they reflect the students' lack of facility at some prerequisite skill, such as the ability to select important information? Second, student idiosyncracies and preferences about which strategy to use sometimes do not coincide with the strategy being experimentally assigned. The experimental strategy may not succeed for reasons of student preference rather than for reasons of lack of utility. Third, there has been disagreement on what is the most relevant outcome measure of effective studying. For example, work on inserted questions has used both task-relevant and task-incidental learning (e.g., Rothkopf, 1966), while other studies have used only one or the other (e.g., Anderson & Biddle, 1975). Using different measures of success makes comparisons between studies difficult, if not impossible.

Some notion is needed of the components of studying, and the role that activities such as note taking and underlining play in determining which information is learned and retained. To accomplish this, an operational model is required that details the nature of and interrelationships among the components of the studying process.

Anderson and Armbruster (1984) have provided the foundations of such a model. They suggest that studying is a special case of reading that involves two sorts of variables: *state* variables and *process* variables. State variables are ". . . those related to the status of the student and the to-be-studied material at the time of study." (p. 1). The state variables of primary interest to recent researchers are the extent of the student's knowledge of the to-be-studied material (Anderson et al., 1977), the structure and density of that material (Rothkopf & Kaplan, 1972), and the nature of the study task. Process variables are ". . . those involved with getting the information from the written page to the student's head." (Anderson & Armbruster, 1984, p. 2). Most prominent among these variables are the focusing of attention on, and encoding of, information (Reynolds & Anderson, 1982; Tulving & Thompson, 1973).

Anderson and Armbruster (1984) surmise that studying is the combination of state and process variables in order ". . . to perform identifiable cognitive and/or procedural tasks." (p. 1). They propose that the interaction between state and process variables in a given study situation will strongly influence the learning obtained in that situation.

A problem with this definition is that it lacks precision; state and process variables are defined but the nature of their interaction is not. Without knowledge of how state and process variables combine, precise predictions and explanations about effective studying are impossible. The prime purpose of the model we are suggesting is to elaborate on how state and process variables interact to influence positive or negative learning outcomes.

Our working hypothesis is that effective use of any traditional study strategy revolves around the student's ability to differentiate important from unimportant information, and to focus adequate amounts of quality attention on the important information in order to learn it. The student also must be able to monitor his/her own studying to determine if task demands are being met. Whether a student underlines, outlines, takes notes, or highlights, his/her first task must be to decide which information to note. If the information chosen is irrelevant or tangential to the main task requirements, any strategy used will be less effective. Even when the most important information is identified, it must be attended to, or it will have little or no impact on what is learned. If the task is not understood or learning is not monitored, important text items may not be consistently identified. The model presented here will concentrate on these three processes: the identification of important text elements, attention focusing, and comprehension monitoring.

An advantage of this approach is that all three of the criticisms previously made about traditional study skills research can be accommodated. Methodological concerns are reduced because this model highlights not only the products of studying but also the underlying processes involved. Hence,

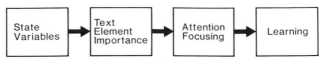

FIG. 1. Model of the role of attention in prose learning.

assumptions about underlying process need not be deduced from the learning data. Student preference for certain study strategies also ceases to be a problem since all traditional study strategies are based on the same underlying processes. Finally, this approach incorporates general learning measures that encompass both task-relevant and task-incidental learning.

Given this orientation, one can develop a definition of "effective studying" slightly different from that of Anderson and Armbruster (1984). State variables such as background knowledge, knowledge of the task, and impression of text density and difficulty combine to produce some ideas in the reader as to which text elements are important (see Fig. 1). These elements are attended to and learned, presumably through some process or processes supported by extra attention. Organization of important text elements by note taking or underlining, etc., should aid the integration of information into memorable knowledge structures, but only after the identification of important text elements and attention-focusing processes have occurred. Students' awareness of what and how they are learning (meta-comprehension) provides continual monitoring and fine-tuning of the entire process. Predictable increments in learning should accrue as students repeat these processes throughout the text.

Using this model as a starting point, research on importance and attention allocation will be examined to determine if these activities are indeed important components of the studying process. Research dealing with the metacognitive aspects of studying will be alluded to here but will not be reviewed due to space limitations.

III. THE PROCESS OF STUDYING

A. IMPORTANCE

1. Components of Importance

Text elements can become important in different ways. They can attain importance because they relate to instructions or objectives stated before studying occurs (Ausubel, 1960; Rothkopf & Kaplan, 1972), because of their relevance to a reader's perspective or point of view (Anderson & Pichert,

1978; Pichert & Anderson, 1977), because of cues inserted into the text by the author (Rothkopf, 1966; Reynolds et al., 1979), because they are interesting to the reader (Asher, 1980; Shirey & Reynolds, 1987), because of the structure of the text in which they occur (Kintsch & van Dijk, 1978; van Dijk & Kintsch, 1983), or because they represent conceptual or relational links between text elements and text ideas (Frase, 1969).

Such distinctions are necessary for looking at the relationship between individual aspects of importance and learning; however, from a theoretical perspective, it seems useful to focus on the more general determinants of importance in the studying situation. The importance of any given text element depends upon the interactions among three variables: the *task* the student receives, the *state* of the student, and the *structure* of the text. Using this general framework, one can account for each of the features of text element importance listed above. Instructions, inserted questions, and experimentally assigned perspectives represent tasks. Yet, each of these tasks must interact with student variables and text variables before an operational determination of importance can be made. Student variables influence how the assigned task is encoded and the student's ability to follow the task throughout the assignment. Text variables such as concept ordering, coherence, and information density can either highlight or obscure task-relevant information. For such student variables as interest, background knowledge, and motivation, this rationale also applies. Student variables are influenced by task and text variables just as text variables must interact with task and student variables before determinations of importance are made. Our notion is that the importance of any text element is quite complex, depending on an interaction of all three major *state* variables: nature of the task, state of the student, and structure of the text.

2. Importance and Attention

Early in the studying process, the effective studier selects important information. The next step is usually engaging in some process or activity to increase the learning and recall of this information. The question is what is the process by which important information is learned and retained better than unimportant information?

One answer is that studiers focus extra attention on important text items and consequently learn and recall them better. Anderson and his colleagues (Anderson, 1982; Reynolds & Anderson, 1982; Reynolds et al., 1979) have suggested a simple theory (the Selective Attention theory) that relates increased attention to the learning of important text information as follows:

1. Text elements are initially processed to some mimimal level and graded for importance.

2. Extra attention is devoted to elements in proportion to their importance.
3. Because of the extra attention, or a process supported by the extra attention, important text elements are learned better than other elements.

Anderson's (1982) model is not the only explanation for why important text elements are well remembered and recalled. Kintsch and van Dijk (1978) and van Dijk and Kintsh (1983) have proposed that important text elements are well recalled because they are retained in working memory longer (for more cycles) than are less important ones. For a discussion of the differentiations between these two theories, the interested reader is referred to Anderson (1982) and Reynolds (1987). It is important to note that regardless of which of these two approaches is used, the notion of selective attention is supported. For purposes of this chapter, the Anderson model will be used because it is much clearer concerning the use of selective attention in learning and studying.

Important implications for understanding the studying process can be derived from the Selective Attention theory. Regardless of whether or not attention is causally related to learning or simply supports processes causally related to learning, the theory predicts a positive relationship between text element importance, attention focused on those elements, and eventual learning. This theory provides the foundation for much of the research discussed in the following section.

B. Selective Attention

The Selective Attention model indicates that important text elements are better learned and recalled because extra attention is allocated to them. The research reviewed in this section tests the validity of that claim. The general approach taken in these studies was to manipulate text element importance by varying external tasks such as questioning, assigning perspectives, and giving students objectives. These manipulations allowed the experimenters to alter importance while still having all students read the same text, thereby controlling the effects of extraneous variables, such as the conceptual difficulty of the text, text content, and text coherence that might have confounded the results.

The general methodology used in the studies was to present the text—a line, a sentence, or a segment (approximately four lines) at a time—on a computer terminal. When the student wanted to see the next line he/she pressed a key on the console and the new text replaced the old on the screen. Attention was measured by timing the interval between key presses. In other words, the amount of time the text remained on the screen reflected the duration of attention given to that unit of text.

1. Reading Time Research

The effects on learning of assigning a perspective to readers before they read have been well documented (Anderson & Pichert, 1978; Pichert & Anderson, 1977). Depending on the perspective, different text elements became more or less important. A text element that was important from one perspective was generally not important from the other. The same text elements were recalled better when they were important than when they were unimportant.

Goetz et al. (1983) attempted to show that the perspective effect on learning was the product of selective attention. They had students (college age) read a text on a computer terminal from either of two separate perspectives or from no perspective. Each text segment contained only information that pertained to one of the assigned perspectives or control information. Student reading time data indicated that selective attention was indeed a likely explanation for the perspective effect. Students who read from Perspective 1 tended to spend a longer time reading segments that contained information relevant to Perspective 1. Those students assigned Perspective 2 followed the same pattern of results for information relevant to Perspective 2.

Research also shows that the facilitative effect on learning of giving college students objectives (goals for studying) before they read most likely rests on a selective attention process. Rothkopf and Billington (1979) have supported this notion. Using reading time and eye movements as their measures of attention, they showed that students paid more attention to those text elements that contained information relevant to the objectives they were given.

Cirilo and Foss (1980) looked at text elements made important through their structural relationship with other text elements. Using the ideas set out by Kintsch and van Dijk (1978), they created sets of stories in which the same sentence was either high or low in the importance hierarchy of the whole story. Their results showed that students spent more time reading a sentence when it was high in the importance hierarchy than they did reading the same sentence when it was low in the hierarchy. Students also remembered the critical sentences almost three times as well when they were high in the importance hierarchy. This is exactly what the Selective Attention hypothesis would predict.

Reynolds et al. (1979) attempted to discover if the facilitative effect of inserted questions on prose learning was due to selective attention or a process supported by selective attention. Subjects were given one of three types of adjunct questions (proper names, numbers, or technical terms) or no questions. The questions were inserted into the text every 4 pages of a 36-page story. The questions always appeared after the text segments that

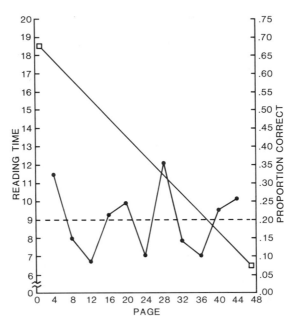

FIG. 2.   Learning and reading time arrayed across a 48-page text. (●——●) Proportion correct, (□——□) reading time in minutes, (- - -) average learning score.

contained the answer. Text elements were seen as important if they were related to the type of question that the student had been asked. For example, it was expected that students who received all number questions would conclude that numbers were important and try to learn them. The results indicated that for both learning and reading time, selective attention seemed to be operating. Students took longer to read and remembered more information from those text segments made important because they contained information relevant to the type of question asked.

Although each of these studies supports the Selective Attention model, some problems remain. If selective attention works as Anderson (1982) suggested, as reading time decreases, learning should also decrease. Figure 2 shows that over the length of the long text, reading time decreased but learning remained constant. Thus, although the selective attention notion was supported, the notion of attention alone causing learning was not. Further research is necessary to resolve this point.

Summary.   The reading time studies reviewed looked at several different ways in which text elements could attain importance. Yet, in all of the studies the notion of selective attention was at least partially supported. As

Anderson (1982) suggested, extra attention was allocated to important text elements when students read or studied texts. These same text elements were also better learned and recalled. Unfortunately, just knowing these two results is not enough to conclude that extra attention is in any way causally related to the increased learning of important information. Indeed, the results of Reynolds et al. (1979; also see Fig. 2) suggest that attention is not causally related to learning. For the Selective Attention hypothesis to remain a viable explanation for how important textual information is learned, the causal mechanism must be explicated.

2.   Probe Reaction Time Research

There may be more than one means by which readers can allocate attention to a specific text portion. While reading time represents attention duration, attention of different degrees of intensity might also be applied to text elements (Kahneman, 1973). An increase in the intensity of attention applied to a text item is thought to indicate a higher quality of attention. On this view, intensity and duration represent two different aspects of attention that can be directed either jointly or separately toward a text element.

Measuring the intensity of attention being used in a reading situation requires using secondary task methodology. Secondary tasks rely on the notion of distractability. The assumption is that if one is easily distracted from a task, one is not intensely involved.

When using this procedure, students are required to read a text passage and answer questions about it (the primary task). While they are reading, a tone or a click is sounded. When they hear the tone, students are instructed to respond as quickly as possible by pressing a key (the secondary task). The time between the onset of the tone and the key press indirectly indicates the intensity of attention being paid to the text at that time. Longer reaction times reflect more attention allocated to the primary task, shorter reaction times reflect less intense attention.

There are several assumptions that underlie the use of secondary task methodology. First, studying, or any other cognitive activity, requires the allocation of cognitive capacity to the task. Second, cognitive capacity is both fixed and limited. Third, when a student directs his/her cognitive capacity to a task, some capacity is retained to monitor the environment. Since capacity is fixed and limited, measuring the amount of capacity retained to monitor (respond to a secondary stimulus) will give an estimate of the capacity being used for the primary task (see Fig. 3).

Britton et al. (1978) attempted to determine if the learning increases associated with inserted questions might be due to the questions causing readers to allocate more intense attention to the reading task. Britton's

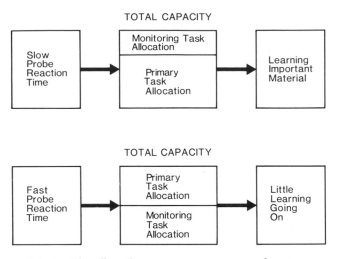

FIG. 3.   The effect of cognitive capacity usage on learning.

hypothesis was that attention intensity was directed at the text in general and not to specific text segments as was suggested earlier (Reynolds et al., 1979). If this assumption is correct, more cognitive capacity, as indexed by slower reaction times to probes, will be allocated to text when inserted questions are present.

In the experiment, college students read the same experimental passage as was described earlier (Reynolds et al., 1979). Subjects followed the general secondary task methodology described above. Britton et al. (1978) found that the questioned group took significantly longer to respond to the clicks than did the no-question group. Britton concluded that this deeper, more elaborate processing accounted for the increments in learning normally observed when inserted question groups are compared to controls. He assumed that the attention that supported this extra processing was global rather than selective in nature. In other words, it reflected increased attention to the text in general and not to any given segment.

Although it is apparent that inserted questions do affect attention in some way, exactly how the effect occurs is still unclear. Reynolds et al. (1979) showed that inserted questions increase reading times for relevant parts of the text (selective attention). Britton et al. (1978) found no difference in total reading time, but an increase in probe reaction time for their inserted question groups (general facilitation). From these results it seems reasonable to assume that both reading time and probe reaction time reflect some difference in text processing between questioned and nonquestioned groups.

In 1982, Reynolds and Anderson reported data that helped resolve the seeming contradiction between the Reynolds et al. (1979) and the Britton et al. (1978) research. Reynolds and Anderson used both reading time and probe reaction time techniques to attempt to determine whether or not selective attention did indeed account for all aspects of the inserted question effect.

A second hypothesis considered was the idea that attention duration and intensity were compensatory in relation to learning. That is, when duration increases, intensity can decrease and learning will still remain constant. Conversely, when attention intensity increases, duration can be reduced and learning will remain constant. Britton et al. (1978) called this idea the Volume-of-Attention hypothesis (intensity × duration).

Reynolds and Anderson (1982) tested the Volume-of-Attention hypothesis in two ways. First, they looked at the relationship among attention duration, attention intensity, and learning over the whole text. Previously, attention duration decreased over the length of a long text while learning tended to remain the same (Reynolds et al., 1979). The Volume-of-Attention hypothesis suggests that attention intensity should increase in this situation. Second, some of the subjects were required to read the text from a speeded, paced format. The Volume-of-Attention hypothesis suggests that as duration is decreased, intensity must increase or learning will decline.

As in the Reynolds et al. (1979) study, the same long experimental passage and inserted questions were used. Reading time and probe reaction times were collected by the computer to an accuracy of 100 milliseconds and 1 millisecond respectively. The results totally supported the Selective Attention model for both the reading time and probe reaction time measures. Both attention intensity and duration were directed at task-relevant text segments and material from those segments was better learned and recalled.

The results also resolved the paradox of the Reynolds et al. (1979) study, that, as readers progressed through the text, reading time decreased but learning remained constant. Figure 4 shows that as students proceeded through the text they decreased attention duration but increased intensity. As the Volume-of-Attention hypothesis predicts, these two aspects of attention are compensatory; hence, learning must remain approximately constant. A second finding that supports the Volume-of-Attention hypothesis was that as duration of attention was reduced (by the paced presentation) both the intensity of attention and learning were reduced. Because the students did not compensate for the reduced duration of attention by increasing intensity, learning should have been reduced.

Summary. Results from both reading time research and probe reaction time research support the Selective Attention model. Probe reaction time research has extended the model with the addition of the Volume-of-Atten-

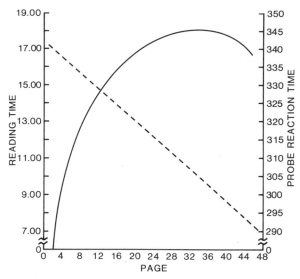

FIG. 4.   The Volume-of-Attention hypothesis: increased attention intensity compensating for decreased attention duration. (-----) Reading time in minutes, (——) probe time.

tion corollary. In combination, both bodies of work give weight to the idea that focusing attention on important text elements is a crucial step in comprehending, studying, and learning.

C.   Causal Relationships

Although much of the research reviewed suggests that selective attention focused on important text elements is a major component of effective studying, whether or not there exist causal relationships among these variables is a question that remains to be answered. Anderson (1982) has suggested that much of current social science research is lacking because experimenters establish relationships among variables but do not establish causal relationships. With an eye to remedying this problem, Anderson established a model for evaluating causal arguments. The model includes four entailments that, if supported, allow researchers to make causal claims for their results. This not only adds rigor to the study but allows the researcher to speculate more strongly because he/she has a more precise notion about the relationships among the variables of concern. Normally, researchers attempt to make the following arguement: ". . . an independent variable, (x), causes changes in a dependent variable, (y), because of an influence on a mediating variable, (m)." (Anderson, 1982, p. 6). Causality for this type of argument can be claimed only if the following four entailments are met:

1. x is related to y at traditional level of significance.
2. x is related to m.
3. m is related to y.
4. When the relations of x to m and m to y are removed, the relationship between x and y has been significantly reduced.

In the research discussed above only the first two entailments were evaluated; hence, conclusions of a causal nature, even if only implicitly made, were premature. The Reynolds and Anderson (1982) study was causally analyzed. In the Reynolds and Anderson paper, the four causal entailments were tested as follows: questions were the independent variable, attention the mediating variable, and learning, both new and repeated information, the dependent variable. For Entailment 1, questions were shown to be significantly related to learning in both the new and repeated items, accounting for 8.3 and 63.6% of the variance, respectively. For Entailment 2, questions accounted for nearly 35% of the variance in probe reaction time. Analysis of Entailment 3 showed that attention contributed significantly to learning of both new items (7.7% of variance) and repeated items (23.8% of variance). The fourth entailment was tested by removing the effect of attention to see if questions and learning were still related. For the new items, removing attention showed a 71% decrease in the variance accounted for. This decrease moved the relationship between questions and learning from a significant to a nonsignificant one. Repeated items showed the same trend. Removing attention caused a 24% decline in variance accounted for. Although the questions were still significantly related to learning, the change in the variance accounted for was a significant one.

From these analyses it can now be concluded that for inserted questions at least, the importance- and attention-based notions offered earlier in Anderson's (1982) model are supported. Studying, using inserted questions, most likely involves the strategy of selecting important text elements, focusing attention on them, and hence, learning more text material.

Reynolds et al. (1987) report another inserted question study that shows slightly different results. The purpose of this study was to see if the causal relationship between inserted questions and learning established by Reynolds and Anderson (1982) was extant in younger students who were less skilled in reading and studying. All of the same procedures described in the Reynolds and Anderson study were used in this study. The major difference was that high school sophomores classified as good (9th- and 10th-grade-level readers) and poor (6th- and 7th-grade-level readers) were the subjects. Initial results indicated that good readers looked very much like the college students in the Reynolds and Anderson study. The poor readers focused their attention on the important text elements but did not show a corresponding increase in learning. Causal analyses were done on both groups. Not surprising is the observation that poor readers showed no causal links between questions and learning, and attention and learning. Questions were, however, related to attention. Since two of the first three causal entailments were not supported, the fourth was predictably also not supported. For the good readers, questions were significantly related to learning, questions were related to attention, and attention was related to learning. Unfortunately, the fourth entailment was not supported. Consequently, we may conclude that even good readers in high school are not yet sophisticated enough to make use of the same types of strategies used by college-level readers.

D. THE PROBLEM OF INTEREST

All of the studies described above have modified the importance of text segments by manipulating specific task parameters or text characteristics. Subjects have been given objectives to consider while reading; they have read text from the point of view or perspective of someone else; they have been given questions to answer while reading; and they have read passages where the importance of the text elements varies because of the structure of the text. Other characteristics that may affect text importance, such as interest, cultural relevance, or background knowledge, reside within the individual reader. To our knowledge, only three studies have been completed that have investigated the effects of reader-based characteristics on allocation of attention and learning. The first is the Goetz et al. (1983) study described previously. Although the results were not overwhelming, the individual's background affected both attention toward and learning of text information. Information that was relevant to the individual's background tended to have more attention allocated to it and was recalled more often. Statistical tests to determine if the increased recall was a direct result of increased attention to important information were not performed.

The other two research projects specifically looked for a causal relationship between attention allocation and learning (Anderson et al., 1984; Shirey & Reynolds, 1987. The Anderson et al. study employed fourth-grade students as subjects while the Shirey and Reynolds study used college-age students. In these studies, the students read a series of sentences that had been rated for interest by a peer group for each study. The computer recorded the time subjects spent on each sentence. Additionally, a secondary task paradigm was employed to allow a measure of intensity of attention to be collected. After reading the sentences, the subjects were administered a cued recall test. In the test, the subject was provided with the first two words of each sentence and then asked to recall the sentence as accurately as possible.

In the Anderson et al. (1984) study, fourth-grade students allocated more attention to and recalled more of those text elements that were related as interesting. However, there was no evidence that attention played a significant causal role in the effects of interest on learning (see Anderson, 1982, for further discussion). Young readers did appear to selectively attend to interesting information, but it was time ineffectively spent because it did not directly result in any increases in learning of the material. Results from the Shirey and Reynolds (1987) study demonstrated that interest also had significant effect on recall of the sentences for college-age students. Very interesting sentences were recalled significantly better. However, there was no significant positive relation between interest and amount of attention allocated. Subjects spent no more time on interesting sentences than they did on sentences they found uninteresting. The results suggest that information that is interesting or culturally relevant to a more mature student is readily learned with no cost in terms of additional expenditure of cognitive resources. This is not a particularly surprising result because other research (Steffensen et al., 1979) has demonstrated that adults spend less time reading and remember more culturally relevant information.

The three studies present a rather confusing picture concerning the effects of person-centered *state* variables on allocation of cognitive resources and learning. First, there are two relatively equivalent subject populations exhibiting very different behaviors. In the Goetz et al. (1983) study it appears that background knowledge affects both the amount of attention allocated to text information and learning of that information. The Shirey and Reynolds (1987) study demonstrates that interesting material (we assume interest to affect processing in a manner similar to background knowledge) is learned better without extra cognitive resources. Second, the interest studies indicated that older and younger students exhibit different patterns of selective attention. Fourth-grade students allocate more attention to and learn more of the interesting information, while college-age students learn interesting information better without this extra allocation of cognitive resources.

At least two explanations may be offered for these apparent discrepancies, both of which may be in operation. First, interest may be confounded with perceived task importance in the Goetz et al. (1983) study. Hints of this confounding were apparent in the earlier perspective work using materials similar to those used in Goetz et al. (Pichert & Anderson, 1977; Anderson & Pichert, 1978). In these earlier studies it was found that burglar information was learned much better than home buyer information regardless of perspective. The implication that we draw from these studies is that burglar information is either more interesting or more familiar than home buyer information. Therefore, interest or familiarity may have effects on learning above and beyond effects evidenced by perspective. This first explanation may address the discrepancies of the two studies involving adult subjects, but does not offer any theoretical account for the developmental differences found in the interest studies.

The second explanation relates to the interaction of task and person-centered state variables, and the effect it may have on importance. In the Goetz et al. study, the adult readers were given explicit and relatively specific task parameters; they were told to read the passages from a particular perspective. In the interest studies, no such task parameters were given. Subjects were simply told to read the information to understand it. The adult readers who were not given the explicit task criteria may have adopted default task criteria in order to effectively learn the presented information. Results of the Shirey and Reynolds (1987) study indicate that adults based their default strategy on external parameters, rather than the interestingness of the material. Consideration of these external task parameters apparently took priority in the allocation of attentional resources. Fourth-grade students also appeared to adopt a default strategy. However, their strategy was based on internal criteria; thus cognitive resources were allocated toward information considered interesting.

Development of Selective Attention

It appears that older students use a different set of criteria than younger students when employing a default study strategy. Research by Myers and Paris (1978) and Miller and Weiss (1982) provides a rather interesting framework within which to organize these findings. Their work has indicated that the young child's understanding of external variables (e.g., task parameters) develops much later than their understanding of internal variables (e.g., interest). Children are aware that such internal variables will have effects on their performance, but do not consider external or task parameters able to affect performance. This evidence is supported by children's self-reports (Myers & Paris, 1978) and performance on incidental learning tasks (Miller & Weiss, 1982). Thus, the ability to use external criteria to assist in learning appears to be a rather late-developing skill.

In most studying situations, students are not required to employ their own default strategy in order to facilitate learning. Generally, some preinstructional strategy such as pretests, behavioral objectives, overviews, or advance organizers are important components of teaching and instruction (Hartley & Davies, 1976). The purpose of these preinstructional strategies is to provide the student with a framework or perspective for the material or task that lies ahead. A valid examination of the development of selective attention should investigate the developmental differences in students' ability to allocate attention to these external parameters. Unfortunately, at least three obstacles stand in the way of such an investigation. First, very little work has addressed the issue of developmental level when assessing the effects of pre-instructional strategies. Indeed, one of the more recent meta-analyses of this literature fails to even mention age or ability level of student (Klauer, 1984). Although most research on the effectiveness of preinstructional strategies has been done with college-age students, Hartley and Davies (1976) did review some research that suggests that developmental differences do exist. Cook (1969) points out that middle-ability students benefit most from behavioral objectives. Additionally, Hartley and Davies (1976) cite two studies demonstrating that advance organizers do not facilitate learning with mentally retarded adolescents, (Neisworth, 1968) and lower-ability elementary school children (Allen, 1970). To our knowledge, however, no concerted effort has been made to investigate developmental differences in effectiveness of preinstructional strategies.

A second obstacle is the confounding of importance and interest in the research that exists. Based on the previous discussion, it appears necessary to take into account information that is relevant to internal and external criteria. The methodology that enables an investigation of the effects of importance on attention allocation and learning has not been often employed in research using younger or less able subjects. All of the work investigating the effects of objectives or perspectives has been performed with adults. The only work using the appropriate methodology with younger students has been the Anderson et al. (1984) study investigating the effects of interest, and one recent study examining the role of stated objectives (Reynolds et al., 1987).

In this study, students read a text about a nature walk during which the plants, animals, and other scenery encountered were described. Many of these descriptions centered around the colors of the particular object. The text was divided into 22 segments, with each segment being two sentences long. The text was presented on a computer screen one segment at a time, with the subject controlling when each new segment was to appear. Subjects were assigned to a control group or a group that received specific instructions to look for colors of things when reading the text. Following the reading of the text, subjects were administered a short-answer test designed to measure comprehension of the story.

Results indicated that, in the specific instruction group, both good and poor ability readers (as measured by a standardized reading test) allocated more attention to text segments that contained colors; however, only the high ability readers in the specific instruction group were able to demonstrate better memory for colors than their control group counterparts. These results suggest that, although both high- and low-ability sixth-grade students are capable of identifying and allocating cognitive resources to information important to the task objectives, only the high-ability students did so effectively. Again, we are unable to determine if interest is confounded with the measures of importance in this study.

The results of the two studies concerned with the cognitive strategies of elementary school students suggest the following two-part conclusion. First, as early as the third grade, students are capable of making predictions about the internal importance (interest) of information and can allocate cognitive resources accordingly. Second, this allocation of attention to interesting information does not appear to be a particularly effective or efficient strategy. Fourth-grade students allocate attention to information that they find interesting, even though it appears that this information would be learned without this added expenditure of cognitive resources. Lower ability sixth graders allocate more attention to information regarded as important, but this strategy appears to be ineffective since it also results in no increases in learning of the information. As stated earlier, this could also be accounted for by the confounding of interest and importance. Either way, the argument that immature learners do not make effective use of attention allocation seems valid. It is only the higher ability sixth graders that appear to make effective use of the attention allocation strategy.

IV.   THEORETICAL CONSIDERATIONS

The development of causal models to explain cognitive processes has had a relatively short history. We have already discussed some of the problems encountered when attempting such a project. Thus, it should come as no surprise that there are very few causal models with solid statistical support. Drawing from the work of Anderson and his colleagues (Anderson, 1982; Reynolds & Anderson, 1982; Reynolds et al., 1987), we have discussed some research within the context of his causal model of selective attention. The most solid support for this model is seen in research using adjunct questions to manipulate text importance (Reynolds & Anderson, 1982). The model has been expressed in the following fashion:

IMPORTANCE→ATTENTION→LEARNING

The importance of the text element to the category of adjunct questions influences the amount of attention allocated which in turn influences how well the text element will be learned. In other words, importance causes a change in learning because of the mediating effects of attention or some process supported by attention.

We have implied in this chapter that there appears to be another step that is necessary to complete this model. In order for the strategy of attention allocation to be effective, the student must have the capability to utilize the parameters of the task and text to determine the importance of text elements. Using conventional terminology, we will call this ability an effective metacognitive strategy. Additionally, the student must keep these task parameters in mind while engaging in the cognitive strategy. Thus the causal model shown previously may take the following form:

METACOGNITION→IMPORTANCE→ATTENTION→LEARNING

It would seem that when the metacognitive strategies are effective, it would make no difference in the model if they were or were not included. If the metacognitive strategies were to fail or become ineffective, however, the model itself would fail in its ability as an explanation of the roles of importance and attention on learning. Therefore, it is not surprising that this factor was not considered when investigating the effects of adjunct questions on adult learning. Because adults are generally effective users of metacognitive strategies, the causal model was successful. We hypothesize, however, that if the role of metacognitive strategies were ignored, the causal model would fail when looking at allocation of attention strategies in children.

Although we have no conclusive evidence to substantiate the above claim, analyses of research in progress (Reynolds et al., 1987) suggest that higher ability tenth graders make more effective use of the cognitive strategy of attention allocation than do lower ability tenth graders. The procedures followed in this study were identical to those in Reynolds and Anderson (1982), the only differences being the subject population and the administration to the students of a test of metacognitive knowledge. One rationale for using a tenth-grade population is that lower ability tenth graders would be at approximately the same reading level as students in the upper elementary grades. Therefore, they should exhibit comparable ineffectiveness in control of their cognitive strategies. Preliminary analyses do suggest that the higher ability tenth graders are more effective than the lower ability group in using the attention allocation strategy.

One area in which data exist to compare results across two divergent ability groups is the effect of interest on attention and learning (Shirey & Reynolds, 1987; Anderson et al., 1984). One study investigated fourth graders and the other looked at college-age students. In neither study was the causal model supported, but we would argue that in this specific instance, the findings in these studies do not disprove the model.

Earlier we offered an explanation to account for the apparent discrepancy between the results of the Goetz et al. (1983) study dealing with prior experience and perspective, and the Shirey and Reynolds (1987) study concerned with interest value of text elements. In the interest study, students may have adopted a "default" study strategy and perhaps attention was allocated according to the criteria of this perceived task. This could account for the finding that adults do not allocate more attention to information that they find interesting. The argument we offer here is that the ability to adopt this default strategy is an indication of effective control of studying behavior. Although no interviews were done with the fourth-grade population, we find it reasonable to assume that these younger students were unable to spontaneously adopt an effective default study strategy (Brown & Smiley, 1978; Pichert, 1979). Instead, the fourth-grade students allocated attention to the text elements that they found interesting; although, as we have emphasized before, this did not appear to be a particularly effective strategy.

The implication that we draw from this data is that there exist two forms of learning in any task-specific learning situation: (1) learning that is relevant to task parameters (instructions, questions, etc.) and text characteristics (titles, boldface print, etc.), and (2) learning that is relevant to the individual learner. Moreover, these two categories of learning are supported by different processes. Task-relevant learning is attention-intensive. In other words, relevant information is learned because of the additional cognitive resources allocated to it. For skilled studiers, person-relevant learning is not attention-intensive. It is more in line with learning posited by the ideational scaffolding hypothesis or slot hypothesis suggested by a number of researchers (Ausubel, 1960; Goetz et al., 1983; Reynolds & Anderson, 1982).

Figure 5 represents an outline of a model of the studying/learning process. In this model, importance criteria are determined by some interaction of the three *state* variables. Incoming text information is then graded for importance against these criteria. Attention is allocated in accordance to the importance rating of the information. As a result of the attention allocation, learning of the task-relevant information occurs. Additionally, information that is relevant to the individual is also learned. The interest study done with adults (Shirey & Reynolds, 1987) demonstrated that this learning is supported by a process quite different from selective attention. Adults learned information that they rated as interesting without allocating additional cognitive resources. Other studies investigating cultural relevance (Steffensen et al., 1979) indicate similar findings. Results show that even though adults read a culturally relevant passage in a shorter time period, more of the cultural-relevant material is learned. The most plausible explanation would involve the effects of an individual's background knowledge or schema on learning. The issues of interest, cultural relevance, and background knowledge, are highly related (Asher, 1980). Because we tend to know more about things in which we are interested or familiar, a more highly developed

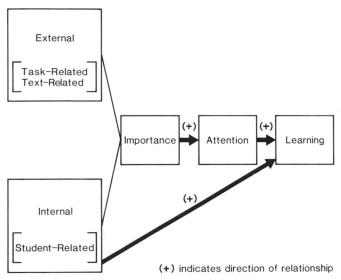

FIG. 5. A model of prose learning reflecting attention-intensive and attention-nonintensive processes.

schema is likely to have been established for this information. If a slot exists in the schema for this relevant or interesting information, the information should be assimilated with relatively little cognitive effort.

Of course, we are by no means suggesting that the learning process is as simple and clear-cut as the outlined model. There are many factors that will cloud this process. One obvious factor is the confounding of task or text relevance and person relevance that will be evident in any learning situation. Thus, it would be futile at present to attempt to break learning into two discrete categories. For now, all we may do is speak of learning in general terms and recognize that it may be supported by either of two distinct processes: (1) an attention-intensive process, and (2) a slot or schema-based process.

ACKNOWLEDGMENTS

The authors would like to thank the following people for their help in preparing this paper: Dr. Nicholas Burbules and Dr. Robert Bullough for reviewing and commenting on earlier versions of the paper, Gregg Schraw and Woody Trathen for stimulating discussions about models of learning, and Shawn Jackson for working on the references. Of course, any errors that remain in the paper are our responsibility alone.

Funding for the various projects discussed in this paper, as well as support for the paper itself, was obtained from the University of Utah Research Committee (grant numbers, 15-332, 15-330, 15-328) and the University of Utah graduate student research fellowship awards.

REFERENCES

Allen, D. (1970). Some effects of advance organizers and level of question on the learning and retention of written social studies material. *Journal of Educational Psychology, 61,* 333–339.

Anderson, R. C. (1982). Allocation of attention during reading. In A. Flammer, & W. Kintsch (Eds.), *Discourse processing.* New York: North-Holland.

Anderson, R. C., & Biddle, W. B. (1975). On asking people questions about what they are reading. In G. Bower (Ed.), *Psychology of learning and motivation.* New York: Academic Press.

Anderson, R. C., & Pichert, J. W. (1978). Recall of previously unrecallable information following a shift in perspective. *Journal of Educational Psychology, 17,* 1–12.

Anderson, R. C., Reynolds, R. E., Schallert, D. L., & Goetz, E. T. (1977). Frameworks for comprehending discourse. *American Educational Research Journal, 14,* 367–381.

Anderson, R. C., Shirey, L. L., Wilson, P. T., & Fielding, L. G. (1984). Interestingness of childrens' reading material, Report No. 323, Center for the Study of Reading, Urbana-Champaign, IL.

Anderson, T. H., & Armbruster, B. B. (1984). Studying. In P. D. Pearson (Ed.), *Handbook of Reading Research.* New York: Longman.

Arnold, H. F. (1942). The comparative effectiveness of certain study techniques in the field of history. *Journal of Educational Psychology, 3 (5),* 449–457.

Asher, S. (1980). Topic interest and childrens' reading comprehension. In R. J. Spiro, B. C. Bruce, & W. F. Brewer (Eds.), *Theoretical issues in reading comprehension.* Hillsdale, NJ: Erlbaum.

Ausubel, D. P. (1960). The use of advance organizers in the learning and retention of meaningful verbal processing. *Journal of Educational Psychology, 51,* 267–272.

Barton, W. A., Jr. (1930). Outlining as a study procedure. New York: Columbia University Bureau of Publications.

Britton, B. K., Piha, A., Davis, J., & Wehausen, E. (1978). Reading and cognitive capacity usage: Adjunct question effects. *Memory and Cognition, 6,* 266–273.

Britton, B. K., Westbrook, R. D., & Holdredge, T. (1978). Reading and cognitive capacity usage: Effects of text difficulty. *Journal of Experimental Psychology: Human Learning and Memory, 4,* 582–591.

Brown, A. L., & Smiley, S. S. (1977). Rating the importance of structural units of prose passages: A problem of metacognitive development. *Child Development, 48,* 1–8.

Brown, A. L., & Smiley, S. S. (1978). The development of strategies for studying texts. *Child Development, 49,* 1076–1088.

Cirilo, R. K. & Foss, D. J. (1980). Text structure and reading time for sentences. *Journal of Verbal Learning and Verbal Behavior, 19,* 96–109.

Cook, J. M. (1969). Learning and retention by informing students of behavioral objectives and their place in the hierarchical learning sequence, USOE Final Report, University of Maryland, College Park, MD.

Distad, H. W. (1926). A study of the reading performance of pupils under different conditions on different types of materials. *Journal of Educational Psychology, 18,* 247–258.

Frase, L. T. (1969). Structural analysis of the knowledge that results from thinking about text. *Journal of Educational Psychology Monograph, 60,* 1–15.

Germane, C. E. (1920). Value of the controlled mental summary as a method of studying. *School and Society, 12,* 591–593.

Germane, C. E. (1921). The value of the written paragraph summary. *Journal of Educational Research, 3,* 116–123.

Goetz, E. T., Schallert, D. L., Reynolds, R. E., & Radin, D. I. (1983). Reading in perspective: What real cops and pretend burglars look for in a story. *Journal of Educational Psychology*, 75, 500–510.

Hartley, J., & Davies, I. K. (1976). Pre-instructional strategies: The role of pretests, behavioral objectives, overviews and advance organizers. *Review of Educational Research, 46*, 239–266.

Howe, M. J. A., & Singer, L. (1975). Presentation variables and students' activities in meaningful learning. *British Journal of Educational Psychology, 45*, 52–61.

Hunter, C., & Harmon, D. (1979). *Adult Illiteracy in the United States*. New York: McGraw Hill.

Kahneman, D. (1973). *Attention and Effort*. Englewood Cliffs, NJ: Prentice-Hall.

Kintsch, W., & van Dijk, T. A. (1978). Toward a model of text comprehension and production. *Psychological Review, 85*, 363–393.

Klauer, K. J. (1984). Intentional and incidental learning with instructional texts: A meta-analysis for 1970–1980. *American Educational Research Journal, 21*, 323–340.

Kulhavy, R. W., Dyer, J. W., and Silver, L. (1975). The effects of notetaking and test expectancy on the learning of text material. *Journal of Educational Research, 68*, 363–365.

Mathews, C. O. (1938). Comparison of methods of study for immediate and delayed recall. *Journal of Educational Studies, 29*, 101–106.

Miller, P. G., & Weiss, M. G. (1982). Childrens' and adults' knowledge about what variables affect selective attention. *Child Development, 53*, 543–549.

Myers, M., & Paris, S. G. (1978). Childrens' metacognitive knowledge about reading. *Journal of Educational Psychology, 70*, 680–690.

National Commission on Excellence of Education. (1982). *A nation at risk*. Washington, D.C.: United States Department of Education.

Neisworth, J. T. (1968). The use of advance organizers with the educable mentally retarded, unpublished doctoral dissertation, University of Pittsburgh, Pittsburgh.

On further examination: Report of the advisory panel on scholastic aptitude test score decline. (1977). New York: College Entrance Examination Board.

Pichert, J. W. (1979). Sensitivity to what is important in prose, Report No. 149, Center for the Study of Reading, Urbana-Champaign, IL.

Pichert, J. W., & Anderson, R. C. (1977). Taking different perspectives on a story. *Journal of Educational Psychology, 69*, 309–315.

Poppleton, P. K., & Austwick, K. (1964). A comparison of programmed learning and note-making at two age levels. *British Journal of Educational Psychology, 34*, 43–50.

Reynolds, R. E. (1987). Studying: theoretical and methodological research, manuscript submitted for publication.

Reynolds, R. E., & Anderson, R. C. (1982). Influence of questions on the allocation of attention during reading. *Journal of Educational Psychology, 74*, 623–632.

Reynolds, R. E., Sawyer, M., & Bliss, S. (1987). Attention focusing in good and poor reading sixth graders, manuscript submitted for publication.

Reynolds, R. E., Goetz, E. T., Lapan, R., & Kreek, C. (1987). Focusing on important text elements: Good and poor reader differences, manuscript submitted for publication.

Reynolds, R. E., Standiford, S. N., & Anderson, R. C. (1979). Distribution of reading time when questions are asked about a restricted category of text information. *Journal of Educational Psychology, 7*, 183–190.

Rothkopf, E. Z. (1966). Learning from written instructive materials: An exploration of the control of inspection behavior by test-like events. *American Educational Research Journal, 3*, 241–249.

Rothkopf, E. Z., & Billington, M. J. (1979). Goal-guided learning from text: Inferring a descriptive processing model from inspection times and eye movements. *Journal of Educational Psychology, 71,* 310–327.

Rothkopf, E. Z., & Kaplan, R. (1972). Exploration of the effects of density and specificity of instructional objectives on learning from texts. *Journal of Educational Psychology, 63,* 295–302.

Shirey, L. L., & Reynolds, R. E. (in press). The effect of interest on attention and learning. *Journal of Educational Psychology.*

Steffensen, M. S., Joag-dev, C., & Anderson, R. C. (1979). A cross-cultural perspective of reading comprehension. *Reading Research Quarterly, 15,* 10–29.

Stordahl, K. E., & Christensen, C. M. (1956). The effect of study techniques on comprehension and retention. *Journal of Educational Research, 49,* 561–570.

Tulving, E., & Thompson, D. M. (1973). Encoding specificity and retrieval processes in episodic memory. *Psychological Review, 80,* 352–373.

van Dijk, T. A., & Kintsch, W. (1983). *Strategies of Discourse Processing.* New York: Academic Press.

Willmore, D. J. (1966). A comparison of four methods of studying a textbook, unpublished doctoral dissertation, University of Minnesota, Bloomington.

III

APPROACHES TO INSTRUCTION IN LEARNING AND STUDY STRATEGIES

COOPERATIVE LEARNING STRATEGIES

Donald F. Dansereau

By interacting with one another students can improve their acquisition of academic knowledge and skills. Such interaction among students, based on equal partnership in the learning experience as opposed to a fixed teacher/learner or tutor/tutee role, has been termed cooperative learning. This type of learning appears to foster two potent activities: active processing of the information (e.g., Reder, 1980; Ross & DiVesta, 1976) and cross modeling/imitation (e.g., Bandura, 1971; Singer, 1978). Additionally, the social context created by a cooperative approach can serve to enhance the motivation and positive affect of the participants (Sharan, 1980; Slavin, 1980, 1983). Cooperative learning also may better prepare individuals to perform "team" activities in the field (Smith et al., 1981). Because cooperative learning requires minimal instructor intervention it is an economical instructional technology that can be easily implemented in a variety of educational settings.

Cooperative learning has been explored primarily in field studies conducted in grade school, high school, and college classrooms (see reviews by Sharan, 1980; Slavin, 1980, 1983). Many of these studies have evaluated cooperative learning scenarios (general procedures for interacting and processing the target material) in comparison with traditional teaching techniques (e.g., lecture). Evaluations of strategies such as the Jigsaw classroom (Aronson et al., 1978), Teams-Games-Tournaments (DeVries & Slavin, 1978), and the Student-Teams and Academic Divisions (Slavin, 1978), have typically indicated positive post-experience effects on academic achievement and social/affective variables (e.g., race relations and mutual concern). Also, a recent meta-analysis indicates that cooperative learning (where peer tutoring is encouraged) promotes higher achievement and productivity than does individualistic effort regardless of age or subject matter (Johnson et al., 1981).

A smaller number of studies have focused on specific parameters of cooperative learning (e.g., group size and ability mixtures within the group). In most of these experiments, the students were not given formal methods for processing the material. Generally, they were instructed to help each other

LEARNING AND STUDY STRATEGIES: ISSUES IN ASSESSMENT, INSTRUCTION, AND EVALUATION

study (occasionally under grade contingencies) and were allowed to utilize their own strategies in accomplishing the objective. Although these investigations typically indicate overall positive effects due to cooperative learning, there are generally no significant effects due to group size on concept acquisition or academic performance (e.g., Beaman et al., 1977; Klausmeir et al., 1963; Lemke et al., 1969) and equivocal results with regard to the matching of abilities within groups (e.g., Hurlock & Hurlock, 1972; Webb, 1977).

Only a few prior studies have been designed to determine if there is transfer of skills from cooperative to individual learning. In these cases, cooperative learning has not led to positive transfer (McClintock & Sonquist, 1976), and in situations where relatively novel tasks were used, it has often produced negative transfer (e.g., Lemke et al., 1969).

Although the prior studies have provided evidence that cooperative learning methods are potentially effective, they have often suffered from a lack of experimental controls and have not made use of current theories and empirical findings associated with cognitive approaches to learning. Consequently, very little reliable information exists about the important dimensions and educational potential of cooperative learning. Controlled laboratory studies using ecologically valid learning materials are needed to provide a basis for the development of viable cooperative learning programs. The research to be reported in subsequent sections of this chapter is designed to be a step in this direction.

DEVELOPMENT OF A DYADIC COOPERATIVE LEARNING STRATEGY

The present research program was designed to remedy drawbacks of prior cooperative learning studies by systematically analyzing the effects of learning strategies and individual differences on the acquisition of scientific knowledge and learning skills in the context of a dyadic learning situation. Student dyads were chosen as the unit of analysis because larger groups make it more difficult to delineate processing and interaction parameters, and may promote the formation of coalitions thus encouraging competition rather than cooperation (e.g., Peterson & Janicki, 1979; Webb, 1980).

The cooperative learning strategy used in the present research was originally developed as an individual text learning strategy (Dansereau et al., 1979). This strategy was modified for use in a dyadic learning situation. In general, the strategy requires each pair member to read approximately 500 words of a 2,500-word passage. One pair member then serves as recaller and attempts to orally summarize from memory what has been learned. The

TABLE 1   A Cooperative Learning Strategy: First Degree MURDER

Mood	Establish positive mind-set for reading and studying
Understand	While reading, grasp main ideas and facts
Recall	Without looking at text, summarize what was read
Detect	Check for errors and omissions in recall (metacognitive activity)
Elaborate	Facilitate memory by adding mental imagery, prior knowledge, etc.
Review	Go over material to be remembered

other member of the pair serves as the listener/facilitator and attempts to correct errors in the recall (i.e., metacognitive activities) and to further facilitate the organization and storage of the material (i.e., elaborative activities). The partners alternate roles of recaller and listener/facilitator. To make the strategy easy to learn and follow, it was broken down into six steps and given the acronym "First Degree MURDER," as illustrated in Table 1.

The major components of this strategy are supported by basic research findings in cognitive and educational psychology. Ross and DiVesta (1976) conducted a study that supports the oral summarization aspect of this strategy. In this experiment, one treatment group studied text with the expectancy that they would later present an oral summary. Another group studied the same material without this expectancy. Following acquisition, one third of the subjects in each group presented oral summaries, another third listened to oral summaries, and the remainder did not engage in any review activity. The results indicated that verbal participation facilitated retention and that the highest mean performances were achieved by verbalizers and observers who expected to give an oral summary.

Based on orientation (Frase, 1970) and mathemagenic (Rothkopf, 1970) notions, Ross et al. (1976) suggest that expectation of oral presentation facilitates acquisition by inducing awareness of objectives and of appropriate learning strategies by which these objectives can be achieved. Further, oral summary as an activity provides a review that serves (through further encoding) to consolidate and strengthen what was learned. It also provides the learner with an opportunity to assess the degree to which mastery and understanding were achieved.

Unlike the Ross et al. (1976) study in which a single summary was required, the cooperative learning strategy requires multiple oral summaries exchanged between pair partners. In addition to providing the effects on processing suggested by Ross and DiVesta (1976), the multiple summary approach potentially allows for a subsequent reduction in presentation anxiety due to increased familiarity with the task situation (Zajonc, 1966), an increase in the quality of the production and interpretation of summaries, and an improvement in study processes due to self-generated feedback on the quality of the summaries.

In addition to advantages gained from oral summarization, the pair partners can monitor and provide feedback on the accuracy and effectiveness of the summary. More specifically, in the Dansereau et al. (1979) strategy, the participants are taught to detect and correct errors and omissions and to make importance judgments about the ideas presented. These activities have been examined by other investigators under the rubric of metacognition. Recent research in this domain has indicated that students tend to have difficulty performing these monitoring activities on their own (Baker, 1979; Markman, 1979; Schallert & Kleiman, 1979). Although attempts have been made to train metacognitive activity, they have met with only moderate success (Brown, 1978). The inclusion of monitoring activities in cooperative learning may impact on the acquisition of information by pair partners and also create the possibility of positive transfer of metacognitive skills to individual learning.

In the cooperative strategy being investigated, the partners are also trained to elaborate on each other's summaries. This involves creating images, making analogies, and personalizing the information to make it more understandable and more memorable. A number of experiments have shown that training students on elaborative activities has led to improved comprehension and retention (e.g., Weinstein et al., 1979). It is expected that even greater gains may accrue in a dyadic learning situation where partners can share in the creation of effective elaborations.

In summary, it was expected that training on using a cooperative strategy with these characteristics would improve performance on tests covering material studied in pairs and provide students with transferable skills to employ in individual learning. In the next sections, experimentation with this cooperative strategy and its modifications will be reported.

A.   INITIAL EVALUATIONS OF THE COOPERATIVE STRATEGY: EFFECTS ON ACQUISITION AND TRANSFER

To provide an initial evaluation, two experiments were designed to answer the following questions:

1. Is cooperative learning more effective than individual learning in initial acquisition of college textbook material?
2. Do students learn more effectively in a cooperative learning situation if they are given systematic instructions for pair interaction?
3. Does cooperative learning transfer to individual study?

For a detailed presentation of these experiments see McDonald et al. (1985).

1. Experiment 1

The first experiment employed three groups of college students: (1) the System (formal pair) group ($n = 20$); (2) the No-System (informal pair) group ($n = 20$); and (3) the Individual Study group ($n = 20$). The strategy described earlier was taught to the System Pair group; students in the No-System Pair group were asked to discuss and decide on a method of pair learning; students in the Individual group were instructed to use their normal study methods. Students in the two pair groups were randomly assigned learning partners.

The experiment consisted of three sessions: (1) 1 hour of training and practice on the strategies; (2) studying of two 2,500-word passages extracted from basic science textbooks (each passage studied for 50 minutes; the first cooperatively, and the second individually); (3) essay, short-answer, cloze, and multiple-choice tests on both passages 5 days after the study session.

A one-way analysis of covariance was performed for both the initial learning and transfer tests separately with overall grade point average used as the covariate. The results indicated that there are significant between-group differences on total scores (sum of the four subsets) for both passages after the effects of the covariate were removed; for the initial learning test, $F(2, 56) = 3.65$, $p < .03$; and for the transfer test, $F(2, 56) = 3.39$, $p < .05$.

Post hoc tests on the initial learning data showed that the System Pairs and the No-System Pairs significantly outperformed the Individuals ($p < .01$, $p < .05$, respectively). The transfer test *post hoc* analysis showed that the System Pairs significantly outperformed the No-System Pairs and the Individuals ($p < .01$). All other differences between groups were not significant.

In general, the results of this study suggest that cooperative learning is effective in initial acquisition of prose material whether or not students are given specific instructions for pair interaction. This finding extends the previous literature on pair learning to the initial acquisition of academic material. In addition, results show that the use of a systematic cooperative learning strategy leads to increased performance in a subsequent individual learning situation relative to the untrained pair group and the individual study group. It appears that the systematic pair group employed strategies during their pair interaction that transferred to individual learning. This finding suggests that systematic cooperative learning may serve as an effective strategy training vehicle. Because of scheduling problems and limited subject availability at the time the study was conducted, however, a group that received the experimenter strategy on an individual basis was not included. It is therefore impossible to determine if the observed transfer was a result of the experimenter strategy, the systematic cooperative experience, or a combination of both. As a consequence, a second study was conducted.

2.   Experiment 2

Three groups of college students were employed in this experiment: (1) System Pairs ($n = 30$; pairs using the experimenter-provided strategy), (2) System Individuals ($n = 27$; individuals using the experimenter-provided strategy), and (3) Own Strategy Individuals ($n = 30$; individuals using their own study methods). The experimenter-provided strategy and experimental procedures were analogous to those described in Experiment 1. The essay test was employed as the only dependent measure in this experiment.

Since the intent was to look at initial learning and transfer separately, two analyses of covariance were conducted. Results revealed a significant main effect of strategy for the initial learning passage, $F(2, 84) = 4.62$, $p < .01$, and approached significance for the transfer passage, $F(2, 84) = 2.81$, $p < .06$. The results of the *post hoc* analyses for the initial learning test showed that the System Pairs were significantly different from the System Individuals and the Own Strategy Individuals, $p < .01$. The *post hoc* analyses for the transfer test also showed that the System Pairs significantly outperformed the System Individuals and the Own Strategy Individuals, $p < .01$. All other group differences were not significant.

Results of the replication of Experiment 1 suggest that students who study in pairs using a systematic learning strategy outperform students who study alone in an initial learning task. In addition, those individuals who studied in pairs during initial learning outperformed the individuals who studied alone in a subsequent individual learning situation. These results suggest that the pair members gained beneficial skills/strategies from the pair learning situation and from each other which transferred to an individual learning situation.

The combined results of the two experiments presented indicate that the cooperative strategy facilitates initial learning and leads to positive transfer on a subsequent individual learning task. It appears that it is not the strategy or the pair interaction alone that contributes to the transfer effect, but a combination of the two that enhances an individual's solitary learning following a cooperative experience.

B.   EXPLORATION OF THE COMPONENTS OF THE COOPERATIVE LEARNING STRATEGY

In this section, two experiments designed to examine critical components of the cooperative learning strategy will be described.

Effects of Role Activity Level of the Learners

This experiment had four major purposes:

1. To provide more information on the relative importance of recalling/summarizing and listening/facilitation during cooperative learning by comparing students assigned fixed roles as "recallers" with those assigned fixed roles as "listeners" and with those who alternated roles.
2. To assess the effectiveness of metacognitive (e.g., comprehension error correcting, importance judging) and elaborative (e.g., integrating information with prior knowledge) activities by comparing dyads who engaged in these activities during studying with dyads who did not.
3. To determine the effectiveness of the cooperative learning techniques in comparison with individual study techniques.
4. To assess the subjective evaluation of the cooperative learning experience as rated by each pair member. These types of evaluations are clearly important in the continued, nonsupervised use of this technique.

In order to conduct this experiment, 126 students from general psychology classes at Texas Christian University were randomly assigned to one of five groups: Fixed Role/Summary + Facilitation Activity ($n = 36$); Fixed Role/Summary Only Activity ($n = 36$), Alternating Role/Summary + Facilitation Activity ($n = 18$); Alternating Role/Summary Only Activity ($n = 18$); and Individual Study Method (18 students used their normal study techniques). Within the four treatment groups, students were randomly assigned to same-sex pairs.

Each of the five groups of participants were given different processing instructions. In the Fixed Role/Summary + Facilitation Activity group, one member of the cooperative pair was randomly assigned the role of recaller. After approximately each 500-word segment of the passage, this person orally summarized the material studied since the last recall (this summary was done from memory). The other member was assigned the role of listener/facilitator and was instructed to correct errors in the recall and to facilitate the organization and storage of the material.

The Fixed Role/Summary Only pairs were given similar instructions except that the listener was instructed not to provide any overt input/facilitation to the cooperative interaction.

In the Alternating Role/Summary + Facilitation group, one randomly selected member of the pair served as the recaller for the first segment of the passage, and the other member served as the listener/facilitator. After reading each passage segment, the pair partners switched roles. In all other respects the procedure was the same as for the Fixed Role/Summary + Facilitation Activity group. The Alternating Role/Summary Only group were given instructions similar to the Alternating Role/Summary + Facilitation Activity group except that the listener provided no facilitative activities. The participants in the Individual Study Method group were told to use their normal strategy for processing the text material.

This study was conducted in three 1½-hour sessions using basically the same materials described previously. During the first session, the Delta Reading Vocabulary Test (Deignan, 1973) was administered, the participants were given instructions about their assigned roles, and then were given a 2,500-word text passage to study for 55 minutes. Two days later, the participants were administered a free-recall test on the passage. Utilizing the same procedures, the participants then studied a second text passage for 55 minutes. After a five-day delay, a free-recall test on the second passage was given and the Group Embedded Figures Test (GEFT) (Oltman et al., 1971), and the Learning Questionnaire were administered. The Learning Questionnaire was designed to assess the participants' subjective reactions to cooperative learning. Due to logistics, the delay lengths between passage presentations and testings could not be equalized.

Two two-way analyses of covariance (ANCOVA) (Delta and GEFT as covariates) were conducted on each of two dependent variables: totaled main ideas scores from both passages and totaled detail ideas scores from both passages. The scores were combined across passages in order to increase the robustness of the dependent measures. Recallers, Listeners, and Alternaters served as the role factor, and Summary + Facilitation and Summary Only served as the listener activity factor for both ANCOVA.

The analysis of covariance using totaled main ideas as the dependent measures revealed significant role and listener effects, $F(2, 100) = 3.92$, $p < .02$; $F(1, 100) = 4.09$, $p < .04$, respectively. Post hoc comparisons indicated that the Recallers significantly outperformed the Listeners, $p < .01$. An examination of means indicated that the Summary + Facilitation group outperformed the Summary Only group on the totaled main ideas. No significant effects were found for the ANCOVA using totaled detail ideas.

To compare the cooperative learning technique with the individual study techniques, two planned one-way ANCOVA were conducted for each of the two levels of the listener activity factor. Recallers, Listeners, Alternaters, and Individuals were included as the role factor, Delta and GEFT used as the covariates, and totaled main ideas and totaled detail ideas were included as the dependent measures for each set of ANCOVA.

The Summary + Facilitation Activity ANCOVA with totaled main ideas as the dependent measure was significant, $F(3, 66) = 3.06$, $p < .03$. Post hoc comparisons revealed that Recallers significantly outperformed the Individuals on the free recall of main ideas, $p < .05$. No significant effects were obtained with the Summary + Facilitation Activity ANCOVA with totaled detail ideas as the dependent measure or with the two Summary Only ANCOVA.

The participants' evaluations of the cooperative learning experience were assessed by the Learning Questionnaire. A principal components analysis produced one factor accounting for 46.6% of the variance. Factor scores consisting of an unweighted total of the eight relevant questions were then utilized as the dependent measure in a Role × Listener Activity ANCOVA (Delta and GEFT as covariates). The role factor was the only significant effect obtained, $F(2, 100) = 5.17$, $p < .01$. *Post hoc* comparisons showed that Alternaters felt they learned more and had increased motivation and concentration by studying in pairs than did Listeners, $p < .01$. Examination of the means revealed that listeners who had no overt input into the learning experience evaluated the situation as being less beneficial than any of the other groups.

The present study investigated the effects of role and activity of students participating in cooperative dyads on free recall of scientific text passages. The results indicated that the students who were assigned the fixed recaller role had significantly higher recall scores for main ideas than students who were assigned the fixed listener role. This finding supports the McDonald et al. (1985) study, the Ross and DiVesta (1976) study, and a number of earlier studies (e.g., Gates, 1917). All of these studies suggest that intermittent recalling (or summarizing) is an activity that increases subsequent recall. This finding is also supported by the Alternaters' performance. Individuals in the Alternating dyad summarized half of the passage and listened for the other half of the passage. The mean performance of the Alternater group is approximately halfway between the Fixed Recaller group, who summarized the entire passage, and the Fixed Listener group who did not summarize at all. Therefore, the more summarization activity produced by the student, the better the recall performance.

The Summary + Facilitation listener activity groups were found to out-perform the Summary Only groups on free recall of main ideas. The meta-cognitive and elaborative activities of the listener appeared to enhance performance of both the listener and the recaller. Examination of the mean performance on free recall of main ideas indicates that the Recallers whose partners provided elaboration had the best performance. Not only does the facilitative activity improve performance, but the combination of summarization and facilitative activity leads to even better performance.

Comparison of the cooperative learning situation with individual study techniques showed that Recallers in the Summary + Facilitation groups outperformed individuals who used their own study technique. Although not significant, the Alternaters in the Summary + Facilitation group also exhibited substantially better mean performance than did the individuals.

The results of the subjective evaluation of the cooperative learning experience revealed that the Alternaters were more enthusiastic about the experience than either the Listeners or Recallers. This finding is important when applying the cooperative learning techniques to real classroom settings. Even though the Recallers had the best performance, the Alternaters also had good performance and they evaluated the situation more positively. In the long run, the alternating technique may benefit more of the students than the fixed recaller technique that allows only one member of each pair to recall. For a detailed description of this experiment see Spurlin et al. (1984).

C. EFFECTS OF METACOGNITIVE AND ELABORATIVE ACTIVITY ON COOPERATIVE LEARNING AND TRANSFER

The results of the previous experiment indicated that both roles (fixed vs. alternating) and listener activities (active vs. passive) are important variables in cooperative learning. On free recall of text main ideas, fixed recallers outperformed fixed listeners, and pairs that incorporated an active listener (one who engaged in metacognitive and elaborative activities) outperformed those that did not.

The purpose of the present experiment was to examine further the importance of listener activity by assessing the performance of three types of dyads: those in which metacognitive activity was emphasized, those in which elaborative activity was emphasized, and those in which the listener remained silent. (For a more detailed discussion of this experiment see Larson et al., 1985.) More specifically this experiment was designed to answer the following questions:

1. What is the relative contribution of metacognitive versus elaborative activity to text processing performance during cooperative learning? (In the previous experiment the "active" listener did both of these processes.)
2. What impact does the activity of the listener during cooperative learning have in subsequent transfer to individual learning? (In the previous experiment, effects on transfer were not assessed.)

One hundred twenty students from general psychology classes at Texas Christian University were randomly assigned to one of three groups: Metacognitive Listener, (n = 42), Elaborative Listener (n = 43), and Control Passive Listener (n = 36). Within the treatment groups, subjects were randomly assigned to same-sex pairs.

The basic learning method used for all three groups was the alternating cooperative strategy described previously.

The study was conducted in three 2-hour sessions. During the first session each of the three groups was given different training packets on the listener activities. In the Elaborative Listener group, participants were instructed and given practice on exploring different methods of elaborating on the material: (1) how to use imagery to help remember the material; (2) personalizing information; (3) using mnemonics such as rhymes; and (4) representing the information in another form, such as drawings and graphs. The Metacognitive Listener group was given instructions and practice on the following: (1) correcting inaccurate information; (2) detecting omissions; and (3) detecting key ideas. Participants in both groups were instructed to perform their respective activities upon each summary completion. The Control/Passive Listener participants were instructed in and given practice on alternating recall of segments of the passage. The listener was instructed to remain silent throughout all recalls. During training all participants regardless of group affiliation were given exposure to the same two short practice passages.

During the second session (conducted 2 days after the first), participants were reminded about their roles and activities and were given one of two 2,500-word test passages to study for 55 minutes using the cooperative method relevant to their group assignment. To assess transfer, all participants then studied a second passage alone for 55 minutes (the two passages were counterbalanced between the two study sessions).

After a 5-day delay, all participants were administered free-recall tests (18-minute tests) on both passages. In addition, participants were administered the Delta Reading Vocabulary Test and the Group Embedded Figures Test.

All free-recall scores were standardized within passages and preliminary analyses were conducted to determine if there were any interactions involving the passage factor. Because no significant passage interactions were found, the data were collapsed across passages. A 3×2 repeated measures ANCOVA (groups as the between factor and task as the repeated measures factor) was performed. Delta and GEFT served as the covariates, and total recall score was the dependent measure. The results of the ANCOVA revealed a significant groups $\times$ task interaction, $F(2, 117) = 4.53$, $p < .01$. All other effects were not significant.

Post hoc analyses revealed that the Metacognitive group significantly ($p < .05$) outperformed the Elaborative group during initial learning, whereas the Elaborative group significantly ($p < .05$) outperformed the Metacognitive group on the individual learning transfer passage.

It should be noted that the Metacognitive group performed better than the control group on initial acquisition. In addition, the Elaborative group performed better than the control group on transfer.

These results suggest that an emphasis on metacognitive activity facilitates cooperative learning and an emphasis on elaborative activity facilitates transfer to individual learning. It appears that students can effectively assist each other in correcting comprehension errors and detecting key ideas. However, the lack of positive transfer for the metacognitive group indicates that the participants are not learning improved ways of conducting these activities on their own. Apparently in this situation, monitoring and correcting each other's productions does not lead to improved self-monitoring and correcting behaviors. It is possible that this lack of transfer arises from the fact that the participants were not directly instructed to focus on the improvement of their individual skills. They were told to help each other to learn a particular body of material using the method required, so any skill transfer was primarily incidental to the stated goals. With metacognitive activity, direct instructions and individual feedback may be needed to foster positive transfer.

On the other hand, in the group receiving the elaborative emphasis, the opposite scenario was indicated by the data. The lack of positive effects on performance under a cooperative situation indicates that the partners were not able to help each other effectively elaborate on the text information. This may not be particularly surprising because elaborations largely involve personalizing the information in an idiosyncratic manner. Attempts at arriving at mutually agreeable elaborations may produce information that is not particularly useful to either participant. However, the elaborative activities during the cooperative experience may give students new approaches to elaborations that they can effectively use when studying alone.

These findings have educational implications regarding the tailoring of cooperative learning strategies to instructional goals. If the goal is to learn specific text material, the use of cooperative learning with a focus on the metacognitive activity of the listener helps performance, whereas if the intent is to facilitate transfer of learning to other materials and situations, the elaborative activity of the listener within cooperative learning should be emphasized.

D.   ROLE OF INDIVIDUAL DIFFERENCES IN COOPERATIVE LEARNING

In all of the experiments reported previously there were large differences among pairs of students receiving the same experimental treatment. It is very likely that this within-group variation is due to individual differences associated with aptitude, style, prior knowledge, and personality variables. This variation may be due not only to an individual's characteristics but also due to his/her partner's characteristics. Because cooperative learning is based on student–student interactions, it is likely that the aptitudes and styles of each member of the pair influence the impact this strategy has on the students' acquisition of information. Two experiments were conducted to explore this possibility. See Larson et al. (1984) for further information on these experiments.

1. Experiment 1

The individual difference variables selected for the present study were drawn from the domains of cognitive style, verbal ability, prior knowledge, and personality. Representative measures of each dimension were chosen based on prior studies relating individual differences to academic learning. Due to the limitations of this chapter the entire set of measures will be listed without description. A discussion of the significant measures will be presented at a later point.

Cognitive style. Field Dependence–Independence—Group Embedded Figures Test (Oltman et al., 1971); Cognitive Complexity—Role Construct Repertory Test (Bieri, 1955); Educational Set Scale (Siegel & Siegel, 1965).

Verbal ability. Delta Reading Vocabulary Test (Deignan, 1973).

Prior knowledge. Two specially developed measures designed to tap students' prior knowledge of the testing materials.

Personality. Internal/External Locus of Control (Rotter, 1966); Test Anxiety (Sarason, 1956).

The major focus of the study was to examine how the individual's and partner's scores on each of the above individual difference measures affect the cooperative learning experience as measured by delayed recall on an essay test on a 2,500-word passage.

Eighty-eight students from a learning strategy class at Texas A&M University provided the data for this study. All students completed the individual difference measures listed previously. They then received approximately 4 hours of cooperative learning training distributed over four sessions. The cooperative learning strategy was a slightly modified version of the one described earlier. In a subsequent session they cooperatively studied a 2,500-word test passage for 45 minutes. Two days later they individually responded to a 20-minute free-recall test on the passage.

All free-recall tests were scored for correct recall of main and detail ideas according to a predetermined key. All individual difference measures were scored using standard procedures.

An examination of the raw data plots relating free-recall performance to the individual difference measures indicated that the salient relationships appeared to be curvilinear. To determine the best fitting form of these relationships, several data transformations were performed and entered into linear regression analyses. In examining these analyses, it appeared that in all cases log–log functions provided the best predictability. In these analyses the log of the individual's score and the log of his/her partner's score on each individual difference measure were entered to predict the log of the individual's performance on the free-recall test for both main and detail ideas. With regard to these analyses, the individual's scores on the Group Embedded Figures Test (GEFT), the Delta Reading Vocabulary Test, the Test Anxiety Scale (TAS), and one of the prior knowledge questionnaires significantly ($p < .05$) predicted recall of detail ideas. The partner's score on the GEFT also contributed significantly ($p < .01$) to the equation using detail ideas as the criterion. In addition, the individual's scores on the GEFT, Delta, and TAS significantly ($p < .01$) predicted recall of main ideas.

To determine which variables or combination of variables were most salient in the cooperative learning situation, all variables that were found to be significant in the log–log transformations were entered into a single, multiple-regression equation. All data were subjected to log–log transformations.

The individual's GEFT scores and Delta scores made significant predictions for detail ideas ($p < .05$) as did the partner's scores on the GEFT ($p < .01$). For main ideas, an individual's performance was signficantly predicted by his/her GEFT score ($p < .05$) and Delta score ($p < .01$). All other relationships were not significant.

The results suggest that within the domain explored, the major predictors of cooperative learning performance are the GEFT and the Delta. The results of increasing performance with increasing vocabulary ability are not surprising. The results with the GEFT, however, are somewhat more complicated and more interesting. An analysis of the salient log–log relationships suggest that the attribute of field independence is particularly beneficial in the recall of detail ideas for those individuals scoring below the median. In addition, especially for those individuals scoring below the median on the GEFT, it appears that having a field-independent partner facilitates the individual's recall of detail ideas. This finding suggests that field dependents will benefit from being paired with field independents and that the field independents will not be adversely affected by such pairings.

2. Experiment 2

Supplementary analyses of the data emerging from the previous individual difference study suggested that students who demonstrate moderate verbal skills (as measured by the Delta) tend to demonstrate more enhanced recall when paired with a high-verbal-ability partner.

The purpose of the present study was to further examine the verbal ability variable with regard to the heterogeneity/homogeneity issue within cooperative learning. In addition, the impact of homogeneity/heterogeneity of verbal ability on transfer to individual learning was examined.

Seventy-eight students from introductory psychology courses at Texas Christian University volunteered to participate in this experiment for course credit. All participants were randomly assigned same-sex pair partners.

The experiment took place in three sessions. In Session 1, all participants were administered the Delta Reading Vocabulary Test and were randomly assigned pair partners. They were then given instructions and practice using the cooperative learning method. Two passages unrelated to the dependent measures passage were used during practice.

In Session 2, participants were reminded of the cooperative learning method and then studied a 2,500-word text passage cooperatively for 45 minutes. Following a short break, all students studied a second 2,500-word text passage individually for 45 minutes.

In Session 3, which occurred 5 days after Session 2, all participants were administered free-recall tests for both passages (18 minutes/test).

The dependent measures were scored for main and detail ideas according to predetermined keys.

Participants were divided into high and low groups on the Delta Reading Vocabulary Test (median split). Two-way analyses of variance were conducted on the main, detail, and total ideas recalled for each passage, using the individual's verbal ability (high/low) and the partner's verbal ability (same/different) as the two factors. This ANOVA approach was used to provide a clearer picture of heterogeneity/homogeneity effects (see Das & Kirby, 1978, for a rationale for this approach).

A main effect was observed for the individuals' scores on the "initial learning" main ideas, $F(1, 82) = 3.43$, $p < .05$, and detail ideas, $F(1, 82) = 13.68$, $p < .01$, indicating individuals high in verbal ability outperform those low in ability. This same effect was also observed for the transfer detail ideas, $F(1, 82) = 13.16$, $p < .01$, and for transfer total, $F(1, 82) = 9.58$, $p < .01$.

The effect of the partner was significant for transfer main ideas, $F(1, 82) = 4.41$, $p < .05$, indicating that individuals who had "different" partners scored higher than those who had partners within the same ability range. All other effects were not significant.

The effects of an individual's verbal ability on his/her free-recall performance were expected and are relatively uninteresting; however, the effect of the partner's verbal ability on an individual's main idea score on a subsequent transfer test is of potential importance. It suggests that heterogeneous pairs learn something from the cooperative experience that aids them in individual study. The lower verbal ability student may learn by observing the strategies of his/her partner, while the higher ability student may learn new methods by being placed in the role of "teacher."

The results of this experiment, combined with the results of the previously reported experiment on individual differences, suggest that heterogeneous pairings based on vocabulary level and field independence are more effective than homogeneous pairings in a structured cooperative learning situation.

E. SUMMARY AND FUTURE DIRECTIONS

To date, the results of the present research program indicate that:

1. cooperating pairs, using the previously described strategy, outperform individuals both during cooperative learning and during transfer;
2. active listening is more effective than passive listening in the cooperative situation;
3. metacognitive activities are more effective for initial acquisition of material but elaborative activities are more effective for transfer;
4. dyads who are heterogeneous with regard to cognitive style and verbal ability outperform homogeneous pairs.

Although the use of this dyadic cooperative learning strategy has yielded consistently positive results, the strategy does appear to have weaknesses that may inhibit its effectiveness. More specifically, informal observations of participating dyads point to a number of apparent difficulties. Some dyads appear to focus on content at the expense of accurately performing the strategy while others do the opposite. In addition, some dyads do not appear to adequately understand and implement the strategy. Finally, some of the dyadic interactions are characterized by a misuse of the available study time through extraneous conversation, concentration on unnecessary details, and occasional arguments.

We have speculated that some of these problems may be ameliorated by including a third person or microcomputer in the learning unit. This person or microcomputer could serve as a process monitor to facilitate strategy usage and appropriate on-task activity. We have conducted some exploratory experimentation to examine both of these possibilities. Our findings suggest that a triadic strategy has potential, but that care must be taken to keep the interaction patterns simple enough to avoid overloading the participants. We plan to continue these explorations of more complicated cooperative interactions, and to extend their applicability to learning from sources other than pure text (e.g., visual schematics, videotapes, and laboratory demonstrations).

REFERENCES

Aronson, E., Stephan, C., Sikes, J., Blaney, N., & Snapp, M. (1978). *The jigsaw classroom.* Beverly Hills, CA: Sage Publications.

Baker, L. (1979). Comprehension monitoring: Identifying and coping with text confusions. (1979). Technical Report 145, Center for the Study of Reading, University of Illinois, Urbana, IL.

Bandura, A. (Ed.) (1971). *Psychological modeling: Conflicting theories*. Chicago: Aldine-Atherton.

Beaman, A. L., Diener, E., Fraser, S. C., & Endreson, K. L. (1977). Effects of voluntary and semivoluntary peer monitoring programs on academic performance. *Journal of Educational Psychology, 69*, 109–114.

Bieri, J. (1955). Cognitive complexity-simplicity and predictive behavior. *Journal of Abnormal and Social Psychology, 4*, 263–268.

Brooks, L. W., & Dansereau, D. F. (1983). Effects of structural schema training and text organization on expository prose processing. *Journal of Educational Psychology, 75*, 811–820.

Brown, A. L. (1978). Knowing when, where, and how to remember: A problem of metacognition. In R. Glaser (Ed.), *Advances in instructional psychology*. Hillsdale, NJ: Erlbaum.

Dansereau, D. F., McDonald, B. A., Collins, K. W., Garland, J. C., Holley, C. D., Diekhoff, G. M., & Evans, S. H. (1979). Evaluation of a learning strategy system. In H. F. O'Neil, Jr., & C. D. Spielberger (Eds.), *Cognitive and affective learning strategies*. New York: Academic Press.

Das, J. P., & Kirby, J. R. (1978). The case of the wrong examplar: A reply to Humphreys. *Journal of Educational Psychology, 70*, 877–879.

Deignan, G. M. (1973). *The Delta Reading Vocabulary Test*. Lowry Air Force Base, CO: Air Force Human Resources Laboratory.

DeVries, D., & Slavin, R. (1978). Teams-games-tournaments: A research review. *Journal of Research and Development in Education, 12*, 28–38.

Frase, L. T. (1970). Boundary conditions for mathemagenic behaviors. *Review of Educational Research, 40*, 337–347.

Gates, A. I. (1917). Recitation as a factor in memorizing. *Archives of Psychology, 6*, 1–104.

Holley, C. D., Dansereau, D. F., McDonald, B. A., Garland, J. C., & Collins, K. W. (1979). Evaluation of a hierarchical mapping technique as an aid to prose processing. *Contemporary Educational Psychology, 4*, 227–237.

Hurlock, R., & Hurlock, J. (1972). Paired students trained by CAI. *Proceedings, American Psychology Association*, 495–496.

Johnson, D. W., Maruyama, G., Johnson, R., Nelson, D., & Skon, L. (1981). Effects of cooperative, competitive, and individualistic goal structures on achievement: A meta-analysis. *Psychological Bulletin, 89*, 47–62.

Klausmeir, H. J., Wiersma, W., & Harris, C. W. (1963). Efficiency of initial learning and transfer by individuals, pairs, and quads. *Journal of Educational Psychology, 54*, 160–164.

Larson, C. O., Dansereau, D. F., O'Donnell, A. M., Hythecker, V. I., Lambiotte, J. G., & Rocklin, T. R. (1985). Effects of metacognitive and elaborative activity on cooperative learning. *Contemporary Educational Psychology, 10*, 342–348.

Larson, C. O., Dansereau, D. F., O'Donnell, A. M., Hythecker, V. I., Lambiotte, J. G., & Rocklin, T. R. (1984). Verbal ability and cooperative learning: Transfer of effects. *Journal of Reading Behavior, 16*, 289–295.

Lemke, E., Randle, K., & Robertshaw, C. S. (1969). Effects of degree of initial acquisition, group size, and general mental ability on concept learning and transfer. *Journal of Educational Psychology, 60*, 75–78.

Markman, E. M. (1979). Realizing that you don't understand: Elementary school children's awareness of inconsistencies. *Child Development, 50*, 643–655.

McClintock, E., & Sonquist, J. A. (1976). Cooperative task-oriented groups in a college classroom: A field application. *Journal of Educational Psychology, 68*, 588–596.

McDonald, B. A., Larson, C. O., Dansereau, D. F., & Spurlin, J. E. (1985). Cooperative dyads: Impact on text learning and transfer. *Contemporary Educational Psychology, 10,* 369–377.

Oltman, P. K., Raskin, E., & Witkin, H. A. (1971). *Group Embedded Figures Test.* Palo Alto, CA: Consulting Psychologists Press, Inc.

Peterson, P. L., & Janicki, T. C. (1979). Individual characteristics and children's learning in large-group and small-group approaches. *Journal of Educational Psychology, 71,* 677–687.

Reder, L. (1980). The role of elaboration in the comprehension and retention of prose: A critical review. *Review of Educational Research, 10,* 5–53.

Ross, S. M., & DiVesta, F. J. (1976). Oral summary as a review strategy enhancing recall of textual material. *Journal of Educational Psychology, 68,* 689–695.

Rothkopf, E. Z. (1970). The concept of mathemagenic activities. *Review of Educational Research, 40,* 329–336.

Rotter, J. B. (1966). Generalized expectancies for internal versus external control of reinforcement. *Psychological Monographs, 80* (1, Whole No. 609).

Sarason, I. G. (1956). Effect of anxiety, motivational instructions and failure on serial learning. *Journal of Experimental Psychology, 51,* 253–260.

Schallert, D. L., & Kleiman, G. M. (1979). *Some reasons why the teacher is easier to understand than the textbook.* (Reading Education Report No. 9). Urbana: University of Illinois, Center for the Study of Reading, (ERIC Document Reproduction Service No. ED 172 289).

Sharan, S. (1980). Cooperative learning in small groups: Recent methods and effects on achievement, attitudes, and ethnic relations. *Review of Educational Research, 50,* 241–271.

Siegel, L., & Siegel, L. C. (1965). Educational set: A determinant of acquisition. *Journal of Educational Psychology, 57,* 1–12.

Singer, R. N. (1978). Motor skills and learner strategies. In H. F. O'Neil, Jr., (Ed.), *Learning strategies.* New York: Academic Press.

Slavin, R. E. (1978). Student teams and comparison among equals: Effects on academic performance and student attitudes. *Journal of Educational Psychology, 70,* 532–538.

Slavin, R. E. (1980). Cooperative learning. *Review of Educational Research, 50,* 315–342.

Slavin, R. E. (1983). *Cooperative learning.* New York: Longman, Inc.

Smith, K. A., Johnson, D. W., & Johnson, R. T. (1981). The use of cooperative learning groups in engineering education. In L. P. Grayson, & J. M. Biedenback (Eds.), *Proceedings Tenth Annual Frontiers in Education Conference* (pp. 29–32). Washington, D.C.: American Society for Engineering Education.

Spurlin, J. E., Dansereau, D. F., Larson, C. O., & Brooks, L. W. (1984). Cooperative learning strategies in processing descriptive text: Effects of role and activity level of the learner. *Cognition and Instruction, 1,* 451–463.

Webb, N. M. (1977). Learning in individual and small group settings, (Technical Report No. 7. Personnel and Training Research Programs, Office of Naval Research, and Advanced Research Projects Agency, Washington, D.C.

Webb, N. M. (1980). A process outcome analysis of learning in group and individual settings. *Educational Psychologist, 15,* 69–83.

Weinstein, C. E., Underwood, V. L., Wicker, F. W., & Cubberly, W. E. (1979). Cognitive learning strategies: Verbal and imaginal elaboration. In H. F. O'Neil, & C. D. Spielberger (Eds.), *Cognitive and affective learning strategies.* New York: Academic Press.

Zajonc, R. B. (1966). *Social psychology: An experimental approach.* Belmont, CA: Wadsworth.

DIRECT INSTRUCTION OF READING COMPREHENSION STRATEGIES: THE NATURE OF TEACHER EXPLANATION

Peter Winograd and Victoria Chou Hare

This chapter examines, in some depth, one aspect of one approach to strategy instruction—the nature of teacher explanations provided during direct instruction of reading comprehension strategies. Our intent is to better understand what is meant by direct instruction of reading comprehension strategies and to learn why such an approach seems to yield such consistently positive results. First, we make our task manageable by analyzing the components of direct instruction as it is currently used and then we concentrate on the important element of teacher explanation, for this seems to be where strategy instruction is most direct in nature. Second, we evaluate how teacher explanations have been addressed in selected successful comprehension strategy instruction studies. Third, we close with a discussion of the strengths and limitations of teacher explanations in improving reading comprehension strategies.

We wish to stress from the start that our focus on the teacher's explanation does not imply that we view the student as a passive recipient of the teacher's wisdom. If we have learned anything from the recent research on reading comprehension, it is that fluent reading depends as much upon the reader's involvement and purposes as it does upon the reader's skills. We strongly believe that the student must take an active role in his or her own learning. We also believe that a teacher's explanation should be evaluated in terms of how well it helps the student to become an active participant in the learning situation.

I. THE NATURE OF TEACHER EXPLANATION

Direct instruction is very difficult to define. There is, of course, the Oregon Direct Instruction model composed of very specific design features (e.g., Carnine & Gersten, 1983; Carnine & Silbert, 1979). But there is also a

121

LEARNING AND STUDY STRATEGIES: ISSUES IN
ASSESSMENT, INSTRUCTION, AND EVALUATION

more general, often careless use of the term "direct instruction." Maggs and
Maggs (1979) provide a tongue-in-cheek view of the ambiguity surrounding
the term when they define "direct instruction" as sitting in front of a child
and directly giving him instructions. Perhaps the advertisement contained in
the 1984 PRO-ED educational materials catalog (PRO-ED, 1984) best illustrates the amorphous nature of the term in defining direct instruction methods as "approaches that work."

Attempting to define direct instruction as it is used in the general sense is
not particularly profitable. Instead, we will focus specifically on those direct
instruction procedures about which investigators have reached consensus
(e.g. Carnine & Silbert, 1979; Good, 1979; Peterson, 1979; Roehler & Duffy,
1984; Rosenshine, 1979, 1983): (1) structuring the learning in terms of clear
academic goals broken down for maximal content coverage into manageable
steps (i.e., conducting a task analysis); (2) brisk pacing and selection of
sequenced, structured materials; (3) providing detailed, redundant instructions and explanations with sufficient examples; (4) asking many questions
and offering numerous overt active practice opportunities; (5) giving immediate, academically focused feedback and correction, especially when new
material is being learned; and (6) active monitoring of student progress.
Rosenshine (1983) helped clarify our understanding of direct instruction by
organizing these procedures into a model of effective instruction composed
of six teaching functions: (1) reviewing and checking the previous day's work;
(2) presenting new content; (3) supervising initial student practice; (4)
providing feedback and correctives; (5) setting up student independent practice; and (6) organizing periodic reviews.

As we reviewed various studies that attempted to teach reading comprehension strategies using direct instruction, it seemed that instruction was
most direct in addressing the second teaching function, the presentation of
new content. It was not that the other teaching functions had been ignored.
Rather, it appeared that training largely focused on providing students with
carefully planned, systematic explanations about new, effective reading
strategies. Indeed, the importance of careful explanations has received so
much attention that Roehler and Duffy (1984) have proposed replacing the
phrase "direct instruction" with "direct explanation."

It is important to note that the enhanced role of good explanations in
direct instruction runs counter to the habit of instruction as "leaving pupils
to achieve competence by virtue of repeated and relatively unguided exposure to a task" (Duffy & Roehler, 1982, p. 442). This habit is reasonable
only if one believes that teachers' manuals and workbooks provide the necessary instruction. Unfortunately, the view is fallacious; witness recent reviews
of comprehension instruction in basal reader manuals (Durkin, 1981; Hare &
Milligan, 1984; Jones, Ch. 13, this volume; Winograd & Brennan, 1983).

Teachers' manuals are in fact saturated with teacher directives, but limited on teacher explanations.

Why have researchers interested in reading comprehension strategy instruction given so much thought to how new content should be presented? To answer this question, it is necessary to examine the nature of strategies in reading. Several researchers (Johnston & Byrd, 1983; Paris et al., 1983; van Dijk & Kintsch, 1983) have recently defined strategies as deliberate actions that learners select and control to achieve desired goals or objectives. Such a definition emphasizes the active role that the learner has in strategic reading. For the most part, researchers interested in strategy instruction have appreciated the importance of the learner's active participation and have therefore attempted to enlist it through careful and complete explanation of the procedures and values of the strategy under question. As Roehler and Duffy (1984, p. 266) point out:

> . . . teacher explanations of the processes are designed to be metacognitive, not mechanistic. They make students aware of the purpose of the skill and how successful readers use it to activate, monitor, regulate, and make sense out of text, creating in students an awareness and a conscious realization of the function and utility of reading skills and the linkages between these processes and the activities of reading.

What constitutes a careful and complete explanation of a reading comprehension strategy? Certainly, we might consider the following elements, compiled from instructional researchers' programs (Belmont & Butterfield, 1977; Brown et al., 1981; Bush et al., 1977; Duffy & Roehler, 1982; Garner et al., 1984; Hare & Milligan, 1984; Land & Smith, 1979; Pearson, 1984; Roehler & Duffy, 1984). Such explanations would describe:

1. *What the strategy is.* Teachers should describe critical, known features of the strategy or provide a definition/description of the strategy.
2. *Why the strategy should be learned.* Teachers should tell students why they are learning about the strategy. Explaining the purpose of the lesson and its potential benefits seems to be a necessary step for moving from teacher control to student self-control of learning.
3. *How to use the strategy.* Here, teachers break down the strategy, or re-enact a task analysis for students, explaining each component of the strategy as clearly and as articulately as possible and showing the logical relationships among the various components. Where implicit processes are not known or are hard to explicate, or where explanatory supplements are desired, assists such as advance organizers, think-alouds, analogies, and other attention clues are valuable and recommended (Roehler & Duffy, 1984).
4. *When and where the strategy is to used.* Teachers should delineate appropriate circumstances under which the strategy may be employed,

(e.g., whether the strategy applies in a story or informational reading). Teachers may also describe inappropriate instances for using the strategy.

5. *How to evaluate use of the strategy.* Teachers should show students how to evaluate their successful/unsuccessful use of the strategy, including suggestions for fix-up strategies to resolve remaining problems.

To summarize, although the term "direct instruction" is frequently used in the literature, it is not always clearly defined. One essential component of direct instruction, however, seems to be the provision of detailed explanations when presenting new content. Moreover, a review of recent strategy instruction research indicates that careful explanation is also a critical component of these studies. Let us now examine, in more detail, how teacher explanations have been addressed in some successful reading comprehension strategy instruction studies.

II. TEACHER EXPLANATIONS IN SUCCESSFUL INSTRUCTIONAL STUDIES

For this discussion, we searched for examples of comprehension studies using direct instruction procedures. As mentioned before, however, what two investigators mean by direct instruction can vary widely. Thus, we chose to cast our net over a wide area by reviewing studies that explicitly claimed to be direct instruction, those referred to as direct instruction by others, and those that incorporated elements featured in descriptions of direct instruction. Because our review is meant to be more illustrative than comprehensive, we limited our review to seven studies. Table 1 lists the studies by authors, samples, and strategy taught.

The Adams et al. (1982); Alexander and White, 1984; Baumann (1984); Hare and Borchardt (1984); and Patching, et al. (1983) studies explicitly mention using direct instruction procedures. The Hansen and Pearson (1983) study and its predecessor study, Hansen (1981), are often cited as examples of direct instruction studies (e.g., Patching et al., 1983; Pearson, 1984). The Garner et al. (1984) study uses procedures similar to those espoused by direct instruction advocates.

A. STUDY SKILLS

In the study conducted by Adams et al. (1982), teachers taught fifth-grade students a study strategy for 30 to 40 minutes daily for 4 days. Over the period of 4 days, students individually learned to master the six-step strategy for reading content area texts. Teachers initially modeled the strategy steps, and students repeated teachers' models and received corrective feedback.

TABLE 1   Seven Reading Comprehension Strategy Studies

Study	Sample	Strategy taught
Adams et al. (1982)	45 5th-grade poor studiers with adequate decoding skills; 15 students each assigned to systematic instruction, independent study with no feedback, and no intervention groups.	A study skills strategy composed of lessons concerning: (a) Previewing headings, (b) Reciting subheadings, (c) Asking questions for subheadings, (d) Reading to find important details, (e) Rereading subheadings and reciting important details, and, when the whole selection has been studied, (f) Rehearsing, or reading each subheading and reciting important details.
Alexander & White (1984)	21 4th-grade students of average reading ability.	An analogical reasoning strategy composed of lessons concerning the component processes of: (a) Encoding, (b) Inferring, (c) Mapping, (d) Applying.
Baumann (1984)	66 6th-grade students of high, middle, and low reading achievement; 22 each assigned to strategy, basal, or control groups.	A main idea comprehension strategy composed of lessons on: (a) Locating explicit and implicit main ideas in paragraphs, (b) Locating explicit and implicit main ideas in brief passages, and (c) Constructing outlines of main ideas for brief passages.
Garner et al. (1984)	24 upper-elementary and middle-grade students with adequate word recognition and poor comprehension; 12 assigned to a strategy training group and 12 assigned to a control group.	A text lookback strategy, composed of lessons on the nature of and proper use of text lookbacks.

TABLE 1   (Continued)

Study	Sample	Strategy taught
Hansen & Pearson (1983)	40 4th-grade readers, 20 good and 20 poor, 10 students of each ability level assigned to either a strategy group or a traditional instructional group.	An inference strategy composed primarily of prereading questions designed to: (a) Raise students' consciousness about tying new information to old information, and (b) Have students relate personal experiences to text events and to predict text events.
Hare & Borchardt (1984)	52 minority high school juniors with adequate decoding abilities; 22 students assigned to either a deductive or inductive strategy group, and 10 students assigned to a control group.	A summarization strategy composed of lessons describing rule-checking suggestions, summary rules, and a polishing rule. Rule-checking suggestions included: (a) Be sure you understand the text. (b) Look back, (c) Rethink, and (d) Check and double-check. Summary rules included: (a) Collapse lists, (b) Use topic sentences, (c) Get rid of unnecessary detail, and (d) Collapse paragraphs. The polishing rule requires summary editing.
Patching et al. (1983)	39 5th-grade students with adequate decoding abilities; 13 each assigned to strategy workbook with corrective feedback, or non-instruction groups.	A critical reading strategy composed of lessons on: (a) Detection of faulty generalizations, (b) Detection of false causality, and (c) Detection of invalid testimonial.

The summary of the procedures in the Adams et al. (1982) study suggests that all components of complete explanations were taken into account. The *what* feature of the study strategy was incorporated into the actual steps of the strategy, derived from a task analysis of how fluent readers study expository text (see Table 1). Within each step, the *why the strategy should be learned* was addressed. For instance, in Step 2, "Recite the subheading," students learned, "The subheading in a textbook serves to highlight and introduce a new topic" (p. 33). *How to use the strategy* was also clearly delineated within each step, e.g., also for Step 2, "In this step of the procedure, students were instructed to read the subheading, look up, and try to say it themselves, then check to see if correct. If not correct, they were to repeat the process until correct" (p. 33). *When and where* information about strategy use was included in the procedures of the Adams et al. study, but not for every step. The authors also attended to the limitations of instructed steps, when necessary. For example, in Step 4, the authors acknowledged that most texts included important information, in addition to information for answers to preposed questions, and thus directed students to seek both answers to questions and sometimes to also seek other important information. Finally, instruction in *how to evaluate* independent use of the study strategy was provided by suggesting self-checking routines, such as the ones mentioned for Steps 2 and 6. Thus, Adams et al. (1982) handled all aspects of a complete presentation and handled them well.

B. ANALOGICAL REASONING

Alexander and White (1984) taught fourth-grade students analogical reasoning skills in two phases. The first phase involved four sessions of intensive training and the second phase involved 8 weeks of intermittent training. Sessions were organized to lead students from simple to more complex reasoning problems. During the initial phase, students were taught what analogies and their component processes were (see Table 1), and to apply the processes to solving both nonlinguistic and linguistic analogies. During the intermittent training phase, students devoted 1 week of study to each of the component processes and then spent the remaining 4 weeks learning how the component processes integrated with regular basal lessons.

Many aspects of complete explanations were incorporated into the lessons. For example, *what* information was entailed in descriptions such as: "Analogy—special kind of thinking problem; a way of comparing two objects, events, or ideas" (Alexander & White, 1984, teacher script, p. 1). Further, students were told *why* analogical reasoning was important, i.e., that analogies "allow us to learn new things by comparing them to things that we already know" (teacher script, p. 1). *How-to* information regarding each of the component processes (encoding, inferring, mapping, and applying) was directly conveyed to students. For example, in the introductory lesson, students learned that "encode" meant examining each term of the analogy, that "infer" meant relating the terms, that "map" referred to trying out the inferred relationship on the second pair, and that "apply" suggested making a guess. In Alexander and White's study, *when and where* elements were emphasized heavily in the intermittent training segment. Here, students were provided with step-by-step information demonstrating how reading is like solving an analogy in that the same four component processes are functional in the act of reading. Overall, Alexander and White addressed four of the five components of a complete explanation.

C. MAIN IDEA COMPREHENSION

Baumann (1984) developed and tested a series of eight lessons for teaching sixth-grade students how to identify the main idea. The content of the eight 30-minute lessons was hierarchically arranged so that students learned how to find the main idea in increasingly more difficult materials (see Table 1). A five-step instructional procedure was used during each of the lessons to help children learn how to find the main idea. It is the content of this five-step procedure that is most relevant for our purpose, for it is here that the children were told *what* the strategy is, *why* the strategy is important, *how to use* the strategy, and *when and where* to use the strategy.

Most components of complete explanation were captured in Baumann's (1984) instruction. Students were explicitly told in each lesson *what* information about main ideas. For example, in Lesson 2: Main Ideas and Details in Paragraphs—Implicit, students learned, "Yes, there are several different ways of saying what the main idea is . . . But the main idea tells us about all the details in the paragraph; that is, the biggest, most important, idea in the paragraph" (p. 109). In the same lesson, students were provided with information as to *why* it is important to know how to find the implicit main idea in a paragraph:

> This is an important reading skill because many paragraphs have unstated main ideas, and if you can figure out what these main ideas are, you will understand and re-member the most important information in the material you read. (p. 108)

Information concerning *how to use* the strategy was integrated with *what* information in this lesson. The teacher reminded students about how to figure out the topic of the paragraph, then asked students to help list paragraph ideas related to the topic, and finally requested students to think about, "Now what would be a main idea sentence we could come up with that goes with all these details?" (Baumann, 1984, p. 109). To help children make the requisite inferences, Baumann used the analogy of a tabletop supported by legs. His sample script indicated that the teacher used a transparency to display a picture of a table before engaging in the following dialogue:

> Just as a table is supported by legs, so too, a main idea is supported by details. So let's put the main idea on the table and the supporting details on each of the legs. Who can help us get going? Let's start with the details on the legs. . . . When you try to

figure out the main idea of a paragraph, think of a table and legs to help you understand
how supporting details and main ideas relate to one another, or go together. (p. 109)

Baumann addressed *when and where* components of explanations by
stressing application of main idea skills in many different contexts. Students
received many chances to generate as well as recognize important ideas for
both paragraphs and passages, at least some of which were modeled or
adapted from naturally occurring texts. Beyond practice with different texts,
however, the sample script included in the description of the study does not
mention explanation of *when and where* particulars for specific texts. Similarly, the script does not mention *how to evaluate* information.

D.   TEXT LOOKBACKS

The Garner et al. (1984) study focused on teaching a text lookback strategy. Text lookbacks occur when readers reaccess portions of a text in order to
overcome perceived difficulties in comprehension. Upper-elementary and
middle-school remedial readers received three "hints" about lookback use
over three sessions. Hints were explicitly introduced to students, one at a
time, with a summary of the hints at training's end.

Several components of useful explanations were addressed in the hints.
On day one, *what, why,* and *how to* information was intertwined in the first
hint:

> Most people do not remember everything they read in an article. That is *why* it is a
> good idea to look back at the article to find information needed to answer some
> questions. People who want to answer questions correctly often spend many minutes
> searching for answers to questions. Let's look at the first article you read. When you
> had (if you had) some difficulty answering question (#), you (could have) looked back
> in the article and found the answer (_____) here. Do you understand *why* looking
> back to the article for information works? (Garner et al., 1984, training script, p. 2).

Clearly, defining a lookback in this instance partially informs students
about how to look back. Hint two dealt with *when* to use lookbacks, i.e., for
text-based questions and not for reader-based questions. Last, hint three
dealt with *where* to use lookbacks, actually an instance of how to use lookbacks. Students were told to skim the entire text to locate a key part to be
reread. Thus, the hints addressed four of the elements found in complete
explanations.

E.   DRAWING INFERENCES

Classroom teachers in the Hansen and Pearson (1983) study taught fourth-
grade readers an inference strategy by helping students realize the importance of noting relationships between new and known information, having

students explicitly discuss personal experiences related to the text and then make predictions about text events, and asking students inferential questions. Project-related instruction took place 2 days a week over a 10-week period. Teachers emphasized the *why* aspects of a complete explanation when they discussed with students the importance of "using your own life" to help understand what was being read. The sample dialogue (Hansen & Pearson, 1983, p. 823) illustrates their approach:

> Teacher: What is it that we have been doing before we discuss each story?
> Focus of responses: We talk about our lives and we predict what will happen in the stories.
> Teacher: Why do we make these comparisons?
> Focus of responses: These comparisons will help us understand the stories.

Next, teachers modeled the *how to use* portion of the presentation by leading students through a thinking strategy. For each of three important ideas in a selection, two questions were discussed by readers. The first question called for readers to bring up personal, related experiences; the second question called for readers to speculate what might happen under similar circumstances in the selection. One example of such a question pair is: (1) "Tell us about a time when you were embarrassed about the way you looked," and (2) "In our next story there is an old man who is embarrassed about the way he looks. What do you think is the thing that embarrasses him?" (Hansen & Pearson, 1983, p. 823). The report of their study does not mention whether the children were explicitly told *what the strategy was, when and where the strategy should be used,* or *how it should be evaluated.*

F. WRITING SUMMARIES

Hare and Borchardt (1984) taught high school students a summarization strategy based upon Day's (1980) work that demonstrated how summarization rule training, combined with self-control training, enhanced students' summarization skill. Hare and Borchardt adapted and expanded Day's procedures to produce a series of summarization rules, questioning steps, and a rewrite rule as a basis for their summarization program (see Table 1). Direct instruction was delivered in three 2-hour sessions. Students were shown first how to apply the summarization strategy, rule by rule, to easy, contrived materials and then to unaltered high school texts, before they learned how to coordinate and integrate rule usage.

All five components of complete explanations were captured in Hare and Borchardt's (1984) instruction. Teachers provided students with a definition of a summary and with a rulesheet highlighting the summarization rules, questioning steps, and rewriting rule. In addition to *what* information, students also received *why* information when they were told that the rules would help them write better summaries. *How to* information was extensive and, because of the number of rules, was supplemented by numerous "help-sheets." Initially, teachers described and explained each of the four rule-checking suggestions, four summarization rules, and the polishing rule. The summarization rule "Get rid of unnecessary detail," for example, was explicated as follows:

> Some text information can be repeated in a passage. In other words, the same thing can be said in a number of different ways, all in one passage. Other text information can be unimportant, or trivial. Since summaries are meant to be short, get rid of repetitive or trivial information. (p. 66)

To show students when and where rules should be applied, teachers modeled rule application for both a good and a poor summary in one task. By modeling rule application with many different kinds of materials, teachers hoped to convey *when and where* information about rule usage. Similarly, for the *how to evaluate* component, teachers modeled appropriate behavior rather than directly explain it. For instance, in one activity, teachers "discovered" a list which had not been collapsed the first time around during the doublechecking step. As in the Adams et al. study, coverage of the various components of explanations was thorough.

G. CRITICAL READING

Patching et al. (1983) taught fifth-grade students critical reading strategies (see Table 1) on a one-to-one basis. Intervention occurred in three 30-minute lessons, and included eight to ten learning tasks per minute, corrective feedback, and teaching until the student demonstrated mastery. Teacher prompts were gradually faded, as students reached mastery.

The published description of the procedures in the Patching et al. (1983) study is far less complete than that provided by Adams et al. (1982). Only one portion of a lesson is available for review. Within this segment, we can see clearly that the *what* component is covered for the rule for detection of false causality: "Just because two things happen together, it doesn't mean that one causes the other" (Patching et al., 1983, p. 410). *How-to* information that is difficult to explicate is conveyed via an inquiry line of questioning, wherein students are led to reinvent the rule for teachers, and thus, learn how to apply the rule, as in, "Do you know that Mary won the race because she wore her lucky ring? . . . Why not?" (p. 411). Whether *why, when, and where,* or *how to evaluate* components of the critical reading strategy were made available to students is not mentioned in the published article.

In summary, our review of seven instructional studies revealed some interesting commonalities and differences in how various reading com-

TABLE 2 Explanation Components Addressed by Various Instructional Studies[a]

| | Explanation components | | | | |
	What the strategy is	Why a strategy should be learned	How to use the strategy	When and where the strategy should be used	How to evaluate use of the strategy
Adams et al. (1982)	X	X	X	X	X
Alexander & White (1984)	X	X	X	X	
Baumann (1984)	X	X	X	X	
Garner et al. (1984)	X	X	X	X	
Hansen & Pearson (1983)		X	X		
Hare & Borchardt (1984)	X	X	X	X	X
Patching et al. (1983)	X		X		

[a]An X in a column indicates that the component was explicitly addressed as part of the strategy instruction.

prehension strategies were presented. Table 2 presents a graphic summary of this information.

As the information in the first column of Table 2 indicates, most of the investigators attended to explaining *what* the strategy is. The investigators had decomposed their strategies into component steps and then provided a description of some sort for each step. It is important to emphasize that the data presented in column one mark a definite change from the kind of instruction noted by Durkin (1978–1979).

The data presented in the second column also indicate that many of the investigators addressed *why* a strategy should be used. This is not surprising given our understanding of the essential relationship between the reader's motivation and effective strategy use (Covington, 1983; Johnston & Winograd, 1985; Paris et al., 1983).

As the data in column three indicate, all of the investigators addressed *how to use* the strategy. This information ranges from fairly straightforward information (Garner et al., 1984) to more complex information (e.g., questions of determining importance in Adams et al., 1982; Hare & Borchardt, 1984). Where steps are amenable to easy description, explanations are made (e.g., "Collapse lists," Hare & Borchardt, 1984). Where steps are more difficult to explicate, more modeling, analogies, and examples seem to be the rule (e.g., the two-step questioning procedure, Hansen & Pearson, 1983).

When one considers the information in the fourth and fifth columns of Table 2, it is evident that the *when and where* information is used somewhat less often than the first three components and the *how to evaluate* component is addressed even less frequently in presentations. Whether this may be attributed to the difficulty of making good explanations of these components or to other factors remains to be studied.

Each of the studies reviewed in this chapter reported significant gains in the use of the strategy taught. Thus, the results of this review indicate that explicit explanation is an effective way to improve student's use of reading comprehension strategies. In the next section we will examine more closely some of the strengths and limitations of explicit explanations.

III. THE VALUE OF COMPLETE EXPLANATIONS IN STRATEGY INSTRUCTION

Theoretical support for the assertion that explicit explanations are an effective way to teach reading comprehension strategies comes from a number of researchers including Brown et al. (1981), Roehler and Duffy (1984), Paris et al. (1983), and Pearson (1984). For example, Paris and his colleagues (Paris et al., 1983) have identified three kinds of knowledge that are important if a student is to use reading strategies fluently: (1) declarative knowledge, (2) procedural knowledge, and (3) conditional knowledge.

Declarative knowledge is the kind of knowledge that includes information about task characteristics and task goals. As such, it seems reasonable to address some kinds of declarative knowledge through explanations of *what* the strategy is and *why* it should be learned.

Procedural knowledge is defined as the reader's understanding of how to perform various actions, for example, how to study, how to deal with analogies, or how to write summaries. In the studies cited in this chapter, it is procedural knowledge that is most directly addressed through presentations on *how to use* the strategy.

Conditional knowledge refers to the learner's understanding of why and when to engage in various procedures. Conditional knowledge is necessary if a reader is to know whether or not a certain action (e.g., text lookback) is appropriate. What Paris et al. (1983) refer to as conditional knowledge appears to be similar to what others (e.g., Sternberg, 1981) refer to as executive skills, that is, those skills used in identifying a problem, selecting an appropriate strategy, and evaluating its effectiveness. Conditional knowledge is communicated when the teacher explains to students *why* a strategy is important, *when and where* to use the strategy, and *how to evaluate* its effectiveness.

Experimental support for the assertion that explicit explanations are effective in improving children's use of reading strategies comes, of course, from the successful studies cited in this chapter. In addition, there is some research that has examined the relative effectiveness of the degree of instructional explicitness. We refer, here, to Day's (1980) work. Day compared four instructional conditions that varied in the explicitness of the training procedures. In the least explicit training condition, *self-management*, junior-college students were provided with a definition of a summary and encouraged to write good ones, but were given no information on how to proceed. Students in the second instructional condition, *rules alone*, were provided with a definition of a summary and given explicit rules for how to write one. Students in the third instructional condition, *rules plus self-management*, were given the same general encouragement as the first group of students and the same rules as the second group of students, but were not provided with any explicit information on how to integrate the two sets of information. Students in the most explicit instructional condition, *rules integrated*, received instruction in what a summary was, how to write one, when and where to use each of the summarization rules, and how to evaluate the efficacy of the strategy. In general, results from Day's study indicated that the more explicit and complete the training, the more the students, especially the poorer students, improved.

Although theoretical and experimental support for the assertion that explicit explanation should be an integral part of reading comprehension strategy instruction is plentiful, there are also some important considerations that may limit the usefulness of teacher explanations (e.g., Doyle, 1983; Winograd & Johnston, 1987). Doyle (1983), for example, identifies three problems that could affect the value of direct instruction in general, and direct explicit explanation in particular: (1) some processes cannot be communicated to learners in understandable terms, (2) some processes used by experts have yet to be identified or at least specified, and (3) determining the most effective level of specificity for direct instruction is difficult because many processes operate at different levels.

The second consideration, that some processes used by experts have yet to be explicated, appears to be particularly problematic in the field of reading. Fluent readers use a number of strategies that researchers cannot explain to each other, much less teach to children. For example, researchers still do not understand how fluent readers identify the important ideas in text (Winograd & Bridge, 1986). Recall that Adams et al. (1982) addressed this issue by having their students pose questions to help them differentiate important information from less important information. They also acknowledged that:

> However in most texts, there is often additional important information besides the answers to the preposed questions. Therefore, in this step students were instructed both to read to find answers to their questions and to sometimes find other important information. (p. 34)

Instructing students to "sometimes find other important information" does not qualify as explicit instruction, and yet it is this essential procedure that students need to learn.

Doyle's (1983) third consideration, determining the most effective level of specificity, is also likely to prove troublesome for investigators interested in teaching reading comprehension strategies. How far should a strategy be decomposed and how explicit and complete should the explanation be for each step? For example, is it necessary to discuss with students the value of each step in a strategy? Are all five components of a complete presentation (i.e., what a strategy is, why it is important, etc.) necessary for all kinds of strategies? Are complete explanations necessary for all kinds of students? Some general guidelines to deal with these questions seem necessary if direct explanation of reading strategies is to gain widespread acceptance in classrooms.

In addition to the concerns raised by Doyle (1983), there is another consideration that may limit the effectiveness of teacher explanations in strategy instruction. Recall that strategies were defined as deliberate actions that learners selected to achieve desired goals. The words "deliberate," "selected," and "desired" in this definition all reflect the important affective aspect of strategies. As Paris et al. (1983, p. 304) aptly state, "strategies combine components of both skill and will." At present, only a few instructional studies (e.g., Palmer & Goetz, Ch. 4, this volume; McCombs, Ch. 9, this volume) have concerned themselves with the affective aspects of reading comprehension strategies. In general, there seems to be an implicit assumption that motivation will be an important side effect of successful instruction of cognitive skills. It is not unreasonable to assume that removing some of the obstacles to comprehension will result in more reading. We believe, however, that the motivation to read springs from a deeper source than simply the ability to comprehend. The reader must be comprehending something meaningful; that is, the learner should experience the attraction of "task-involvement" (Nicholls, 1983) that results from reading interesting, worthwhile materials. This may be especially true for those children who have experienced early failure in reading and whose subsequent reading difficulties are compounded by learned helplessness and other characteristics of passive failure (Johnston & Winograd, 1985). Perhaps by combining more complete explanations with high-interest, meaningful materials, teachers can more fully address both the cognitive and affective factors so essential to becoming a fluent reader.

Roehler and Duffy (1982, p. 477) speculate that teachers may also be able to use direct instruction to address the affective aspects of reading comprehension strategies by engaging in presentations that include:

> . . . discussions of the enjoyable and recreational functions of reading, modeling of personal reading, sharing of children's literature with the class, presentation of guidelines for selecting appropriate books, explaining techniques for sustaining silent reading, and discussing strategies for relating literature to experience.

Discussions of the enjoyable and affective aspects of reading do have a place in the classroom, but such discussions should be conducted in a sensitive manner that nurtures rather than replaces or restricts the children's aesthetic encounters with reading (Winograd & Johnston, 1987). Clearly, strategy instruction will truly be effective when it produces students who not only have learned how to learn, but who also use what they have learned (Sternberg, 1981).

IV. SUMMARY

Our purpose in this chapter has been to examine what is involved in the direct instruction of reading comprehension strategies. We closely examined one specific aspect of strategy instruction: the nature of the explanations given when new strategies are presented. Five components of teacher explanations were identified: (1) what the strategy is; (2) why a strategy should be learned; (3) how to use the strategy; (4) when and where the strategy is to be used; and (5) how to evaluate use of the strategy.

Next, we reviewed seven instructional studies to learn how they addressed the instructional function of presenting new material. Our review revealed that all of the investigators explicitly addressed the *how to use* the strategy component in their presentations. *Why* a strategy should be learned and *what* the strategy is were explicitly addressed in six of the studies. However, *when and where* a strategy should be used, and *how to evaluate* the use of a strategy were addressed less frequently. Nevertheless, the instructional explanations constructed by all of the researchers represent a radical departure from the "repeated exposures" conceptions of instructional practice. In general, the results from the studies indicate that direct teacher explanation seems to be a useful approach for teaching complex comprehension skills.

Finally, we explored some of the strengths and limitations of using explicit explanations. We noted that the usefulness of direct teacher explanations may depend upon how easily the strategy under consideration can be described or modeled. We closed by emphasizing that both cognitive and affective aspects of fluent strategic reading must be addressed if any instruction, direct or not, is to be successful.

ACKNOWLEDGMENTS

The authors would like to thank Connie Bridge, Marilyn Greenlee, Peter Johnston, George Newell, Jean Osborn, and Laura Roehler for their helpful comments on earlier versions of this chapter.

REFERENCES

Adams, A., Carnine, D., & Gersten, R. (1982). Instructional strategies for studying content area texts in the intermediate grades. *Reading Research Quarterly, 18,* 27–55.

Alexander, P., & White, C. (1984). Effects of componential approach to analogy training on fourth graders' performance of analogy and comprehension tasks: An exploratory investigation, unpublished manuscript, Texas A & M University, College Station, TX.

Baumann, J. (1984). The effectiveness of a direct instruction paradigm for teaching main idea comprehension. *Reading Research Quarterly, 20,* 93–115.

Belmont, J. M., & Butterfield, E. C. (1977). The instructional approach to developmental cognitive research. In R. V. Kail, Jr., & J. W. Hagen (Eds.), *Perspectives on the development of memory and cognition* (pp. 437–481). Hillsdale, NJ: Erlbaum.

Brown, A. L., Campione, J. C., & Day, J. D. (1981). Learning to learn: On training students to learn from texts. *Educational Researcher, 10,* 14–21.

Bush, A. J., Kennedy, J. J., & Cruikshank, D. R. (1977). An empirical investigation of teacher clarity. *Journal of Teacher Education, 28,* 53–58.

Carnine, D., & Gersten, R. (1983). The effectiveness of direct instruction in teaching selected reading comprehension skills, paper presented at the annual meeting of the American Educational Research Association, Montreal.

Carnine, D., & Silbert, J. (1979). *Direct instruction reading.* Columbus, OH: Charles E. Merrill.

Covington, M. C. (1983). Motivated cognitions. In S. G. Paris, G. M. Olson, & H. W. Stevenson (Eds.), *Learning and motivation in the classroom* (pp. 139–164). Hillsdale, NJ: Erlbaum.

Day, J. D. (1980). Training summarization skills: A comparison of teaching methods, unpublished doctoral dissertation, University of Illinois, Champaign, IL.

Doyle, W. (1983). Academic work. *Review of Educational Research, 53,* 159–200.

Duffy, G. G., & Roehler, L. R. (1982). Commentary: The illusion of instruction. *Reading Research Quarterly, 17,* 438–445.

Durkin, D. (1978–1979). What classroom observations reveal about reading comprehension instruction. *Reading Research Quarterly, 14,* 481–533.

Durkin, D. (1981). Reading comprehension instruction in five basal reader series. *Reading Research Quarterly, 16,* 515–544.

Garner, R., Hare., V., Alexander, P., Haynes, J., & Winograd, P. (1984). Inducing use of a text lookback strategy among unsuccessful readers. *American Educational Research Journal, 21,* 789–798.

Good, T. L. (1979). Teacher effectiveness in the elementary school. *Journal of Teacher Education, 30,* 52–64.

Hansen, J. (1981). The effects of inference training and practice on young children's reading comprehension. *Reading Research Quarterly, 16,* 391–417.

Hansen, J., & Pearson, P. D. (1983). An instructional study: Improving the inferential comprehension of good and poor fourth-grade readers. *Journal of Educational Psychology, 75,* 821–829.

Hare, V. C., & Borchardt, K. M. (1984). Direct instruction in summarization skills. *Reading Research Quarterly, 20,* 62–78.

Hare, V. C., & Milligan, B. (1984). Main idea identification: Instructional explanations in four basal reader series. *Journal of Reading Behavior, 16,* 189–204.

Johnston, P., & Byrd, M. (1983). Basal readers and the improvement of reading comprehension ability. In J. A. Niles, & L. A. Harris (Eds.), *Searches for meaning in reading/language processing and instruction* (32nd yearbook of the National Reading Conference, pp. 140–147). Rochester, NY: National Reading Conference.

Johnston, P., & Winograd, P. (1985). Passive failure in reading. *Journal of Reading Behavior, 17,* 279–301.

Land, M. L., & Smith, L. R. (1979). The effect of low inference teacher clarity inhibitors on student achievement. *Journal of Teacher Education, 30,* 55–57.

Maggs, A., & Maggs, R. K. (1979). Direct instruction research in Australia. *American Journal of Special Education Technology, 3 (2),* 26–33.

Nicholls, J. G. (1983). Conceptions of ability and achievement motivation: A theory and its implications for education. In S. G. Paris, G. M. Olson, & H. W. Stevenson (Eds.), *Learning and motivation in the classroom* (pp. 211–237). Hillsdale, NJ: Erlbaum.

Paris, S. G., Lipson, M. Y., & Wixson, K. K. (1983). Becoming a strategic reader. *Contemporary Educational Psychology, 8,* 293–316.

Patching, W., Kameenui, E., Carnine, D., Gersten, R., & Colvin, G. (1903). Direct instruction in critical reading skills. *Reading Research Quarterly, 18,* 406–418.

Pearson, P. D. (1984). Direct explicit teaching of reading comprehension. In G. G. Duffy, L. R. Roehler, & J. Mason (Eds.), *Comprehension instruction: Perspectives and suggestions* (pp. 222–233). New York: Longman.

Peterson, P. L. (1979). Direct instruction reconsidered. In P. L. Peterson, and H. J. Walberg (Eds.), *Research on teaching: Concepts, findings, and implications* (pp. 57–69). Berkeley, CA: McCutchan.

PRO-ED (1984). *1984 Catalog.* Austin, TX: PRO-ED.

Roehler, L. R., & Duffy, G. G. (1984). Direct explanation of comprehension processes. In G. G. Duffy, L. R. Roehler, & J. Mason (Eds.), *Comprehension instruction: Perspectives and suggestions* (pp. 265–280). New York: Longman.

Roehler, L. R., & Duffy, G. G. (1982). Matching direct instruction to reading outcomes. *Language Arts, 59,* 476–480.

Rosenshine, B. V. (1979). Content, time, and direct instruction. In P. L. Peterson, and H. J. Walberg (Eds.), *Research on teaching: Concepts, findings, and implications* (pp. 28–55). Berkeley, CA: McCutchan.

Rosenshine, B. V. (1983). Teaching functions in instructional programs. *The Elementary School Journal, 83,* 335–351.

Sternberg, R. J. (1981). Criteria for intellectual skills training. *Educational Researcher, 10 (2),* 6–12.

van Dijk, T. A., & Kintsch, W. (1983). *Strategies of discourse comprehension.* New York: Academic Press.

Winograd, P., & Brennan, S. (1983). Main idea instruction in the basal readers. In J. A. Niles, & L. A. Harris (Eds.), *Searches for meaning in reading/language processing and instruction* (32nd yearbook of the National Reading Conference, pp. 80–86). Rochester, NY: National Reading Conference.

Winograd, P., & Bridge, C. (1986). The comprehension of important information in written prose. In J. F. Baumann (Ed.), *Teaching main idea comprehension* (pp. 18–48). Newark, DE: International Reading Association.

Winograd, P., & Johnston, P. (1987). Some considerations for advancing the teaching of reading comprehension. *Educational Psychologist, 22,* 213–230.

Motivational Skills Training: Combining Metacognitive, Cognitive, and Affective Learning Strategies

Barbara L. McCombs

What are the mental processes that underlie motivation to learn? What skill domains (metacognitive, cognitive, affective) are represented by these processes? What types of learning strategies in each of these domains can be identified and taught to students who are deficient in those processes and skills required for motivation to learn? This chapter explores answers to these questions and their implications for motivational skills training. The discussion first focuses on the role of motivation in strategic behavior, as derived from current theoretical and empirical research. The next section integrates this research in the form of a model of underlying components and processes involved in continuing intrinsic motivation to learn. Implications of the model for learning strategies training in general and for motivational skills training in particular are discussed. The final two sections (1) describe the design and evaluation of a skills training program to promote self-motivation based on this model, and (2) identify further research questions and issues.

I. ROLE OF MOTIVATION IN STRATEGIC BEHAVIOR

In current views of learning, the learner is seen as responsible for attending to instruction and for actively constructing the mental elaborations that make learning personally meaningful. In order for learners to accept responsibility for their own learning, they must be motivated as well as possess the skills and abilities to actively engage appropriate metacognitive, cognitive, and affective (motivational) strategies. A learning strategies training program has, as one of its most important functions, the purpose of promoting self-control of learning or self-directed learning. Centrally involved in the self-control of learning is the motivation to learn. As has been argued by Paris et

LEARNING AND STUDY STRATEGIES: ISSUES IN
ASSESSMENT, INSTRUCTION, AND EVALUATION

al. (1983), if we want learners to be self-controlled and self-motivated in learning situations, we need to directly address processes that relate to perceptions of personal control in these situations. We need to understand what makes up the *skills* and the *will* to maintain motivation and use appropriate strategies. The self-controlled and self-motivated learner is one who can plan, regulate, and evaluate his or her own skills and strategies. Because strategic behaviors involve intentionality and self-control, they combine both skill and will (motivated intent) to accomplish a goal (Paris et al., 1985).

Viewing the learner as an active processor and modifier of information has contributed to a trend in recent theorizing to identify and explain specific processes that mediate learning and achievement. These processes include motivations, belief systems, perceptions, expectations, and attributions (Wittrock, 1986). Some exciting theoretical and empirical evidence is now emerging that further defines the processes that underlie intrinsic or self-generated motivation to learn.

A. THEORETICAL PERSPECTIVES AND EMPIRICAL SUPPORT

It is clear that continuing motivation to learn is in large part a function of the learner's perceptions of self-efficacy and self-control in learning situations. In turn, motivation may serve the functional role of preserving the learner's sense of self-worth to the extent that the outcomes of motivated behaviors are judged by the learner to be "self-enhancing," or at least consistent with his or her self-views, personal values, or goals. We know from personal analyses and evaluations that we enter learning situations with positive motivation when we expect positive outcomes, however varied those expected outcomes might be as a function of our different self-views, beliefs, values, attitudes, and personalities. An important functional role of motivation, then, is to contribute to the maintenance of positive self-views and perceptions of self-efficacy and personal control that underlie the ability to change negative attitudes and orientations toward learning. Support for this position can be found in a variety of theoretical perspectives, some of the more pertinent of which are highlighted here.

1. Competence Motivation

Early recognition of the central role of competence and self-control in motivation can be found in White's (1959) competence motivation theory. White defined competence as an individual's capacity to interact effectively with his or her environment. He argued that there is a competence or "effectance" motivation that is directed, selective, and persistent and which satisfies an intrinsic need to deal with the environment. He further argued that a feeling of efficacy is the subjective and affective result and also the aim of competence motivation. In fact, White (1959) contended that it is this *feeling of efficacy*, rather than the learning that comes as its consequence, which can lead to continuing interest. The intrinsic need being met by competence motivation is to bring environmental factors under greater *control* and thus enable an individual to become more self-determining. In meeting this need, competence motivation serves the function of not only producing feelings of efficacy, but also of directing attention and organizing actions that will result in effective interactions with the environment.

Building on White's (1959) theory, Harter's work has represented an attempt, from a developmental perspective, to understand processes underlying self-concept formation, self-regulation, and intrinsic motivation to learn in children and young adults (Harter, 1978, 1981, 1982, in press; Harter & Connell, 1984). Harter (1981) defines intrinsic motivation as a domain-specific motivational and informational orientation toward classroom learning and mastery, rather than as interest or activity level in a given task. Perceived competence is defined as a dynamic, multidimensional construct involving perceptions of one's competency in cognitive, social, and physical domains (Harter, 1982). Perceived control is defined as a dynamic cognitive variable that refers to one's understanding of who is responsible for task outcomes, i.e., an understanding of the contingencies responsible for success and failure (Harter, 1982). Knowledge of these contingencies, along with attributions of internal control or personal responsibility, are said to be critical to motivation and achievement in particular content domains.

Harter's theoretical and empirical work has verified that critical correlates of an intrinsic motivational orientation are domain-specific perceived competence and perceived control. Through causal analysis procedures, she has verified the following model: perceived control → actual achievement level → evaluation of cognitive competence → affective reaction → motivation to engage in further mastery attempts (Harter, 1982, 1985, in press; Harter & Connell, 1984). Supporting evidence includes findings that an understanding of self-regulatory behaviors (self-observation, self-evaluation, self-rewards) must include a view of self as an active agent in engaging these processes as well as an object or cognitive construction to which these processes are applied (Harter, 1982). In addition, she contends that general feelings of self-worth are primarily based on discrepancies between domain-specific competency evaluations and attitudes about the importance of success in particular domains, i.e., self-worth arises out of perceptions of competency and control (Harter, in press; Harter & Connell, 1984). Particularly important in this work is the concept of the self and feelings of self-worth as these relate to perceived control and competency, and as an integrating self-system in motivation and learning.

In keeping with this perspective, Thomas (1980) argues that what motivates learners to seek out or avoid learning activities is their perceptions of their competence, their perceptions of the value or rewards associated with successful task completion, and their perceptions of the extent to which their effort will lead to success. Motivation-related behaviors (those involved in accepting responsibility for self-control of learning) are said to contribute indirectly to learning by facilitating a positive motivational state or sense of agency, and are necessary in order for learners to discover and use learning strategies. Thomas (1980) states,

> It seems reasonable to assert that the spontaneous use of learning strategies is a matter of disposition: the disposition to perceive a learning task as controllable, to feel responsible for the outcome, and to search actively for ideas for solving the problem posed by the task. (p. 235–236).

The importance of this position is that it establishes the rationale and purpose of motivational skills training as necessary for the acquisition and use of other cognitive and metacognitive learning strategies. This position is similar to that of Baird and White (1982), who have argued that the purpose of affective (motivational) strategies is to change learner attitudes and orientations toward learning, while the purpose of cognitive strategies is to encourage learner-initiated use and practice of active information processing strategies.

2. Self-Efficacy Theory

Bandura's (1978, 1982a, 1986) self-efficacy theory also emphasizes the role of perceived competence (self-efficacy) and perceived self-control (personal agency) in motivation and performance. Bandura (1982a, 1982b) has argued that for individuals to have a strong sense of self-control, it is necessary for them to develop a range of competencies, self-perceptions of efficacy, and self-regulatory capabilities that can increase their self-directedness. Bandura (1982a) defines perceived self-efficacy as personal judgments about how well we can execute the courses of actions that are required to handle particular situations. Judgments of self-efficacy are said to be strongly affected by individuals' perceptions of their abilities to exercise adequate control over their actions, thereby affecting the amount of effort expended in a given learning situation. Exercising adequate control requires what Bandura (1982a) refers to as the tools of personal agency and the self-assurance to use these tools effectively. In other words, perceptions of personal control and self-efficacy reciprocally influence each other and are a function of an individual's developed competencies and capabilities of self-regulation.

Much of Bandura's empirical work has focused not only on hypothesized relationships between self-efficacy, personal agency, effort, and performance, but also on the underlying processes and skills that contribute to the development of positive judgments of self-efficacy and personal control. For example, Bandura (1982a) has verified that self-efficacy judgments come from four principal sources of information. These are enactive attainments (actually performing the task successfully), vicarious experience (watching others perform successfully), verbal persuasion (hearing and believing in one's capability to perform successfully), and physiological state (being able to adequately assess one's stress level, fatigue, or other types of arousal). In addition, he has found that to develop self-regulatory functions, individuals need to adopt personal standards against which to evaluate their performances. These standards are acquired by perceiving and integrating self-evaluation standards modeled by others (Bandura, 1978). When personal standards are fulfilled, the resulting satisfaction is said to lead to the development of interest and to increase the sense of personal efficacy (Bandura, 1982a). Bandura (1982a) argues that the processes of goal setting and self-evaluation can be important cognitively based sources of motivation in that they allow people to create self-incentives and enhance self-efficacy through successful goal attainment.

Bandura and Schunk (1981) evaluated the effectiveness of proximal and distal goal-setting conditions in cultivating competence, self-efficacy, and intrinsic interest. In part, this study sought to verify that the development of positive self-efficacy judgments requires internal comparison processes which, in turn, require personal standards or goals against which to evaluate performance. The study also sought to verify that proximal subgoals promote and authenticate perceptions of personal causation, thereby heightening intrinsic interest. Their research substantiated the underlying reciprocal relationship of: proximal subgoals → self-efficacy perceptions → personal causation → intrinsic interest → performance. Bandura and Schunk (1981) also established the purpose of goal setting as a process that allows self-evaluation against internal standards, and via this metacognitive activity, increases self-efficacy, personal control, motivation, and performance.

Working from the framework of Bandura's self-efficacy theory, Locke et al. (1982) found self-efficacy to affect goal level, task performance, goal commitment, and specific quantitative goal choice. Their research supported Bandura's theory not only in finding self-efficacy to be a key causal variable in performance, but also in finding self-efficacy to be affected by training in task strategies (i.e., goal setting). In discussing training approaches, Locke et al. (1982) argue that attribution retraining may not be sufficient because self-efficacy is determined by many factors other than effort, such as ability to function under stress and adaptability. In line with this view, Schunk (1984a) has recently summarized research supporting relationships between self-efficacy, motivation, and achievement as a function of differing educational practices. Important contextual influences on students' efficacy judgments include specific attributional feedback strategies, goal setting, social comparison strategies, and reward contingencies. Not only do variations in these processes exert differential contextual influences on self-efficacy judgments, but specific strategies and processes are used by children at different ages and stages of development (Schunk, 1984a).

Schunk (1984b) further explicates the processes contributing to self-efficacy assessments, which include self-perceptions of task outcomes, ability, effort expenditure, task difficulty, situational circumstances, and the pattern of successes and failures. From this view, it follows that self-efficacy appraisals are subsequent to perceptions of task requirements and assessments of prior successes and failures. Schunk (1984b) contends that prior successes or failures will not necessarily lead to positive or negative impacts on perceptions of efficacy, in that educational practices and resulting student beliefs that they can effectively process information can convey perceptions of personal control over learning outcomes. It is the combination of educational practices and students' perceptions of personal control that further strengthen perceived self-efficacy for learning. His research indicates that explicit strategy training not only helps students acquire and use these skills, but also helps them develop self-efficacy. In addition, other educational practices shown to influence self-efficacy include methods of instructional presentation, performance feedback, attributional feedback, goal setting, social comparison, and rewards. Although these interventions are primarily external instructional modifications, rather than interventions directed at helping learners modify their own internal processes and perceptions, this research supports the reciprocal relationship between perceptions of personal control and self-efficacy and its central role in motivation and learning.

3. Attribution Theory

Unlike competence motivation theory and self-efficacy theory, both of which assume that the underlying motivators of human behavior are perceptions of personal control and competency, attribution theory assumes that the underlying motivator of human behavior is the search for a causal understanding of failures (Weiner, 1976, 1979, 1980, 1983). These explanations or attributions students give for their performance (i.e., ability, luck, effort, task difficulty) will differentially influence their emotional responses, performance, and motivation depending on the locus of causality, stability, and controllability of these attributions. Higher performance and motivation are said to result from viewing academic successes as personally caused, likely to recur, and under one's control.

On the other hand, Ames (1984) has suggested that students who tend to be self-regulated and strategy-focused are those that are mastery-oriented and attribute failures to variable and controllable factors (lack of effort, not using appropriate strategies). She argues that there is some evidence that effort attributions are linked to cognitive activities involved in self-monitoring and self-regulation. The point is made that self-directed and individualized learning contexts encourage a sense of personal responsibility which facilitates effort attributions and the use of or focus on strategies (Ames, 1987). Grabe (1984) takes an integrative position and argues that perceptions of ability and effort covary such that the amount of effort expended provides a salient cue for judging ability. He found that low-achieving students who believe both their ability and their effort contribute to their grade were more persistent than those who made either ability or effort attributions. Grabe (1984) suggests that achievement change programs need to address not only student performance attributions, but they also need to help students view their life experiences as under their control and as resulting from their efforts.

Clifford (1984) has recently presented a theory of constructive failure. Relevant aspects of her theory for this discussion include the prediction that failure is more likely to produce constructive effects if students have high expectations for control. She also argues that more attention should be given to encouraging strategy explanations for failure. This argument is based on the rationale that strategy explanations can turn failure outcomes into problem-solving situations and students can focus on finding more effective strategies rather than focusing on negative implications of failure. By increasing students' knowledge and awareness of strategies (a metacognitive level of training) and training them to discriminate between strategy, effort, and ability attributions, perceptions of control can be increased.

White's (1959) contribution in defining competence motivation has also been acknowledged by Nicholls (1979) who has related this concept to the role attributions may play in motivation. He takes the position that ability attributions for success may be the most important determinants of achievement affect, expectancies, and behavior. This conclusion is arrived at from two different assumptions: (1) success is positively valued and failure is negatively valued, and (2) people are inherently motivated to behave in ways that produce feelings of competency. Attributing successes to ability allows one to derive a feeling of personal efficacy that is more stable but less controllable than effort attributions; however, ability vs. effort attributions may perform the valuable function of affecting persistence and the use of appropriate strategies during learning. This latter position has also been advocated by Goetz and Palmer (1983; also see Palmer & Goetz, Ch. 4, this volume) who present evidence that ability attributions significantly predict future performance expectancies as well as affect persistence and the development of learned helplessness. They also present evidence that indicates that students' perceptions of their own personal attributes (abilities, efficacy) and strategy attributes (strategy efficacy in light of personal attributes) contributes to the use of study strategies. The implied underlying relationship is that high self-concepts of ability will lead to high expectancies for success, ability attributions for success, persistence, and the continued use of relevant strategies.

Some links between Bandura's self-efficacy theory and Weiner's attribution theory have been explored by Schunk (1981, 1982, 1983, 1984a). Although both theoretical frameworks emphasize the role of cognitions in assessing environmental information, deriving inferences about factors affecting performance, and generating expectancies that influence achievement behaviors, they differ in the types of judgmental factors that are held to directly influence expectancies (Schunk, 1984a). Within self-efficacy theory, attributional judgments provide an important source of efficacy information that influences performance through its intervening effects on perceived self-efficacy (Schunk, 1982, 1983). Thus, attributions are sources of efficacy information and have an impact on the reciprocal relationship between perceptions of personal control and self-efficacy throughout the learning process.

4. Importance of Self-Control

Two recent meta-analyses have indicated that learners' perceptions of themselves and their perceptions of control over learning show consistent relationships with educational achievement (Findley & Cooper, 1983; Hansford & Hattie, 1982). Watkins (1984) found that if students perceive they have control over their own learning, they are more likely to use deep information processing approaches in which they focus on the content as a whole, try to see connections between the parts, and actively think about the structure of the information. When a lack of control is perceived, students are most likely to focus on parts of the content and view learning tasks as memory tasks. Learners who use deep processing approaches have been found to have well organized study methods, deep and elaborative processing approaches, intrinsic motivation, broad-based understanding, and preference for building understanding on the basis of logic vs. intuition (Watkins, 1984). Similarly, Schmeck (1983, Ch. 10, this volume; Schmeck & Meier, 1984; Schmeck & Phillips, 1982) has found that a personality dimension, labeled self-efficacy, is positively correlated with deep processing. This dimension includes confidence in one's learning potential, communication ability, and perceptions of personal control.

Stipek and Weisz (1981) have argued that perceptions of personal control are essential for the development of a sense of competence following successful mastery attempts. McCombs (1982a) has also noted that a growing body of theoretical and empirical literature clearly supports the view that increasing students' perceptions of personal control can increase motivation and achievement (e.g., Baird & White, 1982; Bandura, 1982a; Schunk, 1984a; Stipek, 1981; Stipek & Weisz, 1981; Thomas, 1980; Wang, 1983; Weiner, 1979, 1980, 1983), and can contribute to positive development in the direction of responsible, mature adulthood (e.g., Brown et al., 1981; Paris et al., 1983). It has also been found that strategies for increasing perceptions of control also increase judgments of self-efficacy—judgments that positively affect motivation and achievement (e.g., Bandura, 1982a; Bower, 1981; Hetenna & Ballif, 1981; Schunk, 1984a, 1984b; Stipek, 1981; Thomas, 1980; Wang, 1983). In addition, evidence exists that persons with developed senses of personal control and competency are more inclined to use previously learned skills and strategies in new learning situations (e.g., Lefcourt, 1976, 1982; Paris et al., 1983; Paris et al., 1985; Ryan et al., 1983; Thomas, 1980; Wang, 1983; Wittrock, 1986).

Several researchers have also found empirical support for the theoretical position that learning outcomes are determined by learner decisions which are, in turn, influenced by learner perceptions and interpretations (Baird & White, 1984; Benware & Deci, 1984; Wang & Lindvall, 1984). Treatments that increase perceptions of control and active orientations to learning have been found to increase intrinsic motivation and conceptual learning. The central component in successful treatments appears to be a metacognitive training component in which students are directly trained in activities such as planning, continuous self-monitoring, and self-evaluation. All in all, the current research and theory in this area indicate the importance of self-perceptions and self-evaluations (including self-efficacy, self-competence, locus of control, and self-responsibility) in fostering continuing motivation for learning new skills. In addition, Nicholls (1983, 1984) reports that a task-involvement vs. ego-involvement orientation to learning results in higher levels of intrinsic motivation and more effective performance, even for students with low perceptions of ability.

Interventions that have proven successful in modifying a sense of personal control and enhancing achievement in Wang's (1983) research include direct instruction in self-management skills (planning, information organization, goal setting, scheduling, and time management) and providing opportunities for self-managed learning (carrying out learning plans with increasing responsibility, self-evaluations of learning, learner selection of subject matter, working with others and sharing classroom resources, and taking responsibility for helping others in carrying out learning plans). It is argued that if learners are placed in carefully structured learning environments that provide opportunities for both self-management skill acquisition and opportunities for self-direction, self-initiation, and self-evaluation, their sense of self-efficacy and personal control will be enhanced along with task performance.

5.   Metacognition and Self-Regulated Learning Processes

Critical to self-control of learning is students' development of metacognitive skills for planning, monitoring, regulating, and evaluating learning activities. Baird and White (1982) have stated that self-control during learning requires learners to engage in self-evaluations of understanding, self-evaluations of competence, and a variety of other metacognitive activities including being aware of the nature and process of learning, personal learning styles and deficiencies, and conscious self-monitoring and decision making (planning) during learning. In fact, it can be argued that metacognitive skills provide the basic structure for the development of positive self-control. These skills are, by definition, involved in the knowledge (awareness) and control (self-regulation) of cognition and affect (Belmont et al., 1980; Brown et al., 1983; Brown et al., 1981; Paris et al., 1985; Paris et al., 1983; Schwen & Sisakhti, 1983). Furthermore, Wang (1983; Wang & Lindvall, 1984) has argued that metacognitive activities contribute to the development of self-regulatory and self-management skills as well as a sense of personal agency. Self-monitoring, in particular, has been found to contribute not only to improved acquisition, but also to improved generalization and transfer of knowledge and skills (Wang & Lindvall, 1984).

Metacognitive activities for regulating and overseeing learning defined by Brown et al. (1983) include planning (e.g., predicting outcomes, scheduling time/resources), monitoring (testing, revising, rescheduling), and checking (evaluating outcomes). Brown et al. (1981) have argued that training in these self-control activities is the most successful because students "are not only instructed in the use of a strategy, but are also explicitly instructed in how to employ, monitor, check, and evaluate that strategy" (p. 15). The basis of self-regulation is said to be self-awareness, which can be accomplished by training in various self-testing, self-monitoring, and self-questioning strategies. Through such training, students can be taught to be aware of what learning activities are appropriate, what their unique characteristics and limitations are, the nature of the materials to be learned, and what the critical tasks of learning are (Brown et al., 1981). Schwen and Sisakhti (1983) elaborate on Brown's work and make the further point that to train general and durable strategies, it is necessary to teach metacognitive skills in conjunction with cognitive skills. Similarly, Belmont et al. (1980) and Paris et al. (1985) stress the need to teach students about their own cognitive functions and the ways they can be combined or organized to solve problems. Such training provides the metaknowledge and strategies for self-management and self-control of learning problems by helping students recognize that there is a problem and that there are learnable skills and strategies for solving the problem, thereby enhancing their motivation to solve it.

Within the framework of self-regulated learning, an interpretive process model of motivated learning in classrooms has been advanced by Corno and Mandinach (1983). In their model, a central role is given to self-efficacy judgments and attributions to personal control as two self-regulation processes contributing to motivated learning. Other processes are alertness, selectivity, connecting, planning, and monitoring. These metacognitive, cognitive, and affective processes are related to what the student does while cognitively engaged in learning. Corno and Mandinach maintain that self-regulated learning is the highest form of cognitive engagement, in that it requires the active use of processes and strategies. The amount and kinds of effort (motivation) expended on classroom tasks are said to be influenced by students' active engagement of a wide variety and range of cognitive interpretations of themselves and their environment. In turn, when students carry out tasks in an effortful manner, there is a reciprocal influence on these cognitive interpretations.

The Corno and Mandinach (1983) model assumes that students come to the learning situation with past experiences and knowledge, skills, and different dispositions, as well as differentially developed self-regulated learning schema. The amount and kind of cognitive engagement (alertness, selectivity, connecting) is determined by these "aptitudes" and the students' interpretations of the instructional environment and task demands. Performance expectations and self-efficacy judgments are said to result from the form of cognitive engagement, and these judgments, in turn, influence the planning and monitoring activities undertaken, the resulting performance outcome, and the attributions given for the outcome. If students have engaged in appropriate self-regulation and performed the task successfully, Corno and Mandinach posit that a controllable and internal strategy attribution (e.g., "I used the right approach") should result. They argue that long-term exercising of self-regulated learning activities will help students learn how to learn and develop school aptitude and motivation.

The skills that have been identified for self-control of learning parallel many of the skills Baird (1983) argues are necessary for self-development and motivation, i.e., problem solving, self-evaluation, self-monitoring, self-reinforcement, controlling negative emotional states, planning, goal setting, and decision making. In motivational self-control training, Tesser and Campbell (1982) have suggested that the most effective programs are those that address cognitive/perceptual skills and strategies for helping students maintain positive self-evaluations. The importance of positive self-evaluations has been recognized by Covington and Omelich (1981) who argue that students with low self-concepts of ability are most susceptible to repeated failures because they do not know how to protect their sense of personal competency. This suggests that self-control skill training programs need to specifically address affective (motivational) strategies for maintaining a sense of competency following self-evaluation, in addition to addressing those metacognitive skills involved in self-evaluation (e.g., self-testing, and self-monitoring).

6. Strategy Use and Strategic Behavior

Strategy use and maintenance has been directly addressed by Paris (Oka & Paris, in press; Paris & Cross, 1983; Paris et al., 1983; Paris et al., 1985). These works indicate that strategy use depends on choices and judgments made by students, including contextual appropriateness, intentions, perceived capabilities, available alternatives, and perceived "costs." Strategy use also depends on the concept of instrumentality—the link between means and goals and between agency and purpose (Paris et al., 1985). Students make judgments about strategy utility and economy, as well as judgments regarding personal competency and control in decisions to apply self-regulated strategies. Paris and Cross (1983) point out that motivational influences on strategy use include learners' values, beliefs, and attitudes. Beliefs and attitudes are said to form the basis for meaningful goals and intentions. They energize strategic behavior, whereas goals provide rationales for the behavior. In addition, values, beliefs, and attitudes help students organize strategic allocation of effort and determine intentions. This is similar to Maehr's (1983) point that decisions made during learning tasks, based on learners' values and beliefs, can promote or deter continued motivation and learning for particular tasks. In this view, task performance is the actualization of one's intentions.

The "personalized dimensions" of motivation, which Oka and Paris (in press) argue can allow students to make adaptive choices during learning, include a sense of control, significant goals and values, self-management skills, and interpretations of success and failure. They, like Harter, suggest that motivation may serve the functional role of preserving students' sense of self-worth, a point that has also been made by Covington (1983). In fact, Covington (1983) has advanced the construct of "motivated cognitions" as ego defenses that preserve self-esteem (e.g., attributions, rationalizations, and excuses) and that reflect beliefs and intentions that can preserve feelings of competence and self-worth. Oka and Paris (in press) state that learning can be understood as ". . . motivated behaviors, that is, abilities that are influenced by feelings of efficacy and worth rather than mere cognitive competencies" (p. 5). This cognitive perspective on motivation focuses on attributions, expectancies, and values to explain perseverance or effort on learning tasks.

Brown et al. (in press) and Nickerson et al. (1984) also define strategic behavior as the deliberate application of skills and knowledges in a goal-oriented or problem-solving context. Motivation is thus a necessary component of strategic behavior and a precursor to strategy use. Schoenfeld (1983) argues that strategy training needs to address motivational influences such as values and beliefs, along with training in management and control strategies. In addition, Baird and White (1982) state, "If only (cognitive) strategies are taught, the training may prove no more effective than other types where the learner more passively applied received rules" (p. 245). In line with this view, Oka and Paris (in press) suggest that motivational interventions should help students develop a sense of control, show them how to make academic goals personally relevant, help them acquire adequate self-management skills, and foster a balanced view of success and failure.

B. Summary

Current perspectives on learning, motivation, and the active role of the learner have led to the recognition that for effective learning to take place, the learner must engage in the self-management or self-control of his or her own learning. To assume this responsibility requires that learners have appropriate attitudes and orientations toward learning (i.e., that they possess concepts, skills, and strategies for being self-motivated), and that they perceive themselves to be competent in their abilities to engage appropriate learning strategies (i.e., that they have perceptions of efficacy and the appropriate cognitive, metacognitive, and affective strategies and skills for self-control of learning). The fact that many students are deficient in strategies and skills for self-motivation and self-control of learning underscores the need for an effective skills training program that addresses essential and trainable metacognitive, cognitive, and affective (motivational) strategies and skills.

From the literature presented here, several conclusions relevant to an understanding of integral processes and skill domains underlying continuing intrinsic motivation to learn can be drawn. First, the metacognitive skills of self-awareness, self-evaluation, and self-regulation provide a basic structure for the development of positive self-control. Second, perceptions of personal control underlie continuing motivation and are reciprocally influenced by perceptions of personal competency or self-efficacy such that both contribute to continuing motivation, perhaps in their effects on feelings of self-worth. Third, there is a set of general self-development skills related to the development of self-system structures and processes that appears to be prerequisite to students' ability to assume personal responsibility and control as well as apply specific learning skills. Fourth, skill training programs can be effective in changing both negative self-views, attitudes, and orientations toward learning and specific metacognitive and cognitive skills required for self-regulated learning. Finally, interventions have tended to focus on external educational practices in bringing about desired changes in internal processes, interpretations, or expectations; however, this approach should be combined with interventions that help students change inappropriate cognitively mediated processes and belief systems in order to more directly influence their environment and positively adapt themselves to changing instructional conditions. A necessary first step to the design of such an intervention is the identification of processes and skill domains underlying continuing motivation to learn. Continuing motivation is seen as the end product of effective generative learning processes and activities, and thus, the appropriate integrative framework for conceptualizing those processes and skill domains to be addressed in skills training interventions.

II. AN INTEGRATIVE MODEL OF PROCESSES UNDERLYING INTRINSIC MOTIVATION TO LEARN

Although the preceding theoretical and empirical work goes a long way toward explicating the self-regulated learning activities important to motivation and their relationships to self-efficacy and attributions, the role of perceived personal control or agency and implications for learning strategies and motivational skills training have not been explicitly considered. For this reason, I would like to build on this work and advance a model of the components and processes involved in continuing intrinsic motivation to learn, as well as discuss how this model relates to learning strategies training in general and motivational skills training in particular (cf. McCombs, 1984a). Thus, a major purpose of this model is to provide a research agenda for learning and motivational strategies training.

The model shown in Fig. 1, incorporates concepts from competence motivation, self-efficacy, and attribution theories, as well as concepts from Corno and Mandinach's (1983) model of classroom motivation and Paris and Cross's (1983) learning cycles framework. It begins by assuming that a metacognitive system of executive processes is involved in both the knowledge (awareness) and control (self-regulation) of cognition and affect. This metacognitive system then interacts with both the cognitive and affective systems in the

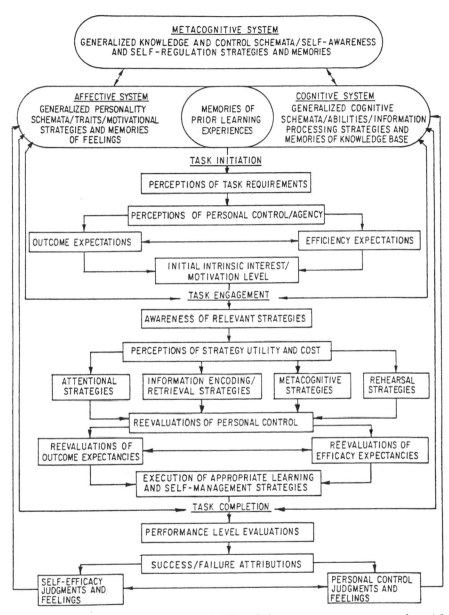

FIG. 1.   Generative model of processes and skills underlying continuing motivation to learn (cf. McCombs, 1984).

generation of perceptions of task requirements. Involved in the generation of these perceptions are generalized knowledge and control schemata and metacognitive strategies for self-awareness and self-regulation, generalized personality schemata and traits, affective (motivational) strategies for self-judgments and acceptance of personal responsibility for learning, as well as generalized cognitive schemata, abilities, and strategies for active information processing. Memories within the metacognitive, cognitive, and affective systems are also involved, particularly as they are combined to form memories of prior learning experiences. The perceptions of task requirements then generate both expectancies for success, failure, and rewards (efficacy appraisals), and perceptions of personal control or agency (assessments of the controllability of task requirements). These perceptions and expectancies form the basis for the generation of a level of intrinsic interest or motivation for (1) accomplishing task requirements and (2) applying appropriate metacognitive, cognitive, and affective learning strategies. Stated differently, when students begin an academic task, they engage in a variety of self-evaluations of their abilities and competencies to succeed at this task. Critical to positive self-evaluations are students' perceptions of how much control they can execute over task requirements. If the task is perceived to be too difficult or to require skills students do not perceive themselves to have, a low perception of personal control will contribute to low competency expectations and low expectancies for success. Without internal strategies or skills for changing these negative perceptions and generating positive affect, interest in pursuing task requirements and resulting effort expended will be low.

Assuming that intrinsic interest or motivation has been generated on the basis of a student's perceptions and expectancies, the metacognitive and cognitive engagement processes necessary for self-control of learning can be called into play (i.e., attention/alertness, selectivity/connecting, planning, performance monitoring, self-evaluation, and rehearsal). Important in this process is an awareness of relevant strategies and perceptions of strategy utility and cost. Depending on the student's repertoire of metacognitive, cognitive, and affective learning strategies, those judged appropriate to task requirements will be executed. Upon task completion, the student engages in self-evaluations of his or her performance level in which comparisons against internal standards (goals), the performance of others, or other external standards are made. Based on these evaluations, attributions for success or failure are generated which, in turn, contribute to the student's judgments (cognitive appraisals) and feelings (affective reactions) of self-efficacy and personal control in meeting task requirements. These task-specific self-efficacy and self-control judgments and feelings reciprocally influence each other and feed back into the metacognitive, cognitive, and affective systems, thereby influencing future perceptions and expectancies that can generate continuing motivation for similar learning tasks. In addition, there is an ongoing reciprocal influence of self-efficacy and self-control judgments, as pointed out by Schunk (personal communication, 1984), wherein these judgments change not only after tasks have been completed, but undergo constant change during task engagement. Thus, changes in self-efficacy and self-control judgments, as a result of self-evaluations during task engagement, can influence affective reactions, alter task motivation, and effect the execution of appropriate metacognitive and cognitive strategies and processes.

Given that the bases for this model have been derived from current conceptualizations of learning and motivation, it shares common elements. It differs from those discussed, however, in several important ways. First, the focus in this model is on the comprehensive set of metacognitive, cognitive, and affective processes that internally mediate learners' continuing intrinsic motivation to learn, generally and in specific situations. Second, a central role has been given to the concept of perceived personal control and its ongoing reciprocal relationship with perceived self-efficacy in both the generation of positive affect necessary for continuing intrinsic motivation to learn and the execution of self-regulated learning skills. Third, the role of outcome expectancies and attributions for success and failure in contributing to perceived self-control and competency and continuing motivation is explicated, thereby clarifying that attribution retraining is necessary but not sufficient for promoting ongoing motivation to learn. Finally, the emphasis on internally mediated processes implies that interventions for enhancing motivation in this context should focus on modifying the learner vs. modifying educational practices.

A. GENERAL INTERVENTION IMPLICATIONS FROM AN INTEGRATIVE MODEL

Using the framework presented in Fig. 1, several general classes of interventions can be specified, within the affective and cognitive systems, for addressing metacognitive, cognitive, and affective skill training needs. Within the *affective* system (i.e., that system generally related to self-knowledge and the manifestations of one's self-view in personality characteristics, emotional and motivational responses, and feelings of self-worth), interventions for learners with a tendency toward inappropriately negative self-views include cognitive tools for generating new self-views (Jordan & Merrifield, 1981). Intervention steps include helping learners (1) identify inadequately perceived, situation-specific self-concept areas that are targets for change; (2) determine those cognitive beliefs and processes that led to inadequate notions about the self and bring these into awareness; (3) make distinctions between evidence and conclusions about the self; and (4) take the risks necessary to transform or cognitively modify old self-views. Metacognitive skill training would be suggested for these intervention steps (e.g., skill training in self-assessment/evaluation, setting realistic self-standards, planning, self-correction, self-rewards), applied in the context of motivational skills training in taking control, knowing yourself, goal setting, and problem solving.

Within the *cognitive* system (i.e., that system generally related to specific intellectual abilities, skills, strategies, and content-based knowledge schemas, as well as higher order executive control processes), interventions for learners with poorly developed metacognitive and cognitive abilities and strategies include many of the same strategies for changing inadequate self-judgments, but are taught in the context of self-evaluations of understanding. That is, metacognitive strategy skill training would be suggested for helping learners to analyze their abilities and knowledge structures, identify what skills and knowledges they can bring to bear on the task, and determine what learning activities are appropriate given the nature of the task and their perceptions of the critical tasks of learning. Metacognitive strategies would include self-testing, self-monitoring, self-questioning, and self-rewards. Motivational strategies would include techniques for maintaining positive self-evaluations of understanding (e.g., cognitive/perceptual tools that combine positive self-talk and imagery to maintain positive self-views) and strategies for self-management and self-control of perceived learning problems (e.g., metaknowledge about assessing one's cognitive functions and ways these functions can be organized to solve problems).

The preceding discussion implies the need for motivational skills training to address general self-control skills and specific skills for maintaining positive self-evaluations. Part of this skill training would help learners become aware of the level of control they have when assessing their personal competencies against their perceptions of task requirements. This level of control is seen to be a product of (1) being aware of particular motivational, metacognitive, and cognitive strategies that can be effectively used in accomplishing task requirements and (2) forming positive self-evaluations of ability. Values clarification training has an important role in this context in that it can help students learn to maintain and enhance self-esteem by understanding their unique mode of conduct against which they can self-evaluate their performance (Rokeach & Regan, 1980). In addition, Chapman (1983) has pointed out that knowledge of one's values provides a necessary context for the teaching of decision-making skills that are required in effective goal-setting and problem-solving strategies.

After helping learners understand the concepts of self-control and personal responsibility and teaching them to engage in appropriate self-evaluation processes, motivational skill training can then be directed at helping learners evaluate task requirements against their cognitive and affective self-knowledge, establish personal meaningfulness of task goals and requirements, and derive positive expectancies for success as well as positive perceptions of personal control. Following these interventions, the next motivational area in the model presented in Fig. 1 focuses on strategies and skills for generating and maintaining intrinsic motivation. Once students have acquired strategies and skills for generating intrinsic interest, cognitive and metacognitive skill training interventions may be required to assist students in self-regulated learning activites such as maintaining attention/alertness, planning, generating personal relevance, performance monitoring, and self-evaluation as well as in executing appropriate learning strategies necessary for successful task completion (see Fig. 1). In addition to these cognitive and metacognitive strategies, a number of motivational strategies can also be identified as helpful. These include goal setting, stress management, problem solving, and to some extent, depending on specific task demands, effective communication skills. Knowing strategies and skills in these content areas can generally assist learners in setting performance standards, establishing personal learning goals, controlling negative emotional states, solving learning problems that arise, and engaging in effective communication necessary to solve particular learning problems. Each of these strategy components also has an underlying function to equip students with self-control skills in areas relevant to maintaining a positive learning climate.

Following task completion (see Fig. 1), students engage in the processes of evaluating performance levels, generating success/failure attributions, and deriving self-efficacy and personal control judgments. Motivational skills training can be helpful in enchancing these processes by teaching students to cvaluate performance outcomes against internal standards and goals, to analyze performance information, to engage in self-correction activities as necessary, to attribute successes/failures to internal and controllable causes, to select and administer appropriate rewards, and to maintain positive self-efficacy judgments in light of positive plans of action for subsequent learning activities. Many of these skills are metacognitive in nature (e.g., self-evaluation, self-correction, planning, self-rewards), thus highlighting the importance of the metacognitive component in motivational skills training.

B. Motivational Skills Training Program

I have designed a program for addressing many of the motivational skills training components identified in the preceding section (McCombs & Dobrovolny, 1982). Since this program has been defined in some detail elsewhere (McCombs, 1983; McCombs & Dobrovolny, 1982), this section will briefly describe the contents and strategies in this program, and discuss evaluation results obtained to date from implementations of the program with military technical training students.

1.   Content and Structure

The content and structure of the motivational program was defined as a result of in-depth quantitative and qualitative analyses of specific motivational, affective, and cognitive skill deficiencies of Air Force trainees in four technical training courses (McCombs & Dobrovolny, 1980). Results indicated that the primary deficiencies (i.e., characteristics that differentiated effective from ineffective learners) in the motivational domain were that low-achieving students consistently had low motivation to learn, had few military or personal goals, and could be classified as being low in maturity, with little self-discipline or the ability to take responsibility for their own learning. In the affective domain, low-achieving students were generally those with high levels of anxiety toward learning and taking tests, and who lacked effective skills for taking personal control and coping with the demands of technical training. In the cognitive domain, low-achieving students were generally those with poor reasoning and comprehension skills, or those who lacked effective decision-making and problem-solving skills in technical or personal areas.

Based on these results, seven skill-training modules were defined to teach motivational skills within a general problem-solving framework (McCombs, 1982a, 1982b). The Introduction Module introduces the concepts of personal responsibility and positive self-control, clarifies the role of these concepts in generating positive feelings of competency, presents rudimentary techniques for controlling negative attitudes (e.g., use of positive self-talk and imagination), and explains the purpose of the skills training package. The Values Clarification Module explains the role of values and beliefs in helping us define ourselves and what is important to us, stresses students' responsibilities in defining their own value system, and helps them explore and resolve conflicts in their values and beliefs. The Career Development Module builds on students' newly acquired self-knowledge and helps them acquire the necessary decision-making skills to explore their career interests and make career goals and plans. The Goal Setting Module formalizes the previously learned goal-setting process by first describing the purpose of goals as directing and motivating human behavior, describing a general model for systematically thinking about and setting personal goals, and helping students work through exercises for setting specific long-term and short-term goals. The Stress Management Module describes the role of perceptions, negative self-talk, and mistaken beliefs in producing stress and presents a number of generalizable strategies for managing stress. The Effective Communication Module describes techniques and strategies for identifying personal communication styles, effectively communicating feelings, wants, and needs, and for dealing with stressful interpersonal situations that may impede goal attainment. Finally, the Problem Solving Module provides a summary of the training package by pointing out that students have been using a problem solving approach throughout the training and by providing a general model for systematically solving problems.

2. Format and Delivery

The choice of format for the motivational skills training materials was based on both practical and theoretical considerations. From the practical standpoint, there was a need for the format to be compatible with the requirements of a self-paced technical training environment in which students have primary responsibility for their own learning, proceeding through modularized instructional materials at their individual paces with limited instructor and group interactions. This set of considerations led to the choice of a printed, self-instructional format, incorporating an easy to read, low-density style conducive to students' reading the materials on their own or in small groups prior to beginning their self-paced technical training course. To enhance students' self-directed learning and understanding of the concepts and strategies in the materials, visuals were included wherever appropriate, as well as periodic embedded questions and practice exercises.

From the theoretical standpoint, format issues of particular importance concerned identifying effective methods and approaches for facilitating students' skill maintenance and generalization following initial training. A review of cognitive behavior modification approaches to skill maintenance indicated that successful techniques include various combinations of self-monitoring/self-assessment with self-reinforcement (McCombs, 1983). Techniques used in self-monitoring include personal diaries, journals, logs, note cards, graphs, progress charts, and other record-keeping procedures that require individuals to frequently evaluate and record positive and negative instances of skills and behaviors in question. Self-reinforcement techniques include engaging in positive self-talk when desired outcomes are attained, recording self-ratings on the effectiveness of new skills, and identifying and applying extrinsic rewards when certain skills and behaviors are successfully implemented.

In addition to the preceding techniques for skill maintenance, our research has indicated that the instructor can play a critical role in skill acquisition, maintenance, and generalization (Dobrovolny, 1982; McCombs, 1982a; McCombs & Dobrovolny, 1980). We found that training instructors in the

role of learning strategies expert/learning facilitator, and using them to aug-
ment the self-instructional format, further enhanced the effectiveness of this
training in other important ways. First, the instructors were able to make
the training content more personally relevant and meaingful by relating
personal experiences. Second, by displaying genuine personal interest in the
students, instructors were able to reduce students' feelings of insecurity,
fear, or anxiety toward interactions with higher ranking instructor personnel. Finally, instructors were able to reinforce the value of the skill training
for positive self-development by explaining its application and benefits in
military situations and experiences, as well as by providing a positive role
model.

Through a blend of cognitive and behavioral approaches, the modules are
designed to be used in a self-paced mode, so that from the beginning,
students become responsible for their own learning. Through extensive behavioral rehearsal, they practice and increase their self-management skills.
Further, throughout the modules, students are asked to commit themselves
to a low, moderate, or high level of effort, underscoring in yet another way
that they must accept responsibility for their progress in the program. Likewise, since the role of the instructor is primarily that of model and motivator,
he or she cannot be blamed for lack of student progress, nor take credit when
students do well. The exercises within each module are practical, graded in
difficulty, and fun to do, so that students will learn because they are active in
the learning process. Finally, group discussions at the end of each module
promote peer modeling and peer pressure to change. Students are encouraged by each other to practice their new skills. In these three ways—behavioral rehearsal, personal commitment, and modeling—the instructional
method matches the content being taught.

3. Evaluation

An initial evaluation of the motivational program was conducted with Air
Force trainees in the Precision Measuring Equipment course. Small groups
of trainees went through the self-paced modules, augmented by instructor
introductions and small group practices, prior to entering their technical
course. Findings indicated that trainees (1) liked the program and found it
helpful in their course work and personal lives and (2) had significantly
higher test scores and lower test failure rates than control group trainees
(McCombs & Dobrovolny, 1982).

Although these initial evaluation findings with the motivational program
clearly pointed to its success, several questions remained. One set of questions concerned the issue of the format of this training package and the use of
instructors and the group process to facilitate trainee acquisition and maintenance of strategies and skills included in the package. For example, could

the cost effectiveness of the program be enhanced by reducing instructor requirements or group interaction requirements through the use of computer-assisted instruction (CAI) for selected portions of the training? An investigation of this question was recently funded by the Army Research Institute (McCombs, 1984b). CAI enhancements were developed to introduce the program and each of the seven modules, and to simulate group practice at the end of each module. An evaluation study with Army trainees in the Electronics Communication School indicated that the program was positively received by both students and instructors, instructor-augmented versions compared with CAI versions of the program contributed to more effective student progress and performance in their technical training course, and experimental compared with control group students tended to report higher self-efficacy following the skill training.

There are other important research questions to be explored with the Motivational Skills Training Program. These include both practical effectiveness issues and a variety of theoretical issues. The final section summarizes conclusions reached in this chapter and outlines important questions to address.

III.   CONCLUSION AND FUTURE RESEARCH RECOMMENDATIONS

In this chapter, the theoretical and empirical bases for identifying processes and skill domains that underlie continuing intrinsic motivation to learn have been described. From these bases, an integrative model was presented, training intervention implications were derived, and progress recently made in the motivational skills training area was described. One important outcome of this recent work is that it is possible to more fully define the concept of *continuing intrinsic motivation to learn.* I would like to define this concept as a dynamic, internally mediated set of metacognitive, cognitive, and affective processes (including expectations, attitudes, and beliefs about the self and the learning environment) that can influence a student's tendency to approach, engage in, expend effort in, and persist in learning tasks on a continuing, self-directed basis. Defined in this way, continuing intrinsic motivation to learn has both a general and a specific connotation. In general, it refers to a student's ongoing tendency to generally pursue learning activities. Specifically, it refers to a student's tendency to maintain interest and implement self-directed and self-regulated learning skills within a particular learning task.

This definition implies that, in order to maintain learning interest and implement specific self-directed or self-motivated learning skills and strategies, it is necessary for students to know themselves, what is important to them, and their learning competencies and abilities. It is also necessary for them to understand that they are responsible for their own learning, that they can take positive self-control in learning situations, and that in so doing, they can increase their sense of personal competency and self-control as well as their learning achievement. That is, a metacognitive self-awareness is an integral component of continuing intrinsic motivation to learn. This self-awareness contributes to perceptions of competency and control in both a general and specific sense. It generally contributes to students' views of themselves as competent and self-directed learners, and it contributes to ongoing feelings of personal efficacy and agency in specific learning situations. In addition, specific self-management strategies and skills are assumed to contribute to self-motivation by instilling the competencies for taking the level of personal control required in self-directed and self-regulated learning. Finally, it is assumed that once generalized perceptions of competency and positive self-control have been developed, students will be more inclined to learn and use other metacognitive, cognitive, and affective strategies relevant to particular learning tasks. In other words, students must learn how to change negative attitudes and orientations toward themselves and the learning situation before they will be motivated to learn and use other, more specific, self-management skills and learning strategies.

A second major outcome of an integration of research on intrinsic motivation and its role in strategic behavior, is that it is possible to describe the functional *purpose of a motivational skills training component* within an integrated learning strategies curriculum. This functional purpose can be stated as that of promoting students' perceptions of self-efficacy and personal causation that underlie ability to take positive self-control and change negative attitudes and orientations toward themselves and learning. Metacognitive skills important in this regard include self-assessment/evaluation, setting realistic self-standards, planning, self-monitoring, self-correction, and self-rewards. Important cognitive components include problem solving, decision making, and higher order analytical skills that can help students evaluate learning task requirements against their cognitive self-knowledge. Affective skills contributing to motivation include goal setting, deriving positive expectancies for success and personal control, managing stress and anxiety, and learning to effectively communicate feelings and needs.

We are on the brink of an exciting research breakthrough in more thoroughly understanding the nature and role of motivation in learning and strategy use. A number of important theoretical and practical research issues and questions need to be addressed. From a theoretical standpoint, research is needed on (1) improved measures of self-efficacy judgments, perceived personal control, and motivation in order to examine underlying relationships between these variables as they are impacted by motivational and learning strategies training and as they impact subsequent learning performance; (2) further identification and substantiation of processes hypothesized to contribute to continuing student motivation, their interrelationships, and effective techniques for helping students acquire underlying skills and strategies for self-motivation; (3) continued integration of theoretical perspectives related to motivation and academic performance, with a focus on the developmental nature of underlying variables; and (4) further identification of specific metacognitive, cognitive, and affective processes related not only to motivation to learn, but also to the development of positive self-system structures, processes, and affective feelings of self-worth.

From a practical standpoint, research is needed on (1) the long-range impact of the type of motivational skills training described here on students' attitudes, performance, self-control skills, and judgments of self-efficacy following initial training and subsequent education or training experiences; (2) the differential effectiveness of various training formats (e.g., CAI, instructor augmentation, and group process) for students with different personality predispositions, learning styles, or other individual differences hypothesized to be impacted by differing training formats; (3) the effectiveness of this type of motivational skills training when combined with training in other metacognitive, cognitive, or affective learning strategies; and (4) the effectiveness of alternative learning strategies training approaches, i.e., presenting this training as a separate initial curriculum vs. an embedded curriculum or a combination of a separate and embedded curriculum approach.

Our continued commitment to research in these theoretical and practical areas promises to be successful in further refinements of interventions for many types of students, including both underachievers and learning-handicapped populations, that can help them maximize their learning enjoyment and achievement levels. Of the greatest significance from our continued efforts in this area, perhaps, is the potential for identifying interventions that will ultimately help students achieve positive self-development and enhanced feelings of self-worth.

REFERENCES

Ames, C. (1984). Attributions and cognition: Essential motivational knowledge for the preservice teacher, paper presented at the annual meeting of the American Educational Research Association, New Orleans.

Ames, C. (1987). Social context and student cognitions, paper presented at the annual meeting of the American Educational Research Association, Washington, D.C.

Baird, L. L. (1983). *Attempts at defining interpersonal competency* (RR–83–15). Princeton, NJ: Educational Testing Service.

Baird, J. R., & White, R. T. (1982). Promoting self-control of learning. *Instructional Science, 11,* 227–247.

Baird, J. R., & White, R. T. (1984). Improving learning through enhanced metacognition: A classroom study, paper presented at the annual meeting of the American Educational Research Association, New Orleans.

Bandura, A. (1978). The self system in reciprocal determinism. *American Psychologist, 33,* 344–358.

Bandura, A. (1982a). Self-efficacy mechanism in human agency. *American Psychologist, 37,* 122–147.

Bandura, A. (1982b). The psychology of chance encounters and life paths. *American Psychologist, 37,* 747–755.

Bandura, A. (1986). The explanatory and predictive scope of self-efficacy theory. *Journal of Social and Clinical Psychology, 4,* 359–373.

Bandura, A., & Schunk, D. H. (1981). Cultivating competence, self-efficacy, and intrinsic interest through proximal self-motivation. *Journal of Personality and Social Psychology, 41,* 586–598.

Belmont, J. M., Butterfield, E. D., & Ferretti, R. P. (1980). To secure transfer of training, instruct self-management skills, paper presented at the annual meeting of the American Educational Research Association, Boston.

Benware, C. A., & Deci, E. L. (1984). Quality of learning with an active versus passive motivational set. *American Educational Research Journal, 21,* 755–765.

Bower, G. H. (1981). Mood and memory. *American Psychologist, 36,* 129–148.

Brown, A. L., Armbruster, B. B., & Baker, L. (in press). The role of metacognition in reading and studying. In J. Oransanu (Ed.), *Reading comprehension: From research to practice.* Hillsdale, NJ: Erlbaum.

Brown, A. L., Bransford, J. D., Ferrara, R. A., & Campione, J. C. (1983). Learning, remembering, and understanding. In J. H. Flavell, & E. H. Markman (Eds.), *Handbook of child psychology: Cognitive development* (Vol. 3). New York: Wiley.

Brown, A. L., Campione, J. C., & Day, J. D. (1981). Learning to learn: On training students to learn from texts. *Educational Researcher, 10,* 14–21.

Chapman, W. (1983). *A context for career decision making* (RR–83–13). Princeton, NJ: Educational Testing Service.

Clifford, M. M. (1984). Thoughts on a theory of constructive failure. *Educational Psychologist, 19,* 108–120.

Corno, L., & Mandinach, E. B. (1983). The role of cognitive engagement in classroom learning and motivation. *Educational Psychologist, 18,* 88–108.

Covington, M. V. (1983). Motivated cognitions. In S. G. Paris, G. M. Olson, & H. W. Stevenson (Eds.), *Learning and motivation in the classroom.* Hillsdale, NJ: Erlbaum.

Covington, M. V., & Omelich, C. L. (1981). As failures mount: Affective and cognitive consequences of ability demotion in the classroom. *Journal of Educational Psychology, 73,* 796–808.

Dobrovolny, J. L. (1982). Transitioning learning strategies research into practice: Focus on the technical training instructor as learning strategies expert. *Journal of Instructional Development, 5,* 17–23.

Findley, M. J., & Cooper, H. M. (1983). Locus of control and academic achievement: A literature review. *Journal of Personality and Social Psychology, 44,* 419–427.

Goetz, E. T., & Palmer, D. J. (1983). Metacognitive awareness in good and poor readers: Knowing when and why you haven't understood and what to do about it. In M. Sadowski, D. Wiseman, & J. Denton (Eds.), *Literacy research: The reader, the text, the teacher.* College Station, TX: Instructional Research Laboratory of the Department of Educational Curriculum and Instruction.

Grabe, M. (1984). Attributions, effort and mastery learning: Do the effort demands of mastery learning reduce perceptions of ability? paper presented at the annual meeting of the American Educational Research Association, New Orleans.

Hansford, B. C., & Hattie, J. A. (1982). The relationship between self and achievement/performance measures. *Review of Educational Research, 52,* 123–142.

Harter, S. (1978). Effectance motivation reconsidered: Toward a developmental model. *Human Development, 21,* 34–64.

Harter, S. (1981). A new self-report scale of intrinsic versus extrinsic orientation in the classroom: Motivational and informational components. *Developmental Psychology, 17,* 300–312.

Harter, S. (1982). A developmental perspective on some parameters of self-regulation in children. In P. Karoly, & F. H. Kanfer (Eds.), *Self-management and behavior change: From theory to practice.* New York: Pergamon Press.

Harter, S. (1985). Processes underlying self-concept formation in children. In J. Suls, & A. Greenwald (Eds.), *Psychological perspectives on the self,* (Vol. 3). Hillsdale, NJ: Erlbaum.

Harter, S. (in press). The relationship between perceived competence, affect, and motivational orientation within the classroom: Processes and patterns of change. In A. K. Boggiano, & T. Pittman (Eds.), *Achievement and motivation: A social-developmental perspective.* Cambridge, MA: Cambridge University Press.

Harter, S., & Connell, J. P. (1984). A model of the relationship among children's academic achievement and their self-perceptions of competence, control, and motivational orientation. In J. Nicholls (Ed.), *The development of achievement motivation.* Greenwich, CT: JAI Press.

Hettena, C. M., & Ballif, B. L. (1981). Effects of mood on learning. *Journal of Educational Psychology, 73,* 505–508.

Jordan, T. J., & Merrifield, P. R. (1981). Self-concepting: Another aspect of aptitude. In M. D. Lynch, A. A. Norem-Hebeisen, & K. J. Gergen (Eds.), *Self-concept: Advances in theory and research.* Cambridge, MA: Ballinger.

Lefcourt, H. (1976). *Locus of control: Current trends in theory and research.* Hillsdale, NJ: Erlbaum.

Lefcourt, H. (1982). *Locus of control: Current trends in theory and research* (2nd ed.). Hillsdale, NJ: Erlbaum.

Locke, E. A., Zubritzky, E., & Lee, C. (1982). *The effect of self-efficacy, goals and task strategies on task performance.* College Park, MD: University of Maryland.

Maehr, M. L. (1983). On doing well in science: Why Johnny no longer excels; why Sarah never did. In S. G. Paris, G. M. Olson, & H. W. Stevenson (Eds.), *Learning and motivation in the classroom.* Hillsdale, NJ: Erlbaum.

McCombs, B. L. (1982a). Enhancing student motivation through positive self-control strategies, paper presented at the annual meeting of the American Psychological Association, Washington, DC.

McCombs, B. L. (1982b). Learner satisfaction and motivation: Capitalizing on strategies for positive self-control. *Performance and Instruction, 2,* 3–6.

McCombs, B. L. (1983). Motivational skills training: Helping students adapt by taking personal responsibility and positive self-control, paper presented at the annual meeting of the American Educational Research Association, Montreal.

McCombs, B. L. (1984a). Processes and skills underlying continuing motivation: Toward a definition of motivational skills training interventions. *Educational Psychologist, 19,* 199–218.

McCombs, B. L. (1984b). CAI enhancements to a motivational skills training for military technical training students. *Training Technology Journal, 1,* 10–16.

McCombs, B. L., & Dobrovolny, J. L. (1980). *Theoretical definition of instructor role in computer-managed instruction* (NPRDC–TN–80–10). San Diego, CA: Navy Personnel Research and Development Center.

McCombs, B. L., & Dobrovolny, J. L. (1982). *Student motivational skill training package: Evaluation for Air Force technical training* (AFHRL–TP–82–31). Lowry AFB, CO: Air Force Human Resources Laboratory.

Nicholls, J. G. (1979). Quality and equality in intellectual development: The role of motivation in education. *American Psychologist, 34,* 1071–1084.

Nicholls, J. G. (1983). Conceptions of ability and achievement motivation: A theory and its implications for education. In S. G. Paris, G. M. Olson, & H. W. Stevenson (Eds.), *Learning and motivation in the classroom.* Hillsdale, NJ: Erlbaum.

Nicholls, J. G. (1984). Achievement motivation: Conceptions of ability, subjective experience, task choice, and performance. *Psychological Review, 91,* 328–346.

Nickerson, R. S., Salter, W., & Herrnstein, J. (1984). *The teaching of learning strategies.* (BBN Report No. 5578). Cambridge, MA: Bolt Beranek and Newman.

Oka, E. R., & Paris, S. G. (in press). Patterns of motivation and reading skills in underachieving children. In S. J. Ceci (Ed.), *Handbook of social and neuropsychological aspects of learning disabilities.* Hillsdale, NJ: Erlbaum.

Paris, S. G., & Cross, D. R. (1983). Ordinary learning: Programmatic connections among children's beliefs, motives, and actions. In J. Bisanz, G. L. Bisanz, & R. Kail (Eds.), *Learning in children: Progress in cognitive development research.* New York: Springer-Verlag.

Paris, S. G., Lipsom, M. Y., & Wixson, K. K. (1983). Becoming a strategic reader. *Contemporary Educational Psychology, 8,* 293–316.

Paris, S. G., Newman, R. S., & Jacobs, J. E. (1985). Social contexts and the functions of children's remembering. In M. Pressley & C. J. Brainerd (Eds.), *Cognitive learning and memory in children.* New York: Springer-Verlag.

Rokeach, M., & Regan, J. F. (1980). The role of values in the counseling situation. *Personnel and Guidance Journal, 59,* 576–583.

Ryan, R. M., Mims, V., & Koestner, R. (1983). Relation of reward contingency and interpersonal context to intrinsic motivation: A review and test using cognitive evaluation theory. *Journal of Personality and Social Psychology, 45,* 736–750.

Schmeck, R. R. (1983). Learning styles of college students. In R. Dillon, & R. Schmeck (Eds.), *Individual differences in cognition.* New York: Academic Press.

Schmeck, R. R., & Meier, S. T. (1984). Self-reference as a learning strategy and a learning style. *Human Learning, 3,* 9–17.

Schmeck, R. R., & Phillips, J. (1982). Levels of processing as a dimension of difference between individuals. *Human Learning, 1,* 95–103.

Schoenfeld, A. H. (1983). Beyond the purely cognitive: Belief systems, social cognitions, and metacognitions as driving forces in intellectual performance. *Cognitive Science, 7,* 329–363.

Schunk, D. H. (1981). Modeling and attributional effects on children's achievement: A self-efficacy analysis. *Journal of Educational Psychology, 73,* 93–105.

Schunk, D. H. (1982). Effects of effort attributional feedback on children's perceived self-efficacy and achievement. *Journal of Educational Psychology, 74,* 548–556.

Schunk, D. H. (1983). Ability versus effort attributional feedback: Differential effects on self-efficacy and achievement. *Journal of Educational Psychology, 75,* 848–856.

Schunk, D. H. (1984a). Self-efficacy perspective on achievement behavior. *Educational Psychologist, 19*, 48–58.

Schunk, D. H. (1984b). Self-efficacy and classroom learning, paper presented at the annual meeting of the American Educational Research Association, New Orleans.

Schwen, T. M., & Sisakhti, G. P. (1983). Aptitude training: A meta-analysis of findings, paper presented at the annual meeting of the American Educational Research Association, Montreal.

Stipek, D. J. (1981). The development of achievement-related emotions, paper presented at the annual meeting of the American Educational Research Association, Los Angeles.

Stipek, D. J., & Weisz, J. R. (1981). Perceived personal control and academic achievement. *Review of Educational Research, 51*, 101–137.

Tesser, A., & Campbell, J. (1982). Self-evaluation maintenance processes and individual differences in self-esteem, paper presented at the annual meeting of the American Psychological Association, Washington, D.C.

Thomas, J. W. (1980). Agency and achievement: Self-management and self-regard. *Review of Educational Research, 50*, 213–240.

Wang, M. C. (1983). Development and consequences of students' sense of personal control. In J. M. Levine, & M. C. Wang (Eds.), *Teacher and student perceptions: Implications for learning*. Hillsdale, NJ: Erlbaum.

Wang, M. C., & Lindvall, C. M. (1984). Individual differences and school learning environments. In E. W. Gordon (Ed.), *Review of research in education* (Vol. 11). Washington, DC: American Educational Research Association.

Watkins, D. (1984). Students' perceptions of factors influencing tertiary learning. *Higher Education Research and Development, 3*, 33–50.

Weiner, B. (1976). Attribution theory, achievement motivation, and the educational process. *Review of Educational Research, 42*, 201–215.

Weiner, B. (1979). A theory of motivation for some classroom experiences. *Journal of Educational Psychology, 71*, 3–25.

Weiner, B. (1980). The role of affect in rational (attributional) approaches to human motivation. *Educational Researcher, 9*, 4–11.

Weiner, B. (1983). Speculations regarding the role of affect in achievement-change programs guided by attributional principles. In J. M. Levine, & M. C. Wang (Eds.), *Teacher and student perceptions: Implications for learning*. Hillsdale, NJ: Erlbaum.

White, R. W. (1959). Motivation reconsidered: The concept of competence. *Psychological Review, 66*, 297–333.

Wittrock, M. C. (1986). Student thought processes. In M. C. Wittrock (Ed.), *Handbook of research on teaching* (3rd ed.). New York: McMillan.

INDIVIDUAL DIFFERENCES AND LEARNING STRATEGIES

Ronald R. Schmeck

This chapter proposes that learning strategies training and research programs should routinely include individual difference measures. The objective would be to study and take advantage of interactions between personal attributes and the treatments used in training. Very few studies of this sort have been conducted.

A brief discussion of terminology is necessary. I define learning as a by-product of thinking, the tracks left behind by our thoughts. We learn by thinking, and the quality of the learning outcome is determined by the quality of our thoughts. In my opinion, the more effective learning strategies are those that have the greatest impact on our thought processes. Thus, drawing a red line under a sentence in a text is less effective than restating the meaning of the sentence in my own words. My work in the learning styles domain reflects this emphasis which I place upon information processing.

There is a difference between the terms *strategy* and *tactic* (Snowman, in press). I like this distinction because it draws attention to the dimension of behavioral specificity–generality, and the study of individual differences often requires that we look at behavior from the more general perspective. The term tactics refers to the specific activities of learners and the word strategy refers to their more general approach or plan. This use of the terms is consistent with dictionary definitions and military usage. Tactics operationalize strategies, i.e., tactics are the observable activities that imply that certain strategies are in use.

I feel that a learning strategy is a higher level cluster of learning tactics that work together to produce a unified learning outcome. A student's choice of tactics is guided by his or her strategy, and this choice determines the learning outcome, e.g., whether it is concerned chiefly with memory or comprehension. This brings me to my final terminological distinction. Levin (1982) grouped learning tactics into those that are "memory-directed" and those that are "comprehension-directed." Memory-directed tactics are concerned with storage and retrieval of information. Comprehension-directed tactics emphasize understanding of the meanings of ideas and their interre-

LEARNING AND STUDY STRATEGIES: ISSUES IN
ASSESSMENT, INSTRUCTION, AND EVALUATION

lationships. The memory-directed and comprehension-directed dimensions are not orthogonal.

To introduce the concept of individual differences that may interact with learning strategies, I present a brief overview of my work in the learning styles domain. I have attempted to develop an individual differences measure based directly upon learning strategies research rather than upon research in the areas of motivation, attitudes, or personality. This was designed to measure an individual's cross-situational preference for using a particular learning strategy, regardless of specific situational demands. Next, I will investigate the limitations that individual differences place upon learning strategies training programs, and ask whether or not it is necessary, in theory at least, to change some of the individual differences that characterize students in order to achieve a lasting change in their learning strategies. Toward the end of the chapter, I will present a broad list of dimensions of individual differences that I believe to be most important in the learning strategies area.

I. LEARNING STYLE AS A DIMENSION OF INDIVIDUAL DIFFERENCE

I begin the discussion of individual differences relevant to the learning strategies area by presenting my own work concerned with learning styles. This work has centered upon those aspects of information processing that have demonstrated relationships with memory measures (e.g., Craik & Tulving, 1975). Unlike some other researchers, I have not been concerned with preferences for environmental conditions such as temperature, noise level, social stimulation, or media.

My work relates to traditional learning strategies research in two ways. The most obvious connection is in terms of Cronbach's (e.g., Cronbach & Snow, 1977) call for studies examining attribute by treatment interactions. Learning styles may provide measures of some new, educationally relevant personal attributes that can moderate either the effectiveness of certain learning strategies or the procedures used to teach those strategies to students. The second connection between my work and traditional learning strategies research relates to Underwood's (1975) suggestion that the external validity of processes uncovered in the laboratory should be supported by evidence of naturally occurring differences among individuals with regard to their use of those processes outside of the laboratory. For example, if we can make the memory of an association more permanent by instructing subjects to use imagery under laboratory conditions, then we should search outside of the laboratory for individual differences in students' tendencies to use imagery in their everyday studying practices. Thus, individual differences research would support the validity of the constructs uncovered in the laboratory. In this sense, it should become clear to the reader that I am studying the same theoretical constructs as those uncovered in the learning strategies laboratory, but perhaps at a less specific conceptual level.

The study of individual differences often requires that we look at behavior from the more general perspective. In addition, I believe that most of our interventions in learning strategies training programs are actually at the more specific level of tactics, and we often fail to give sufficient attention to whether or not the tactics that we teach fit together to produce a coherent learning outcome. I also believe that there are some individuals who would benefit more from interventions aimed at the more general strategies level or, in some cases, an intervention aimed at the level of learning style, or even at the student's general, philosophical orientation toward education. I will have more to say about this later after the discussion of learning styles research.

Psychologists have argued for many years about whether behavior is determined more by the person (e.g., the individual's personality traits) or by the situation to which the person is responding. Those with an extreme behavioristic orientation maintain that the situation is all that we should consider when trying to explain behavior. Those with an extreme psychodynamic orientation argue that individuals are driven to repeat their past within their present situation, thereby giving structure and meaning to the present. Thus, they view self-expression, or expression of the personality, as the chief determinant of behavior. In the domain of education, as in that of psychotherapy, the truth seems to lie somewhere between the psychodynamic and behavioristic extremes. As Jenkins (1979) and Bransford (1979) have noted, the learning outcome is the result of a complex interaction between the person (learner characteristics) and the situation (instructional activities, material to be learned, and type of test used to assess learning).

My research in the area of strategies and tactics of learning has been conducted outside of the laboratory, by asking students true–false questions about the tactics that they use in their normal, everyday study practices, and then factor analyzing their responses to these questions. I have assumed that each of the clusters of tactics revealed by a factor analysis represents a strategy, and cross-situational use of such a strategy represents a style. As the behaviorist suggests, we do see variability in an individual's learning tactics from one situation to another, but we also find some cross-situational consistency, and this consistency is difficult to see if we look only at a few selected tactics. If we look at clusters of tactics, however, i.e., strategies reflected in questionnaire factor scores, then we begin to see consistencies that presumably reflect learning styles.

TABLE 1 A Tentative Model of Learning Style with Suggestions Regarding Causality

Personality, motivation, stages of development →	Learning style →	Learning strategy →	Learning tactics →	Learning outcome
Stable introvert, intrinsic motivation, reflective, field-independent, internal locus of control, high self-confidence, highly individuated.	Deep	Conceptualizing	Categorizing, comparing and contrasting categories, hierarchically organizing ideas in networks, abstracting.	Synthesis and analysis, evaluation of conclusions, subsumption, schema development, theory development.
Stable extravert, both intrinsic and extrinsic motivation, internal locus of control, well-defined self-concept, genuine, impulsive, creative, field-dependent.	Elaborative	Personalizing	Productive thinking, self-referencing concretizing, generating examples, translating into personal language and images, relating current information to prior personal experience.	Application, personal growth, personality development, development of social skill and understanding of people.
Neurotic, extrinsic motivation, anxious, dependent, external locus of control, self-defensive, low self-efficacy, fear of failure as main source of motivation.	Shallow	Memorizing	Repetitive rehearsing of information, using mnemonics, verbatim or literal encoding with little or no translation.	Description of what was studied, literal reproduction.

As Table 1 indicates, I view learning style as lying between personality and learning strategy on the causal continuum that leads to a learning outcome. It is not as specific as strategy nor as general as personality. Learning style is the expression of personality within the situational context, i.e., the school setting. Learning style also reflects the student's preferred learning strategy, but it implies more than learning strategy. For example, it includes elements of motivation, attitude, and cognitive style.

I did not begin my study of the relationship between personality and learning tactics by using traditional personality measures. Past research (e.g., Tallmadge & Shearer, 1969, 1971) had shown that such an approach was not likely to bear fruit. Rather, I developed my own individual differences measure by asking students questions about their learning tactics, and I assumed that when a student consistently claimed to use a particular combination of tactics, it reflected the presence of a strategy, with cross-situational preference for such a strategy reflecting the presence of style. Next, I examined the relationships between traditional personality measures and learning style, as assessed by my newly developed Inventory of Learning Processes (Schmeck, 1983). I want to emphasize once again that, although my individual difference methodology differs from that of the experimental researcher studying learning strategies, I feel we are ultimately studying the same processes.

The theoretical model that I chose to present in Table 1 lists three dimensions of learning style: deep, elaborative, and shallow. My research suggests that the individual with a predominantly deep learning style is likely to adopt a conceptualizing strategy. For example, Schmeck (1983) reported that deep processors profit most from conceptual retrieval cues in a memory experiment. Such a conceptualizing strategy follows from the learner's assumption that learning and education are concerned with the development and refinement of cognitive structures, i.e., concepts. Study time is spent comparing and contrasting abstractions and organizing them to form hier-·archies and theories. The learning outcome produced by the tactics of someone with a deep learning style tends to be at the analysis, synthesis, and evaluation levels in Bloom's (1956) Taxonomy. The reader should compare Tulving's (1985) discussion of "semantic" memory and "noetic" consciousness.

An individual demonstrating a learning style that is predominantly elaborative, on the other hand, prefers a personalizing strategy. For example, Schmeck and Meier (1984) found that students who score high in elaborative processing have a more articulated self-concept and they use self-reference as a learning strategy more frequently than students who score low on the scale. The elaborative individual assumes that learning involves adaptation, application, and the development of coping mechanisms (personal growth), activities that fall in the middle level of Bloom's (1956) Taxonomy. The students of the late 60s and early 70s who called for "relevance" in education were elaborative individuals. The reader should compare Tulving's (1985) discussion of the "episodic" memory system and "autonoetic" consciousness. The learning outcome produced by the tactics listed with this style is one of application.

The person with a predominantly shallow learning style tends to adopt a memorizing learning strategy. The learning outcome is most often at Bloom's (1956) knowledge level, i.e., involving a literal, verbatim description of what has been read. Within Perry's (1970) theory of development, the shallow individual would define learning in a "dualistic" fashion, believing that truth is provided by the school system, and it is the student's job to commit this truth to memory in a literal, verbatim form.

The shallow individual will show the greatest interest in memory-directed tactics. Deep and elaborative individuals will be more interested in comprehension-directed tactics (Levin, 1982). The elaborative student will also appreciate the value of certain memory-directed tactics and will value examples and an opportunity to translate information into his or her own words. The metaphors that he or she uses will most often be personal, concrete, and drawn from experience. The deep student, on the other hand, prefers abstract theoretical metaphors and enjoys networking ideas, whether on paper or simply through mental comparison and contrast. It should be emphasized that the dimensions of deep, shallow, and elaborative processing are not orthogonal. It is likely that most individuals will demonstrate components of all three strategies (conceptualizing, personalizing, and memorizing), but one of them will predominate in most individuals' learning behavior.

II.   INVENTORY OF LEARNING PROCESSES

My initial work in this area was done in 1977 (Schmeck et al.). Operating within the framework of cognition and information processing, with its emphasis on detailed description of cognitive processes, we prepared 121 true–false, self-report questionnaire items that described activities of students writing reports, and preparing for examinations and class discussions. The items were chosen to reflect current research and theory in the area of memory processes (storage, retrieval, organization, etc.).

Factor analyses yielded four interpretable factors that encompassed 62 of the original 121 items. The four scales were labeled Deep Processing, Elaborative Processing, Fact Retention, and Methodical Study. Deep Processing is an information process of verbal classification and categorical comparison and contrast. The deep processor is argumentative when reading and listening; he or she also contrasts opposing explanations and makes comparisons across academic domains. Later work summarized by Schmeck (1983; cf. Lockhart & Schmeck, 1984) established that the Deep Processing scale is related to reading comprehension, critical thinking ability, verbal ability, attention to semantic attributes of words, skill at building conceptual tree structures, and the Wechsler Adult Intelligence Scale (WAIS) digit-span subtests. Also, the individual with a high score on Deep Processing is usually independent, and has an internal locus of control and high self-efficacy (Meier et al., 1984; Schmeck, 1983).

Elaborative Processing personalizes information by translating it into experiential terminology and images. The elaborative processor likes to relate class material to his or her personal life, preferring illustrations that are actual experiences or episodes in the lives of people. Research summarized by Schmeck (1983) showed that the Elaborative Processing scale is related to mental imagery, writing ability, and subjective (personalized) organization of recalled lists of words. Schmeck and Meier (1984) report evidence that elaborative individuals use self-reference as a learning tactic.

Further evidence that the self-report learning style scales of Deep Processing and Elaborative Processing are related to differences in observable behavior comes from a graduate thesis (Shaw, 1984) directed by myself and McCarthy. Shaw (1984) summed scores from the Deep and Elaborative Processing scales to classify subjects as "deep–elaborative" or "shallow–reiterative." Volunteers from this pool of subjects were then engaged in counseling sessions with a counseling psychologist. Blind analysis of the counseling session transcripts by highly trained raters showed that the verbal protocols of the deep–elaborative individuals were rated more deep, conclusion-oriented (rather than description-oriented), elaborative, personal, and clear (rather than vague).

The other two scales on the 1977 Inventory of Learning Processes were Fact Retention and Methodical Study. The items on the Fact Retention scale were characterized by an emphasis on memory, and scores on the scale were related to good performance on multiple-choice tests, retention of verbatim definitions of words, and retention of names, dates, and places. Students with high scores on Fact Retention tended to have more specific classification systems (Schmeck et al.).

The Methodical Study scale contained items that on the surface seemed to suggest a "good," methodical approach to studying, but scores on the scale were negatively related to grades, critical thinking ability, verbal ability, and cognitive development (Schmeck, 1983). The scale was also positively related to the lie scale of the Eysenck Personality Inventory (Schmeck & Spofford, 1983) and negatively related to the Disinhibition measure on the Sensation Seeking Scale (Meier & Schmeck, 1985), suggesting that students who score high on Methodical Study attempt to make a "good impression" by fabricating a false representation of self with regard to study habits and by avoiding the violation of social norms.

Recently, the items of the 1977 Inventory of Learning Processes were combined with those from a British inventory developed by Entwistle (1981; Entwistle & Ramsden, 1982). This item pool was administered to a large sample of university students from a variety of grade levels and academic majors. Factor analysis yielded six clearly interpretable factors and a "hint" of two additional factors. Three of them corresponded to the dimensions in Table 1. The item content of two of these factors suggested the labels Deep Processing and Elaborative Processing, both similar to the 1977 scales. A third factor was labeled Shallow Processing. It contained items suggesting literal memorization, similar to the original Fact Retention scale. The emergence of these three factors supported the model represented in Table 1.

This latter factor analysis also revealed two personality dimensions and one additional dimension that matched the 1977 analysis. The personality dimensions related to "confidence" and were labeled Self-Efficacy:Conceptualizing and Self-Efficacy:Memorizing. Self-Efficacy:Conceptualizing expresses confidence in one's synthetic and analytic skills as they apply to studying, and Self-Efficacy:Memorizing suggests confidence in one's memorization skills. These dimensions of efficacy and personal responsibility are ones that might be fruitfully modified in strategies training programs (see Ch. 9 by McCombs, and Ch. 4 by Palmer & Goetz in this volume). Meier et al. (1984) report that students with more self-efficacy regarding their writing skills tended to demonstrate higher scores on the Deep Processing scale.

The last factor revealed by the latter analysis was Methodical Study. Once again, as in the 1977 analysis, the items suggested an extremely thorough (almost compulsive) approach to studying, and once again, it is likely that some of the students scoring high on the dimension were "lying" while others truly were "compulsive" in their studying (cf. Schmeck, 1983). There was some suggestion in the analysis of two additional dimensions of information processing that have been described by other theorists (e.g., Entwistle, 1981; Entwistle & Ramsden, 1982; Pask, 1976a, 1976b; Gregorc, 1979, 1982). In some ways, these dimensions seemed to assess more general cognitive styles rather than learning styles. The content of the scales suggested the labels Serialist Processing and Holist Processing, with the former being analytic-sequential and the latter more global–random. Following Entwistle (1981), deep processors would probably earn moderately high scores on both of these latter scales suggesting that their processing style is a versatile one.

In the next section, I will discuss the relationship between the theoretical assumptions illustrated in Table 1 and learning strategies training programs.

In particular, I want to draw attention to the causal model implied by Table 1 and discuss the issues of modifiability, retention and transfer of modifications, attribute by treatment interactions, and limitations that we must face when designing learning strategies training programs.

III. SHOULD WE ACCOMMODATE PERSONAL CHARACTERISTICS OR TRY TO CHANGE THEM?

I will make three points with regard to Table 1. First, as we move from left to right in the table, we move from more stable, less modifiable personal characteristics to less stable, more modifiable characteristics. It is easier to teach learning tactics than it is to modify personality. In this regard, the behaviorist would argue that personality is, in fact, irrelevant, and it is the specific behaviors (tactics) to the right in Table 1 that should be the sole concern of any training program. The psychodynamically oriented psychologist, on the other hand, would maintain that lasting change is accomplished only through modifying the personality traits to the left in Table 1, regardless of the obstacles encountered.

Another implicit assumption is that the more stable characteristics on the left-hand side of Table 1 might set limits on the extent to which modifications of the less stable characteristics on the right-hand side can be retained and transferred after leaving a learning strategies training program. If we teach a networking tactic (e.g., constructing tree-diagrams of idea units) to someone with a shallow learning style, the tactic may not fit with the individual's style to yield a unified learning outcome. The tactic may be dissonant. If we want to teach such an individual to make good use of a networking tactic, we may need to consider ways of modifying aspects of his or her shallow learning style. [1]

Once again, the behaviorist would argue that we can change an individual only if we change specific behaviors. Thus, the behaviorist would assume that teaching a networking tactic to an individual with a shallow learning style would change the person's style, perhaps making it "deeper." However, this can be true only if the new tactic is retained and transferred to the student's real-world study situation, and yet the student's stable charac-

---

[1]Biggs (in press) provides evidence that a strategy disembedded from any personological roots becomes merely a group of "short-term props to learning." He reports that, as students develop higher levels of metacognitive awareness and an internal locus of control, their motives and strategies become more congruent and lead to higher qualitative levels of performance. The highest levels of performance and personal satisfaction are associated with congruent, or integrated, packages of personality, motive, and strategy variables.

teristics (e.g., personality) tend to set limits to retention and transfer. Thus, we are faced with a "chicken or egg" dilemma; do we change personality to permit changes in specific behaviors to transfer, or do we change specific behaviors to enable us to change personality? My suggestion is that we pay attention to both possibilities simultaneously when designing a training program. I will elaborate on this later in the chapter.

My final point regarding Table 1 concerns the size of the impact that our strategies training programs can have on the individual. Psychodynamically oriented psychologists emphasize that, although the more stable traits on the left-hand of Table 1 are more difficult to modify, any modification that we are able to accomplish will have far-reaching ramifications at the behavioral level. The psychodynamic psychologist poses an argument which is essentially the opposite of that posed by the behaviorist. Specifically, he or she maintains that we do not need to worry about specific behaviors, because a change in the individual himself or herself (i.e., in his or her personality) will automatically "filter down" to a behavioral level.

My purpose here is not to side with one or the other of these two extreme positions (behavioral and psychodynamic). Rather, I feel simply that we may have failed to fully consider the possibility of changing the more stable characteristics of the individual, and we may also have failed to pay sufficient attention to the ways in which our training procedures interact with those stable individual characteristics.

In general, I feel that we should strive to make the student's style more versatile. This requires a slight mismatch between the tactics that we teach and the strategy that is most comfortable for the individual (i.e., his or her style). On several occasions (e.g., Schmeck, 1981), I have argued that all students should be encouraged to develop a deep style of learning, and I still maintain that deep processing of information produces a learning outcome that is more enduring and transferable. However, I must admit that I am equally convinced that cross-situational use of conceptualizing or personalizing strategies will not always earn the highest school grades. Many instructors want memorization, and those who claim to want comprehension often still test for memorization (cf. Schallert et al., Ch. 11, this volume). Thus, in spite of my own bias favoring conceptualizing and personalizing strategies, we would be doing students a disservice if we encouraged only deep and elaborative styles without teaching some memory-directed tactics for those situations where rote memory will be tested.

I have alluded to the possibility of changing seemingly stable individual differences, but I have addressed the topic only indirectly. Changing the individual's personality is one of the aims of long-term psychotherapy, and it may seem outrageous to mention it in the context of a learning strategies training program. However, even a small amount of change at this level will have far-reaching effects with regard to learning tactics. Consider the individual's philosophical orientation toward education. What might be the effect if every learning strategies training program included a section that addressed questions such as: "What is education? What is learning? and What is the individual student's personal responsibility with regard to these processes?" Change in the student's definition of learning from one centering on memorization to one based upon cognitive restructuring and personal growth could have far-reaching effects upon his or her use of learning tactics. If an individual's shallow learning style becomes more deep and elaborative, it seems likely that he or she will seek out and discover for himself or herself elaboration learning tactics regardless of whether or not we teach them in our training programs. One way to encourage development of such a deep–elaborative learning style is through cognitive restructuring influenced by philosophical discussions centering upon the students' definition of learning, and their assumptions regarding the purpose of education and their personal responsibility for the learning outcome.

I am reminded here of metacognitive research concerned with children's conceptions of reading (e.g., Francis, 1982; Johns, 1980; Meyers & Paris, 1978). Improvement in reading comprehension skills runs hand in hand with increases in metacognitive knowledge. Mayers and Paris (1978) state, "The results of the present study demonstrate that beginning readers have a limited understanding of reading as a cognitive activity and certainly could profit from instruction regarding the means, goals, and parameters of proficient reading" (p. 690). There is some evidence that similar relationships between conception and process exist with regard to learning (Marton & Saljo, 1984; Saljo, 1979). Thus, metacognitive "consciousness raising" might be an appropriate component in a learning strategies training program.

To conclude the chapter I will summarize some of the individual differences dimensions that I have found to be relevant in the domain of learning strategies.

IV. OTHER INDIVIDUAL DIFFERENCES WORTHY OF STUDY

In this final section of the chapter, I will list some of the personality, motivational, and developmental variables that could appear in the extreme left column of Table 1. My purpose is simply to introduce individual differences dimensions that learning strategies researchers may include in their studies. This is intended to be a rough overview, and it is intended to stimulate some new ideas for the study of attribute by treatment interactions. I have selected dimensions based upon my experience, and have grouped the variables to add some conceptual organization to them. I am sure that I have left out some individual differences dimensions that others would include, and I have probably included some that others would eliminate. Also, I have ignored a few of the traditional distinctions between personality, ability, and cognitive style, but I hope that insight stimulated by a reorganization of the dimensions may compensate for these errors. I would suggest that information gathered with regard to the interaction of a training variable and any of the characteristics in a category may be generalizable to the whole category. Also, higher level traits, as assessed by the profiles of scores on lower level measures, may demonstrate (at some meta-analytic level) replicable relationships with training variables even if the relationships obtained with specific lower level measures are less stable.

Table 2 lists those established individual differences variables that I consider worthy of further study in the learning strategies domain. The first column in the table contains commonly accepted labels for the attributes and the second column lists measuring instruments that can be used to assess those attributes. I have not necessarily listed the "best" measures; I have listed those with which I am most familiar. This will at least provide an introduction or overview for the learning strategies researcher. As I noted above, I have grouped the attributes into categories to add some conceptual organizations. I take full responsibility for these categorizations. I will make a few comments regarding each of the categories before closing the chapter.

The categories in Table 2 that I have labeled Separation/Individuation and Neuroticism/Anxiety reflect a psychosocial developmental view of personality. The first category (Separation/Individuation) focuses upon the developmental task that presumably follows initial bonding with a parent figure. People in this stage strive to attain a sense of separateness, individuality, and identity, including a tolerance for being alone, an ability to maintain their own self-esteem, and a trust in their own abilities. Object relations theorists (e.g., Kernberg, 1980) note that very few of us totally complete this task, and the extent to which we complete it will set limits to our creativity, confidence, independence, sense of personal responsibility, and self-expression and self-assertion. Greater separation/individuation leads to less conformity, less need for social approval, and less conventionality, in addition to increasing self-actualization, intrinsic motivation, and internal locus of control. Schmeck (1983) reports evidence that suggests that the extent to which we have moved toward individuation is a determinant of scores on the Deep Processing Scale of his learning style inventory. The more individuated individual would have greater appreciation for the value of comprehension-directed tactics (Levin, 1982). Domino (1971) found that less individuated students required more structure in the learning environment. Such students would tend to be syllabus-bound (Parlett, 1970).

TABLE 2   Some Examples of Personal Attributes That May Be Relevant in the Learning Strategies Domain

Attributes	Measures
I. Separation/Individuation	I. Separation/Individuation
Syllabus-bound vs. syllabus-free (Parlett, 1970).	Approaches to Studying Inventory (Entwistle & Koyeki, in press).
Locus of control of reinforcement (Rotter, 1966).	I–E Scale (Rotter, 1966).
Learning-oriented vs. grade-oriented (Eison, 1982).	LOGO Scale (Eison, 1982).
	California Personality Inventory (Gough, 1957).
Intrinsic vs. extrinsic motivation (Entwistle & Koyeki, 1985).	16 Personality Factor Questionnaire (Cattell & Eber, 1962).
Self-actualization (Shostrom, 1964).	Personal Orientation Inventory (Shostrom, 1965).
Self-esteem (Coopersmith, 1967).	Self-Esteem Inventory (Coopersmith, 1967).
Need for approval (Crowne & Marlowe, 1964)	Social Desirability Scale (Crowne & Marlow, 1964).
Conventionality (e.g., Zuckerman, 1971).	Sensation Seeking Scale (Disinhibition) (Zuckerman, 1971).
Dependence vs. Independence Conceptual level (Hunt, 1979).	Paragraph Completion Test (Hunt, 1979).
Internal vs. external standards of evaluation.	Hidden Figures Test (French et al., 1963).
Fear of success (Tresemer, 1976).	Clinical Analysis Questionnaire (Krug, 1980).
Self-assertion.	Assertion Inventory (Gambrill & Richey, 1975)
Conformity (Krug, 1980).	
II. Neuroticism/Anxiety	II. Neuroticism/Anxiety
Anxiety (Taylor, 1953).	Manifest Anxiety Scale (Taylor, 1953).
Neuroticism (Eysenck & Eysenck, 1964).	Test Anxiety Questionnaire (Mandler & Sarason, 1952).
Optimism–Pessimism.	Eysenck Personality Inventory (Neuroticism Scale) (Eysenck & Eysenck, 1964).
Self-efficacy/confidence (Meier et al., 1984).	California Personality Inventory (Gough, 1957).
Performance and evaluation anxieties (Watson & Friend, 1969).	16 Personality Factor Questionnaire (Cattell & Eber, 1962).
Fear of failure (McClelland, 1961).	Self-Efficacy Scale (Meier et al., 1984).
Defensiveness.	The Social Avoidance and Distress Scale (Watson & Friend, 1969).
	The Fear of Negative Evaluation Scale (Watson & Friend, 1969).
	State-Trait Anxiety Inventory (Spielberger et al., 1970).

TABLE 2   (Continued)

Attributes	Measures
III. Cognitive Development Evaluative thinking Critical thinking Piaget's formalism (Piaget, 1963). Perry's formalism (Perry, 1970).	III. Cognitive Development Watson–Glaser Critical Thinking Appraisal (Watson & Glaser, 1964). Measures of formal thinking (e.g., Inventory of Piaget's Developmental Tasks). Interviews to measure college development (Perry, 1970; Saljo, 1979).
IV. Need for Stimulation (cf. Schmeck & Lockhart, 1983). Eysenck's & Cattell's work with extraversion (cf. Prentsky, 1979). Farley's work in instructional design (Farley & Gordon, 1981). Zuckerman's work with sensation seeking (Zuckerman, 1971).	IV. Need for Stimulation (cf. Schmeck & Lockhart, 1983). The Eysenck personality Inventory (Extraversion Scale) (Eysenck & Eysenck, 1964). Sensation Seeking Scale (Zuckerman, 1971). 16 Personality Factor Questionnaire (Cattell & Eber, 1962).
V. Sequential vs. Holist Styles of Processing Information Serial vs. holistic processing (Pask, 1976a, 1976b). Simultaneous vs. successive processing (Das et al., 1979). Left vs. right hemispheric processes (Ornstein, 1977; Torrance et al., 1977). Cognitive styles (category width, field dependence, tolerance for ambiguity, etc.). Sequential styles vs. random styles (Gregorc, 1979).	V. Sequential vs. Holist Styles of Processing Information Approaches to Studying Inventory (Entwistle, 1981). Your Style of Learning and Thinking (Forms A & B) (Torrance et al., 1977). Inventory of Learning Processes (Schmeck et al., 1977). Cognitive style measures (e.g., field dep., impulsivity, divergence). Gregoric Style Delineator (Gregorc, 1982). Hidden Figures Test (French et al., 1963). Gregorc Style Delineator (Gregorc, 1979).
VI. Prior Experience with the Material Existence of schemata, organizers, subsumers. Interest Level.	VI. Prior Experience with the Material Pretests. Interest inventories. Achievement tests.
VII. Learning Style Philosophy of education. Metacognition. Deep vs. shallow approaches to the material.	VII. Learning Style Approaches to Studying Inventory (Entwistle, 1981). Inventory of Learning Processes (Schmeck, 1983).

TABLE 2   *(Continued)*

Attributes	Measures
Perry's developmental theory (dualist vs. relativist definitions of learning) (Perry, 1970). Marton's conceptions of learning (Marton & Saljo, 1976a, 1976b).	Study Processes Questionnaire (Biggs, 1979). SOLO (Biggs, 1979).

The second category in Table 2 (Neuroticism/Anxiety) reflects later developmental tasks including further condensations resulting from earlier failures to individuate fully. The task at this stage is one of developing an orientation with regard to social comparison, rivalry, and competition. Obviously, having previously attained an acceptably esteemed self-concept does a lot to reduce unhealthy developments during this period. Neuroticism/Anxiety includes the balance (or imbalance) of fear and hope as sources of motivation. It is also related to the presence of excessive inhibitions and defensiveness. Schmeck (1983) reports that the anxious, neurotic, inhibited individual is likely to demonstrate a shallow learning style. Even the individual who is capable of a conceptualizing strategy will resort to sheer memorization when in a state of high anxiety (e.g., test anxiety), and the neurotic individual is in such a state almost all of the time. Trown and Leith (1975) report that students with less anxiety need less structure and more freedom in the learning environment.

The third category in Table 2 reflects the developmental theories of Piaget (1963) and Perry (1970) as well as the views of Marton and his colleagues (Marton & Saljo, 1976a, 1976b, 1984). I have labeled it Cognitive Development to distinguish it from psychosocial development with all of the emotional involvements implicit in the latter label. I am trying to describe a sort of epistemological sophistication. Piaget (1963) spoke of mental operations as proceeding from the "hands-on" sensorimotor stage through a sort of mental "hands-on" or covert trial and error thinking to completely abstract thinking. Perry (1970) spoke of the development of an epistemological theory beginning (at early stages) with the primitive assumption that teachers teach "truths" that students store in memory, and then slowly proceeding to the development of the more advanced assumption that "truth" is, in fact, always debatable. Perry found that critical thinking is especially important in the more advanced stages of development, with the most developed students demonstrating the most acceptance of comprehension-directed learning tactics. As a final point, Marton (Marton & Saljo, 1984; see also Saljo, 1979) speaks of differences in the way one defines or conceptualizes the learning process. In the case of the more primitive conception, the student assumes that to learn is to be able *to describe* what one is taught. With the more advanced conception, he or she assumes that to learn is *to reach conclusions* based on a combination of what is taught and what is already known. In general, the lower a student's level of epistemological sophistication, the more likely he or she will be to gravitate toward memory-directed tactics and demonstrate a shallow learning style.

Eysenck (Eysenck & Claridge, 1962) suggests that the fourth category of individual differences listed in Table 2 (Need for Stimulation) is physiologically based. Eysenck assumed that an individual's need for environmental stimulation depended on the ease with which his or her central nervous system could be aroused. "Introverted" individuals are easily aroused above their optimum level, and thus they tend to avoid excess stimulation. "Extraverts," on the other hand, require extra stimulation just to maintain their alertness and are actually uncomfortable (bored) in a quiet environment. Extraverts tend to prefer discussion and discovery learning. Farley (Farley & Gordon, 1981) and Zuckerman (1971) have proposed alternative conceptualizations, but the implications are essentially the same. Specifically, higher quality thoughts, and thus more enduring and transferable memory traces, occur when the central nervous system is optimally stimulated. For some individuals, this requires a very specific stimulus input and no extrinsic distractions. For others, complicated inputs and extrinsic distractions can be beneficial (cf. Schmeck & Lockhart, 1983). Farley and Gordon (1981) report that students who need more stimulation prefer inductive approaches, discussion, and discovery learning.

The fifth grouping of individual differences in Table 2 encompasses traditional cognitive style measures and concerns preferences for detailed, serialist approaches to building understanding as opposed to holist, global approaches. I have subsumed dependence, impulsivity, and divergence under this heading. Both sequential and holist thinkers can use comprehension-directed tactics, but the holist prefers to begin at the top and then "flesh out" the idea with specifics, while the sequential thinker likes to begin with specifics and gradually build up to the general conception in a serial, step-by-step fashion. Sequential thinkers prefer deductive, step-by-step, sequential tactics (an "additive" approach to comprehension). Holist thinkers prefer inductive, random, global tactics (more of an "insight" approach to comprehension). Entwistle (1981) argues that deep processing requires both holist and serialist thinking used in alternation, i.e., the deep processor would be "versatile," paying attention to both generalizations and detailed evidence.

The sixth category of individual differences is content-specific and relates to differences among experts and novices within a content domain (cf. Voss et al., 1983). In general, the more an individual knows about a particular content area and the more interested he or she is in it, the more capable and the more likely he or she will be to show a deep processing learning style and use comprehension-directed tactics. This relationship would presumably be attributable to the availability of schemata (or "subsumers") resulting from the processing of prior experiences.

The last category in Table 2 is Learning Style. I will not belabor that topic further because the initial section of this chapter was devoted to it.

V. SUMMARY

I am convinced that progress will be stimulated in learning strategies training and research if we include more individual differences variables, thereby permitting the observation of attribute by treatment interactions. We need to know what types of students are most receptive to what types of tactics. We need to know which tactics are slightly "out of character" for a particular student, but close enough to produce some accommodation or growth in style and personality. I discussed the match–mismatch dilemma. Do we teach tactics that are consonant with the students' dispositions, thereby capitalizing on strengths, or do we "stretch" them a bit by teaching tactics that are slightly dissonant with style and personality? I went so far as to ask whether we should attempt to change the personality itself before or while teaching certain tactics.

I began by discussing learning styles because that is the area in which I have done most of my own research. The three styles that I emphasized were deep processing (involving a conceptualizing strategy), elaborative processing (involving a personalizing strategy), and shallow processing (involving a memorizing strategy). With regard to modification of learning style, I noted the limitations imposed by personality development (e.g., individuation). However, I also suggested that cognitive restructuring of the individual's assumptions regarding personal responsibility, definition of learning, and philosophy of education might yield changes in learning style or at least prepare more fertile soil for cultivating new styles.

Several times I drew attention to differences between the behavioral and psychodynamic views regarding the best ways to change people. The behaviorist ignores stable, cross-situational individual characteristics and teaches specific, situationally controlled behaviors. In contrast, the psychodynamic psychologist assumes that specific behaviors will change without our help if we change the stable, cross-situational characteristics of the individual (i.e., his or her personality).

I noted that there is merit in both of the above points of view. Personal characteristics of the individual do set limits on the retention and transfer of newly learned behaviors. I noted, however, that we can change personal characteristics by teaching new behaviors. I then asked whether we should first teach new learning tactics to change learning style or first change learning style to permit the retention and transfer of the new learning tactics. I concluded that neither should be undertaken without the other.

I concluded the chapter by listing individual differences that I have found especially relevant to learning strategies research. I grouped these individual difference dimensions into theoretical categories in order to summarize some trends, and in the belief that corroborative findings are more likely to be obtained from multivariate research focusing on profiles of measures rather than single measuring instruments.

Individual differences measures reflect the same processes that are revealed by experimental contrasts. I recognize, however, that experimental findings have the advantage of revealing causal links. I am not suggesting that a self-report inventory could ever replace an experiment, but I am suggesting that the two modes of research can support one another (cf. Cronbach & Snow, 1977; Underwood, 1975). It is not difficult to routinely collect data regarding some of the personal attributes of the subjects in our learning strategies research. Certainly at the beginning of a learning strategies training program we are confronted by unique individuals who differ in some rather persistent ways. My intention has been to convince you that some of those individual differences are worthy of study because of the limits that they impose upon our training programs, and I have tried to suggest which individual differences are most measurable and most likely to interact with learning strategies.

REFERENCES

Bloom, B. (1956). *Taxonomy of educational objectives.* New York: David McKay.

Biggs, J. B. (1979). Individual differences in study processes and the quality of the learning outcome. *Higher Education, 8,* 381–394.

Biggs, J. B. (in press). The role of metalearning in study processes. *British Journal of Educational Psychology.*

Bransford, J. (1979). *Human cognition: Learning, understanding, and remembering.* Belmont, CA: Wadsworth.

Cattell, R. B., & Eber, H. W. (1962). Manual for Forms A and B of the Sixteen Personality Factor Questionnaire. Champaign, IL: Institute for Personality and Ability Testing.

Coopersmith, S. (1967). *The antecedents of self-esteem.* San Francisco: Freeman.

Craik, F. I. M., & Tulving, E. (1975). Depth of processing and retention of words in episodic memory. *Journal of Experimental Psychology: General, 104,* 268–294.

Cronbach, L. J., & Snow, R. E. (1977). *Aptitudes and instructional methods: A handbook for research on interactions.* New York: Halstead Press.

Crowne, D., & Marlowe, D. (1964). *The approval motive.* New York: Wiley.

Das, J. P., Kirby, J. R., & Jarman, R. F. (1979). *Simultaneous and successive cognitive processes.* New York: Academic Press.

Domino, G. (1971). Interactive effects of achievement orientation and teaching style on academic achievement. *Journal of Educational Psychology, 62,* 427–431.

Eison, J. A. (1982). Educational and personal dimensions of learning and grade-oriented students. *Psychological Reports, 51,* 867–870.

Entwistle, N. J. (1981). *Styles of learning and teaching.* Chichester, England: Wiley.

Entwistle, N. J., & Koyeki, B. (1985). Relationships between school motivation, approaches to studying, and attainment among British and Hungarian adolescents. *British Journal of Educational Psychology, 55,* 1–10.

Entwistle, N., & Ramsden, P. (1982). *Understanding student learning.* London: Croom Helm.

Eysenck, H. J., & Claridge, C. (1962). The position of hysterics and dysthymics in a 2-dimensional framework of personality. *Journal of Abnormal and Social Psychology, 64,* 46–55.

Eysenck, H. J., & Eysenck, S. B. (1964). *Manual of the Eysenck Personality Inventory.* London: University of London Press.

Farley, F., & Gordon, N. J. (1981). *Psychology and education: The state of the union.* Berkeley, CA: McCutchan.

Francis, H. (1982). *Learning to read.* London: Allen and Unwin.

French, J. W., Ekstrom, R. B., & Price, L. A. (1963). Manual for Kit of Reference Tests for Cognitive Factors. Princeton, NJ: Educational Testing Service.

Gambrill, E. D., & Richey, C. A. (1975). An assertion inventory for use in assessment and research. *Behavior Therapy, 1,* 550–561.

Gough, H. G. (1957). *Manual for the California Personality Inventory.* Palo Alto, CA; Consulting Psychologists Press.

Gregorc, A. F. (1979). Learning–teaching styles: Their nature and effects. In J. W. Keefe (Ed.), *Student learning styles: Diagnosing and prescribing programs.* Reston, VA: National Association of Secondary School Principals.

Gregorc, A. F. (1982). Gregorc Style Delineator: Development, technical, and administration manual. Maynard, MA: Gabriel Systems, Inc.

Hunt, D. E. (1979). Learning style and student needs: An introduction to conceptual level. In J. W. Keefe (Ed.), *Student learning styles: Diagnosing and prescribing programs.* Reston, VA: National Association of Secondary School Principals.

Jenkins, J. J. (1979). Four points to remember: A tetrahedral model of memory experiments. In L. S. Cermak, & F. I. M. Craik (Eds.), *Levels of processing in human memory.* Hillsdale, NJ: Erlbaum.

Johns, J. L. (1980). First graders' concepts about print. *Reading Research Quarterly, 15,* 529–549.

Kernberg, O. (1980). *Internal world and external reality.* New York: Jason Aronson.

Krug, S. E. (1980). Clinical Analysis Questionnaire manual. Champaign, IL: Institute for Personality and Ability Testing, Inc.

Levin, J. R. (1982). Pictures as prose-learning devices. In A. Flammer, & W. Kintsch (Eds.), *Advances in psychology: Vol. 8, Discourse processing.* Amsterdam: North-Holland.

Lockhart, D., & Schmeck, R. (1984). Learning styles and classroom evaluation methods: Different strokes for different folks. *College Student Journal, 17,* 94–100.

Mandler, G., & Sarason, S. B. (1952). A study of anxiety and learning. *Journal of Abnormal and Social Psychology, 47,* 166–173.

Marton, F., & Saljo, R. (1976a). On qualitative differences in learning: I. Outcome & processes. *British Journal of Educational Psychology, 46,* 4–11.

Marton, F., & Saljo, R. (1976b). On qualitative differences in learning: II. Outcome as a function of the learner's conception of the task. *British Journal of Educational Psychology,* *46,* 115–127.

Marton, F., & Saljo, R. (1984). Approaches to learning. In F. Marton, D. J. Hounsell, & N. J. Entwistle (Eds.), *The experience of learning.* Edinburgh: Scottish Academic Press.

McClelland, D. C. (1961). *The achieving society.* New York: Van Nostrand.

Meier, S., & Schmeck, R. (1985). The burned out college student: A descriptive profile. *Journal of College Student Personnel,* 63–69.

Meier, S., McCarthy, P., & Schmeck, R. (1984). Validity of self-efficacy as a predictor of writing performance. *Cognitive Therapy and Research,* *8,* 107–120.

Meyers, M., & Paris, S. G. (1978). Children's metacognitive knowledge about reading. *Journal of Educational Psychology,* *70,* 680–690.

Ornstein, R. E. (1977). *The psychology of consciousness* (2nd Ed.). New York: Harcourt Brace & Jovanovich.

Parlett, M. R. (1970). The syllabus-bound student. In L. Hudson (Ed.), *The ecology of human intelligence.* Harmondsworth, England: Penguin.

Pask, G. (1976a). Styles and strategies of learning. *British Journal of Educational Psychology,* *46,* 128–148.

Pask, G. (1976b). Conversational techniques in the study and practice of education. *British Journal of Educational Psychology,* *45,* 12–25.

Perry, W. F. (1970). *Forms of intellectual and ethical development in the college years: A scheme.* New York: Holt, Rinehart, and Winston.

Piaget, J. (1963). *The origins of intelligence in children.* New York: Norton.

Prentsky, R. A. (1979). *The biological aspects of normal personality.* Baltimore: University Press.

Rotter, J. B. (1966). Generalized expectancies for internal versus external control of reinforcement. *Psychological Monographs,* *80,* (Whole No. 609).

Saljo, R. (1979). Learning in the learner's perspective: I. Some common-sense conceptions. Reports from the Institute of Education, University of Goteburg, Sweden.

Schmeck, R. (1981). Improving learning by improving thinking. *Educational Leadership,* *38,* 384–385.

Schmeck, R. (1983). Learning styles of college students. In R. Dillon, & R. Schmeck (Eds.), *Individual differences in cognition.* New York: Academic Press.

Schmeck, R., & Lockhart, D. (1983). Introverts and extraverts require different learning environments. *Educational Leadership,* *40,* 54–55.

Schmeck, R., & Meier, S. (1984). Self-reference as a learning strategy and a learning style. *Human Learning,* *3,* 9–17.

Schmeck, R., & Spofford, M. (1983). Depth of processing and encoding specificity: Does processing depth make a significant independent contribution to recall performance? *Resources in Education,* *1,* 1–2.

Schmeck, R., Ribich, F., & Ramanaiah, N. (1977). Development of a self-report inventory for assessing individual differences in learning processes. *Applied Psychological Measurement,* *1,* 413–431.

Shaw, T. (1984). *Differential effects of information processing style on client verbal behavior,* unpublished master's thesis, Southern Illinois University, Carbondale, Illinois.

Shostrom, E. L. (1965). A test for the measurement of self-actualization. *Educational and Psychological Measurement,* *24,* 207–218.

Snowman, J. (in press). Learning tactics and strategies. In G. D. Phye, & T. Andre (Eds.), *Cognitive instructional psychology: Components of classroom learning.* New York: Academic Press.

Spielberger, C. D., Gorsuch, R. L., & Luchene, R. (1970). *State-trait Anxiety Inventory manual.* Palo Alto, CA: Consulting Psychologists Press.

Tallmadge, G. K., & Shearer, J. W. (1969). Relationships among learning styles, instructional methods, and the nature of learning experiences. *Journal of Educational Psychology, 60,* 222–230.

Tallmadge, G. K., & Shearer, J. W. (1971). Interactive relationships among learner characteristics, types of learning, instructional methods, and subject matter variables. *Journal of Educational Psychology, 62,* 31–38.

Taylor, J. A. (1953). A personality scale of manifest anxiety. *Journal of Abnormal and Social Psychology, 48,* 285–290.

Torrance, E. P., Reynolds, C. R., Riegel, T., & Ball, O. (1977). Your style of learning and thinking: Forms A and B. *The Gifted Child Quarterly, 21,* 563–573.

Tresemer, D. (Ed.), (1976). Current trends in research on "fear of success." *Sex Roles, 2,* Whole issue.

Trown, E. A., & Leith, G. O. M. (1975). Decision rules for teaching strategies in primary schools. Personality-treatment interactions. *British Journal of Educational Psychology, 45,* 130–140.

Tulving, E., (1985). How many memory systems are there? *American Psychologist, 40,* 385–398.

Underwood, B. J. (1975). Individual differences as a crucible in theory construction. *American Psychologist, 30,* 128–134.

Voss, J. F., Tyler, S. W., & Yengo, L. A. (1983). Individual differences in the solving of social science problems. In R. Dillon, & R. Schmeck (Eds.), *Individual differences in cognition.* New York: Academic Press.

Watson, D., & Friend, R. (1969). Measurement of social-evaluative anxiety. *Journal of Consulting and Clinical Psychology, 33,* 448–457.

Watson, G., & Glaser, E. M. (1964). Watson-Glaser Critical Thinking Appraisal manual. New York: Harcourt Brace & World.

Zuckerman, M. (1971). Dimensions of sensation seeking. *Journal of Consulting and Clinical Psychology, 36,* 45–52.

IMPLICIT INSTRUCTION OF STRATEGIES FOR LEARNING FROM TEXT

Diane Lemonnier Schallert, Patricia A. Alexander, and Ernest T. Goetz

Imagine that you are looking through a camera that has a special type of lens that allows you to go from a very close-up look at pieces of the scene in front of you to a very global, all-encompassing view of the whole scene. A zoom lens, effective between the extremes of wide-angle and telephoto lenses, captures what we are describing here. Now imagine that the lens is focused on a printed sentence. What you see are the parts of the sentence and how they are fitted together. The sense of the sentence can perhaps be captured in this shot, but it is difficult to see either its full meaning or its full relevance as language that is communicating thought.

Now the camera zooms back and you can see the other sentences that surround the original line of print that you had in your viewfinder. Not only can you see the immediate sentences nearby, but also the format of the whole message, the way paragraphs are indicated, sections shown, and illustrations positioned next to the print. The familiarity of the format confirms your realization that your camera is focused on how an author has developed a particular message for a particular audience, with the overriding intention of informing the audience.

Your camera lens widens again and you see a young college student holding the textbook. It is at this point that you are reminded of the range of possible interpretations of the text that might result depending upon where your camera is pointed. It could be pointed at either an advanced- or an introductory-level student, at either a motivated or a bored and sleepy reader, at either a sophisticated and strategic learner or at a student who is not. In addition, you realize that the book might have been held by any number of people, an older returning student, a foreign student, a fifth-grader looking for some information for a class report, a teacher deciding whether to use the textbook for a course, an expert considering writing his or her own textbook on the same topic, or a text analyst. Different kinds and

LEARNING AND STUDY STRATEGIES: ISSUES IN ASSESSMENT, INSTRUCTION, AND EVALUATION

amounts of background knowledge and different intentions in reading the text passage might produce very different kinds of interactions with and interpretations of the text.

Once again your lens changes and now you see the student looking at the textbook while the teacher is explaining the diagram that appears on that page. Now you become concerned with how helpful (i.e., informative and readable) the text passage is with respect to fulfilling the needs the student develops as he or she interprets the teacher's instructional intentions for that passage. If the teacher implies or states directly that this portion of the text is very important because it will be the basis for many questions on an upcoming test, then the student may change his or her usual style of reading the textbook. Similarly, other messages from the teacher, such as those relating to importance, accuracy, and appeal, may influence the manner of the student's interaction with the textbook.

For our present purpose, this is the widest angle through which we want you to see. Of course, the lens might be opened further to present the influences that affect the teacher. These influences may include the curriculum package or the community standards and expectations of what to teach and what to accept from students. Perhaps, the lens might capture the social and intellectual milieu in which the textbook author, the teacher, and the student exist, thus allowing us to predict the kinds of information that will be emphasized, overlooked, or discarded as interaction with the text proceeds. With such a perspective, broad sociocultural influences on how information is constructed and transmitted would be the focus. For this particular essay, we want to concentrate on a narrower view of language use yet remain on a broader level than the text–reader interaction. The *shot* we will be discussing is of the textbook as it is used by students for instructional purposes largely determined by their teachers.

One more delimitation of our topic is necessary before we continue. In line with the topic of this volume, we will be discussing those aspects of the teacher's messages that have to do with strategic moves a student might or should make in order to use the textbook most effectively. By "strategic move" we mean differentiated processing activities that a student might employ to fulfill his or her intentions to learn from the text. Thus, we make contact with a growing literature related to metacognition and the role that metacognitive activities play in comprehension and retention. We adopt the distinction often made between reading for comprehension on the one hand, and on the other, reading for retention as well as comprehension, which is often called "studying." Study strategies have themselves been the focus of countless investigations, many of which predate our current conceptions of metacognition (see Anderson & Armbruster, 1982; and Goetz, 1984, for reviews).

These studies are important to theory development related to metacognition and to instructional models. They are also relevant in understanding the numerous programs on college campuses across the country devoted to remediating poor reading skills and ineffectual study habits. These courses and programs have existed for many years and have often remained surprisingly isolated from findings obtained in training studies. At their best, however, they incorporate sound instructional techniques to help students become more effective learners with an ongoing self-evaluation of the program and experimental testing of new components (cf. Dansereau, 1978; Dansereau, et al., 1979; Palincsar & Brown, 1984; Weinstein, 1978, 1982; Winograd & Hare, Ch. 8, this volume).

As effective as special learning strategy courses can be, their impact is limited by two factors. The first is that they reach a growing, but, nevertheless, still small proportion of college students. Thus, most students never make contact with a special curriculum designed to guide their use of textbooks. A second factor is the decontextualized nature of the instruction that is imparted in these courses. As much as instructors may strive to have students see how broadly the skills and approaches discussed in class can be applied to particular study situations, students are notorious for "compartmentalizing" what they are taught. Thus there is a rather large risk that, for many of the students, the training will not transfer to other learning situations, or that the transfer, when it does occur, will be incomplete, inappropriate, and short-lived.

In view of these rather disconcerting considerations, one might wonder how most students acquire purposive control of their reading and study habits. The working hypothesis that guided us in this project was that students may be exposed to contextualized instruction in strategic use of their textbook as an inherent aspect of content courses they are taking. Such instruction, we proposed, might vary widely in terms of its explicitness and extensiveness, but our initial guess was that it would be most often implicit and cursory. Two major sources of such instruction are the instructor who assigns the textbook and evaluates the effectiveness of the students' interaction with the text, and the textbook author who may influence the students by facilitating certain kinds of processing of the text. In this chapter, we will emphasize the role of the instructor and comment more briefly on the role of the author.

In the following sections, we will describe how we proceeded in our analyses of the strategic influences provided by instructors. Because we were attempting to construct a systematic, sociofunctional understanding of the context in which students encounter such influences, we took several approaches. First, we had a group of undergraduate education majors keep a diary for a 1-month period in which they recorded when and how each of their professors used or referred to the textbooks associated with the courses they were taking. These diary entries were coded in terms of empirically emergent categories representing the different ways and the frequency in which the instructors referred to the texts. Second, these same students were interviewed individually and asked to describe for each course, the degree of text–lecture and text–test match and how they used their text-books. Our intent in using the two different sources was that the diaries would provide a concurrent record of what students perceived their instruc-tors were telling them about the text; the interview, by contrast, would provide a summative perspective of the same.

The rationale for using students' perceptions of instructor behavior as the basis of our conclusions about instructors' strategic influences came directly from the system-oriented view we were espousing (cf. Bronfenbrenner, 1979). Since we were interested in messages that would have an effect on students, it seemed logical that those that were perceived as sufficiently clear and/or important to be noted by students would have more influence than messages not so observed by students. From these two data sources, we were hoping to obtain a picture of how students interpret their instructors' messages about strategic textbook usage. As a third data source, we inter-viewed a subset of the students' instructors, teachers of undergraduate liber-al arts and education courses, regarding the use of the textbooks in their courses.

In the following sections, we will describe, for each data source, how we obtained and coded our observations and the major patterns we see in our data. We will then summarize an investigation of college textbooks as possi-ble sources of strategic cues and present some tentative conclusions about how textbooks function in instructional settings and how students' strategic moves are encouraged, discouraged, or neglected in content courses.

I.   STUDENT DIARIES

A.   METHOD

1.   Subjects

The participants were 14 students taking an undergraduate education methods course in reading from the second author (two additional students had to be dropped due to failure to keep a usable diary). The participants were all women, all education majors, and all full-time students. Eleven students were between 19 and 21 years of age, and three were over 22. All were juniors or seniors. Their self-reported GPAs ranged from 2.1 to 3.9 with a mean of 2.97. Their areas of specialization within education were math education (nine students), English education (two), special education (two), and psychology (one).

2. Procedure

At one class meeting early in the semester, the students were given a brief description of our general interest and they were asked to keep a daily record, noting for each class each occasion when an instructor alluded to the textbook. They were told to identify the class and to give the date for each entry. Several times during the next 1-month period, the students were reminded to keep up their diaries. At the conclusion of the period, we collected the diaries as the students came in to be interviewed individually. The diaries were not discussed in the interview.

3. Coding

In coding the diaries, we made some preliminary decisions. We excluded all entries that involved the Reading Methods class itself, those that were in reference to a tutorial self-paced course involving remedial English that two of the students were taking, and the two entries that one student made with reference to her art class. We eliminated entries where the students reported they had been absent, class had been cancelled for the day, or a test had taken up the whole class period. Also, if a student made no mention whatsoever for a particular class, that potential diary entry was not counted. Since the entries coded were a subset of the total possible entries, the categories we formed to represent the kinds of uses of text reported by students, as well as the frequencies we tallied for each category, represent a subset of the students' experiences.

In Table 1, we list the categories we saw reflected in the diaries. The first three are grouped together because these entries indicated that the text had been discussed in detail during classtime and implied that the students had their textbooks open during the lecture. To corroborate this inference, we point to the fact that the four instances where instructors directly requested that students bring their textbooks to class (Category 13) occurred in conjunction with a text reference that fell into one of these three categories. In the following discussion, when we refer to direct uses of the textbook, we mean events that fall into these three categories.

The next five categories are grouped together because they represent more general references to the textbook in relation to course activities. In this instance, the textbook seems to be helping the teacher manage the

TABLE 1 Empirically Emergent Categories from Student Diaries

Function	Category
Direct use of textbook	1. T[a] explains maps, graphs, charts, or photos in textbook. 2. T explains examples, theorems, sections, or appendices. 3. T cites actual lines.
Use of textbook to manage course content	4. T refers to text, indicating its relationship with lecture content or course organization. 5. T refers students to the text for additional information on a topic. 6. T tells students how to read particular portions of text. 7. T gives, changes, or reminds students of reading assignment. 8. T gives homework assignment from text involving other than simply reading the text.
Reference to textbook in relation to tests	9. T gives specific information about sections of chapters that will appear on the test. 10. T gives or reminds students of which chapters to study for a test. 11. T states how much of the test will come from the textbook.
	12. T makes some evaluative comment about the textbook. 13. T asks the students directly to bring their textbooks to class.

[a]T: teacher.

content of the course. The five categories reflect a continuum that represents how relevant the textbook is to the concepts being discussed by the teacher in the lecture.

The third major grouping covers those teacher references that indicate in some way how the textbook will be relevant for tests. Again, a continuum emerges, reflecting, this time, degrees of specificity with which the text is tied to the test. Thus, Category 9 represents instances where an instructor tells students what parts of a chapter will be relevant for a test; Category 10 represents more general assignments on the order of which chapters will be covered by the next test; and Category 11 refers to even more comprehensive statements of how important the textbook is for the test, that is, for example, how much of the test will come from the textbook.

The last two categories could not be grouped, in our opinion, either with each other or with the previous three major groupings. Category 12 was used to code instructor statements that were evaluative in nature (e.g., "Definitions in the book don't thrill me," "Your author did a poor job of Chapter 7," "They do a nice job with the pictures in the book."). Category 13 referred to requests to the students to bring their textbooks to class.

4. Data Grouping

Collectively, the students were taking 56 courses, after the exclusion of Reading Methods, remedial English, and art (see coding section above). Each student contributed from three to five courses, with nine of the 14 participants reporting on four courses. These courses were then aggregated into what we considered reasonably sized groupings reflecting natural divisions according to academic disciplines. Since 12 of the students were taking a course on methods for teaching language arts, and nine were taking a methods course for teaching social studies (though, in neither case, from just one instructor), the data for each of these two courses were analyzed separately, as reflected by the Language Arts Methods and Social Science Methods divisions. Eight students were taking curriculum-related education courses, grouped together as Other Education. The Social Science grouping ($n = 7$) included such courses as educational psychology, sociology, and Texas history. The Other Science grouping ($n = 7$) included such courses as ecology, Texas geography, and human sexuality. Note that none of our students were taking more typical natural science courses in biology, physics, chemistry, or geology. The Mathematics group ($n = 6$) represented courses offered through the mathematics department and the final group ($n = 7$) represented courses offered through English.

B. Results

In Table 2, we report the frequencies with which students reported their instructors' references to the textbook. Each frequency is corrected for the number of student–courses (i.e., one student taking one course) that appeared in course groupings. Thus, the numbers represent the mean frequency with which a student reported a particular kind of textbook reference in one course over the total 1-month period.

Some patterns are worth noting in these frequencies. As one would expect, English literature instructors cite the text verbatim (Category 3) much more frequently than do other instructors. Math professors use sections of the text mainly as a basis of direct explanation during class (Category 2); more so than any other group of instructors. Instructors of Other Education courses (not including the Language Arts and Social Studies Methods) generally refer to the text very infrequently. By contrast, teachers of Language Arts and Social Studies Methods courses make varied and frequent use of the textbooks.

On the whole, teachers made most use of the textbook for managing course content (Categories 4 to 8; 5.13 mean total references per student–course), and they referred least often to how the textbook would be reflected

TABLE 2 Frequency per Student–Course of Instructors' Cues to Strategic Moves as Reported in Students' Diaries[a]

Course groupings	Direct use of textbook			Use of textbook to manage course content					Reference to text for tests				
	1	2	3	4	5	6	7	8	9	10	11	12	13
Language arts methods (n = 12)	.17	3.08	.42	3.92	1.08	.50	1.67	.33	.33	.42	.25	.25	.17
Social studies methods (n = 9)	.11	.56	.11	3.56	.33	.11	1.67	.00	.11	.78	.56	.78	.00
Other education courses (n = 8)	.00	1.00	.25	1.50	.00	.12	.62	.25	.50	.25	.00	.25	.00
Social sciences (n = 7)	.14	.14	.00	4.43	.86	.29	1.14	.14	.14	.57	1.00	.43	.00
Other sciences (n = 7)	3.14	.57	.00	1.43	.86	.00	1.00	.43	.43	.00	.29	.29	.00
Mathematics (n = 6)	.33	7.83	.00	2.50	.17	.00	2.17	2.17	1.17	.17	.00	.33	.17
English (n = 6)	.00	.29	3.00	.42	.00	.00	1.14	.29	.00	.00	.14	.29	.00
Mean total per student course	.50	1.86	.52	2.68	.52	.18	1.36	.45	.36	.34	.32	.38	.05
Mean total per category		2.88				5.13				1.02			

[a]Each type of strategic cue is briefly described in Table 1.

on tests (Categories 9–11; 1.02 mean total references per student–course). As shown in Table 3, the relative weighting of each of these three general functions for the textbook differed across course groupings. Relatively little direct use of the text was reported for the Social Science courses, the Social Studies Methods course, and the Other Education courses. The instructors of these courses were more likely to use the text for course content management purposes. Students in courses represented by the Other Science, Mathematics, and English groupings reported a generally equal number of instances of direct, in-class use of the text, and use of the text for the more general course-management, course-organization function. In these courses, there was a relatively low frequency of reported statements about text–test relationships. The Language Arts Methods course appears much more like this latter grouping of courses than like Other Education or Social Science courses.

In summarizing these findings, we point again to the relative preponderance of teacher statements that reflect reliance on the textbook and its content to organize and manage course activities and the relative dearth of statements about the relationship between texts and tests. Two qualifications should be kept in mind in interpreting these findings. First is the infrequency with which any text reference occurred. In a 1-month period, students reported on the average a little more than nine specific instances per course of the instructors referring to the textbook in any way. Second is the nature of the data. The diary entries depend upon students perceiving that an instructor has alluded to the text and then choosing to note the reference. From these data, we have no way of knowing how often and in what way instructors actually referred to the text.

Given these caveats, we come to a final observation about students' diary records of teacher reference to texts. Rarely did we find in the diaries any

TABLE 3   Proportion of Student-Reported Instructor References to Text

Course groupings	Direct use of textbook	Use of textbook to manage course content	Reference to textbook in relation to tests
Language arts methods (n = 12)	.30	.62	.08
Social studies methods (n = 9)	.10	.72	.18
Other education (n = 8)	.28	.55	.17
Social science (n = 7)	.03	.77	.19
Other sciences (n = 7)	.45	.46	.09
Mathematics (n = 6)	.49	.42	.08
English (n = 7)	.62	.35	.03

report of an instructor giving explicit suggestions of how to go about reading a text. Our closest candidate is Category 6, which we found reflected in only ten of the 532 codeable entries reported by all the students for all the courses. Thus, the type of direction instructors provide to students to help them in using their textbooks strategically is indirect; instructors may identify *what* is important, but not *how* a student might go about studying what is important.

II. STUDENT INTERVIEWS

A. METHOD

The same students who provided the diary records of instructor reference to text were interviewed and asked a number of questions aimed at eliciting, in general, how their textbooks functioned in the courses they were taking. All students were interviewed individually on the same day, in a private office, by the first author. The interviews generally took approximately 30 minutes and followed the same format. Students first listed the courses they were taking. Then, for each course, they were asked the following:

1. How their grade was to be determined;
2. Whether a textbook was associated with the class;
3. How much they needed their textbook to understand lectures, to prepare for tests, and to fulfill other assignments;
4. How much overlap there was between lecture and textbook content, and between test and textbook material;
5. How they went about reading and/or studying their textbook;
6. How much help they received from their instructors in knowing what and how to study from the textbook;
7. Whether they made use of a study guide to help them study their textbook;
8. What their opinion of the textbook was.

Next, the students projected what grade they would receive in each course, whether such a grade would be difficult to attain, and whether they would be satisfied with the grade. Finally, they answered two general questions: (1) what is one feature that would help you use your textbooks better; and (2) do you think that in certain courses you use your textbook in different ways?

Though care was taken to attempt to get students to answer all questions, there were still difficulties. Some students answered more than one question with one statement. Some were very talkative and others were more reticent. Thus, when the interviews were coded, there were frequent occasions when a student's response to a particular question for a particular course could not be determined. The general impression we formed, however, was that students had been interested in the interview and had participated as fully as they were capable. Also, they seemed to find the questions we asked reasonable and to know quite clearly what was going on in each of their courses.

B. RESULTS

For manageability purposes, the data were grouped according to the same course groupings used for the diaries. Throughout all the courses they were taking, none of the students expected a grade lower than a B, and only for Mathematics courses did a clear majority of the students expect a B. Very few students reported they would be dissatisfied with the grade they expected to receive and less than half (46%) of the students thought it would be difficult to get the grade they expected. For most courses, students reported that they had one textbook assigned. For nine of the 56 courses represented, students had two textbooks, and for one course, four textbooks were reported. In three of the courses described, readings from journals and anthologies were used rather than a textbook.

As a way of organizing the students' responses to the interview, we will examine the students' perception of instructor-provided cues to (1) the relationship between the text and the lectures, (2) the relationship between the text and tests, and (3) strategic moves appropriate for text usage.

1. Text—Lecture Relationship

The first set of responses referred generally to the extent to which lectures "covered" textbook content. For the Other Science courses, students reported that most teachers (71%) used the textbook very little during their lectures. Similarly, most Social Science instructors (71%) were reported to show little overlap between textbook and lecture content. Education courses (Language Arts Methods, Social Studies Methods, and Other Education groupings), by contrast, were reported to have a much greater degree of overlap, with students reporting that their instructors used the textbook extensively but also elaborated and extended beyond the text or that their instructors "went exactly by the book" or "taught the book" (67%). The latter comment generally meant something slightly different for the Mathematics (100%) and English (43%) than for education courses. In these courses, students reported that instructors "explained" the textbook or "analyzed" the text.

A second way of exploring the text–lecture relationship was to code whether students mentioned having to read the text before going to class. Students taking Other Science and Mathematics courses reported they seldom needed to read the text before class (14 and 17%, respectively). Education courses, on the other hand, were more likely to be seen as requiring textbook preparation before class (Language Arts Methods: 42%; Social Studies Methods: 44%; Other Education: 62%).

Finally, we looked at whether students reported actually using the textbook during class. Although we were unable to determine the answer to that question in quite a few cases, we point to the 100% reported use in Mathematics courses and the very high (44%) reported use in the Social Studies methods course, with much lower frequencies ranging from 0 to 28% in the other course groupings.

2. Text–Test Relationship

During the interview, students consistently reported that performance on tests and other assignments were important grading components. When asked to comment on the significance of the textbook for performance on the tests, they answered most often by talking about the proportion of the test questions that would come from the textbook. The reported importance of the textbook for test performance was very high for Social Studies Methods (100%), Mathematics (100%), Language Arts Methods (75%) and Other Education (75%), moderate for Social Science and English courses (57% for both), and very low for Other Science courses (28%). In fact, such test–text relationships seemed to have quite practical consequences in that the two students who reported that no questions on the test came from the textbook had not even bought the textbook.

Next, we looked for evidence that students used their textbooks for other assignments in a particular class. The pattern that emerged was similar to that found for the use of textbooks during class time. All students taking mathematics courses reported using the textbook for other assignments and nearly half of those in the Language Arts Methods course did the same. Otherwise, we could not determine from the interviews whether students used their textbooks for any other assignments besides simply reading and studying.

3. Reported Strategic Influence

Here we were looking for any indication from the students that their interactions with the textbook were purposive and active. We looked for such indications by asking the students how they went about reading and studying their textbooks and by looking for evidence of teacher or textbook author guides to strategic uses of the text.

Let us consider the second part of the question first. Across the 56 student courses represented, only one student for one course reported that there was a published study guide available. However, she had not bought it since its use was optional for the course. In terms of helping students read their textbooks in purposeful ways, teachers provided syllabi that had the reading assignments listed. For only nine of the 56 student–courses represented was there no syllabus. However, most syllabi simply gave the reading assignment. Five students, all taking the Language Arts Methods course, reported that their syllabus also listed instructional objectives and nine students reported that, in addition to objectives, their syllabus for a particular course listed study questions (seven in Social Studies Methods, one in Language Arts Methods, one in Other Sciences). When looking for evidence that teachers were directly helpful during classtime in guiding students' reading of their textbooks, we found that students had provided some relevant statement for only half of the student–courses. Their statements indicated that the kind of help teachers gave mostly involved identifying what would be important to study for the test.

Turning next to the question of how students reported they studied their textbooks outside of class, most students told us they highlighted their textbooks, with notetaking (including outlining) also frequently reported (see Table 4). Only for the Mathematics and English groupings of courses were these two methods of studying reported relatively infrequently. Most students in Mathematics courses reported "using" the text rather than studying or reading it. The least active kind of reading seemed to occur for English courses. We find this last observation interesting in view of the fact that students were more likely to report direct, in-class uses of the textbook for English courses than for most other courses. Yet, their reading outside of class seemed to involve them in the least activity. We also found it interesting that some students reported one method of using their textbooks for all their courses, whereas others showed much more differentiated approaches. Of those, the more active kind of studying, as represented in taking notes and making an outline, occurred for courses where the textbook was more important to test performance.

As a final task, students responded to two general questions. The first asked them to recommend an improvement that would facilitate their use of textbooks. The 14 students gave a total of 19 different recommendations, which we reduced to three general problem areas. The first, represented by more than half of the statements, related to a need expressed by the students to know more clearly what was important and what was supplementary in what they were reading. Here, the students requested of textbook authors (and sometimes of their teachers) a better use of objectives, summaries, outlines and study guides. Implicit in their comments was the motivator of having to take tests. The second general group involved recommendations to

TABLE 4   Reported Strategies in Reading Textbooks outside of Class[a]

Course groupings	Did not look at text 1	Read and/or reread 2	Read and highlighted 3	Read and took notes 4	Read only portions 5
Language arts methods (n = 12)	8%	—	50%	42%	—
Social studies methods (n = 9)[b]	—	—	44%	22%	22%
Other education (n = 8)	—	25%	38%	38%	—
Social science (n = 7)	—	14%	28%	57%	—
Other science (n = 7)	14%	—	57%	14%	14%
Mathematics (n = 6)	—	—	—	33%	66%[c]
English[b] (n = 7)	—	43%	14%	—	14%

[a]Percentages represent the proportion of students in each course grouping who gave each response.

[b]For one person in Social Studies Methods and two people in English, interview protocols do not reveal an answer to this question.

[c]Students said they did not read and study the textbook, but used it to do problems to prepare for tests.

change the wording, to make the language more accessible and less "intellectual" as one of our students put it. The last set was represented by just two statements and dealt with the ideas presented. One student asked that authors make sure they explain and not just state their points and another student saw a need to improve the flow from one idea to the next.

When asked whether they saw that textbooks were used differently in different courses, 12 of the students said yes and, of these, six identified mathematics courses as the truly different occasion of use. The remaining six students mentioned that professors differed widely in the degree to which they either lectured "straight from the book" or used the textbook as a supplement.

On the whole, students appeared to be quite sophisticated in determining what was going on in their courses and in regulating their textbook reading to meet their expectations. The strategic influences they reported seemed generally thin, although effective, in getting across teacher expectations. These expectations, from the students' perspective, seemed most clearly to focus on *what* to study and *why* to study, that is, the consequences in terms of evaluation that would follow from studying the textbook. *How* to study did not appear to be an important part of instructors' or of authors' strategic influence, in the students' opinions.

III. INSTRUCTOR INTERVIEWS

A. METHOD

Five of the instructors who had taught courses taken by the student participants were interviewed in a format similar to the one used for the students. Interviews were conducted in the instructors' own offices by the first author and lasted no more than 30 minutes. Questions dealt with the three general areas identified in the student interview data: (1) what is the role of the textbook in lecture and classtime activities; (2) to what degree do tests depend upon material presented in the textbook; and (3) are there specific ways in which the instructor helps students study from their textbooks. Two of the instructors taught courses in our Social Science groupings and one representing each of our Mathematics, English, and Language Arts Methods groupings participated.

B. RESULTS

Instructors varied widely in the reported role of the textbook in determining class time course content. The mathematics and English instructors reported that they spent most class periods explaining in detail what was in the text. For example, the mathematics instructor specifically stated that he felt the book was hard to read for this audience. Therefore, he believed his role in class was to make the exposition of the book less obscure, and to help the students see the logical undergirding of the concepts presented in the book. By contrast, the two social science instructors viewed the textbook as a supplement to lecture content and an overall guide to the choice of topics to be presented in lecture. Both reported that they felt no need for the students to bring their textbooks to class. Finally, the education professor fell somewhere in between. She wanted students to have the textbook in class to have access to certain exercises and samples of curriculum. She reported that she followed the organization of the book but spent the majority of class time in developing applications and extensions of what was presented in the book.

All five instructors claimed that the textbook was significantly represented on tests. Three of the instructors mentioned that questions testing textbook content dealt more with details, with "memory" work, than with generalizations. Four of the instructors also gave essay-type questions that required an integration of lecture and textbook content and an analysis or application of the concepts presented.

In terms of any explicit direction to students in how to study from the textbooks, four of the instructors reported that they made such suggestions, but only in conjunction with preparing students for tests. These suggestions ranged from giving examples of the types of textbook questions that might appear on tests, to telling the students to read the books' lists of objectives, summaries, and key terms before reading the chapters, to telling them to read "with pen in hand" (in mathematics) to work out problems as they appeared in the text. The one instructor who reported giving no strategic help to students said that the textbook itself was unusually helpful in directing students' interaction with it.

To summarize the impression we formed from our interviews with the teachers, we came to the conclusion that students and instructors were in close agreement; instructors do not spend much time training students in *how* to study from their textbooks. Except for the mathematics course, strategic cues are directed more to the identification of *what* to study.

IV.   GENERAL DISCUSSION

We embarked on this project for two related reasons. First, we were concerned that special learning strategy courses, for all the effort their instructors and participants expend, serve only a minor role in improving students' success in using their textbooks effectively in their college program. For one thing, the majority of students do not take these courses; for another, there are problems with the transferability of the skills and strategies acquired to "regular" courses. Finally, the instructional goals of these courses may not be aligned with the actual needs of the students taking them. Therefore, we wanted to examine the instruction in regular content courses to see if students, in fact, receive implicit instruction in how to use their texts strategically.

Second, we were interested in gaining an understanding of how textbooks function in the cognitive, sociofunctional system that is represented by a college course. An examination of how textbooks are used can provide a framework for identifying how well the texts suit the students' needs. Although analyses of the text in isolation may identify features of text that are correlated with student difficulties in learning (cf. Gagné & Bell, 1981; Schallert & Tierney, 1982), it may be that, in actuality, the text is used in such a way that its troublesome features are not an impediment to success in the course (cf. Schallert & Lawrence, 1984).

We chose to pursue these issues by (1) having students record in-class instructor references to the textbooks; (2) interviewing the students regarding the use they and their instructors made of the textbooks associated with their courses; and (3) interviewing the students' instructors to check the degree to which they encouraged strategic use of the textbooks. Through students' diaries, we found that instructors did not allude to the textbook very often and when they did, their statements were more likely to relate to general management of course content than to direct class time use or to how the textbook was to be used in preparation for tests. In their interviews, however, the students clearly indicated that textbook use was determined by its importance for evaluation purposes. Thus we might say that students had gathered from their instructors what to study and why to study (what consequences were associated with studying). The "how" of studying, however, was rarely mentioned. Students reported a reliance on highlighting and outlining the text. Other, "fancier" techniques were not mentioned. Our interviews with the instructors corroborated the view of strategy instruction so far depicted. Instructors were uniformly likely to make textbook reading important by including text-based questions on tests. They were also likely to indicate to students what would be covered on the tests and what portions of the textbooks were critical. However, they were much less explicit in giving students instruction in how to go about reading and studying from the textbook.

A. What about the Textbook Author?

If college instructors provide their students little guidance in how to study their texts, perhaps textbook authors are more helpful. Recently, we examined college texts for strategy cues that authors embedded in their textbooks with the intent of making the text more comprehensible and instructive for their audience (Goetz et al., 1987). We selected five currently popular undergraduate textbooks in both biology and psychology. For each text, chapters from the first, middle, and final one-third of the book were identified and from each chapter, pages at the beginning and end of the chapter as well as a sample of contiguous pages randomly selected from the remainder of the chapter were analyzed. We began our analysis by generating a list of 28 categories of possible strategy cues—cues that reflected author intentions to encourage readers to be actively involved in processing the text. Two of the original categories (advance organizers and guided imagery) were dropped because they never appeared in our samples while two additional types were discovered and added to the list.

We combined the cues into six groups according to their primary function in the text. The first group, comprised of strategy cues that served to focus reader attention on particular concepts in the text, included objectives, questions, boldface, and italics. The second group included strategy cues meant to help the reader see how text material was related to familiar information, including familiar quotes, allusions to common experiences, and comparisons. Cues in the third group—humor, unreferenced illustrations, and photographs—all seemed intended to arouse and keep the interest of readers. The fourth group involved the use of graphics (e.g., referenced drawings and photographs, graphs, and tables). In the fifth group, we included examples of authors' restatement or elaboration of a concept by giving examples, paraphrases, applications, and marginal comments. The final grouping of strategy cues were those that signaled the content or organization of a portion of text and included titles, headings, summaries, overviews, outlines, intertextual references, and text-to-graphic references.

Analysis of the text samples revealed a fair number and variety of strategy cues, ranging from fewer than eight to more than 16 per page for the texts analyzed. In terms of the relative frequency of cues, we found that psychology authors, on the average, employed 45% of their strategic cues to focus attention, 28% to give organization, 10% to transform information textually, and then much smaller and relatively equal numbers of cues to relate the text to the reader (3%), enhance interest (6%), or transform information graphically (5%). Biology authors used the organization aids and attention-focusing cues nearly equally (31 and 29%, respectively) and the two information transformation strategies comparatively more often than psychology authors (textual: 22%; graphic: 11%). Their use of strategy cues involved in relating the text to the reader (5%) and enhancing interest (2%) was much lower.

Thus, despite differences across disciplines among the texts we analyzed, it appeared that the types of cues represented generally required little effort and activity from readers. Pictures and graphics were provided. Directed imagery, where an author might ask readers to imagine or construct a mental representation, was never used in our sample. Summaries were provided, but readers were not asked to summarize for themselves. The application strategy was used very infrequently. The most effort-demanding cues that were used with any substantial frequency were questions to be answered by the reader. These usually were found at the ends of chapters and may have been easily overlooked during studying. It should be noted that such a passive view of readers is not inherent to the textbook format. A few textbooks exist (see, for example, Bransford's *Human Cognition*, 1979, and E. Gagné's *The Cognitive Psychology of School Learning*, 1984) where authors are much more forceful in encouraging students to be active in processing the text.

Our examination of strategic cues suggests that, like college instructors, authors attempt to mark for students important information to be studied but provide little direction or prompting regarding how it might be studied. Thus it appears that authors, like instructors, have done little to implement the recent emphasis on the role of active, elaborative, generative processing by the student in effective learning (cf. Goetz, 1984; Weinstein, 1982; Wittrock, Ch. 16, this volume). With respect to the students' suggestions for improving the utility of textbooks (in our interviews), authors seem responsive to some degree to the desire of the students for organizational guides and importance markers, but less forthcoming with respect to their desire for more accessible text. Cues directed at relating the text material to familiar information and enhancing student interest would seem particularly germaine, but such cues were used sparingly in our sample of texts.

B. CONCLUSIONS

A summary compiled by Brown et al. (1984) of the functions of strategies likely to be of some importance when readers are attempting to learn from text, allows us to understand more clearly what our students, instructors, and authors were doing in terms of strategic use of textbooks. The list includes:

1. Clarifying the purposes of reading, i.e., understanding the task demands, both explicit and implicit.
2. Activating relevant background knowledge.
3. Allocating attention so that concentration can be focused on the major content at the expense of trivia.
4. Critical evaluation of content for internal consistency and compatibility with prior knowledge and common sense.
5. Monitoring ongoing activities to see if comprehension is occurring by engaging in such activities as periodic review and self-interrogation.
6. Drawing and testing inferences of many kinds, including interpretations, predictions, and conclusions (p. 263).

In our data, we found that in regular college-level content courses, most instruction about strategic interactions with text was related to the first three functions in the above list. Our students seemed to have a clear idea of why they might need to read their textbooks. Textbook authors did make use (however slight) of cues that might have helped readers activate relevant background knowledge. Finally, authors, students, and instructors seemed to concentrate their efforts toward strategic use of text by focusing their attention on key ideas and concepts, number three in Brown, Plincsar, and Armbruster's list. The other three types of strategies did not appear in our data.

A second way of understanding our results is to analyze them in view of a model of studying presented by Biggs (1984). The critical component of the model we see reflected is that of differential strategies that students choose depending upon their motives. Students will not choose to fully understand a text (what *this* means in all its complexity is still being investigated), except under rather rare circumstances where such understanding is made important to fulfill students' intentions either to get the grade they find acceptable or to understand the material to the degree they find satisfying. In a student's life, where time is a most precious commodity, many interactions with text are less than perfect. Yet, most still allow students to be generally satisfied with their performance.

C.   Recommendations

The last topic we want to discuss involves recommendations we might make to textbook authors, to instructors of content courses, and, finally, to instructors of special strategy courses to help them be more effective with students. Authors and instructors must be aware of the fact that the books they write, and the books that they employ in their instruction, do not function in isolation. Textbooks are but one component in the instructional system. Therefore, it is essential to look at the text in light of the function it serves within this system.

Specifically, to textbook authors we would recommend that they embed more elaborative processing cues in their textual content. In the texts we examined, it seems apparent that the emphasis fell most heavily in the attention-focusing category. While this is not, in and of itself, detrimental, it would seem that more emphasis could be directed toward strategic cues within the categories of "Information Transformation," or "Relating Text to Reader." Helping readers to process the information in some alternate form, to apply what has been read, or to relate it to their prior experiences would seem likely to enhance learning. In addition, textbook authors should be mindful of the audience to whom they are writing. In the various textbooks we analyzed (Goetz et al., in press), we frequently felt that the student was overlooked. For example, most of the prefaces and introductions we read were addressed to instructors considering adoption of the text rather than the students who would be learning from that text.

There are additional recommendations that we can make to content area teachers. First, teachers might provide more explicit instruction to students as to how they should use the text. If the goal is to enhance students' learning from text, then it may not be sufficient to assign readings. Even in college, most students may require more guidance and for younger, less experienced students, the need for additional guidance is still greater. While we would not expect regular classroom teachers to become study skills instructors, it does seem that they could provide students with some direct instruction in studying as it relates to a particular text and content. From what we have found, even a *small* increase in this type of explicit instruction would probably be a significant improvement. Regular classroom teachers cannot assume that this type of knowledge is possessed by students, nor can they assume that textbooks will provide learners sufficient strategic cues.

Finally, to instructors of special strategy courses, we offer several recommendations. As was pointed out in various chapters within this text and elsewhere, strategy training should be integrated into the instructional system if we expect learners to acquire the habit of being strategic. As long as we isolate learning and study strategy training from the rest of the instructional system, it is not likely that learners, especially those enrolled in study skills courses, will naturally transfer that training to other domains. Study course instructors can assist in this transfer by making contact with aspects of the existing instructional system in which their students are immersed. These instructors should refer to the actual learning tasks students are required to perform in their regular content area classes. Rather than having students practice various study skills with contrived texts, they should have them identify and practice strategies that would be appropriate for the texts and for the tasks they are actually involved with in their classes. This would seem to be more readily accomplished by having study course instructors work closely with content area instructors. These two groups can then work cooperatively to identify aspects of texts and of courses that give students problems, so that these aspects can form the basis of study skills instruction. Perhaps, study course instructors would become more effective if they thought of themselves as coaches to students and as consultants to content area instructors to help both function optimally in the instructional system.

REFERENCES

Anderson, T. H., & Armbruster, B. B. (1982). Reader and text: Studying strategies. In W. Otto, & S. White (Eds.), *Reading expository material* (pp. 219–242). New York: Academic Press.

Biggs, J. B. (1984). Learning strategies, student motivation patterns, and subjectively perceived success. In J. R. Kirby (Ed.), *Cognitive strategies and educational performance* (pp. 11–134). Orlando: Academic Press.

Bransford, J. D. (1979). *Human cognition.* Belmont, CA.: Wadsworth Publishing Co.

Bronfenbrenner, U. (1979). *The ecology of human development.* Cambridge: Harvard University Press.

Brown, A. L., Palincsar, A. S., & Armbruster, B. B. (1984). Instructing comprehension fostering activities in interactive learning situations. In H. Mandl, N. Stein, & T. Trabasso (Eds.), *Learning and comprehension of text.* (pp. 255–286). Hillsdale, NJ: Erlbaum.

Dansereau, D. F. (1978). The development of learning strategies curriculum. In H. F. O'Neil (Ed.), *Learning strategies*. New York: Academic Press.

Dansereau, D. F., McDonald, B. A., Collins, K. W., Garland, J., Holley, C. D., Dickhoff, G. M., & Evans, S. H. (1979). Evaluation of a learning strategy system. In H. F. O'Neil, Jr., & C. E. Speilberger (Eds.), *Cognitive and affective learning strategies* (pp. 3–44). New York: Academic Press.

Gagné, E. D. (1984). *The cognitive psychology of school learning*. Boston: Little, Brown & Company.

Gagné, E. D., & Bell, M. S. (1981). The use of cognitive psychology in the development and evaluation of textbooks. *Educational Psychologist, 16*, 83–100.

Goetz, E. T. (1984). The role of spatial strategies in processing and remembering text: A cognitive information processing analysis. In C. D. Holley, & D. F. Dansereau (Eds.), *Spatial learning strategies: Techniques, applications, and related issues* (pp. 47–77). Orlando: Academic Press.

Goetz, E. T., Alexander, P. A., & Schallert, D. L. (1987). The author's role in cueing strategic processing of college textbooks. *Reading Research and Instruction, 27*, 1–11.

Palincsar, A. S., & Brown, A. L. (1984). Reciprocal teaching of comprehension-fostering and comprehension-monitoring activities. *Cognition & Instruction, 1*, 117–175.

Schallert, D. L., & Lawrence, B. J. (1984). The demands of informative text, paper presented at the annual meeting of the American Educational Research Association, New Orleans.

Schallert, D. L., & Tierney, R. J. (1982). Learning from expository text: The interaction of text structure with reader characteristics, final report to the National Institute of Education, NIE-C–79-0167.

Weinstein, C. E. (1978). Elaboration skills as a learning strategy. In H. F. O'Neil, Jr. (Ed.), *Learning strategies* (pp. 31–56). New York: Academic Press.

Weinstein, C. E. (1982). Training students to use elaboration learning strategies. *Contemporary Educational Psychology, 7*, 301–311.

APPLICATIONS OF LEARNING STRATEGIES BY STUDENTS LEARNING ENGLISH AS A SECOND LANGUAGE

J. Michael O'Malley, Rocco P. Russo, Anna Uhl Chamot, and Gloria Stewner-Manzanares

Learning strategies may assist students in mastering the forms and functions required for comprehension and production in second language acquisition (Rubin, 1981). Strategies have been used in learning the language required for integrative tasks, such as speaking or listening, as well as for discrete language tasks, such as vocabulary and pronunciation (Naiman et al., 1978). Learning strategies may be effective for learning foreign languages or for learning English as a second language. However, the types of strategies that are effective for specific language-learning tasks, and the effectiveness of strategy training among second language learners need to be examined in detail before strategy use is prescribed in teaching.

This paper describes two studies designed to examine the usefulness of learning strategies for second language learners. The first study was a descriptive analysis of strategies used by students learning English as a second language (ESL), and the second was an experimental study in which ESL students were trained to use learning strategies on different academic language tasks for vocabulary, listening, and speaking.

I. REVIEW OF LITERATURE

The rationale for expecting that learning strategies may be useful for second language learners lies in part with theoretical developments in second language acquisition and in part with evidence accumulating from recent studies in second language acquisition. In the following sections, we identify selected theoretical positions in second language acquisition that incorporate a cognitive component and discuss some of the literature sug-

LEARNING AND STUDY STRATEGIES: ISSUES IN
ASSESSMENT, INSTRUCTION, AND EVALUATION

gesting that learning strategies play an important role in learning second languages.

A. SELECTED REVIEW OF MODELS OF SECOND LANGUAGE ACQUISITION

Fillmore and Swain (1984) have proposed a theoretical model suggesting that the rate and level of second language learning is due to the interaction of social, linguistic, and cognitive processes. The cognitive component is salient in assisting the learner to identify and learn the linguistic components that are required to use a second language in achieving social purposes. Bialystok (1978, 1981) has proposed four categories of learning strategies as being instrumental in second language acquisition. The categories are inferencing (using contextual cues in guessing), monitoring (reviewing comprehension or production for accuracy), formal practicing (grammar or other classroom drills), and functional practicing (or practicing outside of didactic settings). Bialystok suggests that learning strategies may be useful in gaining both explicit linguistic knowledge (forms and functions) and implicit linguistic knowledge (which is required to produce spontaneous language).

These two theoretical views identify an important part of the coverage given to cognitive strategies in the second language field. Other theories of second language acquisition either fail to mention cognitive processing altogether or deny that conscious cognitive processing is important for second language acquisition (O'Malley, et al., 1987). For example, Krashen (1977, 1983) indicates that classroom learning does not lead to the ability to produce language spontaneously. Teaching is useful only for familiarizing students with language elements and forms that can be used to monitor spontaneous production. Language interactions in unstructured social settings, which entail unconscious acquisition processes, are required for attaining second language fluency.

The central position on which Krashen differs from the other two theories is the importance of cognitive strategies in second language acquisition, particularly for language production. A resolution of this difference is suggested by Cummins' (1984) model of language proficiency. Cummins indicates that language tasks vary orthogonally along one continuum from cognitively demanding to undemanding, and along a second continuum from context-embedded to context-reduced. Academic tasks are cognitively demanding and usually require language in which context clues for meaning are reduced. Tasks outside the classroom, on the other hand, are relatively undemanding cognitively and are characterized by language that either has rich contextual clues or follows social formulas. Krashen's suggestion that cognitive strategies have little place in acquisition may apply more to undemanding, context-embedded language in social interactions, rather than to the more demanding tasks found in classrooms where deliberation on the use of language rules and forms is not uncommon even among first language students learning to read or studying content areas.

B. RESEARCH ON LEARNING STRATEGIES WITH SECOND LANGUAGES

There is substantial evidence to indicate that learning strategies are, in fact, used during second language learning. Naiman et al. (1978) found that individuals proficient in foreign languages recalled using strategies while learning tasks associated with speaking, listening, reading, and writing. Rubin (1981) confirmed the use of strategies in comprehension and production tasks with second language learners who maintained journal accounts of their use of strategies. Rubin identified a variety of discrete strategies such as monitoring, requesting clarification or verification, inferencing, deductive reasoning, and memorizing strategies. Cohen and Aphek (1981) found positive effects over an extended time period that were associated with reported strategy use for vocabulary learning. Similarly, Politzer (1983) found a positive relationship between strategy use and learning among adult students of English as a second language. Wenden's (1983) use of interviews revealed that second language students may be self-directed in analyzing their knowledge of language, planning for language exchanges that promote learning, and evaluating the success of their learning activities. Wenden's strategies are comparable to the definition Brown and Palinscar (1982) gave to metacognitive strategies.

This body of research indicates that learning strategies can be identified and described by second language learners and that the strategies range from direct cognitive manipulations of learning materials to metacognitive analyses of learning. What the studies leave unanswered, however, is the classification of strategies, the frequency with which different strategies are used in second language learning, and the effectiveness of strategy training for generating strategy use and for improving language proficiency.

The two studies to be reported here were performed to gain an improved understanding of learning strategy applications with individuals learning a second language. The first study, a descriptive study, examines the range and type of strategies used with specific language tasks by beginning and intermediate ESL students (O'Malley et al., 1985a). This study also identifies the frequency of strategy use with language tasks. The second study was designed to determine the effectiveness of learning strategies training with vocabulary, listening, and speaking tasks in an academic setting for intermediate-level ESL students (O'Malley et al., 1985b).

II. DESCRIPTIVE STUDY

A. Purpose

The first investigation involved the design and implementation of a descriptive study undertaken in a public school setting. The basic intent of this study was (1) to determine the types and range of strategies used by high school students for language learning tasks found typically in English as a second language (ESL) classrooms and in the daily experiences of these students, and (2) to determine if strategy use interacts with the type of language task or activity and the level of English proficiency of the students.

B. Method

1. Subjects

The subjects in the descriptive study were 70 ESL students and 22 of their teachers in three suburban high schools close to a major metropolitan area in the mideastern United States. Except for five Vietnamese students, the students interviewed were from Central and South America and Puerto Rico. Students were approximately equally divided between boys and girls, and their ages ranged from 14 to 17. They had been classified by their school as beginning or intermediate level in ESL, and were nominated by teachers as representing the higher academic ability students at each proficiency level.

The high school teachers interviewed held secondary teaching certificates and had a minimum of 2 years of teaching experience. Teachers employed a variety of methodologies, ranging from audiolingual to grammatical and communicative approaches in ESL classes, and from lecture to demonstration and small hands-on activities in content classes.

2. Instruments

Data were collected through the use of a Student Interview Guide and a Teacher Interview Guide that asked the interviewee to describe strategies used to facilitate learning and retention in eight language learning activities. Six of these were activities typically found in ESL classes: pronunciation exercises, oral grammar drills and exercises, vocabulary learning, instructions and directives, listening to a teacher's lecture, and formal classroom speaking. The two other language-learning situations, typically occurring outside the classroom, were social communication and operational or functional communications (applying for a job or requesting directions).

3. Procedures

The general approach used in the descriptive study was to collect interview data from students and their teachers regarding students' use of learning strategies for language-learning activities both in and out of the classroom. Interviews with high school students were conducted in groups of three to five. When necessary, interviews were conducted in Spanish for Hispanic students with limited English proficiency. The teacher interviews were conducted individually. All interviews were taped and rated afterwards by the person conducting the interviews. An average interrater reliability of .79 was determined by comparison of the interview's individual strategy classifications with four independent raters.

C. RESULTS

Project staff had considerable success in identifying learning strategies through interviews with students, but less success in interviews with teachers. Students understood readily the request for information about approaches they used to assist their language learning, and provided numerous examples of the ways in which they applied strategies to specific learning activities. On the other hand, teachers tended to confuse learning strategies with teaching strategies. Teachers could describe in detail how they taught, but in most cases were uncertain how students actually went about learning the materials presented. Nevertheless, teachers were intrigued with the concept of learning strategies and later sought additional information concerning their use through teacher workshops.

1. Range of Strategies

The range of strategies found in the interviews extended a preliminary list of strategies identified in an initial review of the literature (O'Malley et al., 1983). By almost doubling the number of strategies, the data collection (particularly the interviews with students) proved to be a useful and informative approach for gaining information about the ways in which students attack language learning. A final list of 25 strategies and their corresponding definitions are shown in Table 1.

2. Strategy Classification and Student Proficiency

The basic classification scheme proposed by Brown (1982) that was comprised of metacognitive and cognitive strategies proved useful for the strategies identified in this study. A third category, social affective strategies, was added to account for strategies used by students requiring social interaction.

TABLE 1   Learning Strategy Definitions

Learning strategy	Description
Metacognitive	
Advance organizers	Making a general, but comprehensive preview of the concept or principle in an anticipated learning activity
Directed attention	Deciding in advance to attend, in general, to a learning task and to ignore irrelevant distractors
Selective attention	Deciding in advance to attend to specific aspects of language input or situational details that will cue the retention of language input
Self-management	Understanding the conditions that help one learn and arranging for the presence of those conditions
Functional planning	Planning for and rehearsing linguistic components necessary to carry out an upcoming language task
Self-monitoring	Correcting one's speech for accuracy in pronunciation, grammar, vocabulary, or for appropriateness related to the setting or to the people who are present
Delayed production	Consciously deciding to postpone speaking to learn initially through listening comprehension
Self-evaluation	Checking the outcomes of one's own language learning against an internal measure of completeness and accuracy
Cognitive	
Repetition	Imitating a language model, including overt practice and silent rehearsal
Resourcing	Defining or expanding a definition of a word or concept through use of target language reference materials
Directed physical response	Relating new information to physical actions, as with directives
Translation	Using the first language as a base for understanding and/or producing the second language
Grouping	Reordering or reclassifying and, perhaps, labeling the materials to be learned based on common attributes
Note taking	Writing down the main idea, important points, outline, or summary of information presented orally or in writing
Deduction	Consciously applying rules to produce or understand the second language
Recombination	Constructing a meaningful sentence or larger language sequence by combining known elements in a new way
Imagery	Relating new information to visual concepts in memory via familiar, easily retrievable visualizations, phrases, or locations
Auditory representation	Retaining the sound or similar sound for a word, phrase, or longer language sequence

TABLE 1 (Continued)

Learning strategy	Description
Key word	Remembering a new word in the second language by (1) identifying a familiar word in the first language that sounds like or otherwise resembles the new word, and (2) generating easily recalled images of some relationship with the new word
Contextualization	Placing a word or phrase in a meaningful language sequence
Elaboration	Relating new information to other concepts in memory
Transfer	Using previously acquired linguistic and/or conceptual knowledge to facilitate a new language-learning task
Inferencing	Using available information to guess meanings of new items, predict outcomes, or fill in missing information
Social affective	
Cooperation	Working with one or more peers to obtain feedback, pool information, or model a language activity
Question for clarification	Asking a teacher or other native speaker for repetition, paraphrasing, explanation, and/or examples

Table 2 presents the number of metacognitive, cognitive, and social affective strategies used by beginning and intermediate ESL high school students. A total of 638 strategies emerged from the 19 group interviews with students for an average of 33.6 strategies per interview. These were individual strategy applications averaged across successive interviews. Of the reported strategies, 30.1% (192–638) were classified as metacognitive in nature, 52.8% (337/638) appeared to be cognitive strategies, and 17.1% (109/638) of the strategies were social affective strategies.

Some of the prolific expression of strategy used by students was in part due to multiple strategies. In order to reflect accurately the richness of strategies used by students, project staff sometimes found it necessary to assign multiple strategy names to a single description provided by students. Two or more strategies were used in 20.9% of all strategies reported. There were virtually no differences between beginning and intermediate students in this regard. Further inspection of the multiple strategy uses revealed that metacognitive strategies were combined with cognitive strategies in 7% of all strategy applications. Metacognitive strategies were used alone in an additional 26.7% of all strategy applications, and 66.2% were cognitive strategies alone. The extensive use of metacognitive strategies by students suggested that considerable reflection on the acquisition and function of language was occurring.

TABLE 2   Number of Metacognitive and Cognitive Strategies Used by Public School ESL Students for English as a Second Language

| Learning strategy type | Learning strategy classification | English proficiency | | | | | |
| | | Beginning | | Intermediate | | Total | |
		n	%	n	%	n	%
Metacognitive							
Planning	Advance preparation	24	21.4	20	25.0	44	22.9
	Self-management	22	19.6	18	22.5	40	20.8
	Selective attention	25	22.3	13	16.3	38	19.8
	Directed attention	15	13.4	10	12.5	25	13.0
	Delayed production	8	7.1	2	2.5	10	5.2
	Advance organizers	1	0.9	0	0.0	1	0.5
Monitoring	Self-monitoring	8	7.1	10	12.5	18	9.4
Evaluation	Self-evaluation	9	8.0	7	8.8	16	8.3
Subtotal		112	100.0	80	100.0	192	100.0
Cognitive							
	Repetition	45	20.0	21	18.8	66	19.6
	Note taking	43	19.0	20	17.9	63	18.7
	Imagery	31	14.0	11	9.8	42	12.5
	Translation	29	13.0	9	8.0	38	11.3
	Transfer	23	10.2	12	10.7	35	10.4
	Inferencing	21	9.3	11	9.8	32	9.5
	Resourcing	11	5.0	7	6.2	18	5.3
	Contextualization	7	3.1	11	9.8	18	5.3
	Elaboration	9	4.0	2	1.8	11	3.3
	Auditory representation	3	1.3	2	1.8	5	1.5
	Grouping	1	0.4	3	2.7	4	1.2
	Recombination	1	0.4	1	0.9	2	0.6
	Deduction	1	0.4	1	0.9	2	0.6
	Key word	0	0.0	1	0.9	1	0.3
	Directed physical response	0	0.0	0	0.0	0	0.0
Subtotal		225	100.0	112	100.0	337	100.0
Social affective							
	Cooperation	34	47.0	18	49.0	52	48.0
	Questions for clarity	38	53.0	19	51.0	57	52.0
Subtotal		72	100.0	37	100.0	109	100.0
Total		409	100.0	229	100.0	638	100.0

Results presented in Table 2 reveal that intermediate level students tended to use proportionately more metacognitive strategies than students with beginning level proficiency. Whereas intermediate level students used 34.9% (80/229) metacognitive strategies, beginning level students used 27.4% (112/409) metacognitive strategies. However, both beginning and intermediate level students used more cognitive than metacognitive strategies overall.

Individual metacognitive strategies displayed in Table 2 are differentiated in terms of Brown's (1983) categories for regulation of learning—planning, monitoring, and evaluation. The greatest differentiation and heaviest use of strategies appears in planning, regardless of English proficiency. Overall, 82.3% (158/192) of the metacognitive strategies were used for planning learning activities, primarily in self-management, advance preparation, directed attention, and selective attention. Self-monitoring comprised 9.4% overall of all metacognitive strategies, while 8.3% involved self-evaluation.

Cognitive strategies used by students in acquiring speaking and understanding skills in English are also presented in Table 2. The strategies are presented from most to least frequently occurring strategies. The pattern of use is similar for beginning and intermediate level students. The two most frequently used strategies overall were repetition and note taking. The appearance of a rote strategy among the most frequently mentioned strategies is of considerable interest in that it indicates that students are not transforming or otherwise engaging the learning materials in an active manner. The next strategies in frequency were cooperation and questions for clarification, both of which involve contact with another person for additional source information. The next group of strategies in terms of frequency consisted of imagery, translation, transfer, and inferencing. All of these strategies entail active manipulation or reworking of the learning materials, although translation is generally accepted as a highly inefficient strategy for language learning. Among the lower frequency strategies cited by students were a number that entail a high level of active involvement with the learning materials, such as elaboration, the key word method, deduction, grouping, and recombination. In general, it seemed that some of the more frequently used strategies entailed less active manipulation of the learning text, and the active strategies that should lead to greater learning were infrequently used.

3. Interaction of Strategies with Learning Activities

The proportion of learning strategies reported by students varied depending on the learning activity, as shown in Table 3. By far the most strategies were reported for vocabulary learning, virtually twice as many as for the other activities such as making an oral presentation and for drawing inferences from listening, and substantially more than for operational communications and analysis in listening comprehension. The other activity for which students reported numerous strategies was pronunciation. Thus, strategies were most frequently mentioned with relatively less conceptually demanding language-learning activities in comparison to the more complex activities such as analysis, inferencing, and making an oral presentation.

TABLE 3   Number and Percentage of Strategy Uses among Beginning and Intermediate
Level Students for Different Learning Activities

| | English proficiency | | | | | |
| | Beginning | | Intermediate | | Total | |
Learning activity	n	%	n	%	n	%
Listening comprehension: inference	34	8.3	12	5.2	46	7.2
Oral presentation	22	5.4	30	13.1	52	8.2
Operational communication	46	11.2	17	7.4	63	9.9
Instructions	42	10.3	25	10.9	67	10.5
Social communication	42	10.3	28	12.2	70	11.0
Listening comprehension: analyzing	49	12.0	24	10.5	73	11.4
Oral drills	52	12.7	21	9.2	73	11.4
Pronunciation	51	12.5	37	16.2	88	13.8
Vocabulary learning	71	17.4	35	15.3	106	16.6
Total	409	100.0%	229	100.0%	638	100.0%

One of the reasons why a strategy might have appeared with low frequency with a particular language-learning activity was that the activity itself occurred with low frequency in the student's experience. For example, many students did not regularly engage in more complex language activities, such as social communication or classroom oral presentations. Further, the students were infrequently assigned communicative interactions outside the classroom, such as talking to a clerk in a store, which precluded extensive experience in activities such as social and operational communications. Nevertheless, over 20% of all strategy uses were with language occurring in nonclassroom environments, that is, with contextualized language.

D.   Discussion

Overall, ESL students were able to identify and describe a wide range of learning strategies used in gaining command over the English language. The strategies used proportionally most often entailed minimum conceptual manipulation—such as repetition and note taking—while strategies used less regularly involved a higher level of cognitive processing such as inferencing and elaboration. Furthermore, the tasks with which strategies were used most regularly were the less complex language tasks—such as vocabulary and pronunciation—as contrasted with language tasks that required integrative skills, such as listening or using language in social contexts. Since the students interviewed were considered by their teachers to be better language students, this suggests that even the more effective language students infrequently use strategies with complex language tasks and infrequently use learning strategies requiring conceptual integration of new information. Opportunities for strategy instruction to strengthen existing strategies, to broaden the range of strategies in a student's repertoire, and to expand the types of tasks with which strategies are used, appear evident in these findings.

III. TRAINING STUDY

A. PURPOSE

The purpose of the training study was to evaluate the effectiveness of learning strategies training among intermediate level ESL students for vocabulary learning, listening comprehension, and academic speaking tasks.

B. METHOD

1. Subjects

The subjects, who were different from those used in the Descriptive Study, were 75 high school ESL students. The subjects were randomly assigned to one of three groups: a metacognitive group ($n = 27$), a cognitive group ($n = 26$), and a control group ($n = 22$). About one-third of the students were Hispanic (mostly from Central and South America), another third were Asian (mostly from Southeast Asia), and the remainder were from various other ethnolinguistic backgrounds (mostly European and Middle Eastern). Each of the three treatment groups contained a roughly equal number of boys and girls and a representative selection of students from all the ethnolinguistic groups in the study.

2. Instruments

The data collection instruments used in the study were curriculum specific tests in vocabulary, listening comprehension, and speaking. These instruments were administered at both pretest and posttest. Only the speaking test was individually administered; all others were group administered. Four daily tests that were similar in format to the pretests and posttests were administered in each of the three language tasks during the course of the training sessions.

3. Procedures

Training lessons were planned around three language-learning activities: vocabulary learning, listening comprehension, and oral presentations. The two experimental groups were trained in the use of different combinations of learning strategies which they then applied to the three language tasks, while the control group completed the language tasks using whatever regular approaches they preferred. The *metacognitive* experimental group received training in a combination of metacognitive, cognitive, and social affective strategies, while the *cognitive* group received training only in cognitive and social affective strategies. Table 4 identifies the strategies taught to each experimental group for each language task.

Instruction in the use of strategies for vocabulary, listening, and speaking tasks was provided to students for 1 hour daily for eight successive days with an additional hour devoted to a pretest and a posttest. For the treatment groups, the same learning strategies were always repeated with each language activity, although new content was presented each time a language activity recurred. Students therefore could practice strategy applications with new materials. Explicit directions and cues for using the strategies were faded on successive days of treatment for each activity, until at the posttest, only a reminder was given to use the same strategies they had rehearsed before. The extension of strategy training to new language tasks of a similar type, while cues for strategy use were faded, was intended to test for transfer.

C. RESULTS

The posttest results for the three groups on the tests for vocabulary, listening, and speaking appear in Table 5. An analysis of covariance was used to compare the posttest performance of the metacognitive, cognitive, and control groups. For each, the covariate was the pretest score corresponding to each type of test. The table shows the group-adjusted mean scores, standard deviations, probability values, and a measure (R^2) that provides an association between the treatment and the outcomes.

The results of the speaking posttest were encouraging and significant beyond the .01 level. The metacognitive group outperformed the cognitive group, which in turn was judged more highly than the control group. Even though the judges of the speech samples were not told the purposes of the study or given any inkling about the training procedures for the experimental groups, they evaluated the groups receiving training as higher on the criteria of delivery, appropriateness, organization, and accuracy. A separate analysis of Hispanic, Asian, and the other ethnolinguistic groups indicates that all who were trained in the metacognitive group were judged superior in the speaking task to students from the same ethnic groups who did not receive the metacognitive training.

The listening comprehension posttest scores show that the metacognitive

TABLE 4 Language Learning Activities and Accompanying Strategies for the Metacognitive Group[a]

Language task	Strategy type	General description of strategy and task instruction
Vocabulary (20-item list)	Metacognitive	*Self-evaluation:* each student completed a journal in which they recorded the number of words they learned each day, the words they found to be difficult, and the method they used to remember the words
	Cognitive	*Grouping:* students were taught that a long list of words can often be separated into parts and labeled to show semantic or other similarities
		Imagery: students closed their eyes and created a vivid image that incorporated the words they had grouped together and their English equivalents
Listening (5-minute lecture on academic topic)	Metacognitive	*Selective attention:* students were instructed to listen selectively for key words typically used in lectures to present an overview, to introduce a main topic, main point, example, or conclusion
	Cognitive	*Note taking:* students used a T-list, entering main points on the left and corresponding details adjacently on the right
	Social affective	*Cooperation:* students interacted with peers to verify the accuracy of their notes, fill in gaps in information, and clarify areas of confusion
Speaking (2-minute presentation on familiar topic)	Metacognitive	*Functional planning:* students were taught to analyze a communication for the functions that must be accomplished, and to determine if they had the language needed to perform those functions. Then they could learn new language as required to perform the communication
	Social affective	*Cooperation:* students practiced their presentation with one or more peers and received feedback on volume, pace, organization, and comprehensibility

[a]The cognitive group received instruction in all strategies *except* for the metacognitive ones; the control group had the same language tasks but received no strategy training.

TABLE 5   The Effect of Learning Strategy Training on Selected Language Skills Controlling for Pretest Score

Variable	Metacognitive ($n = 27$)		Cognitive ($n = 26$)		Control ($n = 22$)		p value	R^2
	Adj. mean[a]	SD[b]	Adj. mean	SD	Adj. mean	SD		
Posttests								
Speaking	3.60	0.88	3.04	0.80	2.88	0.73	0.008	0.20
Listening	8.25	2.12	8.18	2.00	7.30	2.31	0.162	0.30
Vocabulary	22.66	4.76	21.41	4.23	23.21	4.90	0.349	0.17
Daily tests on listening								
Listening 1	6.03	1.29	5.91	1.45	5.46	1.47	0.096	0.26
Listening 2	6.25	1.48	6.54	1.22	5.45	1.50	0.004	0.36
Listening 3	6.27	2.33	6.95	1.61	5.17	2.31	0.043	0.29
Listening 4	5.25	1.32	5.10	1.68	5.09	1.57	0.626	0.10

[a]Adjusted mean score.
[b]Standard deviation.

group was superior to the cognitive group, which performed better than the control group. However, these scores only approached significance. The second part of Table 5 shows an analysis of the daily tests for listening comprehension, in which the treatment groups performed significantly better than the control group on two out of four tests. Several explanations could clarify the disappointing performance of the treatment groups on the fourth daily listening test and on the posttest. One explanation could be that when the listening task was more difficult, and the cues for strategy use less structured, transfer of strategy training to new listening tasks was not significantly improved. Process analyses of both listening and speaking strategies indicated that students in the treatment groups were using the strategies on which training had occurred, except when cues were too rapidly faded on the listening task. Based on observation and analysis of work sheets, it was found that the control group generally failed to use any visible strategies at all.

Difficulties were encountered in implementing vocabulary strategies that required midtreatment modifications in the instructional approach. Nevertheless, some of the findings for vocabulary instruction were meaningful. Although no significant differences were found overall between treatment and control conditions in vocabulary learning, subsequent analyses revealed differences among ethnic groups. Hispanic students in the metacognitive treatment group performed much better than their corresponding controls on the vocabulary task, whereas Asian students in the control group outperformed the Asian treatment group students. These findings confirmed informal observations by instructors which suggested that Asian students used rote repetition effectively and resisted attempts to modify this preferred strategy, while Hispanic students seemed to accept applying the new strategies to vocabulary learning.

D. DISCUSSION

Findings from the training study indicate that learning strategies can be embedded into a second language curriculum, that students can be taught to apply learning strategies to a variety of language tasks, and that some success can be expected from linking certain strategies to specific tasks. Results of these investigations also suggest that there may be preferences for the selection and use of strategies based on ethnic background. Learning strategies cannot be expected to be equally effective for all students. Individualization of strategies or providing a menu of strategies may be useful approaches to extending strategy repertoires.

The type and duration of training needed to introduce new strategies to students require further investigation. There were indications that the difficulty of the listening skills tasks and the explicitness of directions to perform the strategies may both be important determinants of performance. Students presented with a task that is too difficult may find little assistance in using learning strategies either because the initial communication is too complicated or the information is too unfamiliar.

Transfer of strategies to new tasks may require continued prompts and structured directions until the strategies become autonomous. In order to assess the effect of the use of strategies, both training and difficulty level may need to be adjusted to match the student's abilities. Additional investigations of the factors affecting strategy transfer are needed to identify the training components necessary to facilitate strategy use by students when confronted with new learning tasks.

E. CONCLUSIONS

Findings from the descriptive and the training studies suggest that current models of second language acquisition and learning should be refined and expanded to incorporate cognitive structures and learning strategies. Strategies were reported in the descriptive study in both academic and non-academic language-learning contexts, indicating that conscious processing is occurring during what has been referred to as an unconscious process of language acquisition (Krashen, 1983). This indicates, consistent with Bialystok (1978), that learning strategies may be effective for both explicit linguistic knowledge and implicit linguistic knowledge. Findings in the training study on classroom applications of strategy instruction suggest that the priority given by Fillmore and Swain (1984) to cognitive processes in second-language learning will be a useful avenue to explore in additional theory development.

ACKNOWLEDGMENTS

This research was conducted for the U.S. Army Research Institute for the Behavioral and Social Sciences in Alexandria, Virginia under Contract No. MDA-903-82-C-0169. The views, opinions, and findings contained in this report are those of the authors and should not be construed as an official Department of Army position, policy, or decision, unless so designated by other official documentation.

REFERENCES

Bialystok, E. (1978). Theoretical model of second language learning. *Language Learning, 28,* 69–83.

Bialystok, E. (1981). The role of conscious strategies in second language proficiency. *Modern Language Journal, 65,* 24–35.

Brown, A. L., Bransford, J. D., Ferrara, R. A., & Campione, J. C. (1983). Learning, remembering, and understanding. In J. H. Flavell, & E. M. Markham (Eds.), *Carmichael's manual of child psychology* (Vol. 1). New York: Wiley.

Brown, A. L., & Palinscar, A. S. (1982). Inducing strategic learning from texts by means of informed, self-control training. *Topics in learning and learning disabilities, 2,* 1–17.

Cohen, A. D.,& Aphek, E. (1981). Easifying second language learning. *Studies in second language acquisition, 3,* 221–235.

Cummins, J. (1984). *Bilingualism and special education: Issues in assessment and pedagogy.* Clevedon, England: Multilingual Matters, Ltd.

Fillmore, L. W., & Swain, M. (1984). Child second language development: Views from the field on theory and research, paper presented at the annual meeting of the TESOL Convention, Houston, TX.

Krashen, S. D. (1983). *Principles and practice in second language acquisition.* New York: Pergamon Press.

Krashen, S. D. (1977). The monitor model for adult second language performance. In M. Burt, H. Dulay, & M. Finocchiaro (Eds.), *Viewpoints on English as a second language.* New York: Regents.

Naiman, N., Frohlich, M., Stern, H. H.,& Todesco, A. (1978). *The good language learner.* Toronto: Modern Language Center, Ontario Institute for Studies in English.

O'Malley, J. M., Chamot, A. U., Stewner-Manzanares, G., Kupper, L., & Russo, R. P. (1985a). Learning strategies used by beginning and intermediate ESL students. *Language Learning, 35,* 21–46.

O'Malley, J. M., Chamot, A. U., Stewner-Manzanares, G., Russo, R. P., & Kupper, L. (1985b). The effects of learning strategies training on the development of skills in English as a second language. *TESOL Quarterly, 19,* 557–584.

O'Malley, J. M., Chamot, A. U., & Walker, C. (1987). The role of cognition in second language acquisition. *Studies in Second Language Acquisition, 9,* (3).

O'Malley, J. M., Russo, R. P., & Chamot, A. U. (1983). *A review of the literature on learning strategies in the acquisition of English as a second language.* Rosslyn, VA: InterAmerica Research Associates.

Politzer, R. L. (1983). An exploratory study of self reported language learning behaviors and their relation to achievement. *Studies in Second Language Acquisition, 6,* 54–68.

Rubin, J. (1981). Study of cognitive processes in second language learning. *Applied Linguistics, 11,* 117–131.

Wenden, A. (1983). Learning training for L2 learners: A selected review of content and method, paper presented at the annual meeting of the TESOL Convention, Toronto, Canada.

TEXT LEARNING STRATEGY INSTRUCTION: GUIDELINES FROM THEORY AND PRACTICE

Beau Fly Jones

How do you apply research to maximize student achievement? While many approaches are possible, the answer given in this paper reflects not only recent research but also the needs, perspectives, and resources of specific educational systems. The purposes of this paper are (1) to define text learning strategy instruction from the perspective of developing instructional materials for two giant educational systems—the Chicago Public Schools and the U.S. Army, (2) to describe the interaction of theory and practice in efforts to develop instructional materials in real world settings, and (3) to delineate the principles of instructional design that emerged from that interaction.

The paper will be divided into three parts. Part 1 briefly describes the key characteristics and needs of the Chicago Public Schools and the U.S. Army. Part 2 discusses the major theoretical and practical issues that have driven the development of instructional materials over the years. Part 3 elaborates on four general principles.

I. EDUCATIONAL CONTEXTS

A. CHARACTERISTICS

The Chicago Public Schools and the U.S. Army must provide instruction for hundreds of thousands of students taught by thousands of teachers. Many of the students in both settings are low achieving. The teachers may not be the most able in terms of prior achievement and talent (National Commission on Excellence in Education, 1983). Many, if not most, were trained before recent models of knowledge acquisition, learning, and teaching were widely communicated. Further, the Army and the Chicago schools, like most other schools, involve extensive use of instructional materials, many of

LEARNING AND STUDY STRATEGIES: ISSUES IN
ASSESSMENT, INSTRUCTION, AND EVALUATION

which are poorly constructed and poorly aligned (Cavert et al., 1980;
Davison, 1984).

B.   MATERIALS DEVELOPMENT VERSUS STAFF DEVELOPMENT

The extraordinary size of these systems, the mobility of teachers, and the
dependence on materials almost preclude a heavy dependence on staff development. That is, given the preponderance of textbook materials whose
quality is problematic, a major way to change the quality of instruction is to
change the quality of textual materials. If we provided the best possible staff
development program using traditional methods such as workshops, cadre
trainers, and masters for 5,000 teachers, there would still be three overwhelming problems. First, there would be many thousands of teachers who
did not receive the training. Second, a substantial number of those teachers
would be displaced within a year due to various reasons such as transfer or,
in the case of the Army, contract bidding. Third, the available commercial
materials pose important problems, which we discuss below, even for well-
trained teachers.

For these reasons, the approach we developed for the Chicago Public
Schools and the Army has emphasized the development of research-based
instructional materials that (1) embed explicit learning strategy instruction;
i.e., what we termed an *embedded curriculum* (Jones, 1980); (2) seek to be
maximally comprehensible; (3) represent a diversity of instructional strategies; and (4) must serve low- and high-achieving students. If such materials
were widely available, they would serve as a means of instruction for students as well as a means of staff development for teachers. Moreover, once
such materials were developed, they would be easily transportable and implementable in other school systems.

C.   RESEARCH AND DEVELOPMENT PROJECTS

The projects listed below are the products of various research and development efforts. The first five are embedded curricula. The sixth provides for
developing embedded curricula.

1. *Chicago Mastery Learning Reading (CMLR):* grades 5–8, see Campione
   & Armbruster, 1985; Jones et al., 1985a; Sternberg, 1984, descriptions.
2. *Applying Comprehension Instruction to Fiction and Nonfiction (ACI):* a
   teacher's guide.
3. *Vocabulary Learning Strategies (VLS):* grades 1–8, see Jones et al., 1984,
   description.
4. *Collaboration to Improve Reading in the Content Areas (CIRCA):* see
   Jones et al., 1985a, description.

5. *Reading Is Thinking: A Literature Anthology (RIT/LIT):* grades 4–6, see Jones, 1985a.
6. *Content-Driven Comprehension Instruction (CDCI): A Model for Army Training Literature:* (Jones et al., 1984).

D. RESEARCH QUESTIONS

Research that is based in school systems obviously proceeds in very different ways from research that emerges from academic settings. The latter often focuses on isolating and testing specific variables from a given body of research to obtain precise knowledge. School research, in contrast, frequently must address very broad issues and weave a complex fabric from a diversity of separate research strands to form a synthesis, often without a clear-cut body of research to provide guidelines.

The following list comprises the basic questions and problems we had to address for each project. Each question will be addressed in the next section.

1. What is already known from recent research regarding learning and comprehension?
2. What assumptions can be made about instruction given the knowledge base in comprehension and learning?
3. What is the domain of learning strategies? That is, how does one define the scope of possible strategies from which to choose for specific tasks?
4. How does one develop strategy instruction when there are no existing models?
5. What provisions should be made to train for transfer of training and independent learning?
6. How do you control the level and quality of the content materials if you reject the idea of using traditional readability formulas?
7. What provisions should be made for assessment?
8. How do you provide instruction for all phases of learning before, during, and after reading that is appropriate for both homogeneous and very heterogeneous classrooms grouped by chronological age?

II. MAJOR THEORETICAL AND PRACTICAL ISSUES

A. COMPREHENSION AND LEARNING

Most fundamentally, instruction should reflect recent models of comprehension and learning. Specifically, our model welds together assumptions from schema theory (e.g., Anderson et al., 1984; Spiro, 1980; Rumelhart, 1980), especially the focus on the role of prior knowledge and the need to link new learning to previously acquired knowledge; learning strategy research, especially the concept of generative learning strategies (e.g., Wittrock, 1983); text analysis, particularly the concept of frames (Anderson & Armbruster, 1984); the notion that constructing meaning from text occurs before, during, and after reading (Anderson, 1980); and various concepts from reading in the content area strategies (Herber, 1978; 1985), notably, the focus on prereading activities involving prediction (e.g., Stauffer, 1975) and postreading activities involving constructing graphic organizers (Moore & Readence, 1984).

Especially important here is the notion that comprehension emerges from an interaction of the reader, the text, and the context (Anderson et al., 1978). Using their statement as a model, we culled recent research to identify the key characteristics of the reader, the text, and the context that affect comprehension (Jones, 1985a; Jones et al., 1984). Characteristics of the *reader* are (1) the reader's prior knowledge of content and his/her repertoire of reading/thinking strategies (Rohwer, 1971); (2) metacognition, the reader's capability for planning, comprehending, and evaluating what is learned (Armbruster et al., 1983); and (3) individual differences (Spiro, 1980). The main characteristics of the *text* that influence comprehension are factors related to the prose text: the organizational structure, unity, coherence, and age appropriateness (Anderson & Armbruster, 1984; Armbruster, 1985; Meyer, 1982; Shimmerlik, 1978). Additionally, graphics and their relationship to the text (Alesandrini, 1984; Jones et al., 1984; Levin, 1982; Schallert, 1980) and text design (e.g., Duchastel, 1982) seem to influence comprehension. Characteristics of the *context* are: (1) the purpose for reading and the information available, (2) the teacher, and (3) policy variables such as textbook adoptions, grouping, and pacing.

B. ASSUMPTIONS ABOUT INSTRUCTION

From the outset, we assumed that the instructional materials we developed should be based on research on comprehension and learning as well as on principles of instruction gleaned from successful training studies. Using these two sources, we determined that instruction should provide:

1. Comprehension instruction that focuses on helping students understand the meaning of what they read (Durkin, 1978–1979; 1985);
2. Explicit learning strategy instruction (e.g., Brown et al., 1981; Weinstein & Mayer, 1986; Winograd & Hare, Ch. 8, this volume);
3. Sustained direct instruction that specifies clearly what is to be learned

and how to learn it (Jones, 1980; Rosenshine, 1983) and provides for a progression from teacher-directed activities to independent practice and transfer of learning (Brown et al., 1981; Jones, 1980; Pearson & Leys, 1985);

4. Instructional materials for the students and teacher for all three phases of comprehending the text and responding to questions (Jones, 1985a; 1985b);

5. Provisions for teaching vocabulary terms and concepts, using principles from concept attainment theory (e.g., Markle, 1975; see also Anderson & Jones, 1981, summary);

6. Provisions for organizing instruction into learning units that are addressed to specific objectives, have tests aligned to the objectives, and include reteaching procedures using a different teaching/learning strategy (Bloom, 1976) for students who do not pass the tests.

C. LEARNING STRATEGIES

1. Learning Strategies in Training Studies

Learning strategies are the various mental operations that the learner uses to facilitate learning. Learning strategies, therefore, are specific behaviors that are goal-oriented, either consciously or unconsciously. Definitions of the domain of learning strategies exist in both research and practice. Both the Army and the Chicago Public Schools, for example, already had a well-defined study skills curriculum that included such learning strategies as finding the main idea, summarizing, and inferring meaning from context. However, this domain was not based on recent research on reading or learning strategies. It was derived largely by examining other curricula, hiring curriculum researchers to serve as consultants, and field testing. We needed to know how the scope of study skills defined by these institutions matched the domain of learning strategies defined by recent research on reading and learning. To address these issues, Jones (1980; Jones et al., 1985a) re-examined the learning strategies literature to establish the domain of learning strategies and the tasks to which they apply, and to determine precisely how learning strategies instruction in experimental studies was conducted. To do this, the strategies and texts used in the various training studies were defined and classified.

This analysis was most revealing. First, and most important, it was not possible to define the strategies without reference to the characteristics of the texts to which they applied. Consider categorizing, for example; it is not possible to explain how to categorize without assuming or explaining that this strategy is only appropriate for information that is categorizable. This fact has important implications for learning and instruction. Specifically, it means that the developer/teacher should provide instruction regarding the text characteristics required for using each strategy so that students understand (1) how the strategy works and (2) how to relate different strategies to different texts.

Second, it was necessary to specify the parameters that differentiate different types of text. Amiran and Jones (1982) found that generally texts could be differentiated according to their degree of explicitness, the degree of complexity, and the density. However, to develop a classification scheme that covered not only these text variables but also the task, we had to integrate the classification scheme developed by Pearson and Johnson (1978) to differentiate various question and answer relationships. They argue that questions (tasks) cannot be classified by their content alone. Rather, they must be understood in relation to a specific text. Thus, if the answer to the question is explicit in the text, the question/answer relationship (QAR) is text explicit. If the answer must be inferred, the QAR is text implicit. And if the answer is not there at all or only partly there, the authors called this condition "script" because the students had to develop an answer from prior knowledge. We prefer to call this condition text inadequate because the student may also get the answer by integrating information from another text.

Our most recent analysis of the interaction of text-learning strategies, text characteristics, and text conditions is shown in Table 1. A similar taxonomy was developed for the interaction of vocabulary-learning strategies, text conditions, and word characteristics (see Jones et al., 1985b).

A noteworthy feature of strategy/task relationships in Table 1 is that the order of strategies essentially parallels the taxonomy of educational objectives developed by Bloom et al. (1956), which is also defined in terms of specific text features (e.g., implicit texts, texts having component parts and relations, and multiple texts). Moreover, as with Bloom's taxonomy, in the learning-strategies taxonomy, high-order strategies subsume many of the lower-order ones; notetaking procedures, for example, require paraphrasing and analysis of component parts.

We recognize that the sequencing of strategies from high order to low order is far from perfect. Who is to say, for example, that verbal elaboration is higher or lower order compared to analysis? In practice, the final level of difficulty would be determined by the level of difficulty of the passage and, most important, the level of the reader's prior knowledge. Moreover, we recognize that several learning strategies may be used to construct meaning from text. At the same time, the taxonomy was not developed to sequence the order of learning strategies to be taught. Rather, it is hoped that the definitions in Table 1 will help researchers and instructional developers (1) to define the relationship between learning strategies and the text conditions to which they apply, and (2) to sequence the selection of passages in instances where selection of content can be manipulated to progress from text explicit to text inadequate. Finally, we hope that the taxonomy will encourage developers to provide instruction for the full range of texts, i.e., the range of implicit and inadequate texts that students must comprehend in the classroom.

2. Learning Strategies Instruction in Training Studies

Our analysis of the learning strategies instruction in the same body of literature yielded another important set of discoveries regarding training. First, we found that there were four different levels of strategy training provided in experimental studies:

Level I: studies providing *only LS* (a general instruction to use a strategy such as "categorize" or "take notes"). These are studies in which learning-strategy instructions were given without (a) any reference to the characteristics or context of the text to be comprehended or learned or (b) any reference to how to apply the strategy to the text.

Level II: studies providing *LS* and *DS* (a definition or guideline regarding how to apply the strategy to the text); e.g., Peper and Mayer, (1978) who defined generative underlining in terms of providing the sentence that gives the most information without telling students how to select this particular sentence from the text.

Level III: studies providing *LS, DS,* and/or *STI* (structure of text information); e.g., almost any study purporting to train students to categorize a (scrambled) word list or list of sentences. Any explanation beyond the word "categorize" must necessarily involve identification of the component parts of the text in terms of the need to infer the category label(s) and relate individual instances to each one.

Level IV: studies providing *LS, DS, STI,* and *IPA* (instruction in the process of applying the strategy); e.g., Brown et al. (1981), who provided extended summarizing rules and extended instruction in applications.

Second, and not surprisingly, we found that the more explicit the level of strategy instruction, the greater the effects; this was true not only of studies involving training of average and above average students but also of studies involving the training of low-achieving students. This examination covered studies of strategy training for learning-related and unrelated word lists, categorizable and noncategorizable sentences, as well as connected prose passages. Further, it covered a broad range of strategies from categorizing, paraphrasing, and elaborating to using context clues, taking notes, summarizing, and outlining.

TABLE 1 Text Learning Strategies and Text Conditions[a]

Type of strategy	Strategy operations and cognitive processes	Text condition	Text features
Generative processes	Use of previously learned information and associations to construct new associations and verbal abstractions	**Text explicit**	Discourse or definitions; titles, subtitles, graphics that make explicit propositions
Restatement Paraphrasing Visualizing	Restating new information in terms of previously acquired vocabulary and associations Restating verbal information in terms of previously acquired visual images	Brief descriptions	Organized discourse and definitions; could also be used for diagram/graph explanations
Discourse elaboration Visual Verbal	Creating short verbal stories and/or interactive images to comprehend concepts or integrate component parts of definitions	Extended descriptions and definitions	Discourse containing new vocabulary (English or foreign) accompanied by definitions or English equivalents
Inference Translation Interpretation Prediction Deduction Analogous thinking	Using prior knowledge and information given in the text to make inferences about word meanings, propositions, figurative language, and high-level organization	**Text implicit**	Discourse or graphics containing figurative language and implied meaning
Analysis Content Organization	Identifying the component parts of words, sentences, and passages; examining the relationship between the parts; selecting important information and main ideas; differentiating general and specific; recognizing new information interrelating ideas	Complex information	Discourse containing many component parts, levels of ideas, sequences of types of information; titles, subtitles, or graphics
Summarizing	Selecting important information and making high-level generalizations and abstractions	Paragraphs/multilevel information	Discourse containing two or more levels of information (e.g., main ideas and details)

Strategy	Description	Text type	Text type description
Transformational representations Linear outlining Matrix outlining Network outlining Graphic notetaking	Perceiving *underlying* structure of information plus transformation of prose into charts, tables, networks, maps, graphs, and symbols	Extended multilevel complex discourse	Complex discourse Descriptive information Sequential information Comparative information Causal information
Constructive strategies	Strategies that redefine or create overall meaning and organization when it is not explicit or implicit, or when it is very complex	**Text inadequate**	Discourse that is very complex, abstract, unfamiliar, or unclear; discourse involving more than one prose passage
Constructive inference Comprehension monitoring Hypothesis testing Analogical thinking using other resources	Identifying information that is unclear; constructing and testing hypotheses as to intended meaning; locating and interpreting information from additional resources (teacher's help, additional text, or dictionary)	Unclear discourse	Discourse containing contradictions, ambiguous or inconsistent information, inadequate examples or explanations
Reconceptualization Restructuring Reorganizing Summarizing	Imposing a new organizational structure on complex discourse in which the imposed structure was *not* stated or implied by the author	Very complex discourse	Discourse that is very complex or unfamiliar; poorly organized, or organized in different dimensions from that imposed by the learner
Synthesis	Imposing a single organizational structure on two or more different sets of previously unrelated, unorganized materials		Two or more unrelated passages or stories usually containing extended description, unclear discourse, and/or multilevel discourse

*Source: Jones et al. (1984).

Third, we found that the low-achieving students needed extended instructions. In the Brown et al. (1981) study, for example, the junior college students had difficulty, compared to junior high and high school students, using summarizing rules in spite of receiving the extended training. It is also interesting to note that some of the studies that provided only learning strategy instructions without DS, STI, or IPA were not successful (e.g., a number of studies on note taking). These findings are consistent with numerous studies indicating that there are typically marked differences in learning strategy use between 4-year college students, on the one hand, and 2-year college students and adult learners who lack high school or college education, on the other hand. See correlational studies of 2- and 4-year students, such as Cross, 1969; Jones, 1976, as well as other studies seeking to train 2-year students (e.g., Deffenbacher et al., 1974) or recent studies of military recruits (e.g., Cavert et al., 1980).

3. Learning Strategy Instruction Development

Once it was determined that we had to develop strategy instruction for a given task or skill, we usually tried to search the research literature for a model or guideline regarding the mental operations involved in the strategy. In many instances, there was such a body of literature, especially for traditional study skills, such as inferencing. However, there were two problems. First, most of the existing research was conducted using college students or average students rather than low-achieving students, and experimenters rather than average teachers. Second, in many instances, there were no existing models or guidelines.

To address these problems, we adapted a procedure articulated by Rohwer (1971) for developing strategy instruction when existing models were not available. He recommends the following steps: (1) give the task to persons known to be skilled, strategic learners; (2) interview them afterwards, asking them to "think backwards" to determine the strategy and the specific steps and thought processes used in the strategy; (3) develop instruction based on these interviews; (4) field test the strategy using the target population; (5) revise the instruction based on the field test; (6) evaluate the strategy in experimental designs. Although we did not have the capability to evaluate the instruction experimentally, to this day we use the other procedures with certain modifications to develop instructions for tasks for which there are no models.

One modification concerns a crucial step that is left out by Rohwer and others. This step is specification of the text structure for tasks involving whole texts. Brown et al. (1981), for example, only provide "generic" summarizing rules, but these rules do not work well for text structures such as compare/contrast or cause/effect. Interestingly, Shoenfeld (1985) found similar problems in efforts to apply generic problem-solving strategies to specific math problems. In such instances, it would be important for the student's comprehension of the strategy and his/her capability to apply the strategy, to learn from the outset that there are various text structures that may be summarized in different ways. This lack of specification regarding specific text structures may explain why experimental studies using these and other generic rules have been inconsistent. At any rate, we found it essential to specify to students not only the specific "how to" rules but also the particular text structures to which each strategy applies, and we strongly recommend that guidelines for direct instruction of strategy training include specific references to text structures, not only for prose texts but other structures such as analogies, as well.

Another modification concerning Rohwer's procedures pertains to the notion of field testing. Field testing in academic and school settings may have very different assumptions. Field tests in academic settings frequently aim for ideal conditions and maximum control, often involving the experimenter as teacher. In developing materials for a school system, the curriculum developer has little or no control over how the materials are used and no control over the selection of teachers. Because the materials we developed were intended for low-achieving students and their teachers, many of whom were mobile, it was imperative to develop materials that were sufficiently robust to be used effectively by low-achieving populations as well as by substitute teachers and transfer students. Consequently, Katims and Jones (Jones, et al., 1985a) argued for criterion-referenced field testing. Using this concept, *each* unit of instruction would be field tested using representative teachers and students. If 80% of the students did not master the objective, the unit was revised and field tested repeatedly until this level of mastery was reached. This concept assumes that experimenters and curriculum developers have the technology to provide effective instruction, even for low-achieving students. Therefore, they, not the teachers or students, should be accountable for what is developed.

D. METACOGNITION

The reader's capability to think about and control what is comprehended and learned is crucial to achievement. In fact, numerous studies of these metacognitive capabilities (e.g., Armbruster & Brown, 1984; Paris et al., 1984; Wittrock, 1983) indicate that training which provides explicit instruction in metacognition, may have a powerful impact on reading comprehension. Generally, there seem to be three phases of metacognition: planning, comprehension monitoring to select important information and fill in gaps where necessary, and evaluating the quality and accuracy of what is learned (Armbruster et al., 1983). These issues were addressed in several ways. First, we developed a sequencing model so that student activities progressed from being teacher directed to student directed (Jones, 1980). Second, the instructional materials in all projects provided for (1) informing the students of the objective, (2) step-by-step, thinking-aloud models that spell out the strategy to be used, (3) decreasing levels of reminders to use the strategies, and (4) opportunities for students to review the steps of each strategy.

E.   READABILITY

In light of the extensive literature against using readability formulas to develop and evaluate text (e.g., Davison, 1984), we decided that we would not use them to develop or evaluate text. Naturally, this decision created a serious problem. What were we going to use? After intensive debate and analysis of the texts we were using, we decided to use various criteria: (1) the general criteria developed by Amiran and Jones (1982); (2) the criteria for considerate text developed by Anderson & Armbruster (1984); (3) guidelines for graphics developed by Jones et al. (1984); (4) guidelines from text display (e.g., Duchastel, 1982; Hartley, 1982); and (5) field testing. Additionally, we were determined from the outset that we would try whenever possible to use the most appropriate choice of words, and if those words were inappropriate for the age of the student, we would provide synonyms in parentheses, appositives, or definitions in marginal notes.

F.   ASSESSMENT

What constitutes appropriate assessment of comprehension? Throughout the years, we tried to use instruction-driven testing; that is, we defined units on the basis of what constituted an appropriate unit of instruction, and *not* on the specification of objectives and tests per se. Chicago had selected 276 key objectives and tests in reading from kindergarten through grade 8. If we had constructed separate instructional units for each one, instruction would have been very fragmented, and far too much time would have been devoted to testing and reteaching, causing management problems as well as loss of valuable instructional time. Therefore, in reading, we developed instruction for related objectives and tests, reducing the number of separate tests and instructional units from 276 to 174. In other projects, where we were free to devise assessment as well as instruction, we focused heavily on reviews and/or large instructional units. We also developed study guides and test prompts (such as instructions to make an outline or to use text markers) that are gradually faded out.

G. Individual Differences

1. The Problem

We strongly recommend whole group instruction in relatively homogeneous classes where possible because it is more efficient and because heterogeneous groupings may actually increase the differences between high- and low-achieving students (Commission on Reading, 1985; Jones, 1982; Jones & Spady, 1985). However, the sentiments against tracking are strongly held, and most classes contain ability groups within heterogeneous classrooms. The question arises: how do you develop instruction for a particular classroom, given that it is likely to contain students for whom the instruction is too difficult?

2. Solutions

Different projects involved different solutions. In some instances, we provided direct instruction in prerequisite skills and vocabulary. In other instances, we provided or elicited reviews of prior knowledge of vocabulary, ideas, and skills and then sought ways to link these to the information to be learned (see SPaRC). Other strategies over which we had control involved peer tutoring and building in high-quality extension activities for high-achieving students. Additionally, the schools often added more instructional time to the reading period, accelerated high- and low-achieving students in fast-track programs, reduced class size, or hired extra aides (see Jones, 1982, for further elaboration).

III. CONCEPTS AND PRINCIPLES FROM PRACTICE

In this section, we elaborate on concepts and principles that emerged from our own research and development efforts. These are: (1) organizing instruction in terms of mastery learning units, (2) defining strategy-driven instruction versus content-driven instruction, (3) defining two dimensions of sequencing, and (4) integrating strategy instruction for reading in the content areas.

A. Elements of Instruction for Mastery Learning Units

Jones and her colleagues have argued that mastery learning as stated by Bloom et al. (1976) is a powerful philosophy about learning, teaching, and testing, but it is not a theory of instruction. That is, while it specifies elements such as objectives, learning cues, diagnosis of errors, and correctives, it does not provide clear guidelines for developing instruction—how to conduct the substance of instruction between the objectives and tests. Jones and

Spady (1985) have argued that a close examination of the most successful mastery learning programs in schools reveals that the success cannot be attributed to mastery learning alone because each of these successful programs has research-based elements of instruction and management components that most mastery learning programs lack. These successful schools contrast markedly with numerous mastery learning programs containing serious implementation "flaws."

Because of these problems, Anderson and Jones (1981) developed research-based instructional strategies for teaching concepts, information, procedures, and rules. Additionally, Jones identified the following elements of instruction, culled from various strands of research, to embed within mastery learning instructional materials (see Jones et al., 1985b, for elaboration). These elements are consistent with those identified by Rosenshine (1983). These elements are:

1. Objectives which are given to the teachers and students;
2. Instructional input that is addressed directly to the objectives such as a concept, procedure, information, or rule (Anderson & Jones, 1981);
3. Prerequisite information and skills where necessary;
4. A strategy for processing the input;
5. Examples, explanation, and prompted instruction for applying the strategy;
6. Guided practice;
7. Independent practice;
8. A test that is closely aligned to the objectives and instruction;
9. Corrective instruction and a parallel retest for students who fail the test;
10. Enrichment activities for students who pass the test to extend their previously learned knowledge.

B. Drive: Strategy-driven versus Content-driven Instruction

Instructional units must be driven by something: a concept, a set of information (content), or a skill. That is, once it is determined that instruction should be organized in terms of learning units based on specific objectives, the question arises: what drives the definition of the objectives? In traditional content courses, typically it is the content text that drives the instruction. The teacher seeks "to cover" the content, chapter by chapter, using tests to assess students' understanding of the information in the chapter. In traditional skills-driven instruction, objectives are defined in terms of learning highly specific skills so that skills instruction is often an end in itself, just as content becomes an end in itself in content-driven instruction. Thus, content and skills comprise the two ends of a continuum along which instruction may be defined.

We rejected both of these methods of defining instruction from the outset. Traditional content-driven curricula was too amorphous, lacking in focus and direction, and, in effect, lacking in instructional substance. Most skills programs are so focused on specific, isolated objectives that there is virtually no instruction. Units in such systems consist largely of defining an isolated skill in a single example and then presenting a few practice examples. This type of instruction is very fragmented and has been aptly labeled "skill and drill." Unfortunately, such programs dominate language arts programs and traditional study skills courses. In between these two extremes, what was needed was to provide comprehension instruction for both content and skills curricula. Thus we elaborated the following principles of strategy-driven comprehension instruction and content-driven comprehension instruction.

1. Strategy-driven Comprehension Instruction (SDCI)

This type of instruction is similar to skills instruction in that it focuses on teaching skills or strategies, and it is most appropriate for language arts courses and study skills or learning strategy programs. However, traditional study skills courses might focus on finding the main idea without really defining the main idea for specific types of paragraphs. Or underlining and linear outlining may be taught without really teaching students how to determine key ideas. And summarizing may be taught without providing rules for summarizing. At best, such courses model the process used to find, for example, the main idea, or underline; at worst, such courses merely show one or two examples of main ideas, underlining, and other skills.

SDCI differs from traditional study skills courses in several respects. First, the instruction is research based. Second, the focus is on teaching a broad range of strategies and thinking processes that includes, but goes well beyond, the skills taught in traditional study skills courses. Specifically, research-based learning strategy instruction focuses on such skills/strategies as visual and verbal elaboration, analogous reasoning, complex mnemonics, and various classification skills as well as finding the main idea, underlining, and outlining. Third, such courses provide comprehension instruction in that (1) there is a heavy emphasis on helping students articulate the process of applying each strategy; (2) much attention is given to helping students define specific types of text structures (e.g., sequential, compare/contrast); (3) there is a heavy focus on analyzing the meaning of what is read; (4) metacognitive strategies such as comprehension monitoring are given systematic instruction; (5) information is represented in graphic outlining structures such as flow charts, matrices, logic trees, and maps that reflect the *meaning* and *structure* of different types of text and that have far greater analytical capabilities than linear outlining. Fourth, there is often a great deal more emphasis on the management of time, on strategies for memorizing what is read, and on controlling impulsivity.

Chicago Mastery Learning Reading (CMLR) utilizes the SDCI model in the materials for grades 5–8 and in many units throughout grades 1–8, for the Vocabulary Learning Strategies strand. Figures 1a and 1b are examples of strategy-driven comprehension instruction from the reading program. Figure 1a is taken from the reading program's grade 6 unit on finding the main idea. Note the focus on comprehending the meaning of the paragraph. Figure 1b shows instruction from a grade 6 unit on making inferences from narrative texts using the 5W questions (who, what, where, when, and why). Note that in each figure, the unit is defined in terms of specific strategies, but the focus is on using the strategy to understand the meaning and overall structure of what is read. Other descriptions of SDCI may be found in learning strategy courses developed by Weinstein and her colleagues (e.g., Weinstein & Underwood, 1985), Dansereau and his colleagues (e.g., Dansereau, 1985), Armbruster (1980), Wittrock (1983), and Raphael and Pearson (1985; Pearson & Leyes, 1985).

2. Content-driven Comprehension Instruction (CDCI)

CDCI courses derive largely from research on teaching reading in the content areas and research on comprehension instruction. They are similar to traditional content courses in that covering specific sets of information drives the definition of the objectives, and, typically, the developer/researcher is not free to sequence the passages to be comprehended; that is, the teacher is often obligated to work through a text chapter by chapter because information in later chapters depends on understanding information in earlier chapters. This means that the developer cannot sequence passages from easy to difficult for the purposes of instruction, and many textbooks begin with information that is difficult. CDCI differs from traditional content-driven instruction in that CDCI provides comprehension instruction for the content in each chapter.

Comprehension instruction in CDCI courses or programs is quite variable. Some courses emphasize strategies before reading to activate prior knowledge and to establish a purpose in reading. Others emphasize semantic mapping or some form of graphic notetaking before, during, and/or after reading. Others emphasize the process of forming and testing hypotheses about the meaning of what is read and/or questioning strategies.

There are two types of CDCI courses or programs. On the one hand, there is the classic reading in the content area model that argues against teacher "telling" and providing direct comprehension instruction (Herber, 1985). Instead, such programs emphasize study guidelines, modeling, learning by doing, and other methods of indirect comprehension instruction. On the other hand, there are CDCI models that provide a strong element of explicit strategy instruction as a *means* to comprehending the content. These courses constitute content-driven strategy instruction. Such courses seek to provide a repertoire of strategies for the students to use to help themselves learn. This type of instruction emerged from the CIRCA project because the developers were committed both to reading in the content area and direct comprehension instruction.

Figures 2a and 2b illustrate how CDCI is implemented. Figure 2a shows the lesson overview of one lesson from the CIRCA project. It is evident from this overview that the goal of the instruction is to learn the content stated at the top of the page and that the strategies are used as a means of learning that content. Figure 2b shows the summarizing activity specified in the lesson overview. Other examples of CDCI may be found in the materials developed by Singer and Donlan (1982); Collins et al. (1980); Stein and Glenn (1979); and Tierney (1983).

CDCI and SDCI differ in three important ways. First, in SDCI, the skills objectives determine the sequencing of instruction, whereas in CDCI the content drives it. This single fact alters markedly the way that instruction is conceptualized and developed. Second, CDCI is taught by the content teacher, not a language arts teacher, learning strategies researcher, instructional coordinator, or resource person. Third, CDCI is taught within the context and time periods for content courses and is oriented to comprehending the information in a specific content textbook.

C. Two-dimensional Sequencing

Instruction that is devoid of comprehension instruction is relatively "flat" in that it consists largely of a brief statement about X (a skill or body of content), followed by practice in X if it is a skill, or reading combined with questions assessing comprehension if X is a segment of content. Instruction for the main idea, for example, consists largely of one or two sentences explaining what it is, and a couple of additional sentences that say that the main idea is at the beginning, middle, or end of a paragraph and/or that it must be inferred in some way. Programs containing comprehension instruction may be sequenced in three dimensions: content, strategy, and transfer training.

Review-Topic Sentence

Review-Topic Sentence   Unit 2: SA-5-1   **a**

Name _____   Teacher _____

ANALYZING PARAGRAPHS
Student Activity #5
A Homework Activity

A. Testing Hypotheses as You Read
When good readers begin reading a paragraph, they form an idea in their minds
about the topic of the paragraph. After they have read the first sentence,
they say to themselves, "This paragraph is going to be about such-and-such a
subject." As they continue reading, they sometimes discover that the topic is
what they guessed--that each sentence in the paragraph really is about the
first sentence. But sometimes that find they were wrong--that the first sentence was not the topic sentence and that the paragraph is actually about
something else.

These guesses, which good readers make on the basis of the first sentence or
sentences in the paragraph, are called hypotheses. Good readers are always
testing their hypotheses as they read, even when they do not consciously think
about what they are doing.

EXERCISE A INSTRUCTIONS   Diagrams
---1. TEAR OUT pages SA-4-2 and SA-4-3 from Student Activity #4.
---2. COMPLETE the following diagrams.

EXERCISE A DIAGRAMS   Paragraph A-3

READ PARAGRAPH A-3 AGAIN.

In paragraph A-3, the first sentence is the topic sentence: Every concert
orchestra is made up of many different groups of instruments. The supporting
sentences name the different groups of instruments and tell where they are
located. The last sentence, "Because of the many types of instruments, the
orchestra makes a wonderful sound," ends the paragraph. You may have thought
that it was the topic sentence, but it is not; the other sentences do not talk
about the orchestra's music or sound. The last sentence is the conclusion.

EXERCISE A DIAGRAMS

A-1. | A concert orchestra is made up of different groups of instruments. |

= orchestra is made up of
different groups of
instruments

FIG. 1.   (a) Example of skills-driven comprehension instruction for finding the main idea. (b)
Example of skills-driven comprehension instruction for making references. (Reprinted with
permission.) © Copyright 1983 Board of Education, City of Chicago, and Center for the Study
of Reading, University of Illinois, Urbana-Champaign.

INFERENCES FROM FICTION
Student Activity #3

Passage 3

ANTOINE'S GIFT

This story takes place during the Seven Years War (1756-1763) in Europe and
in North America. The countries of Austria, France, Sweden, and Russia in-
vaded Prussia. Prussia is no longer a nation, but it was located in what is
now northern Germany.

Antoine-Auguste Parentier had been a prisoner of war in Hannover, Prussia,
in 1757. When he returned to France, he found that the war had changed many
things. As he went from village to village, Antoine noticed how barren
(empty) the fields were. Farmers he met on the road were gaunt (thin) and
stared at him through hollow, unseeing eyes. Antoine felt he had to end his
countrymen's suffering.

Then he had an idea. While he was being held prisoner, Antoine had survived
almost entirely on a strange vegetable from the New World (The Americas).
This vegetable not only proved to be nourishing, but could be grown in the
poorest of soils. It could help the starving people, but the trick was to get
them to grow it.

The farmers were fearful of the unknown. They thought that new things would
bring bad luck. Thus, growing a mysterious vegetable from across the world
would be totally out of the question. As far as the farmers were concerned,
no good could come of it. In order to save them from themselves, Antoine
would have to work out a plan based on what he knew of the farmers' beliefs.

Antoine went to see King Louis XVI. It did not take him long to talk the
king into giving him a plot of land outside of Paris. Then Antoine planted
his crop. The local farmers saw how quickly it grew, but still they would
not grow the new vegetable themselves. Antoine had to make the farmers _want_
to grow the new vegetable. All he had to do was somehow make the farmers
think that it was forbidden for them to grow the vegetable; then they would
think it was good.

Antoine paid the king another visit. It was easy to convince the king, once
again, to help in order to save his subjects. The king gave Antoine the use
of his soldiers. Guards were posted (placed) around the field during the day
and withdrawn (taken away) at night. Soon, farmers all over the countryside
were growing similar crops in their own fields. Antoine smiled to himself.
Hunger no longer ruled France. The potato did.

B-6.   Who was Antoine Auguste Parentier?
  (a) <u>Think</u>:   The passage states that he was a prisoner of war.
  (b) <u>Inference</u>: He was probably a _____.

B-7.   Why is Antoine sad at the beginning of the story? _____

_____

B-8.   Why were the farmers suffering?
  (a) <u>Think</u>:   The fields were barren (without crops).
  (b) <u>Think</u>:   The farmers were gaunt and stared at him through hollow (empty) eyes.
  (c) <u>Inference</u>: They were probably _____.

---

a

LESSON 6 OVERVIEW

CONTENT FROM PART 2, REVOLUTION

The colonies establish an independent United States, with strong state governments and a weak national government.

The Articles of Confederation limit the powers of the national government, which results in problems for the new nation.

ACTIVITIES

Activity - Learning about the American Government under the Articles of Confederation [35 min.]

The teacher reviews the SPaRC reading/thinking strategy and directs the students to review what they learned in lesson 5. Then the students survey the graphics in Part 2, Revolution to predict answers to some discussion questions. After summarizing the discussion as predictions about goals, actions, and results for the new American government, the teacher directs the students to read the Summary Text and complete the action frame on SN **.

Reference Box: Action Frame (TM **, SN **)
Reference Box: SPaRC   (TM **, SN **)

Homework - Summarizing the Problems of the Articles of Confederation

The teacher directs the students to follow the instructions on SN ** for homework.

FIG. 2.   (a) Lesson overview from the CIRCA Project. (b) Action frame used in summary. (Reprinted with permission.) © Copyright 1983 Board of Education, City of Chicago, and Center for the Study of Reading, University of Illinois, Urbana-Champaign.

1.   Sequencing Content

In SDCI instruction, there is no body of content to be covered. Therefore, content may be sequenced to progress from easy to difficult in terms of

b

Part 2, Revolution   Unit 3: Lesson 6

Who took these actions?   The Americans

What goals did the Americans have in setting up their government?

(The Americans needed a national government to unite them. They did not
want the national government to have too much power.)

↓

What actions did the Americans take to set up their new government?

(Representatives wrote the Articles of Confederation, which set up a new
national government with very limited powers.
For example, the national government could not tax people, control
trade, or have a president or court system to enforce its policies
or laws.)

↓

What were the results of these actions?

(The first national government in America had very limited powers over
the states.)

Did the Americans' actions meet their goals?
(The actions the Americans took met their goal of having a national
government that was not too powerful.)

Were there other results?
(Yes, there were other results. The national government was too weak to
solve many of the problems America faced. For example, as soon as the
Revolutionary War ended, America began to have trouble with its allies.
There were also economic and political problems that the national
government could not solve because it did not have the powers it needed
to control the 13 colonies or act forcefully against other nations.)

complexity, explicitness, concreteness, familiarity, and length. Content may
be sequenced within a given lesson and/or within a given unit, and there is
no simple formula as to when to do it within a lesson or within a unit. Nor is
it easy to define clearly for writers what elements of text are being varied and

how. It is not possible to do this type of sequencing for CDCI because history texts may be complex, abstract, implicit, unfamiliar, and long from day one.

2. Sequencing Strategy Instruction

Strategies and skills may be conceptualized as *concepts*. Accordingly, it is necessary to provide the domain, critical features, examples, and nonexamples where appropriate. The domain might be text-learning strategies such as mnemonics, or prereading strategies versus postreading strategies or metacognitive strategies. Critical features would be the definition of the strategy and task (e.g., finding the main idea vs. inferring it), the text characteristics (such as compare/contrast), and text condition (e.g., well marked, explicit vs. poorly marked, implicit). Students will also need examples of appropriate and inappropriate applications, as well as some explanation as to why they should use the strategy.

Additionally, the developer may sequence in *four levels of strategy prompts* to use the strategy: (1) thinking-aloud, step-by-step prompts that spell out each step of the thought processes needed to comprehend and/or learn the content; (2) content-specific prompts that show the reader how to apply the steps to specific words, sentences, passages, etc.; (3) generalized prompts that merely remind the students to use the strategy; and (4) no prompts. Note that by definition the four levels of prompts move from instruction that is teacher directed (the step-by-step prompts), through guided practice (the content-specific and generalized prompts), to independent practice (no prompts).

For example, consider teaching how to make inferences from narrative passages in the grade 6 CMLR unit shown previously. Literal and inferential comprehension are treated as two concepts. In the first lesson, literal comprehension is defined and illustrated in an example. The critical features of literal comprehension are given in an explanation following the example, namely that the passage provides the answer to a given question. Then the students are given guided practice, followed by independent practice using passages of increasing difficulty. The same procedures are repeated in the next and following lessons for passages and questions requiring inferential comprehension. Again, with each lesson, the passages move from below grade level toward becoming more difficult in terms of vocabulary, sentence structure, passage length, familiarity, and figurative language; and the strategy prompts progress from step-by-step models to no prompts.

While some of the strategy instruction above may be appropriate for CDCI, most of it is not because it is too cumbersome, and it becomes an end in itself rather than a means to comprehending a segment of content. At the same time, following Anderson's (1980) argument, instruction should provide for each stage of learning. Thus, in CDCI models utilizing direct strategy instruction, there may be explicit strategy instruction before, during, and after reading, but it is not as explicit or generalized as in SDCI models (see Jones, 1985b and the upcoming section on SPaRC for further elaboration of the phases of instruction).

3. Training for Transfer and Student Independence

This type of sequencing refers to efforts on the part of the designer/ developer to train students to have flexible access to their repertoire of strategies. This means that students should be able to select appropriate strategies for different tasks. Accordingly, it may be useful for the teacher to articulate specific strategy labels and information about strategy use and applications.

D. SPaRC: An Integrated Strategy for Content Area Courses

To apply these concepts to instruction, we developed a procedure called SPaRC. SPaRC is an acronym for a procedure that is a variation of the classic SQ3R survey, question, read, review, recite procedures. The steps in SPaRC are (1) Survey and Predict from the titles, subtitles, graphics, and prior knowledge, (2) Read, and (3) Construct a summary outline and/or prose statement of what is read. In spite of similarities to the traditional procedures, several features of SPaRC are innovative.

First, SPaRC brings together the survey/predict phase of a typical directed reading/thinking activity (Stauffer, 1975) with the summarizing and analysis that are typically associated with constructing semantic maps and other interpretive graphics (e.g., Singer & Bean, 1983).

Second, the students use the information obtained from the survey/predict step to select what frame they will use. Frames are sets of content-specific questions that underlie specific units of text (Anderson & Armbruster, 1984). For example, a problem-solving frame for history might ask: what is the problem? What attempts were made to solve the problem? To what extent were the attempts successful? Frame questions are a guide for making predictions about the content of the text. Thus, the survey/ predict stage of SPaRC not only serves to activate schemata but also to establish a purpose in reading that is highly structured.

Third, during reading, the students try to evaluate their predictions (or answer specific questions), infer meaning from words in context, note gaps in comprehension, and so on. The construct step of SPaRC involves what we have termed response instruction (Jones, 1985b), in which the teacher either provides or helps the students generate rules for constructing summaries for different types of text structures (e.g., compare/contrast, problem/solution, and so on).

Fourth, Singer and Donlan (1982) point out that strategies for reading in the content area are exclusively instructional strategies for the teacher. They argue that students ought to be able to use such strategies themselves, and proceed to demonstrate experimentally that students can indeed be taught to do so. We devised SPaRC so that it is ultimately a reading/thinking strategy to be used independently by the students, after extended instruction.

One of the most useful features of SPaRC is that in all phases it involves whole-group instruction. This means that the low-achieving students may benefit greatly from participating in each step with the high-achieving students. That is, the high-achieving students share their knowledge and insight during the survey/predict and construct stages. Further, the high- and low-achievers benefit from the feedback they give each other. Thus, the process is an important equalizer in that everyone has access to the meaning defined by the group. Finally, SPaRC goes a long way toward dealing with the fact that students do not spend much time reading because they cannot take the books home. See Figure 2b above for an example of SPaRC instruction.

IV.   CONCLUDING COMMENTS

In conclusion, we would like to make a final case for university researchers to become more involved in developing instructional materials—either in schools or in school/publisher collaborations. If 70–90% of instruction in schools is based on the use of textual materials, we are not going to change the quality of instruction in schools without changing the quality of textual materials. Equally important, as Anderson and Armbruster (1984) point out, "easy reading is damned hard writing," and it takes a considerable knowledge of theory and research procedures to do it well. Asking publishers to develop research-based instructional materials without utilizing trained researchers throughout the development process is unreasonable and inconsistent with fundamental principles of instruction and change. If we are to expect publishers to provide research-based materials, we must do a better job of disseminating research-based models and guidelines, and we must foster extended school/researcher/publisher collaborations.

ACKNOWLEDGMENTS

This chapter describes over 7 years of applied research and curriculum development for the Chicago Public Schools and the U.S. Army Research Institute. The author wishes to express her deepest gratitude to the individuals and groups involved in this research. Additionally, the author wishes to thank the Center for the Study of Reading, which cosponsored the CIRCA project with the Chicago Public Schools, and the CIRCA staff at the Center who provided technical assistance and much insight.

Thanks should also be expressed to Lawrence B. Friedman, Margaret Tinzmann, and Beverly E. Cox, who coauthored an instructional manual for the U.S. Army Research Institute; many of the concepts developed here are taken from that manual. Finally, thanks are given to Joanne and Robert Freeman who typed many of the instructional materials and all of the professional papers that emerged from these projects.

Since the research and development have emerged from the efforts of many, the "we" used throughout the chapter is not the traditional editorial "we" used in many research papers. Rather, the use of this word refers specifically to all of those involved in the various projects.

References for the figures from published works are as follows: Figure 1: Board of Education of the City of Chicago. (1982). *Chicago Mastery Learning Reading: Comprehension, Gold Book (Grade 6) (Teacher Manual)*, pp. 80, 140. © Reprinted with permission. Figure 2: Board of Education of the City of Chicago, and the University of Illinois, Center for the Study of Reading, Urbana. (1984). *CIRCA Teacher Manual, United States History, Era II, Unit 3, Grade 7*, pp. 44, 49, 50. © Reprinted with permission.

REFERENCES

Alesandrini, K. (1984). Pictures and adult learning. *Instructional Science, 12*, 63–77.

Amiran, M. R., & Jones, B. F. (1982). Toward a new definition of readability. *Educational Psychologist, 17*, 13–30.

Anderson, L. W., & Jones, B. F. (1981). Designing instructional strategies which facilitate learning for mastery. *Educational Psychologist, 1*, 121–138.

Anderson, R. C., Osborn, J., & Tierney, R. J. (Eds.). (1984). *Learning to read in American Schools: Basal readers and content texts*. Hillsdale, NJ: Erlbaum.

Anderson, R. C., Spiro, R. J., & Anderson, M. C. (1978). Schemata as scaffolding for the representation of information in connected discourse. *American Educational Research Journal, 15*, 433–440.

Anderson, T. H. (1980). Study strategies and adjunct aids. In R. C. Anderson, J. Osborn, & R. J. Tierney (Eds.), *Learning to read in American schools: Basal readers and content texts* (pp. 483–502). Hillsdale, NJ: Erlbaum.

Anderson, T. H., & Armbruster, B. B. (1984). Content area textbooks. In R. C. Anderson, J. Osborn, & R. J. Tierney (Eds.), *Learning to read in American schools: Basal readers and content texts* (pp. 193–226). Hillsdale, NJ: Erlbaum.

Armbruster, B. B. (1985). Of living stuff and golden spikes, or why Johnny can't read science and social studies textbooks, paper presented at the annual meeting of the Conference on Reading Research, New Orleans.

Armbruster, B. B. (1980). "Mapping": An innovative reading comprehension/studying strategy, paper presented at the annual meeting of the American Educational Research Association, Boston.

Armbruster, B. B., & Brown, A. L. (1984). Learning from reading: The role of metacognition. In R. C. Anderson, J. Osborn, & R. J. Tierney (Eds.), *Learning to read in American Schools: Basal readers and content texts* (pp. 273–283). Hillsdale, NJ: Erlbaum.

Armbruster, B. B., Echols, L. H., & Brown, A. L. (1983). *The role of metacognition in reading to learn: A developmental perspective* (Reading Education Report No. 40). Urbana, IL: University of Illinois, Center for the Study of Reading.

Bloom, B. S. *Human characteristics and school learning.* New York: McGraw-Hill, 1976.

Bloom, B. S., Engelhart, M. D., Furst, E. J., Hill, W. H., & Krathwohl, D. R. (Eds.). (1956). *Taxonomy of educational objectives: The classification of educational goals. Handbook I: Cognitive domain.* New York: David McKay.

Brown, A. L., Campione, J. C., & Day, J. (1981). Learning to learn: On training students to learn from texts. *Educational Researcher, 10,* 14–24.

Campione, J. C., & Armbruster, B. B. (1985). Acquiring information from texts: An analysis of four approaches. In J. W. Segal, S. F. Chipman, & R. Glaser (Eds.), *Thinking and learning skills: Relating instruction to research* (Vol. 1, pp. 317–362). Hillsdale, NJ: Erlbaum.

Cavert, C. E., Jones, B. F., Shtogren, J. A., Wager, W., Weinstein, C. E., & Whitmore, P. (1980). Requirements and recommendations for learning strategies in the U.S. Army basic skills education program, Technical Report, Delivery Order No. 1585, Department of the Army.

Collins, A., Brown, J. S., & Larkin, K. M. (1980). Inference in text understanding. In R. J. Spiro, B. C. Bruce, & W. F. Brewer (Eds.), *Theoretical issues in reading comprehension.* Hillsdale, NJ: Erlbaum.

Commission on Reading. (1985). *Becoming a nation of readers.* Springfield, IL: Phillips Bros.

Cross, P. K. (1969). *The junior college: A research description.* Princeton: Educational Testing Service.

Dansereau, D. F. (1985). Learning strategy research. In J. W. Segal, S. F. Chipman, & R. Glaser (Eds.), *Thinking and learning skills: Relating instruction to research* (Vol. 1, pp. 209–240). Hillsdale, NJ: Erlbaum.

Davison, A. (1984). Readability—Appraising text difficulty. In R. C. Anderson, J. Osborn, & R. J. Tierney (Eds.), *Learning to read in American schools: Basal readers and content texts.* Hillsdale, NJ: Erlbaum.

Deffenbacher, K. A., Miscik, J. G., & Jarombek, J. (1974). Acquisition and forgetting of information in long term memory as a function of certain hierarchically structured variables. *Bulletin of Psychonomic Science, 4,* 590–592.

Duchastel, P. C. (1982). Textual display techniques. In D. Jonnasen (Ed.), *Principles for structuring, designing, and displaying text.* Englewood Cliffs, NJ: Educational Technology Publications.

Durkin, D. (1978–79). What classroom observations reveal about reading comprehension instruction. *Reading Research Quarterly, 15,* 481–533.

Durkin, D. (1985). Comprehension instruction: An analysis of reading methodology textbooks, paper presented at the annual meeting of the Conference on Reading Research, New Orleans.

Hartley, J. (1982). Designing instructional text. In D. Jonassen (Ed.), *The technology of text.* Englewood Cliffs, NJ: Educational Technology Publications.

Herber, H. L. (1978). *Reading in the content areas. (Text for teachers).* Englewood Cliffs, NJ: Prentice-Hall.

Herber, H. L. (1985). Developing reading and thinking skills in content areas. In J. W. Segal, S. F. Chipman, & R. Glaser (Eds.), *Thinking and learning skills: Relating instruction to research* (Vol. 1, pp. 297–316). Hillsdale, NJ: Erlbaum.

Jones, B. F. (1976). Individual differences in strategy use on diverse learning tasks and achievement in high school, unpublished doctoral dissertation. Evanston: Northwestern University.

Jones, B. F. (1980). Embedding structural information and strategy instruction within mastery learning units. Paper presented at the annual meeting of the International Reading Association, St. Louis.

Jones, B. F. (1982). Key management decisions for implementing mastery learning. *School Administrator, 45–48.*

Jones, B. F. (1985a). Reading and thinking. In A. Costa (Ed.), *Developing minds: A resource book for teaching thinking* (pp. 108–113). Alexandria, VA: Association for Supervision and Curriculum Development.

Jones, B. F. (1985b). Response instruction. In T. L. Harris, & E. J. Cooper (Eds.), *Reading, thinking, and conceptual developments: Strategies for the classroom.* New York: The College Board.

Jones, B. F., Amiran, M. R., & Katims, M. (1985a). Teaching cognitive strategies and text structures within language arts programs. In J. Segal, S. F. Chipman, & R. Glaser (Eds.), *Thinking and learning skills: Relating basic research to instructional practices* (Vol. 1, pp. 259–296). Hillsdale, NJ: Erlbaum.

Jones, B. F., Friedman, L. B., Tinzmann, M., & Cox, B. E. (1985b). Guidelines for instruction-enriched mastery learning to improve comprehension. In D. U. Levine (Ed.), *Improving student achievement through mastery learning programs* (pp. 91–154). San Francisco: Jossey-Bass.

Jones, B. F., Friedman, L. B., Tinzmann, M., & Cox, B. E. (1984). *Content-driven comprehension instruction: A model for Army training literature,* Technical Report, Army Research Institute, Alexandria, VA.

Jones, B. F., & Spady, W. G. (1985). Enhanced mastery learning and quality of instruction as keys to two sigma results in schools. In D. U. Levine (Ed.), *Improving student achievement through mastery learning programs.* San Francisco: Jossey-Bass.

Jones, B. F., Tinzmann, M., Friedman, L. B., & Walker, B. J. (1987). *Thinking skills instruction: English/language arts* (Ch. 2). Washington, D.C.: National Education Association.

Levin, J. R. (1982). Pictures as prose-learning devices. In A. Flammer & W. Kintsch (Eds.), *Discourse processing.* Amsterdam: North-Holland.

Markle, S. M. (1975). They teach concepts, don't they? *Educational Researcher, 4,* 3–9.

Meyer, B. J. F. (1982). Reading research and the composition teacher: The importance of plans. *College Composition and Communication, 33,* 37–49.

Moore, D. W., & Readence, J. E. (1984). A quantitative and qualitative review of graphics organizer research. *Journal of Educational Research, 78,* 11–17.

National Commission on Excellence in Education. (1983). *A nation at risk. The imperative for educational reform.* Washington, D.C.: Secretary of Education, U.S. Department of Education.

Paris, S. G., Cross, D. R., & Lipson, M. Y. (1984). Informed strategies for learning: A program to improve children's reading awareness and comprehension. *Journal of Educational Psychology, 76,* 1239–1252.

Pearson, P. D., & Johnson, D. D. (1978). *Teaching reading comprehension.* New York: Holt, Rinehart, & Winston.

Pearson, P. D., & Leys, M. (1985). Application of an explicit skills model in developing comprehension instruction. In T. L. Harris, & E. J. Cooper (Eds.), *Reading, thinking, conceptual development: Strategies for the classroom.* New York: The College Board.

Peper, R. J., & Mayer, R. E. (1978). Note taking as a generative activity. *Journal of Educational Psychology, 70,* 514–522.

Raphael, T., & Pearson, P. D. (1985). Increasing students' awareness of sources of information for answering questions. *American Educational Research Journal, 22,* 217–236.

Rohwer, W. D., Jr. (1971). Prime time for education: Early childhood or adolescence? *Harvard Educational Review, 41,* 316–341.

Rosenshine, B. (1983). Teaching functions in instructional programs. *The Elementary School Journal, 83,* 335–351.

Rumelhart, D. E. (1980). Schemata: The building blocks of cognition. In R. J. Spiro, B. C. Bruce, & W. F. Brewer (Eds.), *Theoretical issues in reading comprehension.* Hillsdale, NJ: Erlbaum.

Schallert, D. L. (1980). The role of illustrations in reading comprehension. In R. J. Spiro, B. C. Bruce, & W. F. Brewer (Eds.), *Theoretical issues in reading comprehension.* Hillsdale, NJ: Erlbaum.

Schoenfeld, A. H. (1985). *Mathematical problem solving.* New York: Academic Press.

Shimmerlik, S. M. (1978). Organization theory and memory for prose: A review of the literature. *Review of Educational Research, 48,* 103–121.

Singer, H., & Bean, T. (1983). Relationship between ability to learn from text and achievement in the UC and the CSU systems, Technical Report No. 3, Learning from Text Project, Executive Summary.

Singer, H., & Donlan, D. (1982). Active comprehension: Problem-solving schema with question generation for comprehension of complex short stories. *Reading Research-Quarterly, 17,* 166–186.

Spiro, R. (1980). Constructive processes in prose comprehension and recall. In R. J. Spiro, B. C. Bruce, & W. F. Brewer (Eds.). *Theoretical issues in reading comprehension.* Hillsdale, NJ: Erlbaum.

Stauffer, R. G. (1975). *Directing the reading-thinking process.* New York: Harper & Row, Publishers.

Stein, N. L., & Glenn, C. G. (1979). An analysis of story comprehension in elementary school children. In R. Freedle (Ed.), *New directions in discourse processing.* Norwood, NJ: Ablex.

Sternberg, R. J. (1984). How can we teach intelligence? *Educational Leadership, 42,* 38–47.

Tierney, R. J. (1983). *Learning from text* (Reading Education Rep. No. 57). Urbana: Center for the Study of Reading, University of Illinois.

Weinstein, C. E., & Mayer, R. E. (1986). The teaching of learning strategies. In M. C. Wittrock (Ed.), *Handbook of research on teaching* (3rd ed. pp. 315–327). New York: Macmillan.

Weinstein, C. E.,& Underwood, V. L. (1985). Learning strategies: The *how* of learning. In J. Segal, S. Chipman, & R. Glaser (Eds.), *Relating instruction to basic research* (pp. 241–258). Hillsdale, NJ: Erlbaum.

Wittrock, M. C. (1983). *Generative reading comprehension* (Ginn occasional reports). Boston: Ginn.

IV

EVALUATION OF RESEARCH
AND PRACTICE IN
LEARNING AND STUDY STRATEGIES

EVALUATION OF LEARNING STRATEGIES RESEARCH METHODS AND TECHNIQUES

Victor L. Willson

To a great extent, each discipline is informed by the methodology it employs (Kaplan, 1964). This theme has been the topic of study by philosophers of science for the latter half of the century. The extent of the influence of method on accumulation of facts and on development of theory is unknown, but in education some philosophers believe it to be substantial, as reflected in the writings of Stake and Easley (1978) and Smith (1981). They have been critical of the ANOVA-regression paradigm currently dominating educational research. Willson (1980) and Goodwin & Goodwin (1985) have surveyed the major methods and techniques used in education, and their findings supported the critics' contention concerning the dominance of ANOVA methods. The critics have charged that current methods are prescriptive and preordinate, that they focus the inquiry process on things that are already known and miss the unanticipated. It may be instructive to researchers in the study strategies area to examine current research methods and techniques employed in study strategies research.

Kaplan (1964) makes the important distinction between method and technique. A method is a general epistemological tool for research. It is useful across many disciplines (although not necessarily all), whereas a technique tends to be used primarily within one discipline. Examples of methods are randomization of units into experimental conditions and estimation of error of measurement. Examples of techniques specific to certain disciplines are titration in chemistry and use of rat mazes in psychology. Neither of these techniques can be reasonably interchanged between the two disciplines for most research activities. Of course, techniques may be borrowed as disciplines are merged along their common boundaries. Ethnographic field techniques have been extensively employed in educational program evaluations. Econometric techniques are currently being used to examine educational productivity. Sociometric observation techniques are being applied to the study of student school behavior and to learning outcomes. All such techniques are changed to some degree when employed in new areas. Scholars from the root discipline will complain about bastardization of the technique, while those of the recipient discipline will complain about the lack of understanding of the problems and issues in their discipline by the outsiders, and both will be right.

When a technique has been used in many disciplines and is basically used the same way in all of them, it is more properly thought of as a method. Randomization of units in an experiment (a technique which moved from agriculture to psychology in the 1930s and into education in the 1940s), is now considered as a method. Often researchers follow one method exclusively and deny any legitimacy to any others. This failing has been charged against most educational researchers by critics who feel that the ANOVA method has been too deeply entrenched in the teaching and conduct of educational research. Willson (1980) reported that over half of all techniques employed in the research in the articles in a 10-year period of the *American Educational Research Journal* were based on ANOVA or ANCOVA. The dominance of the method is clear.

No study to date has examined the learning strategies research corpus with regard to the research methods and techniques employed. This paper attempts to define purposes for learning strategies research, provides an initial scrutiny of the learning strategies research techniques currently being employed, and suggests some new techniques that might be used by learning strategy researchers to further the discipline.

I.   PURPOSES FOR LEARNING STRATEGY RESEARCH

Two samples of learning strategies literature were examined to determine current purposes for learning strategies research. The review by Weinstein and Mayer (1985) and the empirical work described in other chapters of this volume, including reference lists, were used as the basis for selection of research for investigation.

Four separate strands of research, completely subjectively defined, were encountered. These were:

1. Determination of effective learning strategies;
2. Detection of aptitude–treatment interactions (ATIs);
3. Validation of the effectiveness of learning strategies in actual learning situations (ALS) instead of in experimental settings; and
4. Generalizability of learning strategies across ALSs for students of various ages, with various abilities, for various ATIs, etc.

Because this paper is not directly concerned with the actual outcomes of research in these areas, but with the methods and techniques employed, it is not crucial to focus on the learning strategies research conclusions. The degree of success enjoyed by researchers in each area is important, however, since failure of a method to solve major problems or to advance the field is often the impetus for application of a new method, or, in some instances, for abandonment of the topic.

II. TECHNIQUES AND METHODS USED IN LEARNING STRATEGIES RESEARCH

Nineteen articles which reported new data based on observation of subjects were examined. In all 19, the dominant method used was analysis of variance. Note that I have termed ANOVA a method rather than a technique because, as a method, ANOVA includes the use of comparison groups, randomization, systematic manipulation of treatment, control of incidental environmental conditions, etc. (see Willson, 1980, for a related discussion). In at least two of the studies, factorial design was employed using aptitude of the learners as a crossing factor. The ANOVA method was employed even in those cases, as the learners were dichotomized into two or more groups, leaving the aptitude variable to covary in its original form. Techniques that are part of the ANOVA method were used frequently, such as multiple comparisons, trend analysis, and others.

Interestingly, of the empirical research presented in this volume, only Dansereau (Ch. 7, this volume) employed classical ANOVA methodology. His use of the method is exemplary, however, and is somewhat atypical in its use of sequential experimental studies that systematically explore an instructional variable. Other studies isnployed methods such as stagewise general linear path modeling (Palmer & Goetz, Ch. 4, this volume) and naturalistic methods (Schallert et al., Ch. 11, this volume).

One conclusion to be drawn from this initial examination of techniques employed, is that there have been limits placed upon the kinds of outcomes examined. Even though experimental designs have examined both achievement and effective dependent variables, they have little power to detect unintended and unforeseen outcomes (cf. Smith, 1981; Stake & Easley, 1978). For example, examination of fidelity and duration of employment of a learning strategy might yield new results in even the most carefully controlled experimental setting. In actual learning situations, the activities generated by the employment of experimental learning strategies might include diffusion of the treatment to students not in the study, application in other courses (in which the effects might be different than in the experiment), or individual modification of the strategy in unknown ways. In the early stages of development of a new field of inquiry, the premature closure inherent in

ANOVA design may prevent discovery of important outcomes and inter-actions.

Another outcome of the examination of the 19 articles was the finding that most learning strategy research seems to have a short temporal focus of 1 month or less, although a few studies extended over 3 months. One tentative conclusion to be drawn from this is that there is currently little knowledge about the long-term effects of learning strategies.

The methods employed by Palmer and Goetz (Ch. 4, this volume) and by Schallert et al. (Ch. 11, this volume) are representative of the innovation needed in learning strategies research. Willson (1980) found that ANOVA and regression are the dominant techniques used in education, but impor-tant contributions have been made by employing techniques that were origi-nally developed in biology (chi square, path analysis), psychology (factor analysis, scaling), sociology (survey, sociometry), anthropology (ethnogra-phy, ethology), and economics (simulation, time series experimentation, and productivity analysis). The use by Palmer and Goetz of ordered regression based on theoretical modeling is a good example of an alternative method that provides fresh insight. Reynolds and Shirey (Ch. 6, this volume) also discuss this approach in their review paper on the role of attention and metacomprehension in studying learning. Schallert et al. (Ch. 11, this vol-ume) use techniques that are grounded in the ethnographer's field method when they use subjects' diaries, subject interviews, text analysis, and in-structors' interviews to draw a picture of implicit instructions for strategies of learning from texts. Again, their method gained insights simply not possible in the ANOVA method. Their use of verbal self-report has been discussed quite thoroughly by Garner (Ch. 5, this volume) and further comment will not be made except to recognize that this technique, for all its limitations, has once again become respectable in experimental psychology. The cog-nitive movement simply has no other way at present to explore the processes of cognition, and learning strategies research is squarely in the middle of the movement.

A.   DETERMINATION OF EFFECTIVE STRATEGIES

There has been considerable debate in this area between experimentalists and observationalists. The use of experimental design has a 60-year history of success in determining which treatments are most effective under controlled or static conditions. The extent to which the environments found in current learning strategies research remain constant from occasion to occasion is the point upon which the argument rests. Critics of experimental methods sug-gest that the environments are much too complex to allow such an assump-tion, and that the fixed quality of the levels of an experimental design ren-ders it useless to detect variation in non-experimental field settings. This

produces contradictory and confusing results. These critics promote observational techniques, generally based on ethnographic field method. The
advantages of this method, discussed by Smith (1981), are that it is rich in
description of context, sensitive to departure from specified treatment, and
able to detect unexpected outcomes. Unfortunately, the field method is poor
at comparing competing treatments, since its epistemological preference not
to prespecify outcome measures leads to weak and inconclusive findings. It
is reasonable to conclude that the ANOVA methods currently employed are
the most effective in detecting effective strategies.

The research presented by Dansereau (Ch. 7, this volume) is an exemplary set of research studies using ANOVA to detect treatment effects. The
studies were conducted sequentially, each either replicating the previous
one or building on it to expand the "explanatory shell" (Kaplan, 1964).
Within the limits of the ANOVA method, Dansereau's care in designing
experiments to systematically investigate learning strategies is excellent and
exemplary.

B. DETECTION OF APTITUDE–TREATMENT INTERACTIONS

There have been a few recent studies concerned with the detection of
aptitude–treatment interactions in learning strategies research (Meyer et
al., 1980; Paris & Myers, 1981). The aptitude variable typically has been
reading ability, dichotomized into good and poor. This approach, while
providing evidence for interaction, is inefficient and often misleading. A
major failure of this type of research is its incorrect inference of causation
concerning the aptitude variable. That is, differences between good and
poor readers explain nothing about how to make good readers from poor
readers. Treatment differences tell us about effective learning strategies, but
the interaction between treatment and reading expertise is not informative.
No ANOVA techniques of this sort can provide causal evidence for improvement in poor readers unless the studies are longitudinal, examining pupil
change over time. The same poor readers must be given learning strategy
treatments that prove effective over time in comparison with poor readers
given traditional coursework.

Naturalistic inquiry is likewise misplaced when applied to aptitude treatment interactions. Naturalistic inquiry examines the status quo, and depends
upon serendipity to discover innovations in study strategies that will improve
poor reading skills. Its virtue is that the longitudinal study of subjects is
common, even expected. What is lacking is the availability of controls. The
direct manipulation of learning strategies is required to demonstrate that poor
readers can become good readers in response to the strategies'
implementation.

The use of good and poor readers seems to have been recently related formally to the research on expertise (Chase & Simon, 1973). There is an assumption in expertise research that the novice (a poor reader) can become expert (a good reader) under some observable and manipulable conditions. It is based on experience that some nonreaders become good readers. The assumption is limited by other constraints, including ability of the student. Strictly, the assumption should be refined to condition it upon ability: poor readers at a level of ability X (or set of abilities X_1, X_2) found in grades above 1 or 2 may well be different in abilities from *any* of the good readers at the same grade. In the higher grades, this is likely to be true for most poor readers. The selection process simply excludes direct comparisons that no amount of matching can remedy. Once again, experimental comparisons between random samples of poor readers given different strategies will form the best basis to assess reading improvement.

The dichotomization of aptitudes is often made arbitrarily at some point on the ability continuum. As Cook and Campbell (1979) so convincingly demonstrated, artificial splits of continuous variables can produce any desired relationship between two variables: positive, negative, or zero (Cook & Campbell, 1979). Also, this split of subjects, often excluding readers in the middle range of ability, requires an assumption that all readers in the good (or poor) group all perform identically under the treatment that they are receiving. This prohibits examination of covariation within the group between aptitude and achievement. Thus, such studies tend to miss important information because of the design employed.

The most powerful general technique for use in the detection of aptitude–treatment interactions is the Johnson–Neyman technique (Johnson & Neyman, 1936). In this procedure, a continuous range of ability scores is required for both experimental and control groups. A general linear model is employed that includes intercept, treatment effect, ability effect, and treatment–ability interaction effect. The regression weights for each effect are estimated along with the covariance matrix of the estimates. Tests on the null hypothesis for each effect may be made, and confidence intervals constructed. Of particular interest is the fact that the difference in mean score on the dependent variable between experimental and control groups, D, is a function of the ability of the subjects. Thus, an omnibus test of treatment effect averaged across all abilities is typically not useful, and one must specify the ability level for a student or a range of abilities (typically the entire range observed). The statistical test for a single ability value is termed a nonsimultaneous test; a test over the whole range of ability scores is called a simultaneous test because an infinite number of ability scores in the range are tested at once to see where the treatment group differs from the control and where it does not. This produces a cutoff score or pair of scores that tell us that the treatment was effective on one side of the cutoff and not effective on the other. For example, in an experiment comparing learning strategy method A with a control group, children with IQ scores between 95 and 130 are included. The Johnson–Neyman technique will allow learning strategy researchers to indicate the ability levels needed to profit from method A. Results might show that only for students with an IQ over 115, was method A superior to the control. Recent papers by Willson (1985), Rogosa (1980, 1981), and the text by Pedhazur (1982), provide examples and details needed to compute Johnson–Neyman statistics.

The choice of covariates has become quite important to detection of ATIs. General ability or achievement variables seem not to be sensitive to interaction (Bracht, 1970; Cronbach & Snow, 1977). More recently, however, Snow and his associates appear to have found replicable ATIs by selection of covariates more directly related to task requirements (Snow & Lohman, 1984). They suggest that complex learning tasks will correlate more highly with complex ability tests than with simple ability tests. It appears that some investigation will be required to determine which cognitive variables should be used as covariates in learning strategies research.

C. VALIDATION OF STUDY STRATEGIES IN ACTUAL LEARNING SITUATIONS

One of the consequences of limiting the length of time in experimental research studies is that, as yet, little is known about how the effective study strategies function over longer periods of time in actual learning situations (ALS). It is certainly premature to include learning strategies into secondary or postsecondary curricula when their effectiveness over months or years is not known. Of particular importance is the role of maintenance training in the delivery of effective learning strategies. Research with other kinds of learning activities such as speed reading and direct observation indicate that the activity must be periodically relearned or refreshed if it is to be maintained at a specified level. Paris (Ch. 17, this volume) has stated this point well.

Time series designs offer assistance in investigating long-term effects of learning strategies training. Time series refers to periodic, equally spaced measurements of a variable. Experimental designs that incorporate the idea of time series have fewer units of study (e.g., subjects or groups) and more repetitions of observation. Operant and reversal designs are well known in experimental psychology as time series in which experimental conditions are changed at specific time points. This procedure allows several observations at each condition. In such designs in one group, the experimental condition is observed after a baseline condition, whereas in another it is introduced immediately. For effects that can be extinguished (reversals), the experimental condition is stopped and baseline conditions resumed. Such designs would be quite useful in examining the amount and duration of maintenance training required for implementing learning strategies in classrooms. Glass et al. (1975) discuss the implementation of such designs. Approximately equally spaced observations (perhaps daily) on achievement are required for an initial baseline period, a period of training, and a return to baseline (hypothesized to occur when training is absent), followed by maintenance training periods. Time series analysts recommend at least 50 observations for a stable estimation. Such numerous observations may be impractical unless sampling designs are used. Cooney and Willson (1980) proposed the use of matrix-sampled item and subject frames so that each observation in a time series is constructed from subsample estimates. This procedure has been successfully applied in a junior high school science project by Farnsworth and Mayer (1984), who constructed an item bank of objectives and then constructed a matrix-sampling scheme to exhaust the pool of items and subjects each day, each student receiving three items. Items for a student were not repeated until the item bank was exhausted for that student. They then examined class means over a 56-observation period that included baseline, treatment, and return to baseline. A similar design could be incorporated into most study strategy experiments.

Naturalistic inquiry (Smith, 1981) is designed to examine activities as they occur in the real world. It draws primarily from anthropological and sociological field methods. A key to its success is the great amount of time that is needed for observation of people, collation of data on a daily basis, following of leads, interviewing both important persons and representatives of all groups, review of documents, triangulation of facts and conclusions, and stress on coherent reportage. As mentioned earlier, naturalistic inquiry techniques are excellent for detecting the unexpected and for producing a thick description of the state of things. That is what is needed to validate the way learning strategies are used and to validate their effectiveness in actual learning situations.

Several good reference works have been written about ethnographic field method. Naroll and Cohen (1973) edited a very useful book on techniques in ethnography. Smith (1981) cites a number of applications to educational settings.

D.   DETERMINATION OF GENERALIZABILITY
OF EFFECTIVE LEARNING STRATEGIES

There has not been a serious formal examination of generalizability in the learning strategies research literature. The major methods to be applied are generalizability theory and meta-analysis. Both will provide evidence for the

consistency of treatment across conditions. Generalizability theory will be applied as a secondary analysis technique where possible, while meta-analysis will be tertiary, due to the unavailability of primary data files. A third method may be considered, adopted from the program evaluation area. It has the general name of fidelity of transmission (cf. Welch & Willson, 1977). Borrowing the concept of signal transmission from communications theory, fidelity of transmission evaluation examines the changes that take place in educational programs as they are adopted in new settings. All three methods will be discussed below.

Generalizability theory was developed by Cronbach et al. (1972) and has recently received attention in the educational research community for the power of its conceptualization. The work of Cronbach and Snow (1977) on aptitude–treatment interactions using generalizability illustrates the power of the method to estimate variability between educational treatments across other conditions, such as sex and ability. The method results in computation of generalizability coefficients, which can be considered similar to reliability coefficients, except that these g-coefficients give an indication of the consistency of effects, such as treatments within or across levels of other variables of interest. In ANOVA designs, shown already to be the dominant mode for research in learning strategies, application of generalizability theory will allow researchers to calculate variance components and to estimate the g-coefficients for various experimental conditions. For example, in an experimental design with two treatments, three grade levels, and gender as independent variables, g-coefficients can be constructed to examine the consistency of treatment variance under fixed conditions of sex and grade. Stability of such coefficients for various studies using the same treatments will provide evidence for treatment generalizability across actual learning situations (if the studies are conducted in ALSs). The reader is referred to Rentz (1980) for a good primer on construction of g-coefficients. A recent article by Hopkins (1984) is also helpful, indicating the advantage of retaining item information and of matrix sampling of items in the application of generalizability theory to experimental design.

The limitation of generalizability theory at this time is the lack of a comprehensive theory to link different studies statistically, although an initial theoretical paper on the topic has been written by Willson and Boodoo (1985). The advantage of being able to link studies is that one would be able to examine the amount of variance in treatments under many different conditions. Meta-analysis, a new method, has been developed in the last decade to provide statistical variance component estimates, and does allow examination of treatment effects across studies. The conditions of the studies become independent variables against which standardized treatment outcomes are regressed. This covariation provides evidence for treatment variability

across conditions. For example, in a learning strategies research paper in which two treatments were compared, variables coded might include age of subjects, gender composition, ability ranges, duration of treatment, type of treatments, document source, internal validity rating of the research, number of outcomes, statistical significance, and effect size. These would be variables examined for all studies comparing learning strategies treatments. Both descriptive and inferential statistical analyses would be performed on these variables to attempt to describe the body of literature in a numerical way. Glass et al. (1981) have written a useful text on the conduct of meta-analyses.

The third method potentially useful for generalizing findings about learning strategies is grounded in the sociology of knowledge transmission. The dissemination of knowledge fits in directly to the determination of generalizability. Havelock (1973) proposed a theory of knowledge dissemination and use that asked five questions: who says what, by what channel, to whom, to what effect. Havelock and his colleagues discovered seven factors that are important for the channel in the dissemination and utilization of knowledge. The generalizability of study strategies might be usefully studied in terms of these seven factors that affect the channel (adapted from Welch & Willson, 1977):

1. Linkage. Can direct contact and bicommunications be established?
2. Structure. Is the strategy systematic so that it fits user's schedule?
3. Openness. Is the strategy flexible and can user communicate informally and quickly?
4. Capacity. How much communication between user and designer is possible?
5. Reward. How do both designer and user get rewards for the strategy?
6. Proximity How close physically (or in communication) are the designer and user?
7. Synergy. How many different ways can the user communicate with the designer?

The channel becomes very important to fidelity in transmission of the study strategy to new locations. As strategies become well known and identified for use with certain groups of people, the practical aspects of transmission become more important than they are now. For example, communication using research papers typically ranks low on all seven components of the channel factors. Evaluation of proposed delivery systems might be undertaken to determine ways to disseminate effective study strategies with high fidelity so that variation in treatment effects is not due to inability to teach the study strategies as they are intended to be taught. Evaluation specialists have used this theory to perform logical and observational analyses of the

generalizability of educational treatments (e.g., Welch & Willson, 1977). Its use as an aid to generalizing about effective learning strategies is recommended.

III. CONCLUSION

This paper has focused on four purposes associated with methods and techniques used in learning strategies research. These are (1) determination of effective study strategies; (2) detection of aptitude–treatment interactions; (3) validation of the effectiveness of study strategies in actual learning situations; and (4) generalizability across actual learning situations for various kinds of students. For the first purpose it was concluded that the methods currently being used are probably appropriate, especially ANOVA techniques. They are weakest at detecting unexpected outcomes, for which naturalistic research techniques might be employed. For the second purpose, the use of alternate quantitative methods such as the Johnson–Neyman technique seem warranted, as well as the application of more qualitative, descriptive methods. For the third purpose it seems essential that longitudinal studies be conducted in the actual learning situation and that researchers consider the long-term effects of teaching students new study strategies. Finally, the fourth purpose has not yet been undertaken by researchers in a significant manner, but enough research studies are accumulating to consider at some time both generalizability research and meta-analysis of the significant areas in the study strategies field.

REFERENCES

Bracht, G. B. (1970). Experimental factors related to aptitude-treatment interactions. *Review of Educational Research, 40,* 627–645.

Chase, W. G., & Simon, H. A. (1973). Perception in chess. *Cognitive Psychology, 1,* 55–81.

Cook, T. D., & Campbell, D. T. (1979). *Quasi-experimentation: Design and analysis for field settings.* Chicago: Rand-McNally.

Cooney, J. B., & Willson, V. L. (1980). *A matrix sampled time-series design: An evaluation model.* Paper presented at the annual meeting of the American Educational Research Association, Boston.

Cronbach, L. J., Gleser, G. C., Nanda, H., & Rajaratnam, N. (1972). *The dependability of behavioral measurements: Theory of generalizability for scores and profiles.* New York: John Wiley & Sons.

Cronbach, L. J. & Snow, R. E. (1977). *Aptitudes and instructional methods: A handbook for research on interactions.* New York: Irvington/Naiburg.

Farnsworth, C. H., & Mayer, V. J. (1984). An assessment of the validity and discrimination of the interview time-series design by monitoring learning differences between students with different cognitive tendencies. *Journal of Research in Science Teaching, 21,* 345–355.

Glass, G. V., McGaw, B., & Smith, M. L. (1981). *Meta-analysis in social research.* Beverly Hills, CA: Sage Publishers.

Glass, G. V., Willson, V. L., & Gottman, J. M. (1975). *Design and analysis of time series designs.* Boulder: Colorado Associated Universities Press.

Goodwin, L. D., & Goodwin, W. L. (1985). Statistical techniques in *AERJ* articles, 1979–1983: The preparation of graduate students to read educational research literature. *Educational Researcher, 14,* 5–11.

Havelock, R. G. (1973). Planning for innovation through dissemination and utilization of knowledge, Code No. 2981, Institute for Social Research, University of Michigan.

Hopkins, K. D. (1984). Generalizability theory and experimental design: Incongruity between analysis and inference. *American Educational Research Journal, 21,* 703–712.

Johnson, P. O., & Neyman, J. (1936). Tests of certain linear hypotheses and their applications to some educational problems. *Statistical Research Memoirs, 1,* 57–93.

Kaplan, A. (1964). *The conduct of inquiry.* San Francisco: Chandler Publishing Company.

Meyer, B. J., Brandt, D. M., & Bluth, G. J. (1980). Use of top-level structure in text: Key for reading comprehension of ninth-graders. *Reading Research Quarterly,* 72–103.

Naroll, R., & Cohen, R. (1973). A handbook of method in cultural anthropology. NY: Columbia University Press.

Paris, S. B., & Myers, M. (1981). Comprehension monitoring, memory, and study strategies of good and poor readers. *Journal of Reading Behavior, 13,* 5–22.

Pedhazur, E. (1982). *Multiple regression in behavioral research.* New York: Holt, Rinehart, and Winston.

Rentz, R. R. (1980). Rules of thumb for estimating reliability coefficients using generalizability theory. *Educational and Psychological Measurement, 40,* 575–592.

Rogosa, D. (1980). Comparing nonparallel regression lines. *Psychological Bulletin, 88,* 307–321.

Rogosa, D. (1981). On the relationship between the Johnson–Neyman region of significance and statistical tests of parallel within group regressions. *Educational and Psychological Measurement, 41,* 73–84.

Smith, M. L. (1981). Naturalistic research. *The Journal of Personnel and Guidance, 59,* 585–589.

Snow, R. E., & Lohman, D. F. (1984). Toward a theory of cognitive aptitude for learning from instruction. *Journal of Educational Psychology, 76,* 347–376.

Stake, R. E., & Easley, J. A. (1978). *Case studies in science education.* Urbana, IL: University of Illinois.

Weinstein, C. E., & Mayer, R. E. (1985). The teaching of learning. In M. C. Wittrock (Ed.), *Handbook of research on teaching* (3rd Ed.). New York: MacMillan.

Welch, W. W., & Willson, V. L. (1977). An evaluation of alternative systems for implementing curriculum change. *Journal of Research in Science Teaching, 14,* 223–230.

Willson, V. L. (1985). Analysis of interactions in ATI research. In C. R. Reynolds, & V. L. Willson (Eds.), *Methodological and statistical advances in the study of individual differences* (pp. 275–295). New York: Plenum Press.

Willson, V. L. (1980). Research techniques in AERJ articles: 1969–1978. *Educational Researcher, 9,* 5–10.

Willson, V. L., & Boodoo, G. M. (1985). Redefining meta-analysis in terms of generalizability, paper presented at the Fourth European Meeting of the Psychometric Society and Classification Societies, Cambridge, U.K.

PERSPECTIVES ON STUDY SKILLS TRAINING IN A REALISTIC INSTRUCTIONAL ECONOMY

Ernst Z. Rothkopf*

I intend in this paper to offer a critical perspective of research on learning skills and of the practical significance of this work for the problems of schools and other teaching institutions. My hope is to provide a balanced view of priorities for our research in this area. Are we focusing our efforts on the most important problems? Are the scientific and philosophical models that are guiding our work appropriate for the needs of students and schools? Do we need to correct our course so as to assure that our research leads not only to praiseworthy scientific achievements but also to important practical results?

Scientific goals and the search for the solution of practical problems do not always mesh smoothly. The investigation of learning strategies in the laboratory has produced some very good results, yet several of the attempts to apply such findings in practical educational settings have appeared naively innocent of the circumstances of schooling and have proven ineffective. I do not mean to indict the goals of learning skills researchers. Nearly all have been motivated by a very serious concern with educational issues. I, personally, have been fascinated for over 20 years by learning activities as a scientific problem with practical implications. But I believe that we need to reanalyze carefully how our research relates to educational problems. This reanalysis is needed in order for our work to have important impact on the schools. It may also improve the scientific quality of our research.

I will approach my analysis by looking at learning skills from the point of view of the schools. Then I will examine the models and ideas that have guided our research. Finally I will discuss how our research results fit into the needs of the schools.

I. SCHOOL PERSPECTIVES

The perspective of the schools is clear enough. Academic shortfalls are common. There are at least two kinds of problems. Students may meet

*Present address: Columbia University Teachers College, 525 West 121st Street, New York, NY 10027.

LEARNING AND STUDY STRATEGIES: ISSUES IN ASSESSMENT, INSTRUCTION, AND EVALUATION

academic standards, but what they have learned is insufficient or inappropriate to their needs later in schooling or after they have left school. On the
other hand, many students do not meet academic standards. This is sometimes due to inadequate teaching or inadequate teaching materials. It is
widely held, however, that low academic achievement is frequently due to
insufficient or ineffective learning or study activities. Many students do not
do enough homework or remember little of what they have "studied." Students pay poor attention in class or gain little from instructional episodes
from which other students have profited. Some of these failures have been
ascribed to low abilities. But hardly anyone doubts that the exercise of
appropriate learning activities can improve academic results.

What are these learning skills or learning activities that educators worry
about? What is the nature of the skills that have been proposed for inclusion
in formal learning skill training programs? Are they like bicycle riding or
tumbling? Are they so automatic that highly proficient performers can barely
describe what they do? No, they are not like that. Are they like folding a
parachute? Are they like describing the maneuvers of Nur el Din in the
battle of the Horn of Haddin? They are not. Are they like algebra or calculus,
ready to be used, whenever the situation demands it, except for the erosions
of forgetting? They are not at all like that!

No, they are more like the many skills where the critical characteristic is
not only knowing but also translating knowledge into action. Manners are
like that. Persons in a subway who are staring at an elderly pregnant woman
with a broken leg know they should offer her their seats. Yet sometimes such
women stand all the way to the hospital.

Study skills are like dietary information that diabetics can describe in
fastidious detail, but that they neglect at the dinner table. They are like
knowing how to protect the roses in your garden from aphids, but failing to
do so. They are like knowing about calories and wishing to be thin and yet
continuing to eat too much.

Study skills training is like information about birth control. General educational programs produce results, but a substantial number of unwanted
conceptions persist that are not due to deficiencies of method, or lack of
knowledge or skill, but, simply, from failure to use. Driving safety, indus-
trial accident prevention, village sanitation—all of these involve skills from
the same category as those trained in study and learning skills programs.

It seems very clear that what distinguishes learning activities in practical
settings is that we are concerned not only with whether students know how
to study effectively but also whether they are willing or disposed to do so.
The relative importance of these two components is an interesting question
for debate, analysis, and experiment. But it is fair to conclude that the
disposition to translate learning skill into action is very important. It is very
likely that those who have done research on health and safety education may

have just as much to contribute to the solution of practical learning activity problems as those who study how to teach geometry and physics.

II. THE RESEARCH PICTURE

Two major intellectual stances are identifiable in the scientific work on learning strategies. The first, derived from biological and instrumental learning origins, centers around the research on orienting reflexes (e.g., Sokolov, 1963; Wyckoff, 1952) and mathemagenic activities (Rothkopf, 1982). It started in the late 1950s, although its intellectual history probably can be traced to the investigatory responses of Pavlov. The second state is focused on trained, intentional control of learning strategies. This approach, which has clearly captured the contemporary imagination, began to gather momentum in the latter half of the 1970s. Its intellectual origins can be traced to neo-gestalters, phenomenologists, and to those who favor the computer as a metaphor for mind. This view is intimately intertwined with conceptions of man as a very rational creature.

Research with strong biological roots showed strong concern with conditions that affected elicitation, perhaps because animal subjects have no language and cannot be told what to do. This concern resulted in the careful separation of competence from performance. The distinction between competence and performance was theoretically formalized quite early. Hull, for example, incorporated it into his theory (1943) in the distinction between habit strength and effective reaction potential. Skinner (1938) recognized it by distinguishing between the conditions that shape the topography of an action and those that determine its rate of occurrence.

The rise of cognitive psychology during the past 20 years greatly weakened biological perspectives of human learning and memory. It relegated concern with elicitation of activities into the murky outer domains of motivation and social psychology. Although working researchers commonly make the distinction between competence and performance, the distinction goes almost unrecognized in current theoretical formulations. Rothkopf's (1981) recent macromodel is one exception to this in the realm of applied learning theories. Of course, as I have indicated before, the competence–performance distinction plays an exceedingly important role in determining the practical application of training in learning skills.

COMPETENCE

I intend to define competence and to discuss special aspects of competence in learning skills that are likely to be useful to students in academic settings and beyond.

By competences I mean the learned mental substrates that underlie the performance of learning activity. They are inferred (or perhaps defined by) what is taught to students and from observations of what they do or what they say they do. They may also be inferred from what has been learned. I have referred to these in previous works (Rothkopf, 1972a, 1976) as the topographies of learning activities.

Gross learning strategies that are taught tend to have three general components: (1) selection; (2) mnemonic mooring; and (3) integration (Cook & Mayer, 1983; Dansereau et al., 1979; Jones, 1984; Weinstein, 1978). These and other careful studies have shown that learning maneuvers, executed in any one of a number of variations, can produce gains in academic achievement and in retention. There is little evidence, however, that these learning strategies are universal, portable tools that help students in any learning task.

Learning strategies are neither content independent nor context free. As most are taught today, their value to the learner depends on subject matter and educational goals. They depend on the structure and form of instructional information. Perhaps most importantly, their value depends on the intellectual outlook and style favored by academics and educationists who manage the schools. The latter is, of course, important if the aim of learning strategy training is to foster academic success. But such training will not necessarily be useful in preparation for life and for the world of work. Clearly, a successful experimental demonstration in a particular setting is not a sufficient reason for a school to adopt a training program for a particular set of learning skills. The most important question is whether the targeted learning skills are really useful to the student.

III. LEARNING STRATEGIES AND EDUCATIONAL STYLES

The argument can be made that what certain learning (and some reasoning) strategies accomplish is to reduce information into forms that are currently in vogue in the academic/educational community. Such strategies are of immediate advantage to the learner because academic success depends on approval by members of this community. But it is uncertain whether these learning strategies will be useful in the long run, in the world of work or in more open, less structured learning settings. To put it in blunter language, such learning strategy training teaches students to extract what their teachers want to hear and to put it into an approved form. And what teachers want to hear and the forms that are approved may change from time to time or from circumstance to circumstance. It depends on educational fashions. The notion of the *main idea of a paragraph*, for example, smacks of educationists' cant. It also carries with it the tacit assumption, that the main aim of reading is reproduction of information in a test-like setting. There may be more to education than this. The developer of learning skill training must make sure that what is taught is sufficiently flexible to permit escape from educational traps. Clearly the nature of induced competence requires careful examination before permanent introduction in the classroom.

The critical questions are these: did the choice for a particular set of learning strategies arise from transitory aspects or forms of contemporary schooling? Is learning strategies training determined by the information needs of the learner in the contemporary world?

Historical analysis suggests that current approaches to the training of learning skills may be strongly influenced by current instructional tactics rather than by broad educational strategies or goals. Systematic scientific research on learning skills, except for a few scattered episodes, did not gather substantial momentum until the second half of the 20th century. However, concern with such techniques, particularly mnemotechnics, dates back at least as far as the Babylonian Talmud and to the rhetoricians of the classic Hellenic period. Why did the practice and teaching of mnemonic strategies flourish in classical times and in the late middle ages? The most important single factor was the lack of cheap books. Scarcity of books and manuscripts undoubtedly necessitated extensive memorization. When printing was invented and inexpensive texts and glosses became available, the use of mnemonic strategies declined.

What factor in today's world favors renewed interest in mnemonics and other learning strategies? Is it because of a steep increase in the rate and density of information to which the student is exposed? I do not believe so, because the remarkable accomplishments of computer technology have reduced our dependence on memorized factual detail and are likely to lessen our dependence on such memorized detail even further in the future.

A more plausible reason is that the universities in which teachers are trained have successfully managed to introduce fairly uniform instructional approaches in schools. These universities and the teaching community have also brought about the adoption of relatively stereotyped testing methods. Such methods have made demands on the student readily foreseeable. I am inclined to think that the current testing style in schools is more important than information density in reawakening interest in learning strategies and mnemonic skills.[1]

The view that I am proposing here is the following. Interest in practical

---

[1]There is also another more pessimistic hypothesis. It is that educational researchers believe that our classrooms are filled with students who are not intelligent enough to discover efficient learning strategies.

exploration in learning strategies may have been brought about by scientific discoveries, by experimental work in learning laboratories, and by theoretical conceptions. But the condition that makes learning skill training viable as an academic tool is uniformity of expectations about academic outcomes, the routine application of certain teaching methods, and the nature of currently used instructional media.

We must guard against locking the learning skills we teach too tightly into current educational practices and prevalent academic values. Such values are strongly flavored by a particular intellectual milieu and, perhaps, the outlook of an economic class. Many of our students will spend most of their lives in settings that are very different from academia and with very different intellectual values. It seems reasonable that we examine settings beyond the domains of the academic bureaucracies, such as the world of work, for example, or the learning world of travelers, of hobbyists, and of political and social affairs. The design of a useful learning skills curriculum needs to be a compromise between academic and other needs.

Selecting Learning Strategies and the Strategy of Selection

As indicated before, selection is an important component of learning skill. Selection includes two distinct, but related components. These components are: (1) the choice of strategies appropriate for particular conditions and tasks; and (2) the choice from the instructional content of appropriate elements to which particular learning strategies may be applied.

Selection is a critical component of learning activities because learning maneuvers and mnemonic devices, no matter how skillfully executed, are ineffective if they are inappropriately applied or if applied to inappropriate content elements. Inappropriate applications may result from mismatches between learning goals and the nominal purposes of a study maneuver. The nominal aim of the study maneuver may not be the most efficient method for achieving the actual learning goal, even when the nominal aim of the study maneuver appears to match the actual goal.

Selecting learning strategies according to nominal descriptions of their purposes is not efficient because incidental consequences are sometimes more powerful than intentional, systematic approaches. Everyone wants the learner to acquire intelligent flexibility in the choice of learning maneuvers. Almost every learning skill training program teaches that different learning goals require different learning activities. But broad identification of learning goals may not be sufficient for adapting the most efficient strategies. For example, if the actual study goal is to remember the exact sequence of events in a descriptive passage, it may be more efficient to try to remember the exact wording of the event description. These phenomena were very neatly demonstrated by the classical (and now apparently largely forgotten) study of Postman and Senders (1946). They asked subjects to read a Chekov short story under one of six goal-setting directions, e.g., general comprehension or remembering sequence of events, details of wording, etc. Recall was tested using items appropriate to each goal. While some directions facilitated performance on relevant items, others produced reliable improvements in unrelated items, improvements that were in some cases substantially larger than those produced by directions relevant to the test questions. The Postman and Senders experiment (1946) proved that the student will not necessarily achieve the specific goals intended by the study activities.

The second important selection activity does not involve choice of strategy, but rather choice of appropriate content elements. Skill in content choices is probably the most difficult learning strategy to train because it is so closely tied to the semantics of teaching materials and the pragmatics of the instructional tasks. Much learning material, particularly text, is intended for many uses. Consequently, ordering of content elements with respect to centrality or importance does not depend on the material alone but also on instructional purpose or demand. An encyclopedia article, for example, is not like a blue plate special that can simply be analyzed into the important meat, the accompanying vegetables, and decorative garnishes. In practical settings, particularly when conditions are not as stereotyped as standard classroom text or as in the hackneyed analysis of literary classics, cut and dried selection formulas will very likely flounder on the rocky complexities of human knowledge.

I am proposing two points about selection. The first is that we examine the relationship between actual learning goals and the nominal intent of the learning maneuvers we teach. Postman and Senders' (1946) work suggests that effective intentional control of learning activities can benefit from a little sophistication about the incidental consequences of learning activities. The second point is that learning materials by themselves may not be sufficient guides about what is important information.

IV. ELICITATION AND MAINTENANCE OF LEARNING ACTIVITIES

As pointed out before, the most salient and practically important facts about learning skills are that their academic consequences depend not only on acquiring competence in them but also on the disposition to exercise this competence when needed. There is no need to rely on anecdotes of the classroom for this conclusion, nor to search the rather sparse literature about study activities in school settings. Failure to exercise learning activities is a well-demonstrated experimental fact. It has frequently been observed in well-controlled laboratory settings. Most of these observations were based on experiments with spontaneously adapted learning activities. But there are ample reasons to believe that the appropriate elicitation and maintenance of learning activities is an important element in assuring success of formal learning skills training programs as well (Rothkopf, 1973). Elicitation and maintenance of study activities must be carefully considered in the installation of any study skills training program if it is to realize its full value for students and schools.

Three important characteristics of learning activities pose important practical problems and require special attention. These are: (1) variation in ambient level; (2) deterioration; and (3) lability.

1. Variation in Ambient Level

The disposition to exercise learning-related activities varies very widely among students. In laboratory settings, very wide variations in such indicators of learning activities as reading speed have been observed (e.g., Grambsch et al., 1983). In a typical prose-learning experiment, the fastest subject reads six times faster than the slowest in a particular reading task. Such differences in speed are much larger than what may be expected on the basis of differences in process speed constants among individuals. Friedman and Wilson (1975), using a very interesting unobtrusive technique, namely small glue seals affixed on book pages near the spine, found that as many as 60% of text pages had never been opened. By contrast, in early sections of the book and in sections that were assigned just *after* administration of class tests, only about 4% of the glue seals remained unbroken. This is another quite typical case of large differences in learning activity indicators across time and probably among people. Turning pages in a text book is a fairly basic component element in learning activities. There is nearly always, in these experiments, a moderate positive correlation between indices of study activities and measured achievement. It should also be pointed out that one of the notable differences between American and foreign schools in a recent study was that for American schools a new category had to be created for the status of students at any given time in school. It was *not present in class.* I saw a report of this in *The New York Times,* but I am, unfortunately, not able to provide an exact reference.

2. Deterioration

Hoffman (1946), Rothkopf and Bisbicos (1967), and Rothkopf and Coke (1968) have observed substantial deterioration of learning activities during prolonged study. Such deterioration is marked by changes in eye movement patterns during reading, by decreases in inspection time, and by decreases in measured achievement. Correspondence schools have been contented beneficiaries of this phenomenon. Lessons from later portions of courses can be safely prepared in much smaller quantities than the initial sections. The graph in Fig. 1, obtained from a course on computer programming, is a dramatic example of such systematic deterioration of learning activities.

3. Lability

Rothkopf and Bisbicos (1967) and Quellmalz (1971) have shown that the nature of achievements, i.e., what is learned, changes in accordance with the demands made on students. It is reasonable to infer from such data that these achievement changes were due to changes in learning activity. These changes are not only confined to a particular situation and strictly focused, but also have momentum and carry forward even into study situations that are governed by different task demands. The so-called *forward* effect of adjunct questions is an example of this (e.g., see Anderson & Biddle, 1975; Rothkopf 1982). Another intriguing example of this is the momentum effects associated with changes in the difficulty of instructional material (see Rothkopf & Coatney, 1974).

We know something about the factors that alter learning activities and about what maintains them at a vigorous and effective level. For a recent

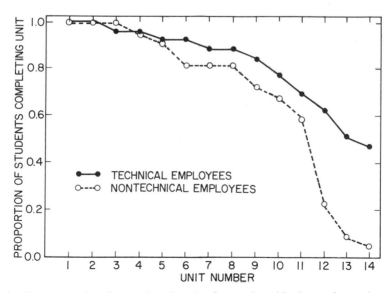

FIG. 1. Proportion of students with technical and nontechnical backgrounds completing successive units of a self-instructional course on computer programming.

review of relevant work in our laboratory and elsewhere, see Rothkopf (1982). A useful generalization is that learning activities, including many of the formal strategies proposed elsewhere is this volume, behave like operants. Learning activities, their vigor and, to a certain degree, their topography, are strongly influenced by their consequences. Such consequences are determined by immediate results produced by the learning activities themselves, and also by the circumstances and demands of the school settings. Educationally relevant contingencies have to be established in the classroom if educationally relevant learning activities, and with them, educationally relevant achievements, are to be maintained.

It is therefore very important to make sure that the educational environment provides learners with consistent and appropriate consequences for study activities. If teachers do not check what students should have learned or if classroom interaction and various exercises do not strongly involve the knowledge that was supposed to be gained by the student, then the activities that produced the knowledge will be extinguished or modified, regardless of the artful training that students may have received in these activities.

In short, competence in learning skills is not sufficient for continued academic success. What is needed, in addition, is a supportive instructional environment. We do not have much information about the relative importance of (1) the topography as compared to (2) the conditions or dispositions that control elicitations. The two factors are not necessarily independent. Perhaps the consequences produced by effective topographies tend to maintain these topographies better than those generated by less adequate learning strategies.

Direct, deductive methods are used to train learning activities in programs such as those used by Weinstein and Dansereau. But the conclusions to be drawn from the research of Rothkopf and his co-workers (see Rothkopf, 1982) are that learning activities are flexible and adaptive. They are also changed by induction whether the learner is aware of it or not. The instructional environment has the last word. If we want learning activity training to work, we have to provide a proper instructional environment or find out how to maintain effective learning activities, even in an undesirable setting. Teaching flexible, productive study strategies is useful, but the goal is to create schools that are properly demanding and are sensitive to the achievements of their students.

V. CONCLUSIONS

I have argued elsewhere that a demonstration of the efficiency of a technique in the laboratory is not sufficient reason for installing the method in practical settings. An educational decision is a balanced judgment in which one must weigh many factors against the size and importance of gains in achievement, learning speed, and retention. It is an engineering decision that should be determined more by needs than by intellectual hobbyhorses, be they ever so handsome and spirited.

Installing a training program for learning skills does not appear to require very substantial resources. The cost to the school is small (smaller than subject matter teaching, no doubt) and it is not too demanding of time. We need to guard vigorously against two potential problems. The first is excessively high and erroneous expectations of the schools. They must not rely exclusively on conveniently available learning skills training to solve achievement problems. The exercise of learning skills is not a problem of competence alone, but a matter of a beneficially sustaining instructional environment. Creating such an environment is a difficult technical and administrative task. Rather than face this task, many schools will be inclined to boast too readily about their shiny new learning skills program, be it from Austin, Dallas, or Illinois. If the programs are to succeed, the schools must also commit themselves to creating environments that will sustain the learning activities of their students.

The second problem is the nature of the competences that are targeted in learning skills programs. We want to make certain that they transcend narrow academic formalisms and unduly idealized conceptions of man. I have discussed the formalism problem earlier in this paper.

Learning skills training ought to provide students with widely applicable skills that are portable beyond narrow classroom demands. And we also need to recognize that much valuable learning is accomplished without deliberate intent and without much awareness. We need to find ways to help students become more effective spontaneous learners as well as deliberate practitioners of finely honed learning arts.

REFERENCES

Anderson, R. C., & Biddle, W. B. (1975). On asking people questions about what they are reading. In G. Bower (Ed.), *Psychology of learning and motivation* (Vol. 9, pp. 89–132). New York: Academic Press.

Cook, L. K., & Mayer, R. E. (1983). Reading strategies training for meaningful learning from prose. In M. Pressley, & J. R. Levin (Eds.), *Cognitive strategy research: Educational applications*. New York: Springer Verlag.

Dansereau, D. F., Collins, K. W., McDonald, B. A., Holley, C. D., Garland, J., Dickhoff, G., & Evans, S. H. (1979). Development and evaluation of a learning strategy training program. *Journal of Educational Psychology, 71*, 64–73.

Friedman, M. P., & Wilson, R. W. (1975). Application of unobtrusive measures to the study of textbook usage by college students. *Journal of Applied Psychology, 60*, 659–662.

Grambsch, P., Clark, L., DeSarbo, W. S., & Rothkopf, E. (1983). An analysis of individual differences in reading, unpublished paper, ATT Bell Laboratories.

Hoffman, A. C. (1946). Eye-movements during prolonged reading. *Journal of Experimental Psychology, 36,* 95–118.

Jones, B. F., Friedman, L. B., Tinzmann, M., & Cox, B. E. (1984). Content-driven comprehension instruction: A model for army training literature, Technical Report, Army Research Institute, Alexandria, VA.

Hull, C. L. (1943). *Principles of behavior,* New York: Appleton-Century-Crofts.

Postman, L., & Senders, V. L. (1946). Incidental learning and generality of set. *Journal of Experimental Psychology, 36,* 153–165.

Quellmalz, E. S. (1971). Effects of three characteristics of text-embedded response requirements on the development of a dominant focus in prose learning. Ph.D. dissertation. University of California, Los Angeles.

Rothkopf, E. Z. (1972a). Structural text features and the control of processes in learning from written materials. In R. O. Freedle, & J. B. Carroll (Eds.), *Language comprehension and the acquisition of knowledge,* Washington, D.C.: V. H. Winston and Sons.

Rothkopf, E. Z. (1972b). Variable adjunct question schedules, interpersonal interaction and incidental learning from written material. *Journal of Educational Psychology, 63,* 87–92.

Rothkopf, E. Z. (1973). Course content and supportive environments for learning. *Educational Psychologist, 10,* 123–128.

Rothkopf, E. Z. (1976). Writing to teach and reading to learn: A perspective on the psychology of written instruction. In N. L. Gage (Ed.), *The psychology of teaching methods* (The seventy-fifth yearbook of the National Society for the Study of Education, pp. 91–129). Chicago, IL: The National Society for the Study of Education.

Rothkopf, E. Z. (1981). A macroscopic model of instruction and purposive learning: An overview. *Instructional Science, 10,* 105–122.

Rothkopf, E. Z. (1982). Adjunct aids, and the control of mathemagenic activities during purposeful reading. In W. Otto, & S. White (Eds.), *Reading expository material* (pp. 109–138). New York: Academic Press.

Rothkopf, E. Z., & Bisbicos, E. E. (1967). Selective facilitative effects of interspersed questions on learning from written materials. *Journal of Educational Psychology, 58,* 56–61.

Rothkopf, E. Z., & Coatney, R. (1974). Effects of readability of context passages on subsequent inspection rate. *Journal of Applied Psychology, 59,* 679–682.

Rothkopf, E. Z., & Coke, E. U. (1968). Learning about added sentence fragments following repeated inspection of written discourse. *Journal of Experimental Psychology, 78,* 191–199.

Rothkopf, E. Z., Fisher, D. G., & Billington, M. J. (1982). Effects of spatial context during acquisition on the recall of attributive information. *Journal of Experimental Psychology: Learning, Memory, and Cognition, 8,* 126–138.

Skinner, B. F. (1938). *The behavior of organism.* New York: Appleton-Century-Crofts.

Sokolov, E. N. (1963). Higher nervous functions: The orienting reflex. *Annual Review of Physiology, 25,* 545–580.

Weinstein, C. E. (1978). Elaboration skills as a learning strategy. In H. F. O'Neill (Ed.), *Learning strategies.* New York: Academic Press.

Wyckoff, L. B., Jr., (1952). The role of observing responses in discrimination learning, Part I. *Psychological Review, 59,* 431–442.

16

A CONSTRUCTIVE REVIEW
OF RESEARCH ON
LEARNING STRATEGIES

M. C. Wittrock

I.   INTRODUCTION

We share a noble goal. It is to educate everyone.

The authors of this volume also share a method for attaining that noble and age-old dream. The method consists of conducting research on the teaching of learning strategies to students.

This volume contains excellent papers by educational psychologists, experimental psychologists, clinical psychologists, and educational researchers who study human cognition, including learning strategies and metacognitive processes. From their chapters it is clear that these researchers believe that the design and teaching of learning strategies play a critical role in realizing the nearly impossible dream of educating everyone. I share that dream and that method of attaining it by applying principles of cognitive psychology to the construction of effective and teachable learning strategies. These important ideas have a history dating to antiquity.

II.   THE TEACHING OF LEARNING STRATEGIES

In the days of ancient Greece and Rome, teachers, authors, and rhetoricians, including Cicero and Quintillian, also shared an interest in the teaching of learning strategies. Learning how to remember information was an important part of higher education, because most of higher education was devoted to the art of public speaking, which they called rhetoric. An important part of rhetoric was learning how to memorize the sequence of the points in speeches, because paper and pencil were not readily available for writing notes, scripts, and outlines. Instead, teachers and orators used well-developed imagery mnemonics derived from Aristotle's model of memory, which emphasized putting points in a linear sequence, with each point represented by an image involving an interaction with an easily retrievable familiar object.

From this beginning came the ancient imagery mnemonics with which all of us are familiar. They have been regularly used by students, teachers, lawyers, politicians, statesmen, and other professionals. The architects of ancient Greece and Rome, and later of medieval times, used vivid imagery to represent important events and concepts. For example, in cathedrals, good and evil were clearly and concretely depicted by the use of imagery.

Those pedagogical uses of imagery mnemonics persevered until about 100 years ago, when their use began to decline. Not many people remember that a *finagler* was originally one who used Gregor von Finagle's 19th century imagery mnemonic system to win card games by remembering which cards in the deck had already been played. Today we look upon that technique as something just short of dishonesty, hence the implication of the term *finagler*. We do not often appreciate imagery memory strategies; and we do not use them much in schools. Other than in some elementary schools, you will see little use of imagery, such as paintings and statues in classrooms.

Now we have a different way to remember information, a more cost-effective way: the book and all its derivatives. But along with an increased use of books has come a decline in the pedagogical use of imagery to enhance memory or understanding.

Only recently are we beginning to study again the thought processes involved in stimulating learning, memory, and comprehension. Research on verbal learning strategies, including the facilitation of attention and comprehension is increasing, as is the research on the use of imagery. Recently, images, for example, were used to facilitate memory, by use of pegword mnemonics. Infrequently, imagery has been used to enhance comprehension by having people integrate information, such as by imaging an interaction among the characters in a play.

Underlying the renaissance of interest in learning strategy are modern derivatives of ancient principles of cognitive psychology that appeal broadly to clinicians, educators, researchers, and experimental psychologists. The essential concept uniting these principles is that the central function of the mind is to build representations of events and models of experience. It uses these mental representations and models to solve problems, and to give meaning to experience by relating it to knowledge. The mind functions, in essence, to make sense of experience. This is an oversimplification, but it is the gist of the idea.

Research on learning strategies and metacognitive processes fits within this context. We study ways that can be, or that are, used to acquire knowledge, to solve problems, to build mental representations, and to make sense of experience. We study how people learn these fundamental thought processes.

We study these processes to build models of them. We build models of them so that we can teach them. Our first goal is to understand the processes and our ultimate goal is to teach them.

Stated alternatively, we should not teach learning strategies without thoroughly understanding them, without conceptualizing the network involved in learning the materials we give students. By becoming aware of learning strategies, by measuring them, by naming them, and by trying to teach them to students, we believe that we can enhance learning in class and also performance on the job. We are making substantial progress in these areas. We are moving toward an understanding of thought processes and toward an understanding of how we might give learners an awareness of them, and some self-control over them.

III.   A MODEL OF LEARNERS' THOUGHT PROCESSES

Our noble aspiration—to improve education through knowledge about learning strategies—leads us to study cognition in a number of areas, all of which contribute components to the model of learners' thought processes that I see coming from this volume. I will now try to summarize the fundamental concepts presented in the chapters of this book by stating the model of thought processes that I constructed when I read these papers.

The chapters discuss essentially three cognitive processes or aspects of cognition. Some of the chapters discuss attention, e.g., the chapter by Reynolds and Shirey (Ch. 6, this volume). Others discuss motivation, e.g., the chapters by Palmer and Goetz (Ch. 4, this volume) and by McCombs (Ch. 9, this volume). Most of the papers describe reading comprehension, or at least, comprehension in general.

There are chapters about measuring learning strategies, e.g., the one by Weinstein (Ch. 3, this volume). Garner (Ch. 5, this volume) discusses using verbal reports to measure strategies, and what sense we can make out of verbal reports. Willson's chapter (Ch. 14, this volume) discusses the research methods we use; and Schmeck's chapter (Ch. 10, this volume) relates learning strategies to learning styles.

The model of learning strategies emerging from the papers in this volume looks very good to me. The model centers on active learners (1) who attend to instruction; (2) who attribute results to their own effort; (3) who, at least in large part, relate tasks and materials to their knowledge and experience; and (4) who construct meaning from that interaction. These model learners are aware of their own learning strategies, choose among them, and employ them appropriately for the tasks and the context.

Basically, the model consists of these three cognitive processes—attention, motivation, and comprehension. I want to discuss them one at a time, relating these three processes to research in related fields.

A. ATTENTION

In the chapter by Reynolds and Shirey (Ch. 6, this volume) on attention, some fundamentally important concepts were presented. In the *Annual Review of Psychology* (1977), I discussed how an attentional model explained the operation of adjunct questions and behavioral objectives. That idea, of course, was not original with me—other people had been saying the same sort of thing. According to an attentional model, prequestions should be better than postquestions, in some contexts, and postquestions better than prequestions, in other contexts. The prequestion directs attention to those facts or concepts that are mentioned. The postquestion directs attention only in subsequent paragraphs, and therefore does not lead to specific responses. Yet postquestions do facilitate behavior according to the concept that is mentioned repeatedly in them. Objectives seem to work in much the same way.

Another line of research also shows the value of attentional models for understanding teaching processes. In the new edition of the *Handbook of Research on Teaching* (Wittrock, 1986), there is a chapter by Brophy in which he reports some interesting findings about how reward works to direct attention in the classroom. Reward does not seem to be good positive reinforcement, because it is not given frequently enough to students. Instead of changing the behavior of the child to whom it is given, the reward seems to change the behavior of the children who observe it being given. Reward conveys a teacher's notion about what is correct, about what the teacher expects from the students.

In this example, attention is useful for explaining classroom learning. Unfortunately, attention might come to explain nearly all learning and comprehension. We need to ensure that we do not use attention as a synonym for learning.

In the Reynolds and Shirey chapter (Ch. 6, this volume), attention was not used loosely as a synonym for learning. It is an excellent paper, with important findings to report. The research follows a productive line, builds a model, tests it, and develops causal links. That is a kind of research we need on attention.

Other research on attention has developed useful training programs. Bonnie Camp (1980), Virginia Douglas (1976), and Donald Meichenbaum (1978) have developed metacognitive training programs that give some hyperactive children who are on stimulant drugs hope of getting off the medications. Sometimes these strategies do not work, but sometimes they work remarkably well. Their research is a good example of how one can take a theory and use it to develop a training program.

B. Motivation

The second part of my model, the process of motivation, has probably been studied more than almost any other area of research on learning, with, perhaps, the exception of comprehension.

This volume includes several stimulating chapters on motivation. For example, the Palmer–Goetz paper (Ch. 4, this volume) deals with how learners select strategies according to their ability and their history of success and failure and McComb's paper (Ch. 9, this volume) deals with instilling motivation. Underlying each of these papers on motivation is an emphasis on attributional processes and self-efficacy. These reports show how people behave differently if they attribute their actions to effort rather than to ability, luck, or other factors. Indeed, attribution does make a difference in their performance. It seems to increase the learners' sense of self-efficacy if they succeed through their own efforts.

The research on motivation discussed in this volume by Palmer and Goetz (Ch. 4, this volume), and McCombs (Ch. 9, this volume) fits well with that performed recently by some other researchers. Research on attributional retraining programs, such as Carol Dweck's research on learned helplessness (1975), and Richard deCharms's work on locus of control and self-efficacy (1972), report complementary findings about the improvement of learning due to changes in motivational patterns.

C. Comprehension

The third and final cognitive process is comprehension. Many of the chapters in this volume deal with research on reading comprehension. To facilitate reading comprehension, we often return to some of the ancient techniques used to enhance memory (Wittrock, 1974).

Our methods for stimulating understanding of text ask people to relate the text to their past background. We have them build a structure, and assemble the units of the text into some larger wholes. We ask them to do something actively with the text (Wittrock, 1981, 1986).

Some of the chapters of this volume deal with writing summaries, elaborating on the text, inserting cues into textbooks, working in pairs, and constructing curriculum materials to stimulate comprehension and metacognitive thought processes. In all cases, the emphasis is on getting people to understand text by doing something with it, such as writing summaries or inferences, to generate relationships between it and their knowledge.

IV. THE TEACHING OF READING COMPREHENSION

During the past 2 years, at the Army Research Institute, I have been studying the same processes and techniques. I want to briefly discuss that research (Wittrock, 1984) before I come to my concluding remarks, because it shows relationships among attention, motivation, and comprehension, the components of the model that I am using to summarize this volume.

My research was intended to help enlisted men, who had failed reading comprehension tests, to learn how to read better. We soon learned that these three processes that we have discussed—attention, motivation, and comprehension—were critical to improving reading comprehension. We soon found that we needed to know in detail the learner's interests, motivations, and models of reading comprehension. Without that knowledge, we would make serious mistakes in designing instruction.

When we first worked with these young men, we learned that some of their motivations were quite different from what we expected. Many of them had given up on themselves. Because many of them had been told from childhood that they could not read, they believed that they were never going to learn how to read. They also believed that nobody could ever teach them how to read. When some of them came to class, they would quickly find reasons why they did not want to do what we had assigned them. They would say things such as, "This is too long a reading," or "We are not interested in this reading." We learned quickly that we had to know much about their attributional patterns, and their feelings of self-efficacy.

Many of their attributions were bad from our point of view. They did not believe that by putting forth effort they would ever learn to read. Reading seemed beyond their ability. They often had poor self-concepts. A few of them would make statements such as, "I cannot get married because I know I cannot support a family."

They were often the opposite of the stereotype that people have of many young soldiers. They were anything but fun-loving, fast-living people. They were discouraged. They showed a learned helplessness in their behavior.

We quickly learned that we had to give them brief readings that they felt were within their grasp. We found that they did not, at first, want to work with a microcomputer, because they thought somebody would take their data from it and report their poor scores to their sergeants. Instead they wanted to work in small groups composed only of marginally literate soldiers and a supportive, nonpunitive teacher.

Some topics we thought they would be interested in reading did not interest them. We thought that passages on Martin Luther King, sports cars, and movie stars would interest them, but many of the soldiers were not interested in these topics. Because the particular class we worked with was interested in reenlisting in the army, they wanted to read only army manuals. They were interested in topics such as "how to lubricate your tank." Their motives were all admirable and quite understandable, if one practices the model I am presenting here.

We then developed written materials from army manuals and gave them to the next class of remedial readers in the army. Unfortunately for us, that second class consisted of soldiers who were waiting to get out of the army. They wanted to read about Martin Luther King, sports cars, and movie stars, but not about lubricating army tanks. The interaction between learner and context variables, on the one hand, and instructional materials and strategies, on the other, is critical. We must know the learners' interests, backgrounds, and aspirations.

We also learned that their concepts of their ability to read were quite limited. We originally gave them a lengthy booklet of passages to read in 2 weeks, 1 hour per day. Many of them took one look at the booklet, put it down, and gave up. We quickly learned that attention to details, such as handing out reading material no more than 1 page long, was critical for motivation. Any material longer than that seemed beyond some of them. Many of them would not attempt to read it.

These points may sound mundane, but they are neither mundane nor trivial. I hope that the reader can see the deeper issues that underlie them. One has to know much about the learners, their backgrounds, and their interests.

I could develop this point further by discussing attention. I am going to omit that elaboration because the reader can see that the same kind of reasoning applies to all parts of the model, including attention.

In the area of comprehension, we started with the typical educational psychologist's method of "laying learning strategies on them." We had several excellent strategies for them, all based on literature on reading comprehension. We gave them a metacognitive strategy, a strategy for building inferences, and a strategy for writing summaries.

At first, we did not ask them what they thought reading comprehension was all about. They were willing enough to go along with our teaching methods. They did the things we asked them to do, although they did not understand why they were doing them. Initially, we made little progress.

We began to make progress with them later, when we asked them what they thought reading comprehension entailed. Their model of reading comprehension was one which is fairly common among beginners, although it surprised us. They believed that to read with comprehension, you need only to learn the meanings of all the words in the text and to say all the words aloud in their correct order. As soon as you know the vocabulary, you can read with comprehension. That seems to be a common model of reading comprehension among novices.

What is interesting about the novice model is that there is enough truth in it to make it a fairly good model, because vocabulary is essential for reading comprehension. But the model is not a sufficient one for reading comprehension. We needed to enlarge their model of reading comprehension because the activities we were asking them to perform seemed to them a waste of time. Who wants to write summaries or create images when you are trying to read a passage? Who wants to look at the structure of the text, and who wants to reread and recall text? None of these activities makes sense until one has an appropriate model of comprehension.

As Table 1 indicates, we showed a sizable increase in reading comprehension—about 20% with most of these groups of soldiers after 9 hours of instruction. As is indicated by the t ratios and the p values, these results were statistically significant and probably did not occur by chance. We learned some critical points about materials, about learners' interests, about their self-concepts, and about their models of comprehension. Most impor-

TABLE 1   Means, Standard Deviations, and Gain Scores of the Experimental and Control Groups

Treatment	Pretest	Posttest	Gain	t	Level of significance	% of gain over pretest
Summaries, headings, and inferences strategy ($n = 29$)	18.9 (4.1)	22.6 (3.9)	+3.7	5.9	$p < .0001$	19.6
Metacognitive strategy ($n = 26$)	20.5 (3.6)	23.1 (4.2)	+2.6	4.2	$p < .001$	12.7
Metacognitive + examples strategy	17.9 (5.7)	22.1 (4.6)	+4.1	6.7	$p < .0001$	22.9
Control group ($n = 16$)	21.1 (5.4)	20.8 (5.4)	−0.3	0.4	nonsignificant	—

tantly, we learned to study and to know our learners before we taught them learning strategies and before we designed reading instruction.

V.   A RESEARCH STRATEGY

The shared goal and the model of teaching that emerges from this volume is productive. To develop it further, I suggest we invest time and effort in studying the learners' thought processes. We are building a sound model of learning and teaching, focused upon the areas of motivation, attention, and comprehension. Now we need to study the ways learners understand the interventions we present to them, their purposes in learning, and their models of the cognitive processes we want to facilitate. We also need to learn to measure learning strategies and metacognitive processes that learners bring to instruction because, important as our shared goal might be, and effective as our strategy for attaining it might be, we need greater emphasis on research strategies that go beyond the choosing, designing, and teaching of sensible, research-based learning strategies worldwide to teachers and students. We need to conduct research on the learners, the strategies and the knowledge they have, as well as the models they bring with them to educational settings. Then we can design our teaching interventions in accord with our findings about learners. That strategy means, of course, that we must do more research, such as that which Claire Weinstein reports (Ch. 3, this volume), on the measurement of learning strategies and learning styles.

The research strategy I am suggesting also implies that we need to study how, when, where, and why people use learning strategies. We need to study metacognitive processes and the awareness and self-control of one's learning strategies and other thought processes, to develop coherent systems and models of learning strategies. Several chapter authors, such as Barbara McCombs (Ch. 9, this volume), are already using this research strategy and are reporting excellent results with it. My point is only that we need to do more of that type of important research, as it relates to instruction.

Perhaps most importantly, we must focus our research on the critical problems of teaching. Our results or findings depend much on the different kinds of problems and subject matters we study, as I have just found in the research on reading comprehension that I have been conducting for the Army Research Institute. The learning strategies that are effective vary greatly, depending upon seemingly insignificant learner or contextual variables. In our quest to educate everyone, these learner and contextual variables are critical.

The research strategy that I am suggesting seems particularly appropriate for the new opportunities we have to contribute to our society. Now is the time for us, as psychologists, educators, and researchers, to think about the enhanced roles we can play in our society. In other professions, there is an awareness of the role of educational psychology and educational research that has never before been present in the span of my career. For example, many of the students in my first graduate course in learning and cognition now come from departments other than education, including nursing, architecture, linguistics, psychology, management, kinesiology, physical education, and public health. They want to study cognition and learning strategies because they are beginning to reconceptualize their respective roles. Nurses are now being taught in schools of nursing that they are more than people who care for the sick. They are also teachers who educate the ill about how to care for themselves after they leave the hospital or clinic. In other words, nurses teach those who are ill some strategies to change their behaviors to control their health more effectively.

Briefly, a wide variety of professions now realize that they have teaching responsibilities. They also realize that cognition and learning strategies are studied by researchers, such as those represented in this volume, whose findings relate to the improvement of teaching.

VI. SUMMARY

We want to educate all people. We have a new way to begin to attain that noble goal of education. Our strategy goes beyond the design of instructional materials to include changing the behavior of learners by giving them new strategies, and new ways to think about learning and knowledge acquisition.

I suggest that we complement our effective research strategy with greater emphasis on the study of learners' knowledge and thought processes. This complementary strategy seems particularly appropriate as we expand our research into a variety of new fields and professions interested in developing their teaching functions through the application of results from research on the teaching of learning strategies.

We can then turn to the fundamental questions of how, where, when, and why learning strategies are used. From that sound basis, we can design meaningful interventions appropriate for the learners. We can also build and study useful models for teaching learning strategies that will help us attain our noble goal of educating everyone.

REFERENCES

Camp, B. W. (1980). Two psychoeducational treatment programs for young aggressive boys. In C. K. Whalen, & B. Henker (Eds.), *Hyperactive children: The social ecology of identification and treatment* (pp. 191–219). New York: Academic Press.

deCharms, R. (1972). Personal causation training in the schools. *Journal of Applied Psychology, 2,* 95–113.

Douglas, V. I., Parry, P., Martin, P., & Garson, C. (1976). Assessment of a cognitive training program for hyperactive children. *Journal of Abnormal Child Psychology, 4,* 389–410.

Dweck, C. (1975). The role of expectations and attributions in the alleviation of learned helplessness. *Journal of Personality and Social Psychology, 31,* 674–685.

Meichenbaum, D., & Asarnow, J. (1978). Cognitive-behavior modification and metacognitive development: Implications for the classroom. In P. Kendall, & S. Hollen (Eds.), *Cognitive-behavioral interventions: Theory, research, and procedures.* New York: Academic Press.

Wittrock, M. C. (1974). Learning as a generative process. *Educational Psychologist, 11,* G7–95.

Wittrock, M. C. (1981). Reading comprehension. In F. J. Pirozzolo, & M. C. Wittrock (Eds.), *Neuropsychological and cognitive processes in reading.* New York: Academic Press.

Wittrock, M. C. (1984). *Teaching reading comprehension to adults in basic skills courses* (Final Report Basic Skills Resource Center Project, Three Volumes). Los Angeles: University of California.

Wittrock, M. C. (Ed.). (1986). *Handbook of research on teaching* (3rd Ed.). New York: Macmillan.

MODELS AND METAPHORS OF LEARNING STRATEGIES

Scott G. Paris

People rely on cognitive strategies to promote learning, remembering, and problem solving. The use of internal tactics, such as rehearsal and paraphrasing, as well as external aids, such as notes and lists, help to reorganize information and ensure retention. Not all learning is controlled by cognitive strategies, certainly, but tasks that are complex or demanding can be simplified by systematic evaluation of the problem and selection of appropriate strategies. Cognitive strategies are particularly valuable in academic settings in which students must master large amounts of new information. They are important tactics in the minds of students as well as prominent instructional objectives for teachers. Indeed, cognitive strategies are embraced so enthusiastically in theories of cognitive development and educational psychology that today it is conventional to differentiate skilled from less-skilled students according to the strategies they are able to generate and apply appropriately to problems (Brown et al., 1983).

The surge of enthusiasm reflects partly the waves of the cognitive revolution and partly the enduring educational concern for teaching students how to think effectively. The seeds for studying cognitive strategies were planted by Binet, Baldwin, Piaget, Dewey, Thorndike, and others early in this century but they took a long time to germinate. The popularity of sensible study strategies such as SQ3R (Robinson, 1946) and pioneering studies on hypothesis testing in children (e.g., Bruner et al., 1956) nurtured research on strategies that blossomed later. Instructional research on mathemagenic activities (e.g., Rothkopf, 1970), generative learning (Wittrock, 1974), and elaboration (Rohwer, 1970) coincided with developmental research on mnemonic and imaginal strategies (Flavell, 1970). Research on individuals with below-average IQs revealed significant differences in such strategies (Jensen & Rohwer, 1963; Paris & Haywood, 1973; Turnure & Thurlow, 1973). Changes continued swiftly during the 1960s, nurtured by research on strategies of mnemonic organization (Tulving, 1962), imaginal coding (Paivio, 1970), learning to learn (Postman, 1969), and behavioral self-control (Thoreson & Mahoney, 1974).

LEARNING AND STUDY STRATEGIES: ISSUES IN
ASSESSMENT, INSTRUCTION, AND EVALUATION

However, the greatest influence on cognitive strategies was undoubtedly the major advances in models of memory. Although mnemonic devices had been investigated for years (Bower, 1970), the multistore model of memory proposed by Atkinson and Shiffrin (1968) assigned major roles to subject-controlled processes like encoding and retrieval strategies. Subsequent models of memory based on "depth of processing" (Craik & Lockhart, 1972) or "spread of activation" (Anderson, 1983) emphasized how information is transformed during learning and remembering. Each of these models has contributed distinctive metaphors to pluralistic research on cognitive strategies.

The explosive proliferation of research on cognitive strategies can be divided generally into three categories; analytic, comparative, and instructional. Analytic research aims to reveal how particular strategies, such as elaboration and organization, influence learning (c.f. Weinstein et al., 1979). Comparative research is designed to show how subjects who vary in certain characteristics such as age, IQ, background, or style use cognitive strategies. The results of analytic and comparative research often form the bases for instructional studies in which less-skilled students are trained to use cognitive strategies. Direct instruction, elaboration, feedback, and modeling have all been shown to improve the cognitive performance of subjects who are ineffective learners (Pressley & Levin, 1987).

These three kinds of research have continued to flourish in many fields including cognitive, educational, and developmental psychology. However, the scope of research, guiding principles, underlying purposes, and meta-theoretical assumptions often differ widely among researchers studying learning strategies. Consequently, models and metaphors used to describe and explain learning strategies have proliferated to the point that there are dozens of different frames of reference used.

This chapter provides a summary of the volume and includes a commentary on the rich and diverse research conducted in the field. The discussion is organized around the use of models and metaphors that characterize learning and instruction because they illustrate differences among approaches. One purpose of this chapter is to provide a catalog of commonly used metaphors in order to stimulate awareness of the contrasting characterizations. Another purpose is to provoke scrutiny of the usefulness of various metaphors for describing essential features of learning and instruction. The chapter is organized to include: (1) an examination of functions served by metaphors in cognitive psychology, (2) a catalog of popular models and metaphors, and (3) a discussion of the advantages and disadvantages of metaphors. The final section includes a summary of instructional research discussed during the conference and an evaluation of various metaphors.

I. DESCRIBING THE UNKNOWN

Part of the scientific difficulty in charting new territory or making new discoveries is finding appropriate terms to describe the events. Quite often new phenomena are compared to familiar things to highlight similarities between them. Consider how people historically have tried to characterize the unseen qualities of memory. Aristotle compared remembering to etchings on a tablet, Plato created the analogy of capturing a bird from an aviary, and Freud used the metaphor of searching the rooms of a house. Roediger's (1980) analysis of metaphors used throughout history to describe remembering includes these examples, as well as a gramophone, purse, switchboard, workbench, tape recorder, library, garbage can, cow's belly, and computer. These comparisons are rich (and amusing) in their technological progression through history as they draw attention to various conceptions of memory. Gentner and Grudin (1985) analyzed mental metaphors used during the past 90 years and found that systems metaphors based on computers, mechanics, mathematics, and symbols have increased dramatically since 1955.

Metaphors are powerful aids to science because they help to describe and explain new phenomena. They all provide a set of features in a well-known base system (sometimes called the vehicle) that correspond to features in an unfamiliar system (sometimes called the tenor). The purpose of the metaphor is to illuminate similarities and dissimilarities between the two domains by mapping the correspondence of objects, attributes, and relations (Gentner, 1982). For example, a workbench metaphor for memory includes corresponding objects (e.g., locations for work), similar attributes (e.g., limited capacity, space, or work), and comparable relations between objects (e.g., tools for assembling and disassembling objects operate like strategies for encoding and retrieving information). Because metaphors have proliferated so rapidly in cognitive psychology and because the analogies are rarely examined, it seems fitting to analyze how they operate.

How do metaphors work and what functions do they serve? These questions are the source of considerable debate (c.f. Ortony, 1979), but some consensus is available. Most current notions of metaphor accept Black's (1962) argument that metaphors do not simply substitute one domain for another. The utterance, "Man is a wolf" does not suggest that all qualities of wolves are shared by men. Nor do metaphors serve as point-by-point comparisons of attributes and relations. The eating behavior of men and wolves, for example, may be described as ferocious or rapacious, but the actions are not too similar and many other characteristics are not at all alike. The prevailing view of the metaphor is interactive whereby individuals are stimulated to compare the tenor and vehicle in order to notice the similarities and dissimilarities in the mapping of relations and beliefs. This interanimation is said to give rise to semantic tension that is resolved as the similarities are apprehended.

The interanimation of domains precipitated by metaphorical comparisons serves many functions. First, it is informative. By analogy we come to know how a new object is like or unlike something familiar. Second, it is provocative. Metaphors force us to consider phenomena in new frames of reference. They compel us to notice and question similar relations and force us to repackage old beliefs according to new structures (Tourangeau, 1982). Metaphors promote constructive and inventive thinking that is motivated by the satisfaction of resolving the tension between two domains and understanding the analogical relations.

Third, metaphors are entertaining. They include figurative language that can be aesthetic or humorous. During the conference, one participant remarked that cognitive skill training sometimes seemed to follow lessons from agronomy—the more fertilizer used to cultivate learning, the better the yield. Clearly metaphors invite elaborated relations that can be amusing. Finally, a fourth and overarching purpose of the metaphor is to communicate. Linguists argue that a primary function of a metaphor is "catechresis" or lexical gap filling. Metaphors provide expressions for actions, events, and phenomena that are beyond experience or difficult to describe.

> The motivation for wishing a well-designed theory of metaphor to accompany realist philosophies of science should now be more clear. The theoretical sciences experience crises of vocabulary. If the progress of science is seen to require the attempt to describe real things, some of which are beyond all possible observation, then one must concede the need to give an account of the terms which are used to describe these things, their properties and relations not available to experience. (Martin & Harre, 1982, p. 96)

The semantic richness and economy of metaphors contribute to their popularity to the point that many metaphors achieve consensus as ways of representing phenomena, e.g., the man in the moon, the wheels of time, electrical current, and food for thought. Scientific metaphors achieve acceptance if they are rich enough to inform, provoke, entertain, and communicate in novel and useful ways, but truth value is not a criterion by which metaphors are judged. (Metaphors are always falsifiable.) Consequently, metaphors can also constrain, misrepresent, or misdirect scientific inquiry. That is why we need to evaluate and revise metaphorical characterizations of learning strategies in order to enhance useful descriptions and to minimize misrepresentations.

A. A Catalog of Popular Models and Metaphors

Theories invite but do not require models, just as some models permit but do not require metaphors. According to Martin and Harre (1982), scientific models are nonlinguistic analogies between two domains while metaphors are figures of speech transported from a familiar to a novel domain. For example, fluid dynamics may serve as a model of electricity and it spins off metaphorical expressions such as electrical "current, flow, and resistance." In this fashion, metaphors provide language to articulate models, that is, to embellish relations between the two domains and to communicate them in comprehensible terms. For convenience, the ensuing discussion of metaphors is organized around five kinds of models: strategies, tasks, learners, teachers, and instructional settings. Common metaphors derived from each type of model are discussed briefly, but citations are limited deliberately in order not to misrepresent people's work.

B. Models of Strategies for Learning and Studying

One view of learning, derived mainly from models of memory in cognitive psychology, is that expertise involves the acquisition of a repertoire of cognitive strategies, such as cumulative rehearsal, imagery, elaboration, and organization. Analytic research has shown that these strategies aid learning and comparative studies have revealed that young, low IQ, and unskilled people fail to use them. Therefore, a key to successful learning involves the collection of these "tools." Two general models of expertise are prevalent although there are many variations and metaphors associated with each one. One model delineates ideal or optimal performance in a characterization of the rules, algorithms, and hierarchical procedures that aid problem solving. The other general model identifies relevant "tools" possessed by experts, but not novices.

Some researchers compare strategies to sequential steps performed in routine tasks. These rules, or algorithms, are often described as formulas, recipes, lists of mental directions, laundry lists, army maneuvers, or how to lists. Often they are domain specific. Procedural knowledge, or how to execute successive mental operations, is the key attribute of these models. Siegler's (1981) method of rule assessment (that is derived from task analyses) has popularized this model in the field of cognitive development. As Winograd and Hare (Ch. 8, this volume) note, these rules are often the substance of direct instruction in studies designed to promote strategies for reading comprehension. Here, it is possible also to include strategies to manage anxiety and impulsivity, to cope with failure, and to preserve positive feelings of self-worth. Although coping rules may be different from learning rules, these strategies are often characterized as lists of procedures to follow so that you can "pull your own strings." Some researchers, though, regard strategies as more general or abstract. Rather than mental algorithms, strategies are metaphorically compared to executive managers, rule-of-thumb tactics, or general heuristics. These global rules are given status and power as general problem-solving aids when they are designated as meta-strategies (Chi, 1981), metacomponents (Sternberg, 1979), or metacognitive skills (Brown et al., 1983).

A related model of expertise compares cognitive strategies to the skills displayed by experts. In this model, lists of rules are organized and auto-mated, yet still specific to tasks. For example, riding a bicycle, playing tennis, or typewriting demand hierarchical integration of elementary re-sponses into automatic sequences of routine actions just like skilled control processes of learning and studying. And gymnastics, whether mental or physical, requires years of practice to become smooth, effortless, and auto-matic. Slightly different metaphors focus on operant habits rather than skilled motor patterns. Rothkopf (Ch. 15, this volume), for example, asks if strategies are like army maneuvers, riding a bicycle, or folding a parachute and he answers with a resounding "No!" He says that strategies are more like manners (e.g., giving up your seat on the bus to an elderly lady), practicing birth control, or following a healthy diet. Rothkopf says that educators should try to enhance the conditions that elicit these judicious actions and appropriate habits.

But models of learning strategies that emphasize rules, habits, or automat-ic skills only identify relevant tools; they seem insufficient for illuminating how students initially learn to use strategies. The first group of metaphors asserts the importance of acquiring them and the second category attends to conditions of practice and consequences that elicit the habits once they are acquired. It should be recognized that metaphors derived from these models are inadequate for understanding learning, development, and instruction because those dynamic relations are not evident in the vehicles (e.g., tools) to which the unknown strategies are compared.

C. TASK ANALYSIS

Models of strategies as "things to acquire" often follow from representa-tions of tasks. That is, the decomposition of a complex task into smaller steps to master provides a model indirectly of possible strategies that could be used along the way. The presumed isomorphism between the structure of the task and the cognitive operations required for mastery is a critical assumption in these models because the structure of the task becomes a model of the mind. The most popular example is the information processing system model for cognitive tasks. System models can be represented in a variety of formats, such as flow charts, production systems, schematic diagrams, or scripts, but they all have in common an abstract representation based on a model of successive steps in handling information (Siegler, 1983). Flowcharts, for example, invite expressions such as "rule-following, executive processing, and downward branching," to represent performance. Task models spin off seductive metaphors because they unpackage complex tasks into series of comprehensible and manageable steps that *might* be mastered in the sequence and scope postulated by the model. But the model does not confirm that people should or can act congruently and, even if some of the task model is confirmed behaviorally, we must be cautious in accepting it as a performance analogy.

D. MODELS OF LEARNERS

The previous models of strategies and tasks are depersonalized views of learning that characterize steps to task mastery and tools that aid performance. The implication is that young, naive, or unskilled students can benefit by following these tactics. This view is inadequate for at least two reasons. First, the goal of training or education becomes the acquisition of strategies rather than the effective use of various strategies for further ends, such as learning and studying. Second, the metaphors do not provide analogical processes for learning and teaching, only the prescription that students ought to behave in this fashion. Models of learners confront these problems head on; some even consider the hearts as well as the minds of learners. Five representative characterizations are discussed; novice–expert comparisons, developmental growth, mental orthopedics, motivational models, and artisans.

A simple model depicts the acquisition of cognitive strategies as an outcome of experience or extended practice. For example, the novice–expert comparison is a popular metaphor for distinguishing the knowledge and skills of successful versus unsuccessful performers. Novices are often characterized as naive, inexperienced, "virgins" who may also be confused or poorly motivated because they have such limited understanding of the tasks they confront. In contrast, experts "have" the knowledge and skills that could transform novices into successful performers. The emphasis on "having" versus "using" knowledge underlies the nominal distinctions between these artificial groups so that the metaphorical process of learning is reduced to accumulation or collection of what experts have. Some principles of learning and development beyond practice and accretion of knowledge are required in order to describe how novices are transformed into experts.

Developmental growth models spin off metaphors based on developmental constraints, such as readiness, stages, capacity, knowledge base organization, mediational abilities, and cognitive structures. In these metaphors, the use of strategies for learning or studying is constrained by developmental limits on competence. A prevalent metaphor of this type is based on hydraulic principles whereby people have fixed capacities of cognitive resources (e.g., attention, strategies) to apply to various functions so that overloads in one area require decreases of resources applied to other areas (Shatz, 1978). Strategic processing increases capacity which, in turn, promotes developing competence. Slightly different metaphors emphasize that workload is a limiting factor and that only a fixed number of mental operations can be performed concurrently until the operations are automated (Case, 1984).

A third kind of developmental model focuses on remediation. Unskilled learners need "mental orthopedics" (Brown, 1984) or "prosthetic devices" (Shatz, 1983), in order to read, communicate, or solve problems more effectively. Provision of crutches or braces for learning, usually the strategies used by experts, is what they need, or perhaps, a little orthopedic surgery will realign their thinking. Remediation metaphors are rich (and humorous), but they carry implicit assumptions about differences between skilled and less-skilled students that are pejorative. A further problem is that most researchers do not provide "orthopedic devices" to the nondisabled. If the provision of special devices and attention aids performance of the nondisabled to the same degree as the less-skilled, then the treatment is simply facilitative to everyone, not remedial to a subclass. These metaphors are potentially harmful because of the assumptions they carry about ability differences and the strong, sometimes unfounded, educational prescriptions for remediation.

Fourth, some models emphasize motivation for success and failure and the subsequent consequences for learning (Dweck & Bempechat, 1983; Weiner, 1979). For example, "the little engine that could" metaphor suggests that students who do not believe they have the ability to succeed, quit trying altogether. But exhortations to try harder do not always meet with success. In fact, students who fail after expending maximum effort *know* that their abilities are limited. They may suffer loss of self-esteem because of the "double-edged sword" of effort and ability attributions (Covington, 1983). These metaphors often portray less-skilled learners as confused, self-defeating, or self-protective students who have difficulty using their potential skills because of misguided self-perceptions and motivation rather than lack of knowledge. The developmental component of the models rests on children's emerging theories of their own performance and abilities.

Finally, some metaphors compare learners to craftsmen and artisans by emphasizing pride and self-fulfillment rather than self-protection or face saving. The processes of creativity, independence, self-evaluation, and esteem derived in the pursuit of crafts and art serve as metaphors for students' goals and their continuing motivation. Such metaphors combine ability and motivation in positive views of intrinsic task orientations, although they are relatively novel (Paris & Oka, 1982).

E. MODELS OF TEACHERS

Teaching can be compared to a variety of other professions, however, three models seem predominant: teachers as motivators, scholars, or coaches. In the first model, teachers are compared to managers who organize tasks and workloads for students while dispensing encouragement and correction. They motivate by exhortation and serve as cheerleaders for achievement.

In a second model, teachers are compared to scholars who collect and share knowledge. As experts and mentors they transmit information by explaining, demonstrating, and lecturing (Winograd & Hare, Ch. 8, this volume). Teachers have also been compared to preachers who provide a "laying on of hands" to teach the uninitiated the academic rites of learning strategies: an academic baptism and revelation. Enlightened students can even become proselytized into future teachers.

The third class of models combines the roles of mentor, manager, and cheerleader into a reciprocal relationship between teacher and student that is often compared to coaching or parenting. Like parents, teachers set standards, monitor behavior, and counsel children in addition to supplying academic information. Like coaches, teachers act as sympathetic coparticipants as well as taskmasters. Coaches and parents evaluate children's progress and encourage development; they share in their charges' successes and failures. The cooperative and reciprocal relationships depicted by coaching and parenting provide rich metaphors for teacher–student relationships. Yet, richness and colorful comparisons do not compensate for the lack of specificity in the metaphors. Which qualities of coaches, scholars, or managers should be extrapolated to teachers and how do these metaphorical comparisons help describe or explain the dynamics of learning and instruction? These metaphors convey expressive vividness because they evoke so many associations between teaching and other professions, but they seem lacking in rigor as explanatory analogies.

F. MODELS OF INSTRUCTIONAL SETTINGS

Recent research on study strategies begins with analyses of what people normally do in instructional settings (Weinstein et al., Ch. 3, this volume). Educational researchers who study how students use strategies often adopt this panoramic view of context because it includes learners, teachers, tasks, and strategies. Michael Cole and his colleagues (Laboratory of Comparative Human Cognition, 1983) argue that the socially assembled situation is the appropriate unit of analysis for learning and development because situations include so many interactive variables. The complexity of the classroom may even require complicated metaphors. It seems to me that the newest metaphors about learning strategies focus on models of instructional settings built on the workplace, investment opportunities, bargaining arrangements, and developmental zones.

Doyle (1983) has popularized the work model of the classroom and, indeed, there are rich analogies between the two domains such as management styles, production schedules and quotas, quality control, and labor/management relations. In some ways students do make contracts to perform certain kinds and amounts of work in order to acquire specified benefits. Strategies can be both instructional methods available to teachers or learning aids to students that facilitate work. A second kind of model extends the enterprise notion to models of personal gain. Students learn to use strategies as investments or collateral for future learning. Note taking, for example, might be handy later and so it is worth learning. In classroom settings, students have a limited amount of time, energy, and resources to allocate to competing activities, so they need to invest wisely in the acquisition of strategies that may prove useful or economical in the future. Sometimes the decisions may be characterized as trades or gambles. For example, students may not expend much effort in learning to use strategies because the risk of failing is too great—they trade attributions of inability for laziness or they may gamble that the consequences of academic failure are less severe than loss of self-esteem. In these metaphors, strategies used for bartering, investing, or gambling become coins whose value are determined by costs/benefits analyses of situations.

A third model of settings involves social reciprocity or cooperative learning. Here the distinction between teachers and students dissolves as roles are blurred or exchanged. Reciprocal teaching used by Palincsar and Brown (1984) or cooperative learning arrangements devised by Dansereau (Ch. 7, this volume) reflect reciprocity and equality akin to town council meetings. Classroom dialogues among teachers and students about reading comprehension strategies is a fundamental aspect of our research and it seems to provoke reflection and debate (Paris et al., 1984). Group dynamics that foster shared discovery and democratic decision making are emphasized in these models.

A final model of instructional settings incorporates developmental characteristics of learners into the context. Certainly the most popular metaphor in this genre is Vygotsky's notion of the relation between learning and development. Vygotsky (1978) asserted that children are typically helped to perform new strategies and to solve new tasks by adults or more capable peers. The zone of proximal development (ZPD) is a metaphor for the "distance" between the levels of performance obtained alone and with guidance. According to Vygotsky, learning pulls development in zones of proximal development and so a wide zone suggests a large potential for change. With regard to cognitive strategies, a wide zone of proximal development implies that children can use strategies successfully with guidance, but do not invoke and apply them well spontaneously. The emphases on emerging developmental competence and the shift from socially supported to independent learning have wide appeal. Critics, however, point out that the width of a zone may be defined by the quality of help provided and that zones cannot be measured easily.

II. THE VALUE OF METAPHORS

This catalog of popular metaphors evident in research on learning strategies reveals that a large variety of metaphors can be derived from models of strategies, tasks, learners, teachers, and instructional settings. Examples of the metaphors are summarized in Table 1 and the catalog at least provides a convenient framework for classifying and distinguishing research. Several caveats are in order, however. The five categories of models do not permit neat or exhaustive classification of all research relevant to learning strategies. Some researchers may claim that the metaphors are exaggerated and not as narrow-minded as they are portrayed. Others might argue that some research encompasses several models and metaphors interactively, such as characterizations derived from task analyses, novice–expert comparisons, and mental orthopedics to derive training studies. Clearly, these protests have merit because metaphors vary widely in their breadth, richness, and intended function. Some researchers use them as loose, amusing, or convenient descriptive frames while others use metaphors as explanations and performance analogies in larger theories or models. The review is intended to provoke debates about appropriate roles of models and metaphors in research and theory rather than to foreclose their use. On the contrary, pluralistic metaphors and scrutiny of their value are at the heart of scientific inquiry.

TABLE 1   Examples of Types of Metaphors Used in
Research on Cognitive and Instructional Strategies

Strategies for learning, studying, and coping
   Cognitive tools, formulas, algorithms
   Lists, recipes, maneuvers
   Habits, heuristics, executives
   Pulling your own strings, being your own boss
Task analysis
   Production systems
   Flow charts
   Scripts
Learners
   Novice–expert
   Fixed capacity, readiness
   Mental orthopedics, prosthetic devices
   Little engine that could, double-edged sword
   Artisans, craftsmen
Teachers
   Managers, cheerleaders, supervisors
   Scholars, mentors, preachers, apprentices
   Coaches, parents, counselors
Instructional settings
   Workplace labor–management relations, contracts
   Investment opportunities, broker, gambler
   Town council, collective bargaining
   Developmental zones, scaffolded interactions

A.   ADVANTAGES AND DISADVANTAGES OF METAPHORS

Metaphors have served valuable purposes in research on learning strategies. They have provided informative analogies that call attention to important characteristics of strategies, tasks, learners, teachers, or settings. New
empirical research and instructional programs have been stimulated by metaphors that repackage ideas. Some metaphors are popular because they are
humorous or easily understood. When training studies are compared to
principles of cultivation or when teachers are portrayed as factory managers,
the metaphors spin off colorful new analogical relations between the domains. Perhaps this is the most valuable function served by metaphors; they
provide language and figures of speech to describe phenomena beyond experience or for which no terminology is available. Metaphors fill lexical gaps to
meet scientific "crises of vocabulary" and, in turn, they provoke new insights. These virtues of metaphors are evident in many models and indeed,
may be implicit dimensions of their popularity.

But metaphors can restrict as well as enlarge our perspectives; they can be seductive by simplicity or richness to the point where alternatives are not considered. As Parker (1982) says,

> Metaphors are 'arresting'; they compel as well as invite us to enter their figurative ground in order to grasp them. But it is often difficult, in this process of 'play', for the reader to perceive that he himself has been 'grasped' or 'occupied.' (pp. 152–153)

Current views of cognitive strategies, for example, rest so firmly on metaphors of algorithms, heuristics, and skilled habits that it is almost impossible to recast them into other frameworks. Martin and Harre (1982) point out that metaphors can act as filters or screens to understanding because they provide a perspective and language that may not be compatible with other metaphors. But there is another way in which metaphors can be restrictive. When a metaphor is appealing, engaging, or colorful, it draws attention to itself. Consequently, we attend to elaborating the relations *within* the base structure rather than charting the analogical processes *between* domains. Task analyses; expertise descriptions, and rule lists all seem vulnerable to this criticism. Dr. Johnson noted that a consequence of diverted attention is that, "The force of metaphor is lost, when the mind, by the mention of particulars, is turned . . . more upon that from which the illustration is drawn than that to which it is applied" (cited in Parker, 1982, p. 152).

Metaphors can also hinder the scientific enterprise by suggesting excessive relations far beyond the similarity originally intended. "Extra baggage" is carried easily by metaphorical expressions that lack clarity because the domains do not map neatly in a one-to-one manner. For example, metaphors of the classroom as workplace or teaching as coaching do not specify which relations cooccur in both domains and which do not; readers are left to import a variety of plausible relations. In fact, metaphors often carry metatheoretical assumptions from their parent models. Metaphors that characterize strategies as general problem-solving routines treat strategies as normative and universal (i.e., everyone could use them to benefit performance on many tasks), while contextual metaphors would assume situational and individual variability in what actions even qualify as strategies. It may turn out that those metaphors more liable to excessive interpretation are those regarded as richer, more entertaining, and more aligned with established models. However, there may be a tradeoff here between appeal and comprehensibility, or richness and clarity.

Finally, metaphors can hinder understanding when they are mixed together. As noted during the conference, "even if a mixed metaphor sings, it should be derailed." The diversity of metaphors is not lessened by concocting assembled metaphors to show "how coaches can use tools to make investments." Mixing theories in the name of eclecticism is just as unacceptable as mixing metaphors. What is required in order to avoid mixed theoretical metaphors is assiduous attention to the consistency of models and metaphors invoked to describe different facets of learning strategies and instruction. The perspectives and assumptions must be compatible among metaphors if theories are to be coherent.

B. CRITERIA FOR EVALUATING METAPHORS

Aristotle observed that metaphors can go wrong in two ways: they can be dull or they can be incomprehensible (Tourangeau, 1982). The paradox is that increased similarity of the two compared domains increases *both* dullness and comprehensibility. For example, describing strategies with a metaphor of cooking recipes may make the step-by-step procedures in both highly sensible but the comparison appears duller than metaphors based on mental orthopedic devices or inclinations to practice birth control. The tradeoff between dullness and comprehensibility reflects two basic aspects of metaphors; (a) the provocative appeal of a rich set of novel relations to be compared; and (b) the need for sensible, familiar relations imported into a new domain. Several theorists have tried to describe the criteria whereby successful metaphors balance these tradeoffs.

Tourangeau and Sternberg (1981) distinguished two kinds of similarity that operate in metaphors. The first is a congruence of domains, that is, the extent to which two subject areas are congruent. The more similar the domains, the more dull the metaphor. The second type of similarity concerns the agreement between prior beliefs about a domain with the projected beliefs afforded by the metaphor. Greater agreement leads to greater comprehensibility. The notion of beliefs focuses attention on the personally relevant and constructive aspects of metaphor, too.

Gentner (1982) postulates four characteristics of the internal structure of mapping relations between domains that contribute to the usefulness of scientific analogies: (1) *clarity* of mapping means that specific relations are mapped between domains; (2) *richness* means that each node, or comparable object between domains, includes many relations; (3) analogies vary in *systematicity* with more hierarchical constraints among relations denoting greater systematicity; (4) *abstractness* increases with the number of higher level, systematic relations that map between domains. Good analogies, according to Gentner (1982), have high base specificity, high clarity, and high systematicity but we should recognize that her criterion for "good" analogies is the value of the metaphor for explicating new phenomena or leading to new hypotheses. Thus, comprehensibility is her main goal and she characterizes rich, entertaining, provocative analogies as expressive rather than explanatory analogies, typical of literary rather than scientific comparisons.

I believe that people consider criteria, such as those delineated by Gentner

(1982) and Tourangeau and Sternberg (1981), but they are usually invoked only intuitively and imprecisely. Certainly, people's preferences for metaphors are also influenced by the scope of their inquiry, the novelty of the metaphor, and their metatheoretical biases. The biological and mathematical metaphors used by Piaget, for example, are not interchangeable with sexual metaphors of Freud or mechanistic metaphors of information processing theorists. Any suggestions that one metaphor is "better" than another will incite vigorous arguments about the relative clarity, richness, systematicity, and abstractness of these core theoretical metaphors and models. Likewise, scientific metaphors will not be discontinued because they cannot be rigorously evaluated and compared.

I would like to suggest four criteria for evaluating the value of metaphors in psychological research. First, the metaphor should be adequate for a specific purpose. The base domain to which the new phenomenon is compared should be rich enough to fulfill the purpose whether that is to inform, entertain, or provoke. Adequacy may be achieved by elementary analogies when loose comparison is the only objective, but analogical explanations of the dynamics of teaching or learning will require more thorough sets of nodes and relations to be mapped between domains.

The second criterion is accuracy. Metaphors should portray the intended behavior accurately and effectively. The analogical relations must inform us about the procedures and conditions that control performance. Third, metaphors should match the level of description and analysis embodied in research and theory. Grand metaphors may not explain detailed performance any better than myopic metaphors explain large psychological events. The value of metaphors will be enhanced if the levels of behavior, theory, and metaphor are comparable. Fourth, the best way to determine adequacy, accuracy, and level of metaphors may be to check how well various metaphors fit empirical data. If the metaphors do not help us interpret data, they are misleading or superfluous.

C. CHARACTERISTICS OF SUCCESSFUL STRATEGY INSTRUCTION

The research on teaching cognitive strategies to students that was discussed at the conference and is included in other chapters in this volume provides an opportunity to match metaphors to data. At the risk of oversimplifying the findings of diverse research, I have summarized eight axioms of successful strategy training. Following a discussion of these characteristics derived from research, the adequacy of various metaphors for characterizing them will be discussed.

1. *The strategies should be functional and meaningful.* A fundamental prerequisite for a successful program is the selection of a strategy (or set of

strategies) that enhances performance on target tasks with a reasonable amount of time and effort. The success of relatively straightforward training programs to teach foreign vocabulary words with the keyword method (Pressley et al., 1982) or to train text summarization rules (Brown et al., 1983), for example, illustrates the importance of selecting useful strategies. The key here is to create a match among the learner's task, context, and strategy so that the action fits into the learner's ongoing behavior readily. This match frequently is not obtained when strategies are transported across different tasks and subject populations. That is why studies of students' customary and useful learning strategies are important for identifying candidates for training (Weinstein et al., Ch. 3, this volume).

2. *Instruction should demonstrate what strategies can be used, how they can be applied, and when and why they are helpful.* As Winograd and Hare (Ch. 8, this volume) point out, most strategy instruction studies provide declarative and procedural knowledge about strategies. Modeling, feedback, and direct instruction all impart this information to subjects who must practice using the strategies. A trademark of proficient students is their greater awareness of learning and study strategies (Brown et al., 1983). But understanding how to use particular strategies when directed and being able to produce them are minimal prerequisites for independent use. Winograd and Hare (Ch. 8, this volume) point out that relatively few studies teach students when and where to use strategies and how to evaluate their use of the skills. Paris et al. (1983) referred to this as "conditional knowledge," knowing *why, where,* and *when* to apply strategies, and it is a prerequisite for the selective use of strategies and transfer. The same set of knowledge was noted by Pressley et al. (1984) as specific strategy knowledge and includes knowledge about: (1) appropriate goals and objectives, (2) appropriate tasks, (3) range of applicability, (4) expected performance gains, (5) effort required, and (6) enjoyment value.

3. *Students should believe that strategies are useful and necessary.* A critical feature of successful training programs is the positive attitudes students develop about the strategies. They become convinced that the strategies are important, helpful and, in fact, necessary for success. If students believe that the tactics are only plausible but not required, or helpful but not efficient or economic, they may not adopt the strategies despite their awareness of how to employ them. Students must believe that the strategies are worth additional time and effort and understand that, with practice, strategies become automated, efficient aids to problem solving (Palmer & Goetz, Ch. 4, this volume). The conviction to use the instructed strategies is at the heart of several successful programs that aim to fuse cognitive skill and motivational will (e.g., McCombs, Ch. 9, this

volume; Paris & Cross, 1983). Without this commitment, it seems unlikely that people will use the strategies independently and possess the
continuing motivation to recruit the strategies.

4. *There must be a match between the instructed strategy and the learner's
   perceptions of the task ecology.* The learning context offers many potential mismatches for instruction (Schallert et al., Ch. 11, this volume).
   Students may perceive the strategies as silly, the task as trivial, or the
   likelihood of success as low. The incentives to use the strategies are tied
   to subjects' perceptions of the relative costs and benefits of trying to learn
   something new. As Palmer and Goetz (Ch. 4, this volume) said, ". . . the
   match between students' perceptions of learner/task attributes and strategy attributes affect their judgments of the personal effectiveness of the
   strategy, and ultimately their decision to use it."

5. *Successful instruction instills confidence and feelings of self-efficacy.*
   Bandura's (1982) view of self-efficacy is that personal expectations about
   one's own ability influence one's choice of activities, the degree of effort
   one will invest, and persistence in the face of failure. Clearly, an individual's perception of his or her own ability to employ strategies effectively will influence performance (Schunk, 1981). Conversely, Licht (1983)
   concludes that learning disabled individuals often do not believe that
   they can succeed on tasks and thus do not even try. Oka and Paris (1987)
   also observed that poor readers with average cognitive skills exhibited
   poorer attitudes toward reading and held lower self-perceptions of their
   abilities than good readers of similar ability. McCombs (Ch. 9, this volume) has an elaborate model for training that makes self-efficacy an objective and not just a byproduct of instruction.

6. *Instruction should be direct, informed, and explanatory.* Direct instruction, according to Rosenshine (1983) includes; (a) presenting material in
   small steps, (b) focusing on one aspect at a time, (c) organizing the material sequentially for mastery, (d) modeling the skill, (e) presenting many
   examples, (f) providing detailed explanations for difficult points, and (g)
   monitoring student progress. While these principles of instruction are all
   important, Winograd and Hare (Ch. 8, this volume) argue that direct
   explanation may be the most significant component of direct instruction.
   Partly because teachers' manuals and basal readers provide so few explanations about cognitive strategies, several programs make informed explanations about reading strategies a principal component of comprehension instruction (e.g., Paris et al., 1984; Roehler & Duffy, 1984).

7. *The responsibility for generating, applying, and monitoring effective
   strategies is transferred from instructor to student.* This principle of
   mediated learning was espoused by Vygotsky (1978) and is central to
   many programs (e.g., Brown et al., 1983; Pearson & Gallagher, 1983).

For example, Palincsar and Brown (1984) designed a cross-tutoring system called "reciprocal teaching" in which students acted first as pupil and then as teacher as they taught their peers how to use strategies such as self-questioning during reading. Successful instruction allows students to interact with teachers and peers and to assume equal partnership in learning. Guided learning is one example and cooperative learning is another (Dansereau, Ch. 7, this volume) for sharing knowledge and beliefs so that each individual internalizes a richer understanding about strategies. A key feature of this dynamic process is that the instruction must be sensitive to the cultural backgrounds and developmental levels of students (c.f., Au & Kawakami, 1984).

8. *Instructional materials must be lucid, considerate, and enjoyable.* Cognitive strategies are not taught by discussion alone. The materials used to teach and practice such strategies as rereading, summarizing, or making inferences must keep the students' attention. Jones and her colleagues (Ch. 13, this volume), report a large project to produce structured materials that embed sequential strategy instruction into reading materials and exercises. Schallert et al. (Ch. 11, this volume) report how students perceive and use some features of textbooks as strategy aids. Effective materials inform and motivate students to use the strategies explained by teachers.

D.   MATCHING METAPHORS TO DATA

If these general conclusions about instructional research are accepted, the task of evaluating myriad metaphors about learning strategies becomes somewhat easier because some of them are inadequate to deal with the findings. For example, researchers have shown that motivation, metacognition, and self-perceptions are important parameters in students' efforts to learn to use cognitive strategies. These factors are absent in models of strategies and tasks that are depersonalized and decontextualized. The metaphors provided by motor skills or flow diagrams may be helpful in characterizing some aspects of strategic performance, e.g., automaticity and sequential processing, but the metaphors do not provide corresponding nodes for motivation, learning, and social interaction. Although the metaphors may aid analytic research that examines fine-grained details of learning strategies, models of strategies and tasks alone are insufficient in scope to encompass findings from instructional research. Thus, metaphors should match the level of analysis and they should not be extended beyond their intended scope.

Likewise, models of teachers or learners in isolation provide insufficient metaphors that can be one-sided. Some metaphors emphasize only learners or teachers, except for reciprocal relations embodied in coaching or zone of proximal development metaphors, while others attend to social and motivational dynamics to the exclusion of tasks and cognitive skills. What seems required for understanding contexts of instruction are metaphors that combine cognitive skill and motivational will within the dynamic interactions of learning and instruction (c.f., Corno & Mandinach, 1983; McCombs, Ch. 9, this volume; Palmer & Goetz, Ch. 4, this volume; Paris & Cross, 1983). For this reason, it appears that models of instructional settings offer the richest metaphors for understanding learning and study strategies. Metaphors of work, investment, or negotiation, for example, include (1) both motivation and cognitive skills, (2) a historical perspective for learning and development, (3) socially dynamic systems of interaction and exchange, and (4) situational variability.

Contextual models of instructional settings are more inclusive than the models of strategies, tasks, learners, or teachers and, thus, they may be both broader in scope and richer in potential relations compared across domains. These metaphors appear to satisfy several criteria better than other metaphors. For example, the results of successful instructional research reveal greater agreement between the beliefs (i.e., facts and relations) evident in strategy learning and situational models (Tourangeau & Sternberg, 1981). Yet the domains have modest congruence which contributes to their appeal while retaining comprehensibility.

Creating metaphors is not the desired end nor is it a substitute for building and testing theories. This chapter has called attention, however, to the popularity of metaphors and their diversity in areas related to learning strategies. Brown et al. (1983) have used a tetrahedral model of learning to call attention to the interactions among characteristics of learners, the activities of learners, features of tasks, and criterial performance goals. A tetrahedron is a skeletal model, at best, and spins off few metaphors for understanding the dynamics of learning. It simply asserts interactions, yet most of the research reviewed fits one, or at best, two dimensions of the tetrahedron. Trying to ascertain why or how an individual could be located at different spatial points within a pyramid is both incomprehensible and dull—a failing metaphor according to Aristotle. More engaging and more sensible metaphors may be more illuminating about how people learn and teach cognitive strategies.

III. CONCLUSIONS

A variety of models and their derivative metaphors were catalogued and evaluated in order to understand their relative merits and biases. Much of this paper is devoted to understanding how metaphors operate in scientific theories and the difficulties they present for interpreting and comparing the phenomenon under study. In the end, it may be that the best test of the adequacy and usefulness of metaphors is compatibility with the data. Metaphors that do not characterize critical aspects of the subject are insufficient for illuminating or explaining relations in the new domain. For this reason, metaphors that encompass instructional settings were seen as promising. The ways in which learning strategies are acquired, instructed, used, and generalized across tasks may be characterized best in terms of metaphors based on dynamic social interactions and instructional settings. It is hoped that the creation and refinement of new metaphors will accompany more comprehensive and powerful theories about cognitive strategies and instruction.

ACKNOWLEDGMENTS

Portions of this paper were written while the author was a visiting scholar at The Flinders University of South Australia. The kindness and stimulation of the psychology faculty during his visit were much appreciated. The paper benefited from the insightful comments of Mary Luszcz, Michael Lawson, Norman Feather, David Cross, David Saarnio, and Ernie Goetz on earlier drafts.

REFERENCES

Anderson, J. R. (1983). A spreading activation theory of memory. *Journal of Verbal Learning and Verbal Behavior, 22*, 261–295.

Atkinson, R. C., & Shiffrin, R. M. (1968). Human memory: A proposed system and its control processes. In K. W. Spence & J. T. Spence (Eds.), *The psychology of learning and motivation: Advances in research and theory* (Vol. 2). New York: Academic Press.

Au, K. H., & Kawakami, A. J. (1984). A conceptual framework for studying the long-term effects of comprehension instruction. *The Quarterly Newsletter of the Laboratory of Comparative Human Cognition, 6*, 95–100.

Bandura, A. (1982). Self-efficacy mechanism in human agency. *American Psychologist, 37*, 122–147.

Black, M. (1962). *Models and metaphors.* Ithaca, NY: Cornell University Press.

Bower, G. H. (1970). Analysis of a mnemonic device. *American Psychologist, 58*, 496–510.

Brown, A. L., Day, J. D., & Jones, R. S. (1983). The development of plans for summarizing texts. *Child Development, 54*, 968–979.

Brown, A. L. (1984). Mental orthopedics: A conversation with Alfred Binet. In S. Chipman, J. Segal, & R. Glaser (Eds.), *Thinking and learning skills: Current research and open questions* (Vol. 2). Hillsdale, NJ: Erlbaum.

Brown, A. L., Bransford, J. D., Ferrara, R. A., & Campione, J. C. (1983). Learning, remembering, and understanding. In J. H. Flavell, & E. M. Markman (Eds.), *Cognitive development* (Vol. III). *Handbook of child psychology.* New York: Wiley.

Bruner, J. S., Goodnow, J. J., & Austin, C. A. (1956). *A study of thinking*. New York: Wiley.

Case, R. (1984). The process of stage transition: A neo-Piagetian view. In R. J. Sternberg (Ed.), *Mechanisms of cognitive development*. New York: W. H. Freeman & Co.

Chi, M. T. H.(1981). Knowledge development and memory performance. In M. Friedman, J. P. Das, & N. O'Connor (Eds.), *Intelligence and learning*. New York: Plenum Press.

Corno. L., & Mandinach, E. B. (1983). The role of cognitive engagement in classroom learning and motivation. *Educational Psychologist, 18*, 88–108.

Covington, M. V. (1983). Motivated cognitions. In S. Paris, G. Olson, & H. Stevenson (Eds.), *Learning and motivation in the classroom*. Hillsdale, NJ: Erlbaum.

Craik, F. I. M., & Lockhart, R. S. (1972). Levels of processing: A framework for memory research. *Journal of Verbal Learning and Verbal Behavior, 11*, 671–684.

Doyle, W. (1983). Academic work. *Review of Educational Research, 53*, 159–200.

Dweck, C. S., & Bempechat, J. (1983). Children's theories of intelligence: Consequences for learning. In S. G. Paris, G. M. Olson, & H. W. Stevenson (Eds.), *Learning and motivation in the classroom*. Hillsdale, NJ: Erlbaum.

Flavell, J. H. (1970). Developmental studies of mediated memory. In H. W. Reese, & L. P. Lippsitt (Eds.), *Advances in child development and behavior* (Vol. 5). New York: Academic Press.

Gentner, D. (1982). Are scientific analogies metaphors? In D. Miall (Ed.), *Metaphor: Problems and perspectives* (pp. 106–132). Sussez: The Harvester Press.

Gentner, D., & Grudin, J.(1985). The evolution of mental metaphors in psychology: A 90-year retrospective. *American Psychologist, 40*, 181–192.

Jensen, A. R., & Rohwer, W. D. (1963). Verbal mediation in paired-associate and serial learning. *Journal of Verbal Learning and Verbal Behavior, 1*, 346–352.

Laboratory of Comparative Human Cognition (1983). Culture and cognitive development. In W. Kessen (Ed.), *Handbook of child psychology: History, theory, and methods* (Vol. 1). New York: Wiley.

Licht, B. G. (1983). Cognitive-motivational factors that contribute to the achievement of learning disabled children. *Journal of Learning Disabilities, 16*, 483–490.

Martin, J., & Harre, R. (1982). Metaphor in science. In D. Miall (Ed.), *Metaphor: Problems and perspectives* (pp. 89–105). Sussex: The Harvester Press.

Oka, E. R., & Paris, S. G. (1987). Patterns of motivation and reading skills in underachieving children. In S. J. Ceci (Ed.), *Handbook of cognitive, social, and neuropsychological aspects of learning disabilities*. Hillsdale, NJ: Erlbaum.

Ortony, A. (1979). *Metaphor and thought*. Cambridge: Cambridge University Press.

Paivio, A. (1970). On the functional significance of imagery. *Psychological Bulletin, 73*, 385–392.

Palincsar, A. S., & Brown, A. L. (1984). Reciprocal teaching of comprehension-fostering and monitoring activities. *Cognition and Instruction, 1*, 117–175.

Paris, S. G.,& Cross, D. R. (1983). Ordinary learning: Pragmatic connections among children's beliefs, motives, and actions. In J. Bisanz, G. Gisanz, & R. Kail (Eds.), *Learning in children*. New York: Springer-Verlag.

Paris, S. G., Cross, D. R., & Lipson, M. Y. (1984). Informed strategies for learning: A program to improve children's reading awareness and comprehension. *Journal of Educational Psychology, 76*, 1239–1252.

Paris, S. G., & Haywood, H. C. (1973). Mental retardation as a learning disorder. In H. J. Grossman (Ed.), *The pediatric clinics of North America* (Vol. 20). Philadelphia: W. B. Saunders Co.

Paris, S. G., Lipson, M. Y., & Wixson, K. K. (1983). Becoming a strategic reader. *Contemporary Educational Psychology, 8*, 293–316.

Paris, S. G., & Oka, E. R. (1982). Schoolcraft. *Academic Psychology Bulletin, 4*, 291–300.

Parker, P. (1982). The metaphorical plot. In D. Miall (Ed.), *Metaphor: Problems and perspectives* (pp. 133–157). Sussex: The Harvester Press.

Pearson, P. D., & Gallagher, M. C. (1983). The instruction of reading comprehension. *Contemporary Educational Psychology, 8*, 317–344.

Postman, L. (1969). Experimental analysis of learning to learn. In G. H. Bower, & J. T. Spence (Eds.), *The psychology of learning and motivation: Advances in research and theory* (Vol. 3). New York: Academic Press.

Pressley, M., Borkowski, J. G., & O'Sullivan, J. T. (1984). Children's metamemory and the teaching of memory strategies. In D. L. Forrest-Pressley, G. E. MacKinnon, & T. G. Waller (Eds.), *Metacognition, cognition, and human performance*. New York: Academic Press.

Pressley, M., Levin, J. R., & Delaney, H. D. (1982). The mnemonic keyword method. *Review of Educational Research, 52*, 61–92.

Pressley, M., & Levin, J. R. (1987). Elaborative learning strategies for the inefficient learner. In S. J. Ceci (Ed.), *Handbook of cognitive, social, and neuropsychological aspects of learning disabilities* Hillsdale, NJ: Erlbaum.

Robinson, F. P. (1946). *Effective study*. New York: Harper.

Roediger, H. L. (1980). Memory metaphors in cognitive psychology. *Memory and Cognition, 8*, 231–246.

Roehler, L., & Duffy, G. (1984). Direct explanation of comprehension processes. In G. Duffy, L. Roehler, & J. Mason (Eds.), *Comprehension instruction: Perspectives and suggestions*. New York: Longman.

Rohwer, W. D. (1970). Images and pictures in children's learning. *Psychological Bulletin, 73*, 393–403.

Rosenshine, B. (1983). Teaching functions in instructional programs. *The Elementary School Journal, 83*, 335–351.

Rothkopf, E. (1970). The concept of mathemagenic activities. *Review of Educational Research, 40*, 329–336.

Schunk, D. H. (1981). Modeling and attributional effects on children's achievement: A self-efficacy analysis. *Journal of Educational Psychology, 73*, 93–105.

Shatz, M. (1978). The relationship between cognitive processes and the development of communication skills. In C. B. Keasey (Ed.), *Nebraska symposium on motivation*. Lincoln: University of Nebraska Press.

Shatz, M. (1983). Communication. In J. H. Flavell, & E. M. Markman (Eds.), *Cognitive development, Vol. III, Handbook of child psychology*. New York: Wiley.

Siegler, R. S. (1981). Developmental sequences within and between concepts. *Monographs of the Society for Research in Child Development, 46*, (2, Serial No. 189).

Siegler, R. S. (1983). Information processing approaches to cognitive development. In W. Kessen (Ed.), *Handbook of child psychology: History, theory, and methods* (Vol. 1). New York: Wiley.

Sternberg, R. T. (1979). The nature of mental abilities. *American Psychologist, 34*, 214–230.

Thoreson, C. E., & Mahoney, M. J. (1974). *Behavioral self-control*. New York: Holt, Rinehart & Winston.

Tourangeau, R. (1982). Metaphor and cognitive structure. In D. Miall (Ed.), *Metaphor: Problems and perspectives* (pp. 14–35). Sussex: The Harvester Press.

Tourangeau, R., & Sternberg, R. J. (1981). Aptness in metaphor. *Cognitive Psychology, 13*, 27–55.

Tulving, E. (1962). Subject organization in free recall of "unrelated" words. *Psychological Review, 69*, 344–354.

Turnure, J. E., & Thurlow, M. L. (1973). Verbal elaboration and the promotion of transfer of training in educable mentally retarded children. *Journal of Experimental Child Psychology, 15,* 137–148.

Vygotsky, L. S. (1978). *Mind in society.* Cambridge, Massachusetts: Harvard University Press.

Weiner, B. (1979). A theory of motivation for some classroom experiences. *Journal of Educational Psychology, 71,* 3–25.

Weinstein, C. E., Underwood, V. L., Wicker, F. W., & Cubberly, W. E. (1979). Cognitive learning strategies: Verbal and imaginal elaboration. In H. O'Neil, & C. Spielberger (Eds.), *Cognitive and affective learning strategies* (pp. 45–75). New York: Academic Press.

Wittrock, M. C. (1974). Learning as a generative process. *Educational Psychologist, 11,* 87–95.

IMPLICATIONS OF LEARNING STRATEGY RESEARCH AND TRAINING: WHAT IT HAS TO SAY TO THE PRACTITIONER

John E. Wilson

The author's present occupation is superintendent of schools in a Texas public school system. In this capacity, as well as assistant superintendent and principal, he has had much experience with the issue of student performance. While he was employed as a high school associate principal, his staff and he attempted to address the problem of low student performance by developing a learning strategies/study skills program.

I. A HIGH SCHOOL LEARNING STRATEGIES/STUDY SKILLS PROGRAM

The motivation for developing a learning strategies/study skills program came as a result of observing the large number of students who were having difficulty performing at their level of capability, particularly in the ninth grade. Time after time, students were observed to falter in their ability to achieve, not because of a lack of intelligence, but, rather, from their low level of organizational and information-processing skills. The students were clearly having difficulty in making the transition from junior high school to senior high school where the amount of information they are required to learn increases dramatically.

To develop the specific program of study we wanted to implement, 1 year was spent in researching, planning, and organizing the curriculum, and training staff members to implement the course. During that time, frustrations were consistently encountered as a result of the unavailability of programs present at that level from which to draw on as models. Further, it was found that most of the programs in existence were at the college and university level. The strong need for study skills courses in the early years of post-

LEARNING AND STUDY STRATEGIES: ISSUES IN
ASSESSMENT, INSTRUCTION, AND EVALUATION

secondary curricula, supported our belief that these skills should be taught to high school students.

The program was endorsed by both the central administration and the Board of Trustees whose purposes embraced the following:

1. To teach ninth graders how to be successful high school students.
2. To assist ninth graders in making the difficult adjustment to the rigorous academic demands of high school.
3. To improve the reading–learning process skills of all students.

To address students' needs in learning strategies, curriculum coordinators and study skills teachers designed 13 units of study differentiated according to students' reading and general intellectual ability. The specific components were:

1. *Organizational Skills:* This unit begins the school year. Teachers assist students in organizing a single, loose-leaf binder into six sections, according to the content-area teacher's specifications. Students learn how to complete a weekly course assignment sheet, organize each section in accordance with course requirements, and develop a reasonable study schedule.
2. *Study/Reading Systems:* Students learn to follow a systematic approach for completing a textbook reading assignment. The method used is a local school district invention called "The Sure-Fire Method Readers Remember" or "T.S.M.R.R." (Think, Survey, Map, Read, and Reflect). Students also learn about the major steps in the FAR Learning System (Focus, Associate, and Review), and about the techniques they can employ to apply the steps as they study. Teachers provide students with numerous opportunities to practice these systems.
3. *Objective-Test Preparation and Test Taking:* Students learn the principles of and techniques for preparing to take objective tests. They study test-taking skills and actually practice answering true–false, multiple choice, matching, and completion questions.
4. *Essay Test Preparation and Test Taking:* All students, regardless of ability, learn something about essay test preparation and test taking. Students with high or exceptional ability learn to compose thesis-controlled essays on a timed test. Students of lesser ability learn to analyze an essay test question, to form the question into a declarative sentence, and to provide supporting detail.
5. *Goal Setting, Attitude, and Time Management:* Following receipt of their first report card in high school, students learn the importance and principles of goal setting, time management, and positive attitude. Each

student analyzes his/her performance in each content area and designs a specific plan for improvement during the next grading period.

6. *Vocabulary Building:* Students broaden their vocabularies through skill development in structural analysis and context clues.

7. *Listening Skills:* This unit of study actually spans the course of the year. However, for a 10-day period, teachers concentrate on improving students' listening skills.

8. *Memory and Concentration Techniques:* Students learn techniques that will improve long-term retention, such as mnemonic devices, simple association, flash cards, and oral recitation.

9. *Basic Reading Skills:* Students who have demonstrated poor reading skills are given extensive practice to: find the main idea, make inferences, draw conclusions, and predict outcomes.

10. *Notetaking:* Students learn various notetaking methods and techniques, such as divided page, mapping, summarizing, and outlining. Techniques students learn to use to highlight important ideas include the use of abbreviations, highlighting, numbering, spacing, and indenting.

11. *Critical Thinking/Problem Solving:* This unit is designed for gifted and academically able students. Students are divided into groups to research current controversial issues, such as gun control, abortion, and use of nuclear power. Each group develops pro and con arguments on the subject and, ultimately, compete against other groups in formal debate.

12. *Library Skills and Research Writing:* All students learn about the variety of resources available to them in a high school library. The activity culminates with all students writing a formal research paper, fully documented, in proper form.

13. *Speed Reading:* Students reading on or above grade level, learn and practice techniques for increasing their reading speed.

The learning strategies/study skills program was successfully implemented and is now in its ninth year of operation. It is a required ninth-grade course at each of the school district's three high schools. In addition, learning strategies/study skills are now taught in the elementary and junior high schools of the district as a part of the regular curriculum. The goal is to incorporate this instruction as part of the curriculum and not have to teach it later as a remedial intervention.

A measurement of success of the program was demonstrated in the significant gains made on a nationally normed achievement test by the students participating in the program compared to those who did not participate. Local surveys were used to gather data from teachers, parents, and students. These results also showed strong support for the program. The SRA

Achievement Test composite percentiles and growth scale values provided the most objective measure of students' improved academic performance. Significant gains on these test scores were observed. The trend of declining test scores that existed for several years prior to the implementation of the learning strategies/study skills program was dramatically reversed for all levels of students. While it is recognized that it is difficult to attribute academic gains to the effectiveness of any single instructional intervention program or component, the inclusion of the learning strategies/study skills program and its content area reinforcement efforts were the only significant changes in the curriculum structure during the evaluation period.

In addition to the standardized testing of students, a variety of instruments and methods were used to clarify how the program was perceived. At the end of each 6-week grading period and each semester, students reported their attitude toward school and learning, and their progress in developing and/or sharpening reading–learning process skills. Approximately three times a year, parents and content-area teachers completed inventories assessing each ninth grader's attitude toward learning and school, his/her management and organization of time, memory and concentration techniques, and learning style. In the study of the end-of-the-year student, parent and teacher inventories revealed the group's overwhelming positive perception of the value and benefits of the Learning Strategies/Study Skills Instructional Program.

LEARNING STRATEGY RESEARCH AND STUDENT INSTRUCTION

The experience of participating in the development of this Learning Strategies/Study Skills Program has also created some concerns about the present developments in learning strategy research and student instruction. First, an important area that still needs to be addressed is the identification and definition of strategies and skills to be taught. Administrators and curriculum designers must have more guidance to identify and select course components. The appropriateness of the skills to be taught must also be determined. Different skills are appropriate for different types of learning tasks and content. We need more guidelines in this area. We must also have better methods of assessing student learning skills. It is important to know about the strengths and weaknesses of individual students, so that we may adapt our instruction to help them meet their individual learning goals. If one is to be successful in teaching attention, motivation, and comprehension skills, one must determine the students' needs, and, therefore, the appropriate instruction.

Another possible issue to resolve in the process of identification and definition of learning strategy/study skills, is the achievement of some type of consensus among researchers as to which skills should be taught. Given the diverse background of the researchers in the field, it is perhaps not possible to develop a consensus. From a practitioner's standpoint, however, it would be very helpful if this could be accomplished. The problem of determining which skills should be taught, how they should be taught, and agreeing on a common definition was an obstacle in developing the learning strategies/study skills course previously described.

Richard Mayer (Ch. 2, this volume) suggests two research issues that support the idea of better definition and descriptions of learning strategies. First, he states that better techniques for describing and evaluating learning strategies, including techniques for describing the cognitive processes and outcomes of learning are necessary. Second, a research base should be developed, concerning the question of whether it is better to provide training in general learning strategies, independent of subject matter domains, or to provide training in specific strategies, within the context of subject matter domains. These and similar questions need attention because they are important to the proper implementation of learning strategy programs in public schools.

II. LEARNING STRATEGIES, PRACTITIONERS, AND PARENTS

Although issues related to identification and definition are very important, there are other concerns that also need to be addressed. A second area has to do with learning strategy research as viewed by the practitioners and parents. Generally, the research literature and the implications for practice that can be derived from it are not known by practitioners and parents. The superintendent, in most instances, is involved in the overall management of the school system. His or her time is stretched between the varied issues that confront a school system such as finance, maintenance, public relations, legal aspects, personnel problems, board meetings, and general management. Unless there is a special interest in learning strategies, it is doubtful that most superintendents would be knowledgeable about current research in this area. Another point is that most of the administrative journals do not publish articles about this topic and if they do, they are very general in content and lack much insight into the research. Also, the journals that do publish this research are very specialized and are not written to attract superintendents or other administrative personnel, but rather, they are written for specialists and researchers in their particular field.

Curriculum directors, on the other hand, would be more likely to be informed about research in the area of learning strategy/study skills. Most tend to be very concerned about the learning process and are generally knowledgeable of current developments in research. Curriculum directors, however, are also primarily involved with curriculum rather than with research, except in areas where there is some personal interest.

Teachers, particularly in the secondary schools, are very content-oriented and do not generally spend much time teaching knowledge acquisition skills. In part, it is believed that this has to do with college training in which teachers receive 24 to 36 credit hours in their major area of study and sometimes substantially fewer hours in learning theory or applied cognition. This emphasis on content learning as opposed to learning how to teach a learning process reinforces the focus on the content teaching. Many teachers believe that it is not their duty to teach students the process of how to learn, thus there is little interest or motivation to teach students these skills and processes.

Parents and members of school boards, in most cases, are not very familiar with learning strategies/study skills. Often, the problem of learning is viewed in relation to how well they perceive their particular child performing in school. They may verbalize that "Johnny just doesn't know how to study," but in many cases they do not understand why. Further, most of the research in this area is not readily available to those outside of the field. Therefore, it is suggested that these two groups would be the most unlikely of all to be familiar with current research in learning strategy/study skills.

Given the lack of knowledge in learning strategy/study skills on the part of superintendents, curriculum developers, school board members, and parents, it is important to find a way to help educate these individuals about learning skills and why they are important. Without administrative support and teacher commitment, programs in the public schools will not be established or supported. Good theories and research are needed, but good implementation will also help to make a difference for thousands of students.

III.   RESEARCH AND PRACTICAL APPLICATIONS

There is a need to convert research into practical applications. Numerous examples of researchers who are trying to address this issue are in this volume. More needs to be done to apply research findings in practical settings. An increasing number of studies demonstrate that improvement in achievement can occur when students are taught to use more effective study strategies (e.g. Kulik et al., 1983). Further, as we continue to increase the awareness of members of the educational community, there is an increased probability that we can "establish the conditions under which study strategies training can be effective, identify the variables that influence the effectiveness of particular strategies, and assess the kinds of changes in cognitive processing that result from students' applications of study habits." (McKeachie, Ch. 1, this volume).

Presently, there are few public schools who truly implement research-based learning strategy problems. This is partly because many researchers do not really try to translate their results into language, formats, and programs usable in the public schools. Teachers and administrators will generally not combine various researched fragments to compile a total program. This makes them vulnerable to the wares of commercial packagers of study skills programs and courses. These commercial programs tend to be attractive to individuals who often look for totally packaged material without consideration for the researched validity of the program. Study skills programs should be implemented by a capable and informed individual. If the program fails, for whatever reason, the faculty will frequently develop a poor attitude about the potential effectiveness of any learning strategy training program.

From another perspective, Rothkopf (Ch. 15, this volume) cautions against excessively high and ill-founded expectations of learning strategy training programs in the schools. These may not, by themselves, solve achievement problems. Rothkopf states that competence in learning skills alone is "not sufficient for continued academic success. What is needed, in addition, is a supportive instructional environment." Rothkopf states that not only is it necessary to teach students portable, productive study strategies, but it is also necessary to create schools that demand excellence and are sensitive to the achievements of their students. Thus Rothkopf suggests that "If the [learning skills] programs are to succeed, [as viable interventions to improve academic achievement, then] the schools must also commit themselves to creating environments that will sustain the learning activities of their students."

IV. TRAINING AND EDUCATING TEACHERS

There is a great need to train and educate teachers as to what learning strategies are and why they are necessary to students. Helping students to process the barrage of information in our society and enhancing their own thinking processes is a major goal in our educational system that will become increasingly important in the future. Thus, a critical task is to train teachers. If teachers are to train students, they must first understand what learning skills are and why they are necessary.

Teachers must also understand how learning strategies can be imbedded in their lesson designs and curriculum, and used to support their teaching

effort. Again, this accomplishment takes effort and training. Continual reinforcement and staff development will also be necessary. Support staff who
conduct in-service sessions will need to assist teachers in developing instructional materials, systems, and models to use for implementing learning strategies. This would include the identification of various kinds of learning
strategies and the variety of situational applications in which their use is
appropriate. Finally, the teachers must have a belief that these strategies
will work. This belief comes from a personal and successful use of these
skills. It would be unrealistic for a school system to expect that a learning
strategies program could be effectively implemented and staffed with faculty
who did not have a belief that learning strategies are effective. This could
happen if a school administration, in its desire to improve achievement,
mandated that a learning strategies program be implemented without considering the attitudes of the staff who would implement the program. This
commitment factor is also important for the faculty to adopt if they are to
teach learning strategy skills successfully to students. Some students who are
exposed to learning strategy techniques will not credit the techniques for
their success. However, it has been observed that over a period of time,
many students who are exposed to a teacher who believes that the skills
will work and who enthusiastically passes on that belief, will also internalize the belief that learning strategies are helpful in promoting academic
achievement.

V. CONCLUSION

The roles practitioners need to play in the implementation of a learning
strategy/study skills program at the secondary level have been discussed.
The need to further identify and define learning strategies has also been
stressed, as well as the need to integrate research and practical applications.
More communication between researchers and teaching individuals is necessary to bridge the existing gap. Finally, teachers must be educated about
the need for and importance of teaching learning strategies. It is unrealistic
to expect that training students in the use of learning strategies will occur
unless a greater emphasis is placed on this area in teacher training institutions and in local district staff development programs.

Books such as this one are an important step in closing the void between
the researcher and the teaching individual. While it is clear that there are
some differences in opinion among the researchers represented in the approaches of what skills should be taught and how, it is important not to let
these differences prohibit the progress of researchers and teaching individuals in achieving a common goal. There is a need for a synergistic ap-

proach to inform and train teachers to instruct their students in the utilization of appropriate study strategies.

REFERENCE

Kulik, C. C., Kulik, J. A., & Shwalb, B. J. (1983). College programs for high-risk and disadvantaged students: A meta-analysis of findings. *Review of Educational Research, 53*, 397–414.

COGNITIVE LEARNING STRATEGIES: IMPLICATIONS FOR COLLEGE PRACTICE

Curtis Miles

This volume has two purposes. The primary and most pervasive one is a sharing, among researchers from an unusually wide array of specializations, of current insights into cognitive learning strategies. The intent is to view this emerging educational force from a richer, broader research perspective. The secondary purpose is to pose questions concerning the ramifications of cognitive learning strategies for day-to-day classroom life.

This chapter explores this latter territory in the form of a practitioner's reactions. As such, it is subject to several constraints. First, the paper reacts to a general conception of "cognitive learning strategies" rather than to the particular aspect of it covered by any one of the other papers in this volume. Second, the paper represents the priorities and knowledge of one who is a practitioner rather than a researcher. Third, this paper represents the views of only one category of practitioner: deans, faculty, and curriculum developers at 2- and 4-year colleges. These views are further influenced by a professional, disciplinary focus on reasoning skills: ways of helping students to learn to think more consciously and clearly.

Finally, and most significantly, this paper is affected by a bias that gives strong priority to almost any meaningful innovation that may help deflect the ship of American education from its current course. That course seems dictated by almost total preoccupation with facts over meaning, passive learning over vitality, and form over contextual substance. As such, it poorly serves its ship's passengers and crew. Researchers and practitioners tend to occupy very different, often nontangential, worlds within the educational universe. Nevertheless, given the growing complexities and demands of our society in comparison with the current direction of America's educational ship, this separation may merely signify that researchers and practitioners inhabit separate decks on the Titanic.

Within this broad context, it appears that widespread infusion of cognitive learning strategies within higher education could provide a partial solution to many long-standing dilemmas. The chapters in this volume trigger myriad

LEARNING AND STUDY STRATEGIES: ISSUES IN ASSESSMENT, INSTRUCTION, AND EVALUATION

ideas about applications to this or that classroom situation. Itemizing and explaining those applications in a clear way, however, would devour pages of text. It would also camouflage the potential value of cognitive learning strategies in much the same way that simply describing the basic chess moves camouflages that game's complexity and power.

It is preferable to invite the reader to engage his or her own imagination. The potential power of cognitive learning strategies lies in their focus on leading the student to become a vital, active part of the educational process. The papers in this volume almost all deal in one way or another with how to make this happen.

I. THE STUDENTS

Generally, cognitive learning strategies function by activating the passive learner: making conscious and more mature those skills that were previously unconscious and often ill developed. It becomes fairly easy to imagine the impact of such strategies, if successful, on different types of students.

A.   ALGORITHMIC THINKERS

These are students who learn and think mechanically and who, like Beatle Bailey's character Zero, seem capable of learning *what* but not when or why.

B.   MENTAL CHIP THINKERS

These are students who treat every idea or bit of information as an isolated, decontextualized event, to be etched on a separate "mental computer chip" which is then dropped into a person's mind. Both a concept and several examples of it, for example, are etched on identical chips, filed side-by-side without consideration of their interrelationships or relative import, and thus sink into some anonymous prairie of data which shows few signs of any organizing structure or schema. For students operating with such a conception, remembering and thinking become merely the act of looking for the appropriate isolated chip, a procedure diametrically opposed to what in fact appears to happen when someone "thinks things through," and a procedure that makes meaningful transfer of learning meaningless.

C.   CATATONICS

These are students who, though perhaps adept with familiar and uncomplicated problems, mentally freeze when confronted with complicated or unfamiliar situations; they do not know what to do or even where to begin in order to "*make* sense" of the situation.

D. MENTAL MUSCLE THINKERS

These are students who, having discovered one learning method (usually memorization) which appears to get them through, practice and use it endlessly to the exclusion of all other approaches. Such students may be convinced to "study harder" but seldom to "study better."

E. MENTAL LOBOTOMIES

These are students who appear to make reasonable progress, but lose much of what they have "learned" during the holidays (or even over a long weekend). Their grasp of knowledge is apparently fragile and tentative.

An educational emphasis on cognitive learning strategies has obvious and perhaps dramatic import for such students. Directly or indirectly it may strike towards the core of many of the misconceptions and bad strategies that underlie such learning inadequacies. Nor are these students the exceptions. These traits seem to reside in almost all students, with a difference mainly of degree, not kind.

II. THE FACULTY

Ultimately, most students will become conscious masters of cognitive learning strategies only if teachers make this possible, appealing, and/or unavoidable. Research such as that reported in this volume will thus have classroom impact only to the degree that it adapts to the characteristics and environments of those teachers. Without such adaptability, research into cognitive learning strategies will join so much other research in the practitioner storage sheds marked "interesting, perhaps true, but mostly irrelevant to practice."

The main focus in this chapter is on those faculty (particularly at 2-year and smaller 4-year colleges) whose primary responsibility is to teach, with research and professional service allocated lesser if any roles. It may be useful to realize that such faculty teach half of all college students (Grant & Snyder, 1984). The vast majority of these faculty are probably, at this point, unaware of the existence of not only cognitive learning strategies but also of the broader realm dealing with deliberately infusing active thinking into daily educational endeavors. This unawareness should be interpreted with care, and be seen more as a lack of exposure to such novel teaching/learning methods than of a fundamental indifference to them.

There *is* strong and growing interest, among a minority of faculty, in what is variously known as reasoning, problem solving, decision making, learning styles, or critical thinking (cognitive learning strategies are newcomers). Evidence abounds. The topic was a novelty at conferences 5 years ago, but now it is a regular feature and even commands its own conferences. Many teaching-oriented groups such as the National Council of Teachers of Mathematics (Krulik & Reys, 1980), the Association for the Education of Teachers of Science (Lawson, 1979), the College Board (1983), and the Educational Testing Service (Benderson, 1984), and many publications such as the *Journal of Developmental Education* and *Educational Leadership*, have promulgated "teaching thinking" through special issues, policy statements, article emphases, special interest groups, and the like. The ground is very fertile, and the weather conditions almost ideal, for seeding concepts such as cognitive learning strategies among classroom faculty.

Such seeding, however, must once again be done with intelligent awareness of who these faculty are and of the constraints under which they operate. Many 2- and 4-year college faculty spend 12–20 hours in the classroom each week, dealing with groups of 20–60 students (rather than a small number of graduate students). Few of them are trained as teachers, though most have opted to make students the focus of their professional lives. Their often excellent teaching skills arise from experimentation and reflection more than from models and training. They tend to operate more from instinct and desperation than from research or theory. They are, as a group, certainly unprepared to deal with the subtleties and complexities of teaching so as to enhance thinking and learning skills (Woditsch, 1978; Moreland-Young, 1983).

These faculty frequently function within institutions where there is little or no reward for innovation, for research, or for reading research findings. Their professional growth comes from within their disciplines far more often than from a search for teaching proficiency. Few are research-oriented (Cohen & Brawer, 1982). Most lack access to or interest in the publications that are most important to those researchers included in this volume. Despite all of this, many practitioners are highly interested in anything that suggests ways of better serving students and, particularly, of ameliorating the types of student behaviors described earlier.

III. THE PROCESS OF INNOVATION

The third critical criterion in weighing the implications of cognitive learning strategies for college practice is the process of innovation within an educational setting. Cognitive learning strategies of the types reported in this volume will have power only to the degree that they become central and long-standing features of the educational process. They can help deflect the course of the American ship of education, if you will, only if they are adopted and maintained.

The question thus becomes: what must an innovation be in order to significantly influence a college's educational practices? There have been a few such innovations in the past two decades. One is individually paced instructional material. Another is what has evolved under the broad umbrella of competency-based education. A third might become computer-assisted instruction, although the auguries are definitely mixed concerning whether or not this innovation will find a natural niche in mainstream educational practices.

Looking at these and other innovations, however, does serve to suggest several characteristics held in common by successful, profound innovations. Here are six of these characteristics of successful innovations.

Successful innovations have strong face validity. Teachers and administrators can understand them, can see how to implement them, and can see their value. Innovations that are murky, highly complex, or dependent upon sophisticated knowledge for implementation or understanding of their relevance do not tend to survive.

Successful innovations hit deep into the core of a problem yet can be very flexibly applied. Simplistic and overly specialized "answers" do not tend to survive. Innovations such as individualized instruction and competency-based education, on the other hand, have a simple underlying theory that can be tailored to fit a very large number of needs.

Successful innovations have top-level administrative support. Innovations can begin at the grassroots (as seems true with most of the initiatives relating to "teaching thinking"), but they become permanent only with strong and consistent backing from mid- and upper-level administrators. Administrative and institutional commitments are needed to support major innovations in the long term.

Successful innovations solve already recognized problems. Manufacturers of weedeaters and food processors can apparently magnify a minor need and then proceed to fill it. This does not seem to work with educational innovations, perhaps because the necessary face validity identified above operates only when a solution fits an already identified or uneasily sensed problem. Computer-assisted instruction may become an example of a solution in search of a problem.

Successful innovations soon appear feasible. Faculty and administrators, like all groups of people, are not likely to make major efforts toward implementing something which they are not sure they can carry out. An innovation can appear questionable at first (e.g., "How would *I* go about helping students learn to think? I don't know anything about it!"). However, very rapidly it must be shown to be something within the grasp of the teacher and student. Otherwise the commitment will waste away.

Successful innovations provide rewards, or at least avoid punishments. Advocating, developing, and implementing an innovation usually requires both work and risk. This makes intrinsic or extrinsic reward important for those who develop and implement the innovation. If there are no extrinsic rewards for such leadership, intrinsic rewards such as self-satisfaction and a sense of service or professional growth and stimulation can suffice. However, for such intrinsic rewards to work in the long term, there must be no major extrinsic punishments such as strong peer or administrative disapproval.

There surely are other hallmarks of successful innovations, but these are crucial. How do cognitive learning strategies stack up as part of a larger advocacy of "teaching thinking?" Interestingly enough, to me it appears that cognitive learning strategies fare better than computer-assisted instruction. They have face validity, solve existing problems, contain the seeds of at least intrinsic rewards, etc. A major question is whether or not they will appear feasible to the average faculty member. This remains to be tested, and may well determine which of the various approaches suggested in this volume (if any) become widely adopted in college classrooms.

IV. MARKETING COGNITIVE LEARNING STRATEGIES

Frequent mention has been made of the wider realm of "teaching thinking," and mention has also been made that cognitive learning strategies are late-comers into that restless movement. At the research level, as Bransford indicates (1979, p. 262),

> The problem of learning to learn is not simply a problem of cognitive psychology, linguistics, or computer science . . . An attempt to understand the problem of learning to learn also requires inputs from educational psychology, social psychology, clinical psychology, and related disciplines.

At the practitioner level, many different approaches compete for attention and for rewards (in the forms of prestige and/or dollars). These approaches also introduce a third group into the equation; between the practitioner and the researcher there are those who might be called "packagers." Packagers are curriculum developers, publishers, consultants, and all of those who standardize an approach in order to disseminate it widely. They occupy yet a third deck on the Titanic, but one that perhaps has more control over the bridge than do the other two.

Cognitive learning strategies present an unusual opportunity to study the relationships among these three groups; this would be intriguing if the stakes were not so high. Many approaches to "teaching thinking" are already packaged in texts or elaborate programs: Feuerstein (1980), DeBono (1976), Whimbey and Lochhead (1984), Lipman et al. (1980), McCarthy (1982), Rubenstein and Pfeiffer (1980), Guilford (1977), etc. Most of those who have gained prominence among college-level practitioners have originally arisen from the practitioners themselves, although they may have obtained a degree of research support along the way. A few, such as Feuerstein, have arisen out of the research community, but not many have.

The work with cognitive learning strategies breaks with this pattern in two ways. First, this work arises more from researchers than from practitioners. Second, it suggests more of an approach to the overall teaching/learning transaction than it does a particular instructional effort; this approach tends to thus be far less "packageable" than most other approaches. These differences highlight some major choices facing both researchers and practitioners in this area, choices that will implicitly be made within the next several years.

The wave of interest in thinking skills will perhaps ebb within the next decade. During that period, most interested college faculty and administrators will either "buy into" one or more approaches or turn to other innovations. If they buy into methods that are not effective (because of poor theoretical foundations, poor development, or poor delivery), they will be unlikely to try again. If they use methods that work marginally, they will gradually discard them yet be reluctant to try to find better approaches. Essentially, then, those seeking to foster particular approaches to cognitive strengthening of students will have but one opportunity to "sell" a particular college faculty and administration.

V. THE ROLE OF RESEARCH

Two fundamental questions must be asked within these implementation decisions: the research question, "What do we know?" and the practitioner question, "What works, and why?" It seems to me that those interested in widespread implementation of cognitive learning strategies, given the awkward packaging capability of the approach, should seek to build up a third, middle-ground question, "What do we know that works, and why?" In essence, such a focus would in many ways accelerate the tendency towards application which is already evident in many of the papers in this volume. It would take as a starting point not the laboratory but the classroom, with an eye to spawning techniques, strategies, and knowledge which are practically applicable but research-based.

For two reasons, faculty and students are almost certainly best served by adopting approaches that are in this way firmly rooted in current research. First, instinct and common sense do not seem to be particularly effective guides when dealing with cognitive operations of students; learning is increasingly being revealed as more complex than we had believed. Second, both students and faculty incessantly fall into the trap of rote learning. Students are supremely capable of transforming any lively concept into memorized fact; they have been taught to do this. Faculty, similarly, fall unwittingly into instructional modes that make lively and flexible learning *seem* mechanical and rote, by emphasizing lectures *about* rather than exploration of the topic. Research-based approaches that expose the fundamental operations beneath pedagogy offer ways to counteract such tendencies by giving clearer indications of the types of teaching/learning transactions that must occur if transferable learning is to occur.

However, research-based approaches such as those underlying cognitive learning strategies suffer from handicaps. The research and researchers are little known among practitioners; on the other hand, the wares of packagers are growing in popularity. Research is seldom "complete" in the sense of offering comprehensive approaches to guide classroom activity. The researchers' instinct to cling to narrow ground and absolute certainty limits the generalizability of their findings, and hence makes their insights less attractive to practitioners who are faced with broad problems today.

There is a marked lack of "translators" who are capable of and interested in revising research findings so that they are understandable to classroom instructors. There are few rewards but many possible penalties within the educational process for researchers who actively seek to influence educational practice or for practitioners who seek to apply research findings. Finally, through tradition and positive reinforcement, the packagers who strongly influence educational innovation tend to look to practitioners rather than to researchers for the new approaches which they will package.

Significant numbers of practitioners are aware of the desirability of adopting research-based approaches to instructional innovation. Far fewer, however, are willing or able to find the researchers' shipboard deck, bargain for the wares, bring them back, translate them, and then apply them in their own classrooms. It is far simpler to choose as wisely as possible from among the ready-to-use wares offered by the packagers. As Molnar (1985, p. x) dryly notes, "It is reasonable to suggest that when practitioners are caught up in difficulties, they rarely expect to find help in scholarly literature."

Cognitive learning strategies, as approaches that are difficult to package and that at this point mainly reside among researchers, are at a particular disadvantage. Within the current dynamics, the probabilities that cognitive learning strategies will become major influences on college educational practices appear slim, *unless* the researchers themselves are willing to adjust their own habits and traditions in order to reach out strongly to practitioners. Given access to prepackaged curricular approaches that possess some degree of evaluative support, have face validity, are immediately implementable, and are being adopted by their peers, few practitioners will be so determined to seek research-certified options that they will be willing to travel more than half the distance to the research campfires.

It should be noted, however, that this volume, and particularly the conference that gave it birth, are clear steps from research towards practice. McKeachie, Wittrock, Weinstein, McCombs, Jones, Dansereau, and others consistently insert concern for application into their research designs, not just in this volume, but in much of their work.

VI.   INCREASING THE RELEVANCE

The concept of cognitive learning strategies has strong face validity and great potential appeal to classroom teachers faced with the types of students described earlier. There are several things, however, that researchers in this area could do in order to increase that appeal *if* they choose to seek adherents among the practitioner community. Three of those actions are explored below.

A.   PUT THE TEACHER BACK IN THE RESEARCH EQUATION

The teacher seems strangely absent from the papers presented in this volume. It would be easy for an outsider to judge that cognitive learning strategies represent some form of interaction only between student and instructional material, perhaps as some mutant form of programmed instruction. The teacher, when mentioned in papers such as the one by Winograd and Hare (Ch. 8, this volume), appears faceless and voiceless, some form of automaton whose styles, foibles, and arts do not affect the transaction.

The paper by Schallert et al. (Ch. 11, this volume) involves the teacher, but here also the methodology and focus is on student interpretations of what the teacher intended. Several instructors were queried as to their instructional intent, apparently to corroborate student reports. The intensity of analysis applied to student reports, however, waned when instructor reports were studied. The conclusions reached were still primarily based on student reports. Once again, the instructor is mostly faceless and irrelevant to the transaction.

Another aspect of such teacher absence can be found in the chapter by Jones and her colleagues (Ch. 13, this volume). It reports on a deliberate project to build learning strategies into materials in such a way that they are "teacher-proof." Such a strategy, which can certainly be defended in terms of the questionable results obtained in many teacher preparation programs, nevertheless again erases the instructor as a significant component of the research.

For a college adopter, the learning equation must involve at least three main actors: student, material, and teacher. Research that focuses on only two of those actors falls short of the mark. To the degree that cognitive learning strategy research fails to give serious attention to the characteristics of the teacher, it is of little practical use to college faculty and administrators. Insights and techniques based on only two legs of a tripod will not appeal to the practitioner, particularly when that practitioner is in fact the unstudied third leg. As McKeachie points out (1978, p. 281), a major flaw in much research related to learning is that "We seldom know how well a particular method was used in experimental studies of teaching methods, but it seems very likely that the effectiveness of a method depends upon the competence and enthusiasm of the teachers in the study."

This is not to suggest that the research reported in this volume is uninteresting or irrelevant. Far from it. It *does* suggest that the research is almost uniformly incomplete, with a common missing dimension. For example, these papers raise potent questions concerning what occurs within student minds when learning does or does not occur and concerning the interactive relationship between student and material. Such research can multiply its relevance and appeal to college practice if it also explores equally potent questions concerning the teacher. Here are some sample questions of merit:

How aware are instructors of their own cognitive learning strategies?

How do instructors' characteristics affect their willingness and ability to actively teach learning processes rather than content?

When exposed to training, how do instructors internalize, understand, and later apply means of fostering student cognitive learning strategies?

What are the relationships between instructional styles, learning styles, and cognitive learning strategies?

What assumptions do cognitive learning strategy researchers make about practitioners?

How do individual instructors modify cognitive learning strategy techniques and research findings when applying them over the long term?

These and similar questions need answers. They acknowledge the role of the instructor as an active and vital part of the teaching/learning transaction.

Answering such questions will benefit cognitive learning strategy proponents in two ways: it will make research conclusions more comprehensive and it will signal to faculty and administrators an intent to make research maximally relevant to practice.

B. CONDUCT RESEARCH INTO LONGEVITY AND TRANSFER OF EFFECTS

One of the more common refrains within these chapters, and within the conversations at the conference which gave rise to them, has been an unwillingness or inability to predict longevity of impact or transfer of effects from the experimental setting into other settings. Retention and transfer of learning, however, are among the very highest of priorities for college faculty. It has even been said that a theory of learning, which presumably directs teaching activities, is in essence a theory of transfer of learning (Bigge, 1976). It can certainly be argued that quality education is essentially no more than these two ingredients: that students retain what is taught, and that students can apply it in other circumstances.

Efforts to help students develop their own cognitive learning strategies require valuable classroom time and effort. This is justifiable only if it appears likely that those strategies will *stick* and be *used*. There are, unfortunately, innumerable study skills programs and materials, for example, that allow the student to learn *about* study skills, pass the tests, and then forget all of it afterwards. Is this likely with cognitive learning strategies? If the student simply memorizes information about cognitive learning strategies and then forgets them rapidly, or fails to see and use them as broad mental tools on an ongoing basis, then the time, effort, and instructor risks are probably not justifiable.

Questions of transfer and retention of learning should not be seen as optional items for cognitive learning strategy researchers (or any other types of educational researchers for that matter) if they wish to significantly influence practice. They need to be viewed as central priorities and be squarely addressed.

C. BROADEN THE SCOPE OF COGNITIVE LEARNING STRATEGY RESEARCH

An observer reading the chapters in this volume and listening to the discussions at the conference that gave rise to them might conclude that cognitive learning strategies are in fact only two-dimensional: cognitive reading strategies and study skills. This apparently constrained breadth of focus may simply reflect the composition of this group of researchers or it may suggest the predilections of the entire cognitive learning strategies community.

A preoccupation with reading and study skills among such researchers may thus be either illusionary or accurate but, in either case, it endangers the ability to impact practice. A seventh, unwritten prerequisite for successful innovation is that the innovation must be *seen* as something different from current practice. If practitioners come to view cognitive learning strategies as "merely" reading and study skills, then they will disregard them. Reading and study skills faculty will tend to judge that, "We are already doing it." Faculty from other areas will tend to judge that, "It is not our job; others are already doing it." In either case, the innovation will not be allowed to take root. It may be significant that during a 6-week period in mid-1985, this author heard three different workshop leaders, who were summarizing for educator audiences the major approaches to "teaching thinking," state or imply that cognitive learning strategies were basically renovated study skills techniques.

Developing cognitive learning strategies can obviously be far broader than developing reading and study skills, at least in concept. The overall sphere of "teaching thinking" is a roiling mass of conflicting but very vital theories, practices, materials, and research findings. It is almost certainly the most lively field of educational research and practice today. Furthermore, it is one that involves all disciplines and all types of educational delivery. To the degree that approaches to cognitive learning strategies share this terrain, then they have the potential for also sharing that allure and breadth.

An undercurrent in these papers deals explicitly or implicitly with the question of whether or not efforts to teach cognitive learning strategies are "domain specific"—limited in their significance to a particular discipline or a specific instructional situation. Certainly there is a sense in which any strategy for thinking and learning is content and context specific, and in which mastery of such skills is best obtained within the context of large amounts of domain-specific knowledge (Ericksen, 1984). Yet as Bruner points out (1985, pp. 5–6),

> It is absurd to insist that each and every theory of learning is utterly domain specific, that nothing general can be said about learners or learning environments. You do not quite need a different model of a learner to talk about learning to play chess, learning how to play the flute, learning mathematics, and learning to read the sprung rhymes in the verse of Gerard Manley Hopkins.

Probably, undue concerns about domain specificity reflect the innate conservatism of the researcher, who designs specialized stilettos to achieve a single precise effect and who is then ill at ease in speculating on other uses or misuses to which the research findings might be applied. Practitioners, unfortunately, are forced by the magnitude of their needs and the urgency of action to employ broadswords rather than stilettos.

As Bloom (1984), Walberg (1984), and others have pointed out, there are dozens of factors that influence the daily teaching/learning process. These factors range from socioeconomic status and TV-watching habits to teaching styles and physical classroom environments. Faced with such complexity, practitioners inevitably lack the time, patience, or inclination to amass and employ hundreds of narrow instructional techniques, each tailored to fit only specialized situations. They necessarily seek generic educational tools that are powerful and adaptable enough to generally do the job in many situations while buffeted by many considerations.

The difference in priorities between the researcher's quest for precision and the practitioner's quest for versatility is not a new conflict. It may be an irreconcilable one. However, in the context of the generalizability of cognitive learning strategies, the gap and its implications are certainly *researchable* ones. What can be usefully researched? Walberg's (1984) strategy of using meta-analysis to integrate and interrelate diverse forms of research is usefully researchable, as is Bloom's (1984) strategy of exploring the effects of multiple combinations of teaching/learning strategies. McCutcheon's (1985) conception of practitioner-oriented "personal theories of action" and research-oriented "generic theories of action" is also usefully researchable. Any of the points of tangency between research and practice dealing with cognitive learning strategies are usefully researchable.

For example, researchers and practitioners in mathematics, science, writing, reasoning, and many other fields are taking steps that appear highly related to cognitive learning strategies. This suggests the rationality of research to establish the degree of commonality. More importantly, it suggests the utility of research designed to look specifically at questions of generalizability among these efforts, to establish, for example, whether metacognitive techniques implanted as a part of reading instruction bear fruit in mathematics performance, and under what circumstances.

Several of the commercially packaged approaches to abetting student cognitive processes are based partly or totally on such theories of generalizability, in terms of assuming that, once becoming conscious of and practicing a particular mental strategy, the student will actually use it in other situations (e.g., Whimbey & Lochhead, 1984; Miles & Rauton, 1985; DeBono, 1977). From the practitioner's perspective, solid research information on the effectiveness of such transfer would be a critical ingredient in deciding whether or not to commit time and resources to learning about and then helping students master these strategies, which are essentially cognitive learning strategies.

VII.   SUMMARY

The concept of deliberately equipping students with a conscious toolkit of cognitive learning strategies is rich with promise for college instruction. It appears useful in challenging many of the student learning tactics that frustrate quality education. It appears to have many of the characteristics required for significant adoption at the college level. It appears to have the potential for becoming one of the more permanent aspects of the general effort to "teach thinking" as a deliberate, central part of educational activities. As such, it offers hope of being one of several forces useful in deflecting the ship of American education from its current course.

The degree to which this promise is realized, however, seems to depend more heavily upon future actions among researchers than upon actions of those who practice or package educational innovations. Cognitive learning strategies suggest more a broad concept than a program, and arise primarily from research activities. Fusion of research with practice in this instance seems to require significant leadership and action on the part of the researcher, to expand research priorities, include research on the teacher as well as the student and materials, moderate conservative habits, and examine relevance to daily classroom environments.

Cognitive learning strategies have enormous potential for benefitting classroom practice. Many of those leading research in this area (as represented in this volume) appear unusually pragmatic, flexible, and concerned with the utility of their discoveries. Those involved in various forms of "teaching thinking" at the practitioner level are motivated, energetic, flexible, and highly attracted to any approach that offers promise. The ingredients are present for an almost classic (if only because rare) symbiotic relationship between research and practice. The initiative rests mainly with the research community.

REFERENCES

Benderson, A. (1984). *Critical thinking*. Princeton, NJ: Educational Testing Service.

Bigge, M. L. (1976). *Learning theories for teachers*. New York: Harper & Row.

Bloom, B. S. (1984). The search for methods of instruction as effective as one-to-one tutoring. *Educational Leadership, 41*, 4–18.

Bransford, J. (1979). *Human condition: Learning, understanding, and remembering*. Belmont, CA: Wadsworth.

Bruner, J. (1985). Models of the learner. *Educational Researcher, 14*, 5–8.

Cohen, A. M., & Brawer, F. B. (1982). *The American community college*. San Francisco: Jossey-Bass.

College Board. (1983). *Academic preparation for college: What students need to know and be able to do.* New York: The College Board.

DeBono, E. (1977). *Teaching thinking.* London: Temple Smith.

Ericksen, S. C. (1984). *The essence of good teaching.* San Francisco: Jossey-Bass.

Feuerstein, R. (1980). *Instrumental enrichment: An intervention program for cognitive modifiability.* Baltimore: University Park Press.

Grant, W. V., & Snyder, T. D. (1984). *Digest of educational statistics, 1983–84.* Washington, DC: US Government Printing Office.

Guilford, J. P. (1977). *Way beyond the IQ.* Buffalo, NY: Creative Education Foundation.

Krulik, S., & Reys, R. E. (1980). *Problem solving in school mathematics.* Reston, VA: National Council of Teachers of Mathematics.

Lawson, A. (Ed.). (1979). *The psychology of teaching for thinking and creativity.* Columbus, OH: 1980 AETS Yearbook.

Lipman, M., Sharp, A. M., & Oscanyan, F. S. (1980). *Philosophy in the classroom.* Philadelphia: Temple University Press.

McCarthy, B. (1982). *Teaching to learning styles using right/left mode techniques.* Oak Brook, IL: Excel Publishing.

McCutcheon, G. (1985). Curricular theory/curricular practice: A gap or the Grand Canyon?" In A. Molnar (Ed.), *Current thought on curriculum: 1985 ASCD Yearbook.* Alexandria, VA: Association for Supervision and Curriculum Development.

McKeachie, W. J. (1978). *Teaching tips.* Lexington, MA: D. C. Heath.

Miles, C., & Rauton, J. (1985). *Thinking tools.* Clearwater, FL: H & H Publishers.

Molnar, A. (1985). *Current thought on curriculum: 1985 ASCD Yearbook.* (Introduction). Alexandria, VA: Association for Supervision and Curriculum Development.

Moreland-Young, (1983). Teaching analytical and thinking skills in a content course. In P. A. Lacey (Ed.), *Revitalizing teaching through faculty development.* San Francisco: Jossey-Bass.

Rubinstein, M. F., & Pfeiffer, K. (1980). *Concepts in problem solving.* Englewood Cliffs, NJ: Prentice-Hall.

Walberg, H. J. (1984). Improving the productivity of America's schools. *Educational Leadership, 41,* 19–26.

Whimbey, A., & Lochhead, J. (1984). *Beyond problem solving and comprehension.* Philadelphia: Franklin Institute Press.

Woditsch, G. A. (1978). Specifying and achieving competencies. In O. Milton et al. (Eds.), *On college teaching.* San Francisco: Jossey-Bass.

INDEX